2315634 15/-

KV-267-799

JOHNSONIAN STUDIES

including

A Bibliography of Johnsonian Studies, 1950-1960

compiled by

James L. Clifford & Donald J. Greene

edited by

MAGDI WAHBA

CAIRO 1962

C620 31805

HERTFORDSHIRE
COUNTY LIBRARY

828/JOH

2315634

Distributed outside the U.A.R. by the
OXFORD UNIVERSITY PRESS

Hertfordshire

828/JOH

1 2 MAY 2005

02/06/05

23 JUN 2005

1 2 JUL 2005

ᴐIEꙅ

Please renew/return this item by the last date shown.

So that your telephone call is charged at local rate, please call the numbers as set out below:

	From Area codes 01923 or 020:	From the rest of Herts:
Renewals:	01923 471373	01438 737373
Enquiries:	01923 471333	01438 737333
Textphone:	01923 471599	01438 737599
L32	www.hertsdirect.org/librarycatalogue	

CONTENTS

PREFACE

This collection attempts to present recent and (except in two cases) hitherto unpublished, essays by Johnsonians anywhere in the world, some of whom have well established reputations, while others are still young scholars, absorbed in the early stages of Johnsonian discovery. This volume is best regarded as a sort of workshop for Johnsonians, where they can try out new methods of approach, or make suggestions, or record new discoveries, or explore the possibilities of some point of detail, which may later be elaborated into a larger piece of work. This is not to say that many of the contributions to this volume are not already highly skilled and final formulations, but an air of enquiry and experiment pervades them, without necessarily detracting from their value.

The reason for wishing to publish this volume in Cairo was originally to make it easily accessible to Johnsonians from either side of our sadly divided world; but, apart from a solitary Indian contribution, the only response has come from the English-speaking world. This is, frankly, a pity — for there are many scholarly Johnsonians in the Far East, in Western and Central Europe and, I am told, in the Soviet Union, who could have enriched this volume with the diversity of their views. Perhaps they will contribute to later collections, which, with encouragement, could appear from time to time, in the future.

"The true Johnsonian will continue to judge Johnson by, above all, his own writings", observed the late Professor David Nichol Smith in his Presidential Address to the Lichfield Johnson Society. This is certainly true of all the contributions to this volume. They are concerned less with the figure of Johnson which appears in Boswell's *Life*, than with the man whose own writings earned him Smollett's appellation of "the great Cham of Literature". Boswell's *Life* is now generally regarded as supplementing the information about Johnson which he provided himself in his own works, and there is a healthy tendency shown in these essays to judge Johnson by what he actually wrote.

In the arrangement of these pieces I have given pride of place to the essay by Dr. L.F. Powell, *doyen* of Johnsonians and Boswellians. Then, apart from an obvious grouping of essays dealing with Johnson's religion and moral thought, no formal pattern has been adopted.

The Bibliography of Johnsonian Studies, 1950-1960, compiled by Professors James L. Clifford and Donald J. Greene, would have deserved separate publication, and I am very grateful for having been allowed to incorporate it in the present volume.

There has been a minimum of editing in this book. I have made no attempt to inflict a uniform spelling convention on American and British contributors. The burden of proof-reading has, in fact, fallen upon the contributors themselves, whose forbearance and understanding during the long delays have been admirable. I have limited myself to being a conveyor of their wishes to the compositors and printers who have truly achieved something of a *tour de force* in this book. I am particularly indebted to Mr. Henri Césaire, for his patience and application during the composing of the text in a language which is not his own. I am also very grateful to Mr. Gabriel Joseph for his almost fanatical diligence in pursuit of misprints, although English is not his mother tongue.

To my wife I owe a debt of gratitude for sensible advice and painstaking help, when she had so much else to do.

Nevertheless errors and imperfections remain, and for these I must assume full responsibility.

M.W.

ACKNOWLEDGEMENTS

"Dr. Johnson and the Literature of Experience" by Ian Watt, was originally broadcast on the Third Programme of the British Broadcasting Corporation, on the 250th. anniversary of Johnson's birth; it was printed in *The Listener*, 24th. September, 1959. The editor gratefully acknowledges permission to reprint it, given by the British Broadcasting Corporation and by the editor of *The Listener*.

∽

"Dr. Johnson and Fanny Burney — Some Additions to the Record", by Joyce Hemlow, was originally printed in the *Bulletin of the New York Public Library*, February 1951. The editor gratefully acknowledges permission to reprint it, given by Mr. David V. Erdman, Editor of Library Publications for The New York Public Library.

L. F. POWELL

Johnson Exhibited

Dr. Johnson made a brave show in New York and in his own Midlands on the 250th anniversary of his birthday. At Lichfield, as is right and proper, the occasion was celebrated, in various ways, by the whole city, led by the Mayor and Corporation and the Dean and Chapter: there was no exhibition of books apart from that in the Birthplace, which has many treasures and is always open. In Birmingham, with which Johnson has many associations, including the writing and production of his first book, Lobo's *A Voyage to Abyssinia*, there were two notable exhibitions of books and manuscripts. The first, held in the Birmingham Library, Margaret Street, (a library founded in 1779 and of which Edmund Hector, Johnson's lifelong friend, was a founder member) displayed fifty works which Johnson is known to have read and consulted, all of them drawn from the library's own shelves. The catalogue 'set and printed by hand', a little jewel of a book, is compiled by the Librarian, Mr. Charles Parish(1). The second exhibition, a very much more ambitious venture, was arranged, as far as the books and manuscripts were concerned, by the Reference Library and held in the Museum and Art Gallery. The organisers attempted to exhibit a complete collection of not only all the works that Johnson wrote and edited, but of all those to which he had contributed. They did not depend upon their own considerable store of over 2000 Johnsoniana but spread their net to include National, University and Public Libraries; over thirty institutions and private collectors collaborated and by eking out with facsimiles and reprints the Birmingham Librarians almost succeeded in their aim.

They assembled, in addition to books, a number of manuscripts, the most important of which were Johnson's epitaph on Goldsmith and the

---

(1) *Johnson's Books. Catalogue of an Exhibition of Books in the Birmingham Library to celebrate the 250th Anniversary of the Birth of Dr. Samuel Johnson.* [Birmingham, privately printed in 100 copies by F.E.P.].

famous protest, the Round Robin, which it called forth, both from Lord
Crawford's library, and a representative collection of portraits of Johnson,
including Reynold's idealised painting of 1769, another version of which,
that presented by Sir Joshua to Johnson's step-daughter, Lucy Porter, was
given the place of honour in the New York exhibition. The books, of which
there were 144, are arranged in the catalogue([1]) in chronological order and
only briefly described; bibliographical points are not given and nothing is
said about the scarcity of a volume, which is sad as some of the exhibits are
very rare indeed. I note, for instance, *A Compleat Vindication of the Licensers
of the Stage* (1739), one of two copies in private hands, *A Commentary on
Mr. Pope's Principles of Morality, or Essay on Man*, by Mons. Crousaz
(1742), of which Johnson himself apparently never had a copy and of which
only four or five copies are now known, the *Evangelical History harmonised*
(1757), by the Rev. John Lindsay, which is very hard to find, perhaps because it is anonymous, and the unique copy, one of the late Dr. Chapman's
happiest discoveries, now in the collection of Lord Rothschild, of *Proposals
for the Publisher* (1744). As one would expect every Shakespearian piece is
included, even the *Proposals* of 1756, which were known to Courtney,
Johnson's bibliographer, from reprints only. There are some exciting association pieces: a copy, signed by the author, Dr. Samuel Madden, of
Boulter's Monument (1745), a panegyrical poem of which Johnson 'blotted
a great many lines', and may have done more; a copy, not now in Oxford
but at Stoke Newington, of *A Journey to the Western Islands* (1775), bearing
the inscription 'To the Master of Pembroke College from the Authour';
and the copy of the collected edition of *The Rambler* (1752), which Johnson
gave to his wife a few days before her death — it subsequently passed to
another Elizabeth, the wife of Francis Barber, Johnson's negro servant,
who entered her signature in one of the volumes.

The exhibition in New York was held in the spacious rooms of the
Pierpont Morgan Library, where the books, manuscripts and pictures were
shown to full advantage. Twelve collectors and Public Institutions, notably
Mr and Mrs Donald F. Hyde, Mr H.W. Liebert and Yale University
Library, co-operated with the Library in making it one of the most remark-

---

(1) *Dr. Samuel Johnson 1709-1784. Celebrations in Birmingham of the 250th.
anniversary of his birth. An Exhibition of Books, Manuscripts, Views, Portraits
arranged jointly by the Reference Library and the Museum and Art Gallery 14
September to 4th. October 1959 in the Museum and Art Gallery.* [Birmingham]

able and successful exhibitions ever held there: it was open for over two months and seen by eight thousand visitors. It attempted, not to show copies of all Johnson's printed works, but "to illustrate in first editions, manuscripts, letters, and portraits, important events and episodes in Johnson's life and literary career." The catalogue[1], a handsome quarto, beautifully printed on handmade paper, provides a permanent record and is an important addition to Johnsonian bibliography. It has a foreword by Herbert Cahoon, who arranged the exhibition, three full-page facsimiles of Johnson's handwriting, and reproductions of three states of Heath's engraving after the painting by Reynolds for Boswell's first edition of the *Life*, the earliest of which raises a problem of Johnsonian iconography.

The exhibition was well-balanced, manuscripts and books being shown in almost equal numbers; the manuscripts included poems or parts of them, such as *London*, the *Vanity of Human Wishes*, Γνῶθι σεαυτόν (1772), the Latin poem written after the revision of the Dictionary for the Fourth Edition, the ode addressed to Mrs Thrale (*Thralia dulcis*), from the Isle of Skye, beginning *Permeo terras*, the actual manuscript sent to Mrs Thrale from the island; prose pieces such as the holograph 'Short Scheme for compiling a New Dictionary' (1746) and the final draft, in a copyist's hand, of the Plan of a Dictionary, with Chesterfield's comments and suggestions and Johnson's corrections (1747), the Dedication to the Queen of Hoole's translation of Tasso's *Jerusalem Delivered* (1763), and the review of Grainger's *Sugar-Cane* (1764) in which it is observed that 'America is well known to be the habitation of uncivilized nations, remarkable only for their rudeness and simplicity', miscellaneous documents connected with his writings, etc., such as the receipt of fifteen guineas, 25 Nov. 1748, for the *Vanity*, the assignment of the copyright of *Irene*, 8 Sept. 1749, the agreement for printing the *Lives of the Poets* 12 March 1781, and the receipt for his pension, signed on the day of his death; diaries and private memoranda, from the earliest extant diary, *Desidiae valedixi*, Oct. 1729, to his record of his first meeting with the Thrales, 9 Jan. 1765, 'At Mr Trails', and his last prayer, 5 Dec. 1784, showing him calmly awaiting death; and a remarkable selection of letters, including the earliest known to have survived, 30 Oct. 1731,

---

(1) *Samuel Johnson, LL.D. (1709-1784). An Exhibition of First Editions, Manuscripts, Letters, and Portraits to Commemorate the 250th Anniversary of his Birth, and the 200th Anniversary of his Rasselas. Sept. 22—Nov. 28. 1959.* New York. The Pierpont Morgan Library. 1959.

in which he declines to write some verses for his correspondent, Gregory Hickman, observing that 'versifying against one's inclination is the most disagreeable thing in the world'; a letter to Cave, the owner-editor of *The Gentleman's Magazine*, some three years later, 25 Nov. 1734, in which, driven by necessity, he undertakes to improve his Poetical Article; the only known letter to 'Dearest Tetty', 31 Jan. 1739–40, rightly given the distinction of reproduction; two copies of The Celebrated Letter to Lord Chesterfield, Feb. 1755, including that which has been accepted as the authoritative text; the original of the equally famous and even more vigorously worded letter to 'Mr James Macpherson' 20 Jan. 1775, which differs materially from the copy printed by Boswell from Johnson's dictation and 'authenticated by a note in his own handwriting'; the short but extremely rough letter to Mrs Thrale, 2 July 1784, on his learning of her intention to marry the Italian musician, Gabriele Piozzi; and the letter to Dr. Burney, 28 Aug. 1784, which contains the first draft of the third paragraph of the Dedication to the King of Burney's *Commemoration of Handel*, (1785), the last of Johnson's writings.

The books included many very rare items, some indeed unique, now exhibited for the first time: the only known copy of Crousaz on Pope, printed for A. Dodd, in 1739; this was withdrawn and reissued with a new title page by Cave in 1742: one of three recorded copies and the only one in America of Johnson's sermon for Hervey, *A Sermon preached at the Cathedral Church of St. Paul before the Sons of the Clergy*... by the Hon. and Rev. Henry Hervey Aston, 1745: one of five recorded copies, not one of which is in Oxford, of *The Prologue and Epilogue, spoken at the opening of the Theatre in Drury-Lane*, 1747; one of three known copies of the tribute to Milton, *A New Prologue spoken by Mr Garrick*... *at the Representation of Comus*, 1750; one of five copies of *Proposals for Printing, by Subscription, the Dramatick Works of William Shakespeare*, 1756; the unique copy, at Yale, preserved by Boswell, who crossed out all of the text that was not written by Johnson, of *Proposals for Printing by Subscription, dedicated to the Queen, a new and elegant Edition enlarged and corrected, of the Original Works of Mrs Charlotte Lennox*, 1775: the projected edition, in three quarto volumes, never appeared; and one of three known copies, the others being in Oxford, in different collections, of *Proposals for Printing by Subscription, inscribed, by Permission, to the Right Honourable the Earl of Eglinton: An Analysis of the Scotch Celtic Language. By William Shaw, Native of one of the Hebrides*, 1777. The copy exhibited, now at Yale, was Boswell's and it provided him with the text for the *Life*. He omitted the paragraph 'As this Book is intended for the Curious and the learned, a few copies more than what are subscribed for will be printed' which may well have been written by Johnson. A special entry in this exhibition was a large collection of the editions of *Rasselas*, arranged by Mr. R.F. Metzdorf, who has devoted a lifetime to the study of this book and shown that it always has been the most popular of all Johnson's writings; over 450 editions have been published since 19 April 1759, when the first edition appeared.

"This is indeed taking prodigious pains about a man".

OXFORD

IAN WATT

Dr. Johnson and
The Literature of Experience

We can hardly talk about literature without using the standard oppositions between art and life, form and meaning, imagination and experience.
But these antitheses are obviously misleading in many ways; one way is to
make us think so highly of 'art', 'form', and 'imagination' that we under-
value the many kinds of writing whose main qualities are not peculiar to
literature, writing whose matter is so close to common experience that we do
not think of it as imaginative, and whose manner is so much that of ordinary
human discourse that it hardly occurs to us to discuss its literary form. The
distinction between the world of art and of life becomes irrelevant in extreme
cases of this kind of writing, because both their subject-matter and their
mode of communication are common to both: such, for example, are the
diary, the letter, the memoir, the prayer; and sometimes these modes of
expression attain a measure of permanence, and thus enter the vast category
of writing to which one can give the name of the literature of experience.
The greatest English writer whose work belongs mainly to this category is
Samuel Johnson.

When, fifty years ago, Walter Raleigh celebrated the two hundredth
anniversary of Johnson's birth, the terms of his eulogy illustrated one way
in which the antithesis between life and art tends to be unfair to the literature
of experience: 'Johnson', he asserted 'was an author almost by accident;
it is the man who is dear to us'.

The question is whether the man is not dear to us mainly through the
greatness of the author; and it cannot be said that the question, though
much debated, has yet been resolved. Raleigh certainly did much to end the
relative decline in Johnson's reputation which set in soon after his death,
and to suggest the main directions which subsequent interest in Johnson

years has confirmed and amplified Raleigh's admiration of the man, it seems to have made it even more difficult to come to terms with the greatness of the author.

Modern trends in the interpretation of Johnson the man are not easy to summarize. Johnson's contemporary, George III, allegedly never discovered how the apple got inside the apple-dumpling; perhaps one can say that new knowledge and new insights have enabled us to uncover in Johnson, beneath the portentous crust of the intimidating portraits, the polysyllabic prose, and the oracular clubman presented by Boswell, a human being who belongs to the world of our own ordinary pleasures and interests and perplexities more completely than any other writer.

Both the difficulties of Johnson's life and the magnitude of his triumph over them were of exceptional proportions. From childhood on he suffered from the King's Evil, a tuberculous infection that scarred his face and left him with one eye almost blind; he grew up in an unhappy home which offered little prospect for the future beyond his father's declining bookshop; he was afflicted with an uncontrollable constitutional nervousness which made him mutter to himself and twitch convulsively; and by the age of nineteen he knew that at any moment what he called his 'vile melancholy' was likely to develop into complete and permanent madness. Then came the brief days at Oxford of the angry young man from the provinces: his contemporaries remembered him as gay, but he knew well enough that 'it was bitterness which they mistook for frolic'.

All this side of the biography, hardly touched on by Boswell, has now been painstakingly filled out by many scholars, and its psychological implications interpreted. Their work makes clear the considerable role which the modern climate of thought, and especially Freud, has played in increasing our understanding of the courage and resource with which Johnson warded off the menace of insanity. In *Johnson Agonistes*, as Bertrand Bronson has called him in a now classic study, we recognize and salute one of the great heroes of the wars of the mind.

Other changes in outlook have increased our sympathetic understanding of Johnson's attitude to life. The Whig view of history, for example, has been sufficiently challenged for us to recognize that there was considerable basis for Johnson's Tory anathemas on the social and political tendencies of his time; while the main events of the twentieth century have vindicated was to take; but whereas the general tendency of thought in the last fifty

Johnson's pronouncement that 'the history of mankind is little else than a narration of designs that have failed and hopes that have been disappointed'.

Johnson's political pessimism was based on his acute understanding of the darker elements in human nature. He could hardly assent to the doctrine of progress when he was convinced that 'there may be community of material possessions, but there can never be community of love and esteem'; and the whole liberal conception of the democratic pursuit of happiness inevitably seemed unreal to someone who, when asked if he really believed that 'a man was not sometimes happy in the moment that was present', answered: 'Never, but when he is drunk'.

Johnson's psychological pessimism — or realism, if you like — enabled him to achieve a posthumous topicality in many other ways. He was, for example, the supreme exponent of One-Upmanship; and Boswell's *Life* is, among other things, a record of the vigour and variety of his tactics: witness, for example, Johnson's rejection of Boswell's offer to tell him all about Allan Ramsay's pastoral drama *The Gentle Shepherd*. 'No, Sir, I won't learn it. You shall retain your superiority by *my* not knowing it'.

Johnson, then, had as keen an awareness of the corruptions of pride and envy as La Rochefoucauld. But he was also, fortunately, aware of much else. His great capacity for cheerfulness kept breaking in on his conviction of human inadequacy; and this, combined with his naturally impetuous and insubordinate nature, did much to qualify the toryism which is the usual result of a pressing sense of man's weakness, greed, and irrationality.

Johnson strongly opposed the 'prevailing spirit' of his time, which he defined as 'a dislike of all established forms, merely because they are established'; but if his view that 'the cure for the greatest part of human miseries is not radical but palliative' made him oppose anything in the nature of radical reform, it did not turn him into a complacent supporter of the *status quo*. He never forgot the need for 'palliatives' and his belief that 'a decent provision for the poor is the true test of a civilization' might well have led him to welcome the Welfare State.

Johnson's philosophical, psychological, and political views, then, have become much more congenial to us than they were to the nineteenth century; our general mistrust of theory makes us welcome Johnson's famous attacks on 'the cant of those who judge by principles rather than perception', while our residual liberalism is satisfied by Johnson's eloquent departure from his own precept when he enunciated one sovereign principle of judgment: 'I am always afraid of determining on the side of envy or cruelty'.

But it may be felt that all this is beside the point; that we can, no doubt—following our personal tastes—applaud Johnson the High Church-man or Johnson the gormandizer, Johnson the patriot or Johnson the punster, but that the only important question is not whether the Great Cham was a great chap, or even the brightest ornament in the casebooks of self-psy-chotherapy, but, simply, whether he was a great writer. The answer, simply, is yes. But the case is difficult to argue, especially in the present critical climates.

For one thing, Raleigh was in a sense right when he said Johnson 'was an author almost by accident'. In the days of his fame, when someone com-plimented Johnson on his legal knowledge and remarked that he might have become Lord Chancellor if he had chosen the law as a career, Johnson was much distressed, and answered: 'Why will you vex me by suggesting this when it is too late?' Most of his published works were commissioned—from the first of them, a translation for a provincial bookseller, to his greatest literary achievements, the *Dictionary* and the *Lives of the Poets*. Johnson is perhaps the supreme example of a great writer with very little sense of a specifically literary vocation. This, however, may not be as disabling as it sounds. For two reasons: first, the notion of the literary vocation as some-thing special and set apart is not necessarily the best one, and is certainly relatively new historically; and, secondly, Johnson had his own conception of his role which, though contrary to some more recent ones, was perfectly adapted to his own particular literary powers.

Soon after Johnson's death the Romantics established their image of the writer as a lonely genius exploring strange seas of thought and feeling; and today this conception retains much of its power. With this stereotype goes a conception of literature as an equally special and separate kind of expression; and this idea, which is strongly supported by symbolist and for-malist doctrines, has only recently been widely challenged in favour of a more literal and rational outlook.

Johnson's idea of literature, and of the role of the writer, was certainly not in the tradition begun by the Romantics. If he thought of himself as an 'artist', it was in its eighteenth-century sense of a skilled craftsman; and his conception of how he should use his craft laid primary emphasis on his kin-ship with his fellow human beings: 'The only end of writing' was 'to enable the reader better to enjoy life, or better to endure it'. So Johnson's best early works in verse—*London* and *The Vanity of Human Wishes*, and in prose the *Rambler* papers—were moral essays, discursive modes of writing which were, as he put it, eminently adapted to 'the propagation of truth' and 'the dignity of virtue'. Their manner was primarily rational and expository; Johnson insisted on the virtues of what he called 'dogged veracity'; his psychological need to control 'the hunger of the imagination which preys upon itself' made him rather uneasy in the presence of the fanciful and the fictional; and it is typical of him that the best parts of his quasi-novel *Rasselas* could easily be essays from the *Rambler*.

This literal and didactic tendency, so out of keeping with recent literary fashion, was undoubtedly an important cause of what has been widely felt as a discrepancy between Johnson's potential and his actual literary achievement. *The Vanity of Human Wishes* is one of the supreme poems of the century, but Johnson obviously fell short of the bulk which is necessary to major poetic status; partly because his sense of moral and religious responsibility was so intense that it did not lend itself easily to poetry—he considered religion 'the great, the necessary, the inevitable business of human life', but he also held that 'contemplative piety, or the intercourse between God and the human soul cannot be poetical'. On the other hand, unlike Boswell, he had little interest in the commonest outlet for the literal and realist habit of mind—self-expression; so it is not surprising that the bulk of Johnson's writings are of a miscellaneous and occasional kind.

Few of us would deny Sir James Murray's estimate that in Johnson's hands the dictionary 'became a department of literature'; nor would we dissent from Logan Pearsall Smith's expert appraisal of Johnson as our supreme aphorist: but we hardly know how to rank these two genres in the literary hierarchy. We like wit and brevity and analytic power, but the definition and the aphorism seem much too short-winded and discontinuous to rank as major literary creations; and both are essentially occasional—supremely so in the *Dictionary*, where every word was a new and unavoidable challenge.

To no one else, surely, can we better apply Johnson's own definition: 'True genius is a mind of large general powers, accidentally determined in some particular direction'; his union of formidable analytic power with immediate command of memorable verbal expression needed only an ap-

propriate eliciting occasion, whether in a literary task or in the occasions of
daily life. This poses further critical problems. First, we must learn how to
deal with writing which was not intended as literature at all. The famous
private *Letter to Lord Chesterfield* is not surpassed by any of his public writings,
and the great gifts found in *The Vanity of Human Wishes* are as fully manifested in some of Johnson's private prayers and in his letters.

Secondly, it is even more difficult to come to critical terms with Johnson's conversation. When Boswell remarked 'But I wonder, Sir, you have
not more pleasure in writing than in not writing', Johnson refused to be
drawn: 'Sir, you *may* wonder'. It seems clear that conversation was Johnson's most natural means of expression—perhaps because there the stimulus
was varied and immediate. In any case, just as Johnson's moral sense made
the distinction between public and private writing unimportant, so it meant
that he put as much seriousness and energy into his conversation as into his
writing. He 'laid it down as a fixed rule to do his best on every occasion and
in every company'; and to 'impart whatever he knew in the most forcible
language he could put it in'. Consequently, Fanny Burney 'could not help
remarking how... much the same thing it was to hear him or to read him';
while Johnson's conversation offers as impressive evidence as his writings
of the variety of his powers, from what Boswell described as 'the majestic
teacher of moral and religious wisdom', to the greatest of the English hum-
orists.

Humour is another literary quality which has not yet received critical
justice. In general it can be regarded as a supremely inclusive response to
the complexities of experience; and a response whose success requires great
gifts of sensitiveness and imagination. Mrs. Thrale tells of a Lincolnshire
lady who was ill-advised enough to show Johnson the underground grotto
in her garden, and then enquire complacently 'if he did not think it would
be a pretty convenient habitation ?' 'I think it would, Madam', he replied
— 'for a toad'. The retort was rude; but not gratuitously so, because as soon
as Johnson was summoned to endorse a grotto as a convenient human habitation he felt himself bound to remind the Lincolnshire lady that civilization
has progressed from living in caves to living in houses only through long and
patient efforts, and that it can continue only on such terms.

To do justice to Johnson's literary achievement, then, we must include
the totality of his recorded utterances: the conversations and the various

marginal kinds of writing, as well as the poems, the essays and the *Lives of the Poets*. This means that we must usually judge Johnson's content on the basis of literal as opposed to imaginative truth. This is what the literature of experience usually demands, but it is contrary to most modern critical theory, with its insistence on the literary artefact as an autonomous verbal structure best considered as separate both from its author and from any relation to real life. Obviously the correspondence of an author's statements to reality or truth is even more difficult to establish than intrinsic literary excellence where we can at least find all—or most—of the evidence on the page before us. We must also remember that there is a real danger in confusing art and life; for one thing, it tends to authorize the common 'let's have no nonsense' sort of Philistinism, and Johnson has had many admirers in this camp: Raleigh himself, as Virginia Woolf noted, in his later years 'ceased to profess literature, and became instead a Professor of Life'.

But the other extreme position is even more impossible; we may not want to go as far as Johnson did in disregarding the distinctions between literature and life, but we obviously cannot disregard the whole tradition of wisdom literature, from the Book of Ecclesiastes to Montaigne and Pascal, or all the other writings in which man has faced and recorded his actual thoughts and feelings. Johnson's own works and reported utterances no doubt constitute a dispersed, untidy, and awkward body of material for the critic to see as a whole; but that whole constitutes an impressively eloquent, consistent, and truthful vision of human experience.

I have said little about Johnson's writings as such, but I will close by letting him speak for himself, all too briefly, in one of the supreme examples of the literature of experience. Perhaps the most famous example of Johnson's literalism is his attack on Milton's *Lycidas*: 'Where there is leisure for fiction', he said, 'there is little grief'. Johnson's elegy 'On the Death of Dr. Robert Levet' is an absolutely direct treatment of the death of a member of his household, described by Boswell as 'an obscure practiser in physic, of a strange, grotesque appearance'. The poem was written hardly a year before Johnson's own death, and in it all his friendship and humanity was framed by a steady awareness of mankind's limitations:

> Condemn'd to hope's delusive mine,
>   As on we toil from day to day,
> By sudden blasts, or slow decline,
>   Our social comforts drop away.

Well tried through many a varying year,
　　See Levet to the grave descend;
Officious, innocent, sincere,
　　Of ev'ry friendless name the friend.

Yet still he fills affection's eye,
　　Obscurely wise, and coarsely kind;
Nor, letter'd arrogance, deny
　　Thy praise to merit unrefin'd.

When fainting nature call'd for aid,
　　And hov'ring death prepar'd the blow,
His vig'rous remedy display'd
　　The power of art without the show.

In misery's darkest caverns known,
　　His useful care was ever nigh,
When hopeless anguish pour'd his groan,
　　And lonely want retir'd to die.

No summons mock'd by chill delay,
　　No petty gain disdain'd by pride,
The modest wants of ev'ry day,
　　The toil of ev'ry day supplied.

His virtues walk'd their narrow round,
　　Nor made a pause, nor left a void;
And sure th' Eternal Master found
　　The single talent well employ'd.

The busy day, the peaceful night,
　　Unfelt, uncounted, glided by:
His frame was firm, his powers were bright,
　　Tho' now his eightieth year was nigh.

Then with no throbbing fiery pain,
　　No cold gradations of decay,
Death broke at once the vital chain,
　　And free'd his soul the nearest way.

UNIVERSITY OF CALIFORNIA, BERKELEY

JEFFREY HART

Some Thoughts on Johnson as Hero

"Maybe there never was anyone so young as Boswell was in the spring of 1763," Christopher Morley remarks in his preface to the *London Journal;* and indeed it is that quality of youthfulness, though of a very special kind, that makes so poignant, so impressive finally, this record of Boswell's early adventures in London. "When we came upon Highgate Hill," writes Boswell of his approach to the city, "I was all life and joy." And a few months later some songs in a play evoke the same emotions: "The songs revived in my mind many gay ideas, and recalled in the most lively colors to my imagination the time when I was first in London, when all was new to me, when I felt the warm glow of youthful feeling and was full of curiosity and wonder." As we read his *Journal* we come to perceive the sources of that joy and that wonder; we see that by joy and wonder he meant an extraordinary awareness of possibility, an awareness that in London, as nowhere else in England, one could, if one had sufficient powers of imagination, be anything one liked.

In Scotland, which lay behind him, his identity was relatively fixed: he must eventually practice the law, preside over Auchinleck, and marry the proper sort of wife. But here in London he can experiment with different selves, each of which is the creation of his imagination. "I patrolled up and down Fleet Street, thinking on London, the seat of Parliament and the seat of pleasure, and seeming to myself as one of the wits in King Charles the Second's time." In such moods as this he plays the rake: "I should have mentioned last night that I met with a monstrous big whore in the Strand..." At another time he imagines himself a blackguard. "It was the King's birth-night, and I resolved to be a blackguard and to see all that was to be seen." And he can be a lover in the highest style – the liaison with Louisa, one feels, was surely invented by Wycherley — or else he can be a literary man, or a respectable and pious citizen, or a friend of Wilkes or of aristocrats, or even – it glitters on his horizon — a commissioned officer in the Guards.

Boswell, we see, was one of the earliest to discover the meaning of the modern city. His *Journal* describes for us the process of that discovery, and the kinds of feelings attendant upon it; and this is a process that is to be central to much of the literature of the next century and a half. The spiritual descendants of Boswell were to explore, as he did, those transformations of self which the peculiar conditions of the modern city make possible: Pip, in *Great Expectations*, becomes a gentleman; Julien Sorel plays a succession of roles and scales the heights of society; James Gatz becomes Jay Gatsby, Oxford man and military hero. Lionel Trilling has called this sort of figure the Young Man from the Provinces: "a provincial birth and rearing suggest the simplicity and the high hopes he begins with — he starts with a great demand upon life and a great wonder about its complexity and promise," and he moves from his obscure position to one of eminence in Paris or London. He touches "the life of the rulers of the earth." It is this story that is told in Boswell's *Journal* and in the *Confessions* of Rousseau, as in some of the greatest novels: *The Red and the Black, Père Goriot, Great Expectations, Sentimental Education, The Princess Casamassima, The Great Gatsby*. The experience with which these books are concerned — the discovery that virtually unlimited possibility is the essence of the modern city — became available at the moment when the modern city was born; sometime, that is, during the middle years of the eighteenth century. Before that time, one supposes, social status was too clearly defined for Boswell's various roles to have much validity: in London, as elsewhere, one might be quickly categorized. The city was, so to speak, an extension of the provinces. But by the middle of the century the city had grown sufficiently — there was the necessary mobility, and just enough anonymity – for an exceptional young man to entertain the diverse possibilities of selfhood that we encounter in the pages of Boswell's *Journal*. This is the discovery that Boswell makes when he comes to London, it is this which produces in him that wonder and joy when he first sees the city from Highgate Hill. He felt about London much as, a century and a half later, Nick Carraway was to feel about New York: "The city seen from the Queensboro Bridge is always the city seen for the first time, in its first wild promise of all the mystery and beauty in the world.... 'Anything can happen now that we've slid over this bridge,' I thought, 'anything at all.' "

The extraordinary popularity of the *London Journal* may be accounted for in part, I think, by the fact that it does express this sense of the city; for now we are more aware of the dehumanizing forces of the modern city than of its promise, more aware of threat than of opportunity. We scarcely feel inclined any longer to celebrate the city as a reservoir of infinite potentiality. And we are therefore inclined to look nostalgically back upon that time, surely the golden age of the city, when it seemed possible to do so. Yet we know, as Boswell eventually discovered, that if one can be anything one wishes one may never achieve any true identity at all. "Know thyself," Boswell says at the beginning of the *London Journal,* "for surely this knowledge is of all the most important." His journals constitute the record of his long search for himself, a search never to be crowned with success. The aging Boswell remains a Young Man from the Provinces, open to all the possibilities of society and intellect, and in the end no doubt defeated by them. We remember him savoring Hume's skepticism, carousing with Wilkes, responding to Ossian, then behaving like a High Tory or else like a disciple of Rousseau. He had even been converted to Roman Catholicism in his youth, and then had renounced it; yet in 1773, amid the ruins of a chapel on St. Kenneth's island, he felt that earlier self return: "I walked out in the dark to the cross, knelt before it, and holding it with both my hands, I prayed with strong devotion ... I said '*Sancte Columbe, ora pro me.*'" Because Boswell in the course of his long search never succeeds in knowing himself, he frequently finds himself plunged into despair. "This was one of the blackest days that I ever passed ... I had lost all relish of London." Again and again this note recurs. As in the case of Gatsby (and how much they have in common, even to the analogous significance of Louisa and Daisy), the dreams the city nurtures have an alarming capacity to turn to ashes.

Johnson had come to London more than twenty-five years earlier than Boswell and unlike Boswell he retained his singular identity to the end. His life in the city turned out to be a long and successful defence of his identity against the contradictory possibilities of his culture. As Carlyle shrewdly observed, Johnson was a moral hero, should be seen, as it was Boswell's greatness so to see him, to have been an exemplary figure. What Carlyle had in mind was Johnson's irreducibility, the courage which enabled him to conquer his "vile melancholy," to hold at bay his fears and his guilt, to fend off all attacks upon his principles. As Boswell observed, accurately and beautifully, Johnson's "mind resembled the vast amphitheatre, the Coliseum at Rome. In the center stood his judgment, which like a mighty gladiator, combatted those apprehensions that, like the wild beasts of the *Arena,* were all around in cells, ready to be let out upon him. After a conflict, he drives them back into their dens; but not killing them, they were still assailing him." Boswell's comparison of Johnson to a gladiator is perfect, for combat was central to his most characteristic activities. As he once remarked to Boswell about the art of conversation, no dialogue can occur "but one or the other will come off superior. I do not mean that the victor must have the better of the argument, for he may take the weak side; but his superiority of parts and knowledge will necessarily appear: and he to whom he thus shows himself superior is lessened in the eyes of the young men." Nor was Johnson combative only in conversation. His defiance of Macpherson is well known: "I hope I shall not be deterred from detecting what I think a cheat by the menaces of a ruffian." Here he was defending the profession of letters against fraud, as he had, in the famous letter to Chesterfield, defended it against the arrogance of a patron. He was humble before the Lord Jesus Christ, as Medford Evans has aptly remarked, but not before any other Lord, not even the Lord Chesterfield; and perhaps the two attitudes are not unrelated.

Nor was this kind of intellectual and moral courage, refined and even delicate though it could become when circumstances demanded, very different in its intransigence of spirit from his extraordinary physical courage. As Boswell tells us, he "feared death, but he feared nothing else, not even what might occasion death." Boswell reports, for example, that Johnson "told me himself that one night he was attacked in the street by four men, to whom he would not yield, but kept them all at bay, till the watch came up, and carried both him and them to the round house." He even seemed to seek out danger in order to prove himself against it: "Mr. Langton told me, that when they were swimming together near Oxford, he cautioned Dr. Johnson against a pool, which was reckoned particularly dangerous; upon which Johnson directly swam into it."

Johnson's undoubted courage, however, was called upon for subtler feats than these, for intellectual tasks imposed upon him, as it were, by his enormous appetite for experience. As we read Boswell, and read Johnson's works themselves, we see that he excluded almost nothing of value from his awareness, and that, as a consequence, he was obliged to hold in precarious balance a whole series of intellectual and emotional antinomies which defined in the fullest way all the possibilities of his culture. It is the agility of his intelligence as well as his strength of will that in the end are so impressive; and perhaps this *agility* accounts in part for his appeal for so many readers: it is surely not the least of his attractions that, like Falstaff and Chesterton, he combined unwieldy physical bulk with intellectual grace, with delicacy and agility of mind.

II

The tasks imposed upon Johnson by his age may be more clearly defined, I think, if we consider very briefly, and with respect chiefly to the rhetoric of poetry, the development of the cultural tradition he inherited. Seventeenth century writers – it is perhaps the first thing to say about them – had been very much aware of the contradictory variety of experience. They did not, however, provided their modes of thought performed their proper tasks, permit it to remain contradictory. The metaphysical conceit is the literary gesture of the process by which one passes beyond the opposition of antinomies to a perception of coherence. Beginning with such antinomies, for example, as lovers and compasses, or lovers and saints, the conceit finally produces a harmonious vision: the lovers *are* in a sense saints or compasses; analogical relations have been reestablished. Examples of this kind of thing in Donne are too well known to require further specification. In Marvell's "The Garden" we see a comparable intellectual operation. Wit, or imagination combined with intelligence, is the means of reconciling man's lowest capacities, his "vegetable soul," with the pursuit of a transcendant ideal, conceived of as the function of his "rational soul." When Pan pursues Syrinx "not as a nymph but for a reed" we understand that he is pursuing one of the "sacred plants," the transcendant ideal of innocence. The end of such pursuits, properly understood, therefore, is the reconciliation of the "vegetable" and the "rational" in man's nature: "a green thought in a green shade." In the final stanza of this poem the circle imagery represents the reconstruction of imaginative wholeness, the transcendance of antinomies. *Paradise Lost*, it will be seen, expands the dialectic to cosmic size, is, in fact, a huge conceit: the antinomies Satan and Eden clash and through their clash produce some·thing new, the "paradise within."

The transition to a rhetoric characteristic of the Augustans may be studied in a variety of ways. Dryden abandons the conceit early in his career, no doubt seeing that his conceits had been merely ornamental, and works for a decade to develop the balanced couplets of his mature works. We understand, as we read his major poems, that his concern was not to *create* coherence, as had been the case with Donne, Marvell, and Milton, but rather to *assert* it: to defend, implicitly as well as explicity, a moral, intellectual and political consensus which he regards as already established. The rhetoric of his mature poetry is the perfect reflection of the characteristic operation of his intellect: to exclude, rather than to assimilate, whatever would disturb the balance of mind or state. In reading Dryden and his greatest followers, one is aware that with respect to diction, as Donald Davie has put it, "a selection has been made and is continually being made, that words are thrusting at the poem and being fended off from it, that however many poems these poets wrote certain words would never be allowed into the poems, except as a disastrous oversight." This, in contrast to, say, Donne, where one is aware of no such pressure. The decorum of the Augustan poem, then, had to be maintained much as the order of the state had to be maintained against an Achitophel, or the order of the mind against an insurgent "fancy" We recall, in this connection, Boswell's image for Johnson's mind: "in the center stood his judgment... like a mighty gladiator..."

Swift forces us to look almost continuously at the unassimilable, at those beasts in their cells around the edges of the arena. He does this in the interest of pressing upon us an awareness of the value of the weapons we have against them: reason, the social order, a belief in providence. The latest interpretations of Swift emphasize, correctly, his seventeenth century affiliations; for, like Donne, he was open to the most heterogeneous ideas — of excrement, and of pure reason, for example — but he scarcely succeeded in yoking these heterogeneous ideas together, whatever the violence of the wit he was able to bring to bear upon them. In "The Mechanical Operation of the Spirit," the higher and the lower, the spiritual and the physical, are seen as related; but the result of this perception is not, as in Donne or Marvell or Milton, a sudden perception of harmony: rather it is the emotion, insisted upon, of outrage. In "The Lady's Dressing Room" Strephon learns that Celia shits and becomes a misogynist. But he ought to anaesthetize this perception, the poet says — "if Strephon would but stop his nose" — for all of experience simply cannot be dealt with in similar terms. Only if he stops his nose can he expect to celebrate Celia's glory, bless

> his ravish'd eyes to see
> Such order from confusion sprung,
> Such gaudy tulips rais'd from dung.

The wit characteristic of the heroic couplet, however, as it reached its perfection in Pope, works to dissipate the tension between the antinomies Swift made us face. Such antinomies, this wit tells us, are what a civilized man must live with. Furthermore, this wit implies that — it is essential to the wit that it need not *say* so — the manners of civilization are capable of dealing with them. Antinomies are comprehended by a civilized order (analogous to a divine order) which is present in the poem — very *much* present — as an exquisitely modulated tone of voice. Just as "the nymph shall break Diana's law,/ Or some frail China jar receive a flaw," so Queen Anne "Dost sometimes counsel take — and sometimes tea," or God, the most civilized individual in Pope's poetry, sees "now a bubble burst, and now a world." *Nil admirari*: the tone functions here as a kind of metaphor, holding in balance those disparities in experience which the metaphysical conceit would have attempted to depict as analogical identities. Surely no more serious task has ever been demanded of civilized tact. Indeed Hume, we recall, regarded such tact as an alternative to his philosophy. And Burke, who began his career as a writer of couplets and as a neoclassical aesthetician, defended in his political theory the circumstances upon which that tact, that tone of voice, depended: "We balance," he said, "we reconcile, we conciliate."

III

Johnson knew, and it is a principal source of his strength that he knew so thoroughly, the variety of forces that had to be reconciled, or at least held in check, if the values of that particular civilization were to be maintained. In literature, in politics, in religion he was aware of, indeed he responded passionately to, the most disparate of possibilities, and yet he strove to comprehend such possibilities within the civilized tradition which commanded his allegiance. As F.R. Leavis has put it, "Johnson is not, like the Romantic poet, the enemy of society, but consciously its representative and its voice, and it is his strength — something inseparable from his greatness — to be so."

Everyone knows, for example, that Johnson admired subordination in society. Men, he observed to Boswell, "are happier in a state of inequality and subordination. Were they to be in this pretty state of equality, they would soon degenerate into brutes." In a similar vein, he once remarked to Mrs. Thrale: "You are to consider, Madam, that it is our duty to maintain the subordination of civilized society; and when there is a gross and shameful deviation from rank, it should be punished so as to deter others from the same perversion." He disinterestedly thought such respect for rank necessary to society: "I am for supporting the principle, and am disinterested in doing it, as I have no such right." And he saw the value of family tradition: "But, surely, it is much easier to respect a man who has always had respect than to respect a man who we know was last year no better than ourselves, and will be no better next year ... riches do not gain hearty respect; they only procure external attention. A very rich man, from low beginnings, may buy his election in a borough; but, *caeteris paribus*, a man of family will be preferred." He considered that "as subordination is very necessary for society, and contentions for superiority very dangerous, mankind, that is to say, all civilized nations, have settled it upon a plain invariable principle. A man is born to hereditary rank; or his being appointed to a certain office, gives him a certain rank." Johnson saw with exemplary clarity that the life of the city was destructive of gallantry and nobility: "Being asked by a young nobleman what was become of the gallantry and military spirit of the old English nobility, he replied, 'Why, my Lord, I'll tell you what has become of it: it has gone into the city to look for a fortune.'" And he saw that it was money that was breaking down subordination, that more and more the relations among people would be defined in terms of money: "I have explained in my 'Journey to the Hebrides' how gold and silver destroy feudal subordination. But, besides, there is a general relaxation of reverence." Johnson also saw, it seems, that his own identity, and perhaps the clarity of his status as man of letters, which constituted a goodly portion of his identity, depended upon a reciprocal recognition of the status of others: "I consider myself as acting a part in the great system of society ... I would behave to a nobleman as I should expect he would behave to me, were I a nobleman and he Sam. Johnson."

On the other hand, and this is not generally recognized, no one knew better than he the wonder of the new kind of society that was emerging in the metropolis, no one has ever expressed in so eloquent a phrase as Johnson's the spirit of the new and insurgent capitalism. When Thrale had died after making his fortune as a brewer, Johnson assisted at the sale of the brewery — Johnson "appeared bustling about, with an inkhorn and pen in his buttonhole, like an exciseman; and on being asked what he really considered to be the value of the property which was to be disposed, of, answered, 'We are not here to sell a parcel or boilers and vats, but the potentiality of growing rich beyond the dreams of avarice.'" He saw long before

Goethe that capitalism was not utilitarian but Faustian, and, perhaps in spite of himself, he responded to its vision. Despite his commitment to traditional values he also felt, as he once remarked, that one should "always fly at the eagle," and he felt at the center of the city itself "the full tide of human existence." "When a man is tired of London," he said, "he is tired of life; for there is in London all that life can afford." Thus, though he was passionately devoted to the traditional order, to the values of subordination, tradition, and reverence, he was also passionately involved with the social forces arrayed against them. He knew the beauty and value of order, but he also knew the excitement of aspiration. For this reason I do not think that it will do to describe Johnson as characteristically common-sensical or utilitarian: though he did indeed have common sense, and though he often judged on the basis of utility, he was too large an emotional entity, too imaginative, to be so defined. His sympathies extended to opposite poles of social possibility.

His judgments concerning literature exhibit when compared with one another a similar tension between contradictory positions. His allegiance was to the main tradition of neoclassicism. That this literary allegiance had wider implications F.R. Leavis has made evident enough: "It is in [Johnson's] ... verse that we can see most clearly the extremely positive civilization to which Johnson belonged expressing itself as literary convention ... For most eighteenth-century verse, and all verse of the Augustan tradition, has a social movement — a movement that suggests company deportment, social gesture, and a code of manners." The Augustan tradition begins for Johnson with Denham and Waller, continues through Dryden, and culminates in Pope. "By perusing the works of Dryden, he [Pope] discovered the most perfect fabric of English verse, and habituated himself to that only which he found the best ... New sentiments and new images others may produce; but to attempt any further improvement of versification will be dangerous." That this is not merely a *literary* judgment, but is involved with a whole series of social assumptions, should be clear enough. Johnson condemns deviations from the mode epitomized by Pope. The metaphysicals "endeavoured to be singular in their thoughts and were careless of their diction." Milton had, both in prose and verse, "formed his style by a perverse and pedantic principle." The language of Gray is "too luxuriant" and "a little ... beyond common apprehension." Collins seemed to think "with some later candidates for fame, that not to write prose is certainly to write poetry." In the famous

tenth chapter of *Rasselas* Johnson gave the most eloquent expression we
have of the neoclassical spirit in poetry. The poet "is to examine not the
individual, but the species. He does not number the streaks of the tulip, or
describe the different shades in the verdure of the forest: he is to exhibit
in his portraits of nature such prominent and striking features, as recall the
original to every mind ... he must disregard present laws and opinions, and
rise to general and transcendental truths, which will always be the same."
We cannot suppose, as some have, that this is Imlac's opinion rather than
Johnson's, for Johnson applies the same standard in his critical essays. "Great
thoughts," he observes in his commentary on the metaphysicals, "are always
general, and consist in positions not limited by exceptions, and in descriptions not descending to minuteness."

Yet even so, when it came to biography, he knew, as Boswell said, the
value of a "minute selection of characteristical circumstances" which serves
to distinguish particular experience from general. Here, as in his *Journey
to the Western Islands,* he shows the influence of that increasing concern
with the *historical* which marked the second half of the century, a concern
with the flux of time and the uniqueness of the moment, which was ultimately so subversive of the neoclassical attempt to focus upon the permanent
in experience, upon the general as distinguished from the particular truth.
Again, when he used the word *nature* to define the difference between
Richardson and Fielding he was adding a psychological, a subjective, dimen-
sion to the neoclassical sense of that word. "Sir," he said, "there is all the
difference in the world between characters of nature and characters of
manners; and *there* is the difference between those of Fielding and those
of Richardson. Characters of manners are very entertaining; but they are to
be understood by a more superficial observer than characters of nature,
where a man must dive into the recesses of the human heart." Here, as in
his social views, we see him, despite his allegiances, attracted to insurgent
and even potentially revolutionary forces. And, oddly enough, it is the
insurgent that evokes his most eloquent, his most memorable, phrases:
"the potentiality of growing rich beyond the dreams of avarice ... a man
must dive into the recesses of the human heart."

It may well be that the range of Johnson's sympathies, and the power
of imagination implicit in such a range, is one of the reasons for the enduring
fascination of Johnson for the most diverse of readers. Like Shakespeare,
he has been claimed by every faction. Even in his religious views one en-

counters a variety of attitude analogous to that in his social and literary opinions. Perhaps his most characteristic, and even his final, allegiance was to
tradition. "Human experience," he told Boswell,

> which is constantly contradicting theory, is the great test of
> truth. A system, built upon the discoveries of a great many
> minds, is always of more strength, than what is produced
> by the mere workings of one mind, which, of itself, can do
> little. There is not so poor a book in the world that would not
> be a prodigious effort were it wrought out entirely by a single
> mind, without the aid of prior investigators. The French
> writers are superficial, because they are not scholars, and so
> proceed upon the mere power of their own minds; and we
> see how little power they have.

Such a position is difficult to distinguish from Burke's: the experience of
many men, or of many generations, counts for more than the experience of
one man or one generation. Nevertheless, his powerful skeptical intelligence
caused him, for example, to persist in searching for further evidence of the
existence of the supernatural, even though that existence seemed to be confirmed by the voice of mankind. He perhaps had more in common with the
analytical Hume than he cared to admit. On the other hand, as we read his
prayers and meditations, we find that his religious temper also had a good
deal in common with the intense and personal religion characteristic of
Methodism. He kept, and advised Boswell to keep, a spiritual diary for the
purpose of self-examination. "Almighty God," he writes in a mood characteristic of his private devotions, "heavenly father, who desirest not the death
of a sinner, look down with mercy upon me, depraved with vain imaginations, and entangled in long habits of sin." Indeed, Boswell went so far as
to observe that "Johnson himself was, in a dignified manner, a Methodist.
In his *Rambler*, No. 110, he mentions with respect 'the whole discipline of
regulated piety'...."

There is no need, it seems to me, to examine in further detail Johnson's
characteristic opinions and attitudes, for the point must now be clear:
Johnson lived at a time when a variety of contradictory possibilities pressed
upon the intelligent awareness, and, despite his allegiance to traditional, to
Augustan values, Johnson responded sympathetically, indeed eloquently,

to whatever was most powerful and valid in the forces, cultural and social, which threatened those values.

His final affirmation of order draws force, indeed, from his awareness of the heterogeneity of that which was to be ordered, in the self as well as in society. Like so many of the great defenders of order he was a violent man. He knew the value of order in the world because he knew what the absence of order meant for the self. When he was twenty, so Boswell tells us, he had a severe nervous collapse: "While he was at Lichfield, in the college vacation year of 1729, he felt himself overwhelmed with a horrible hypochondria, with perpetual irritation, fretfulness, and impatience; and with a dejection, gloom, and despair, which made existence misery. From this dismal malady he never afterward was perfectly relieved ..." Indeed, he afterward found himself threatened by a recurrence: "About this time [1764] he was afflicted with a severe return of the hypochondriac disorder ..." His eccentricity of manner, his impulsiveness, his vast appetites, made all the more firm his commitment to order, for he knew only too well the energies latent in the self: after the conversation with Chambers about Langton's will, "Johnson could not stop his merriment, but continues it all the way till he got without the Temple-gate. He then burst into such a fit of laughter that he appeared to be almost in a convulsion; and, in order to support himself, laid hold of one of the posts at the side of the foot pavement, and sent forth peals so loud, that in the silence of the night his voice seemed to resound from Temple Bar to Fleet Ditch."

In an earlier paragraph, while attempting to characterize the Augustan mode in rhetoric and to distinguish it from the mode representative of the seventeenth century, I observed that the wit characteristic of the heroic couplet works to dissipate the tension between antinomies, works to comprehend them in a civilized order which is present in the poem as an assumption, as a tone of voice. By the time Johnson's style had matured, by the time of *The Vanity of Human Wishes*, we sense that almost intolerable strains are being imposed upon this rhetoric. Of all the poets who developed during the middle years of the century none desired more fervently than Johnson to maintain Augustan literary norms. But his poetic medium, we observe, is far denser than either Dryden's or Pope's, his syntax often tortured and his diction often obscure. We are aware, in reading some of the lines in *The Vanity of Human Wishes*, that he had studied closely and learned from the prose of Sir Thomas Browne — though he censured its lapses of decorum —

and that he had read very widely among the metaphysicals. There are qualities in Johnson's verse which do not seem susceptible of being ordered by
the kind of civilized tact which Pope had employed so triumphantly.

> But scarce observ'd the knowing and the bold
> Fall in the gen'ral massacre of gold.

Why are they "scarce observ'd" ? Because so many are dying that the death
(moral ?) of the knowing and the bold will not be observed ? Is there the
implication here that gold has a levelling effect upon moral distinction,
renders knowledge and boldness invisible ? What is the precise meaning
of "fall" ? And what, precisely, is the "massacre of gold" ? The norms ope-
rating in Johnson's diction quite obviously are not those of Pope, the norms
of polite conversation. Or consider another line: "And restless fire precipitates on death." Not only is this line unusually elliptical because of the
idiosyncratic use of "precipitates," but it cannot be fully understood without
reference to the first line of the *preceding* couplet. The deliberate ellipsis, the
"hard words," the combination of strong verb and personification ("Hate
dogs their flight and insult mocks their end.") all contribute to that "lyric"
quality which Wallace Cable Brown has defined in Johnson's verse, to what
F.R. Leavis has called its "achieved substance ... experience felt by the
reader as movingly present." We are aware here of the sound of the poet's
own voice, of the fact that Johnson's own experience, rather than general
conclusions about experience, is being presented. The difficulty of this
rhetoric, its insistence upon personal experience, defines its difference from
Pope's, and Johnson's distance from the ordering norms of Pope's culture.

IV

The reason why Boswell's relationship to Johnson has what might be
called a *classic* quality ought now to be fairly clear. It is not only that they
were very different and in some respects opposite kinds of men; the point
is that their differences had, as it were, a *representative* meaning. Both came
from the provinces to London. But when Johnson came to London in 1737
he brought with him — and perhaps he was one of the last major figures to
do so — the values of the Augustan tradition, and he committed himself to,
defined himself by, the defence of those values. Boswell, in contrast, adum-
brated the future, felt free to experiment with a variety of selves and to assume, without attempting to reconcile, disparate sets of values. Johnson,

like the other great conservatives of the century — Swift, Pope, Gibbon, Burke — had the ability to view society as a whole, to stand outside of it and view it as a *social order*. By so doing, such thinkers were able to endow the individual act with a wider, a general, significance, to evaluate it in terms of wider relations. As Johnson said, "I consider myself as acting a part in the great system of society ..." But Boswell, like Sterne for example, had little or no sense of society as a social order, could not achieve the imaginative perspective of the great conservatives, could not rise to general meanings. Society did not, for Boswell, impose identity; rather it existed as a limitless reservoir of possible identities. Johnson knows, as we have seen, the social function of the aristocrat but never supposes that he is one. Boswell, in contrast, and with politically sinister implications, is capable of impersonating an aristocrat. Johnson's entire intellectual career was involved with the defence of social and intellectual values which required a man to have a particular character, behave according to established principles. But what Boswell found in London, what evoked in him feelings of joy and wonder, was precisely the liberation from those requirements.

The struggle which gave weight to Johnson's rhetoric, made it the unmistakably personal expression of a self attempting to order its experience, disappears in Boswell and we find instead a perfect, and indeed a selfless, lucidity. The possibilities of experience do not conflict for Boswell as they did for Johnson. They have no implications beyond themselves, no reference to a wider order of meanings. They do not conflict, they merely succeed one another cinematically: Tory, libertine, *littérateur*, Scottish laird, sentimentalist, skeptic, Roman Catholic. And it is the selfless lucidity of Boswell's prose that enables us to see so clearly the unforgettable, the intransigent, selfhood of Johnson.

CCLUMBIA UNIVERSITY

A . R . H U M P H R E Y S

Dr. Johnson, Troubled Believer

To subject oneself to the influence of Johnson is always a strengthening experience; to submit oneself to the influence of his religious thought is to be profoundly searched and moved. Few writers on him have failed to take into account his religious views; these are central to his life, his critical tastes, his moral attitudes. Since Strahan added the *Prayers and Meditations* to the corpus of Johnsonian publications in 1785 there have been these strange but deeply impressive records from within to add to the observations made by other persons; the sum total of material is large, various in implication, and stamped with the impress of a deeply-exploring personality.

The earliest cognisance Johnson records of any religious matter dates from the age of three, and though it apparently had little effect at the time the eschatological dichotomy it embodies was in his later reflective life the deepest of all consciousnesses with him:

> I remember, that being in bed with my nother one morning, I was told by her of the two places to which the inhabitants of this world were received after death; one a fine place filled with happiness, called heaven; the other a *sad* place, called hell. That this account much affected my imagination, I do not remember.[1]

What did affect his imagination was an early and thorough knowledge of the *Book of Common Prayer*, whose phraseology became second nature to him in religious matters, and the 'vile melancholy' inherited from his father, 'which has made me mad all my life, at least not sober' [2] — 'a morbid

---

(1) Boswell, *Life of Johnson*, ed. G.B. Hill, rev. L.F. Powell, 1934, i. 38, fn..

(2) Boswell, *Journal of a Tour to the Hebrides*, ed. Frederick A. Pottle and Charles H. Bennett, London, 1936, p. 174.

melancholy and disturbance of mind', he calls it in the *Diaries* (7 April, 1776)(3) —, resulting often, writes Boswell, in 'a general sensation of gloomy wretchedness'(4). By nature too, when he came to be intellectually self-aware, he had that 'obstinate rationality' which prevented any relaxation in his moral self-inquisition, any comfortable yielding to authority:

> A good man, of a timorous disposition, in great doubt of his acceptance with GOD, and pretty credulous, might be glad to be of a church where there are so many helps to get to Heaven. I would be a Papist if I could. I have fear enough, but an obstinate rationality prevents me. I shall never be a Papist, unless on the near approach of death, of which I have a very great terrour(5).

The Prayer-Book, melancholy, obstinate rationality, terror of death, and what Dr. Cairns has called 'a tender and unwearied charity to all weak and broken creatures'(6) — these constitute the elements of Johnson's troubled faith. Christian duty came upon him with the full force of his reason, but also as the generous outcome of a compassionate nature deeply tried with pain and difficulty.

Though so centrally an Anglican believer he was charitably inclusive in his basic religious sympathies; 'many of his sentiments on religious subjects' — to quote Macaulay's supercilious admission — 'are worthy of a liberal and enlarged mind'(7). They are indeed. He was, as has been seen, not hostile to Roman Catholicism, and he respected John Wesley(8). His detestation he reserved for materialism, free-thinking, deism, or complacent optimism; these concealed the tragic sense of life, and its divine mysteriousness. Faith must admit the mysteries of trial and pain. These mysteries he felt and agonised over in his whole nature. 'I said,' Boswell recorded (though he did not transcribe the record into the *Life*), "'Has any man the same conviction of the truth of Religion that he has in the common affairs of Life?" He said,

---

(3) Johnson, *Diaries, Prayers, and Annals*, ed. E.L. McAdam, Jr. with Donald and Mary Hyde, Yale, 1956, i. 257 (cited as *Diaries*).

(4) *Life*, ed. cit., i. 35.

(5) ibid., iv. 289.

(6) W.T. Cairns, *The Religion of Dr. Johnson and other essays*, Oxford, 1946, p. 1.

(7) T.B. Macaulay, *Works*, ed. Lady Trevelyan, 1866, v. 527.

(8) *Life*, ed. cit., iii. 230 and fn., iii. 394.

"No, Sir".'(9) But like texts of Scripture in St. Augustine's, or Luther's, or Bunyan's mind, Prayer-Book phrases were always in his thoughts; church he attended devoutly though irregularly, often too deaf to hear the sermon, but going over the prayers or Collects, or the devotions he composed himself for the anniversaries he kept — Good Friday, Easter Day, his birthday, his wife's death. He riveted his mind to these things as anchors for a passionate and wilful, though noble, personality.

Anguished in self-searching, he was censorious of foolish faults but most understanding of those which needed understanding. The finest of the *Lives of the Poets*, humanly speaking, is that of Savage, the intransigent Bohemian dependent on yet ungrateful for the help of others. Johnson leaves no doubt about his faults — faults of a proud, rebellious, disconcerting man — but finally sums him up with charity, and an admonition that makes men brothers:

> Those are no proper judges of his conduct, who have slumbered away their time on the down of plenty; nor will any wise man presume to say, 'Had I been in Savage's condition, I should have lived or written better than Savage'.(10)

For the poor, having been one of them, he felt compassion — 'He loved the poor as I never yet saw any one else do, with an earnest desire to make them happy,' is Mrs Thrale's comment.(11) His kindness towards the struggling or destitute provoked his friends' wonder; commenting on the home he provided for the blind Anna Williams, for Mrs. Desmoulins, daughter of his old physician Dr. Swinfen, and for Mrs. Desmoulins' daughter, Boswell observes:

> We surely cannot but admire the benevolent exertions of this great and good man, especially when we consider how grievously he was afflicted with bad health, and how uncomfortable his home was made by the perpetual jarring of those whom he charitably accommodated under his roof.(12)

---

(9) J.W. Krutch, *Samuel Johnson*, London, 1948, p. 478.

(10) Johnson, *Lives of the Poets*, ed. G.B. Hill, Oxford, 1905, ii. 433.

(11) *Johnsonian Miscellanies*, ed. G.B. Hill, Oxford, 1897, i. 204.

(12) *Life*, ed. cit., iii. 368.

He carried home an exhausted prostitute, had her cared for while she was ill, and, writes Boswell, 'endeavoured to put her into a virtuous way of living'.(13) Boswell elsewhere notes his 'uniform and extensive'(14) charity to the poor, and remarks

> Johnson's benevolence to the unfortunate was, I am confident, as steady and active as that of any of those who have been most eminently distinguished for that virtue.(15)

Steevens commented on 'the many bounties he studiously concealed, the many acts of kindness he performed in private'.(16) This kindness came not from eupeptic optimism but from his sense of the gravity of human suffering, the need even of the vicious, and it came throughout a life often tormented with sleeplessness and pain which made him in minor things irascible. 'Impetuous and irritable in his temper', as Boswell remarks, Johnson was 'of a most humane and benevolent heart'.(17)

The opening sentence of Mr Joseph Wood Krutch's admirable biography describes him as 'a pessimist with an enormous zest for living'. If now some stress is to be laid on his melancholia, this should not in the least obscure Johnson's characteristic ardour for life; it should, rather, 'like bright metal on a sullen ground', set that ardour itself forth the more strongly. For the ardour is to be seen against temperamental hypochondria and physical ailments. All but dead at birth, he had an ailing childhood, afflicted with scrofula and, he comments, 'almost blind'.(18) Dr Swinfen testified that 'he never knew any child reared with so much difficulty.'(19) His diary-jottings, in later life, on the aches and ailments of his great awkward body were meant for no-one's eyes but his own; but they move compassion in others. But equally notable is his courage. One finds immediately next to each other in the *Diaries*, first, comments on his pain:

---

(13) ibid., iv. 321-2.
(14) ibid., iv. 132.
(15) ibid., iii. 124.
(16) ibid., iv. 325.
(17) ibid., iv. 426.
(18) *Diaries*, p. 5.
(19) ibid., p. 6.

> I have for some weeks past been much afflicted with the
> Lumbago, or Rheumatism in the Loins, which often passes
> to the muscles of the belly, where it causes equal, if not
> greater, pain ... In the night it is so troublesome as not very
> easily to be born ... One night between the pain and the
> spasms in my stomach I was insupportably distressed.[20]

and next, on the day following, gratitude to God for such health as he has:

> Almighty and everlasting God, who hast preserved me by
> thy fatherly care through all the years of my past Life, and
> now permittest me again to commemorate the sufferings and
> the merits of our Lord and Saviour Jesus Christ ... Make
> me truly thankful for that portion of health which thy mercy
> has restored, and enable me to use the remains of Life to thy
> glory, and my own Salvation.[21]

Though sleepless in Calais, he composes a prayer of gratitude and repentance:

> O God by whom all things were created and are sustained,
> who givest and takest away, in whose hands are life and death,
> accept my imperfect thanks for the length of days which
> thou hast vouchsafed to grant me, [and] impress upon my
> mind such repentance of the time mispent [sic] in sinfulness
> and negligence, that I may obtain forgiveness of all my offen-
> ces.[22]

In Boswell's words, 'his mind was turned to resolution, and never to whin-
ing or complaint'.[23] Physical pains and mental terrors were taken in no
spirit of self-pity or hysteria. A sentence from *The Rambler*, No. 32, which
Boswell never read 'without feeling my frame thrill',[24] has the true Johnsonian nobility:

> I think there is some reason for questioning whether the body
> and mind are not so proportioned, that the one can bear all
> which can be inflicted on the other; whether virtue cannot
> stand its ground as long as life, and whether a soul well
> principled, will not be sooner separated than subdued.

---

(20) ibid., pp. 127-8.

(21) ibid., p. 130.

(22) ibid. p. 228.

(23) *Life*, ed. cit., ii. 357.

(24) ibid., i. 215.

Anguish and terror there are, but not those hysterical depressions of which William James gives accounts in discussing 'The Sick Soul', in *Varieties of Religious Experience*, or the hallucinatory schizophrenia of Bunyan's torments, or panic fear, or suffocating sense of evil. Long-lasting and hardly outlived, Johnson's fears were temperamental but rational also. The 'vile melancholy' excluded him from James's 'healthy-minded' category; but it was reason also, contrasting the high demands of religion with his actual daily performance, which caused him to fear. His very sociability, though partly from generous self-communicatingness, came partly from dread of solitude; even in company he might, he said, 'be cracking my joke, and cursing the sun'.[25] On 21 July, 1763, Boswell first heard from him

> that he had been distrest by melancholy, and for that reason had been obliged to fly from study and meditation, to the dissipating variety of life.[26]

The ring of personal experience is heard in his comment on the merry-makers in *Rasselas*, of whom

> there was not one who did not dread the moment when solitude should deliver him to the tyranny of reflection,[27]

and in that on Rasselas himself, who lived in the crowds of jollity not so much to enjoy as to shun himself, and was only loud and merry to conceal his sadness. Despite his learning and industry Johnson never settled to the methodical life of the scholar because of the self-accusations of his imagination which then, because of the very distraction, and what he perpetually calls his lethargy, found new causes for reproach. If to preside in a tavern was the highest felicity in life, it was so partly because there he had allies against hypochondria.

The causes of his trouble he took to be two, basically. There was agitation as to his sinful nature, and there was inability to succeed in projects of reform. He felt bound to subdue the strong passions of his nature, but fighting these caused great psychological tensions. Boswell records his

(25) ibid., iv. 304.
(26) ibid., i. 446.
(27) *Rasselas*, ch. xvi.

'amorous inclinations ... uncommonly strong and impetuous',[28] and his alternations between abstemiousness and excess:

> many a day did he fast, many a year did he refrain from wine; but when he did eat, it was voraciously; when he did drink wine, it was copiously. He could practise abstinence, but not temperance.[29]

The *Diaries* refer again and again to such matters as 'thoughts clouded with sensuality', and 'appetites [which] have predominated over my reason',[30] 'tumultous imaginations',[31] a mind 'depraved with vain imaginations',[32] 'sinful and corrupt imaginations'.[33] These the American editors equate, rightly no doubt, with sexual fantasies: they occur after Tetty's death. As Johnson struggles, one thinks of St Augustine; one thinks even more of St Paul:

> To will is present with me; but how to perform that which is good I find not. For the good that I would I do not; but the evil which I would not, that I do. Now if I do that I would not, it is no more I that do it, but sin that dwelleth in me. I find, then, a law, that when I would do good, evil is present with me. For I delight in the law of God after the inward man, but I see another law in my members, warring against the law of my mind, and bringing me into captivity to the law of sin which is in my members. O wretched man that I am ! who shall deliver me from the body of this death ?[34]

Examining himself with scrupulous rigour, Johnson applies to his own case the warnings he finds in the Bible. The optimist can disperse the immediacy of the General Confession by sharing his guilt, in the plural, with others — 'We have left undone those things which we ought to have done; And we have done those things which we ought not to have done; And there is no health in us'.[35] For Johnson, his guilt was singular. So, on 31 March, 1771, he prays:

---

(28) *Life*, ed. cit., iv. 395-6.
(29) ibid., iv. 72.
(30) *Diaries*, p. 77.
(31) ibid., p. 46.
(32) ibid., p. 63.
(33) ibid., p. 138.
(34) *Epistle to the Romans*, vii, 18-24.
(35) *Book of Common Prayer*, General Confession.

Almighty and most merciful Father, whose clemency I now
presume to implore after a long life of carelessness and wickedness, have mercy upon me. I have committed many crimes.
I have neglected many duties. I have done what Thou hast
forbidden, and left undone what Thou hast commanded.(36)

This acutely personal conscience is movingly recorded; on 7 April, 1776,
for instance, he receives the communion and comments, 'I was so mollified
by the concluding address to our Saviour that I could not utter it'.(37) This
concluding address is:

O Lord, the only-begotten Son, Jesus Christ; O Lord God,
Lamb of God, Son of the Father, that takest away the sins
of the world, have mercy upon us. Thou that takest away
the sins of the world, have mercy upon us.

As against the occasional relief expressed in the *Diaries* — 'I . . . went through
the prayers without perturbation',(38) 'I had this day a doubt like Baxter of
my state, and found that my Faith, though weak, was yet Faith',(39) 'I went to
evening prayers and was undisturbed',(40) 'Shall I ever receive the sacrament
with tranquillity ? Surely the time will come'(41) — there is an overweight of
a sense of 'habitual wickedness and idleness'(42) and of being 'entangled in
long habits of sin'.(43) He prays repeatedly to shun sloth and negligence;
he records his '*mens turbata*'.(44) On his fifty-ninth birthday he notes:

How the last year has past I am unwilling to terrify myself
with thinking. This day has been past in great perturbation.
I was distracted at Church in an uncommon degree, and my
distress has had very little intermission.(45)

---

(36) *Diaries*, p. 139.
(37) ibid., p. 260.
(38) ibid., p. 105.
(39) ibid., p. 106.
(40) ibid., p. 108.
(41) ibid., p. 132.
(42) ibid., p. 80.
(43) ibid., p. 63.
(44) ibid., p. 316.
(45) ibid., p. 119.

A prayer on his forty-eighth birthday ends with a list of faults which recur as a running theme throughout his life:

> Idleness intemperate sleep dilatoriness immethodical life
> Lust
> Neglect of Worship
> Vain scruples.(46)

Against all these he repeatedly resolves; and repeatedly his resolves are broken. His despondency and courage prompt the following comment, on Good Friday, 14 April, 1775:

> When I look back upon resoluti[ons] of improvement and amendments, which have year after year been made and broken, either by negligence, forgetfulness, vicious idleness, casual interruption, or morbid infirmity, when I find that so much of my life has stolen unprofitably away, and that I can descry by retrospection scarcely a few single days properly and vigorously employed, why do I yet try to resolve again ? I try because Reformation is necessary and despair is criminal. I try in humble hope of the help of God.(47)

In the light of Johnson's total of achievement and charity of nature this self-reproach must seem, as Macaulay unsympathetically declared, 'the tyranny of scruples as unreasonable as those of Hudibras and Ralpho'.(48) Yet it is not mere morbid hysteria. Allowances which Johnson's strong mind and honest judgment generously made for others he would not make for himself. With that 'obstinate rationality' which dispensed with illusion he tested himself against the transcendent demands of Christian faith and performance, and the tension between the rational grasp of what was required of man and the rational perception how far short he fell in performance shook him with terror. 'Too much a believer not to fear divine punishment and too invincibly a sceptic to count his faith sufficient to save him' — as Mr Krutch puts it(49) — he had to pray for deliverance from 'the distresses of vain ter-

---

(46) ibid., p. 64.
(47) ibid., p. 225.
(48) T.B. Macaulay, *Works*, ed. cit., v. 528.
(49) J.W. Krutch, op. cit., p. 1.

rour'.(50) Echoing the last of the Prayer-Book's 'Prayers upon Several Occasions', he noted on 18 September, 1764;

> I went to Church; prayed *to be loosed from the chain of my sins.*
> I have now spent fifty five years in resolving, having from
> the earliest time almost that I can remember been forming
> schemes of a better life. I have done nothing; the need of
> doing therefore is pressing, since the time of doing is short.
> O God grant me to resolve aright, and to keep my resolution
> for Jesus Christs sake. Amen.(51)

On Good Friday, 1765, he comments, 'In reading Nelson, thought on Death cum lachrimis'(52), and Mrs. Thrale records that he would burst into tears over the verse from the *Dies Irae*:

> Quaerens me, sedisti lassus;
> Redemisti, crucem passus;
> Tantus labor non sit cassus !(53)

The state of Johnson's mind, in which dread is based on a rational view of probabilities, is well revealed in Boswell's famous anecdote of his conversation at Merton College, Oxford:

> Dr. Johnson surprised him [a Mr. Henderson] not a little, by
> acknowledging with a look of horrour, that he was much op-
> pressed by the fear of death. The amiable Dr. Adams suggested
> that GOD is infinitely good.
> JOHNSON: 'That he is infinitely good, as far as the perfec-
> tion of his nature will allow, I certainly believe; but it is
> necessary for good upon the whole, that individuals should be
> punished. As to an *individual*, therefore, he is not infinitely
> good; and as I cannot be *sure* that I have fulfilled the condi-
> tions on which salvation is granted, I am afraid I may be one
> of those who shall be damned.' (looking dismally). Dr. ADAMS:
> 'What do you mean by damned ?' JOHNSON. (passionately
> and loudly) 'Sent to Hell, Sir, and punished everlastingly.'

---

(50) *Diaries*, p. 80.

(51) ibid., pp. 81-82.

(52) ibid., p. 91. 'Nelson' refers to Robert Nelson's *Companion for the Festivals and Fasts of the Church of England* (1704).

(53) *Johnsonian Miscellanies*, ed. cit., i. 284.

Dr. ADAMS. 'I don't believe that doctrine.' JOHNSON. 'Hold, Sir; do you believe that some will be punished at all ?' Dr. ADAMS. 'Being excluded from Heaven will be a punishment; yet there may be no great positive suffering.' JOHNSON. 'Well, Sir; but, if you admit any degree of punishment, there is an end of your argument for infinite goodness simply considered; for, infinite goodness would inflict no punishment whatever. There is not infinite goodness physically considered; morally there is.' BOSWELL. 'But may not a man attain to such a degree of hope as not to be uneasy from the fear of death ?' JOHNSON. 'A man may have such a degree of hope as to keep him quiet. You see I am not quiet, from the vehemence with which I talk; but I do not despair.' Mrs. ADAMS. 'You seem, Sir, to forget the merits of our Redeemer.' JOHNSON. 'Madam, I do not forget the merits of my Redeemer; but my Redeemer has said that he will set some on his right hand and some on his left.' — He was in gloomy agitation, and said, 'I'll have no more on't.'(54)

That was just six months before his death; but years before, in the concluding *Idler*, he had written his famous sentence that 'The secret horrour of the last is inseparable from a thinking being, whose life is limited, and to whom death is dreadful'. This fear, says Boswell 'was the result of philosophical and religious consideration'.(55) Struck with the indifference with which Tyburn convicts faced execution Boswell asked him, 'But is not the fear of death natural to man ?', and received an answer penetratingly moving:

JOHNSON. 'So much so, Sir, that the whole of life is but keeping away the thoughts of it.' He then, in a low and earnest tone, talked of his meditating upon the aweful hour of his own dissolution, and in what manner he should conduct himself upon that occasion: 'I know not (said he,) whether I should wish to have a friend by me, or have it all between GOD and myself'.(56)

And in the last year of his life, feeling himself declining, he wrote to Dr. Taylor at Ashbourne, 'O ! my friend, the approach of death is very dreadful. I am afraid to think on that which I know I cannot avoid'.(57)

---

(54) *Life,* ed. cit., iv. 299-300.

(55) ibid., ii. 298.

(56) ibid., ii. 93.

(57) ibid., iv. 270.

His earnestness on this subject was only the most personally-felt aspect
of his sense of ultimate importances, or, as Carlyle put it in his review of Croker's Boswell, his sense 'that Wrong is not only different from Right, but that
it is in strict scientific terms *infinitely* different; even as the gaining of the
whole world set against the losing of one's own soul'[58]. His demolition
of Soame Jenyns for the complacent triviality of his *Free Enquiry into the
Nature and Origin of Evil* is famous. This triviality affronted the tragic dignity
of human nature facing the trials of life and the perils of eternity. To Dr.
Maxwell

> He lamented that all serious and religious conversation was
> banished from the society of men, and yet great advantages
> might be derived from it. All acknowledged, he said, what
> hardly any body practised, the obligation we were under of
> making the concerns of eternity the governing principles of our
> lives.[59]

Converted to a serious attention to religion by reading Law's *Serious Call*
at Oxford [60] he was prompted in his life's work by a deep earnestness of
intention. He prays to God that *The Rambler* 'may promote Thy Glory, and
the Salvation both of myself and others'[61]; he prays before beginning the
study of law[62], politics[63], and languages[64]; he prays for the progress
of the *Dictionary*[65]. His letter to a young clergyman in the country is
practical counsel[66], and he assists many clerical friends. His original work
is seldom far from the sense of ultimate importances, as the noble end of
The Vanity of Human Wishes or the moral material of the periodical essays
may remind us. As Raleigh observes of the essays,

> It is strange to remember, as we read some of the noblest of
> Johnson's sentences, that they were written in periodical
> papers for the entertainment of chance readers. His essay on

---

(58) T. Carlyle, *Collected Works*, London, 1858, iv. 85.
(59) *Life*, ed. cit., ii. 124.
(60) ibid., i. 68.
(61) *Diaries*, p. 43.
(62) ibid., p. 96.
(63) ibid., p. 98.
(64) ibid., p. 58.
(65) ibid., p. 50.
(66) *Life.*, ed. cit., iii. 436-8.

revenge concludes with an appeal not often to be found in the pages of a society journal: 'Of him that hopes to be forgiven, it is indispensably required that he forgive. It is therefore superfluous to urge any other motive. On this great duty eternity is suspended; and to him that refuses to practise it, the throne of mercy is inaccessible, and the Saviour of the world has been born in vain'.(67)

And equally we cannot fail to hear his natural grandeur when, in literary criticism, he goes behind literature to religion, as in the *Life of Milton:*

> We all, indeed, feel the effects of Adam's disobedience: we all sin like Adam, and like him must all bewail our offences; we have restless and insidious enemies in the fallen angels, and in the blessed spirits we have guardians and friends; in the Redemption of mankind we hope to be included; in the description of heaven and hell we are surely interested, as we are all to reside hereafter either in the regions of horrour or of bliss.(68)

This weight of consideration is the characteristic Johnsonian note, his noble and fortifying *gravitas*. Johnson is high among the writers who really make a difference. By facing the reader with first and last things, unobtrusively and with a dignified reticence, yet as part of the ineluctable scale of human life, he gains even from the agnostic the moved recognition of human responsibility of the highest order. To scoff at him, as Taine did(69), is to show one's own deficiency, not his.

(67) W. Raleigh, *Six Essays on Johnson*, Oxford, 1910, p. 16.

(68) Johnson, *Lives of the Poets*, ed. cit., i. 181.

(69) H.A. Taine, *History of English Literature*, trans. H. van Laun, London, 1920, iii. 316-324.

CHESTER F. CHAPIN

Samuel Johnson's "Wonderful" Experience

The religious outlook of Samuel Johnson as he prepared to meet death has been the subject of much controversy. In 1948 Maurice Quinlan argued against the belief, long current among Evangelical groups, that Johnson in his last days experienced a "conversion" to Evangelical religious principles[1]. Quinlan calls particular attention to a remarkable experience of Johnson's during the winter of 1783–84 which, he finds, had the effect of particularly strengthening Johnson's religious ardor. Johnson, experiencing sudden and unexpected relief during the course of a dangerous illness, evidently believed himself, and impressed others with the belief, that he owed his recovery to a special act of divine mercy. Quinlan shows that Evangelically minded persons, misinterpreting Johnson's reaction to this experience, arrived at the belief that Johnson had become a convert to Evangelical doctrines. Such, apparently, was not the case. There is no indication that Johnson ever adopted the central Evangelical doctrine that man is saved by faith *alone*, nor any evidence that Johnson ever "arrived at the typical Evangelical convert's ecstatic assurance of salvation."[2]

If the remarkable experience in question did not signify a conversion to Evangelicalism, what *was* its significance for Johnson ? Granted it had the effect of increasing his religious ardor, can we come to any more precise conclusion than that ? I believe we can, and that the conclusion reached will give us a fuller, more accurate understanding of Johnson's religious outlook as he prepared to meet death.

To gain a clear understanding of what occurred and of its significance for Johnson, it will be necessary to review, but in more detail, some of the

---

(1) "The Rumor of Dr. Johnson's Conversion," *Review of Religion*, XII (1948), 243–261.

(2) *Ibid.*, p. 261.

ground covered by Quinlan. Detail may be further justified in that uncertainty exists concerning the precise date of Johnson's experience(3).

After a paralytic stroke in June 1783, Johnson had so far recovered his health that by November he could exclaim to Sir John Hawkins, "What a man am I ! who have got the better of three diseases ... and can now enjoy the conversation of my friends, without the interruptions of weakness or pain !"(4) Johnson's recovery was followed by a burst of energetic social activity. Within one six-day period in early December he had presided at the first meetings of his revived Ivy Lane club and his newly formed Essex Head club.(5) But this happy state of affairs was not to last. On 13 December, apparently during the third meeting of the Essex Head club, Johnson "was seized with a spasmodick asthma so violent" that it was with difficulty that he managed to get back to his own house.(6) He was not to leave that house again until 21 April, a confinement, as he wrote Mrs. Thrale, "of one hundred twenty nine days, more than the third part of a year, and no inconsiderable part of human life" (955). In addition to the asthma Johnson was suffering from the dropsy, which he rightly considered the more dangerous of the two diseases (932).

Johnson's period of confinement may be divided into three parts: a period of progressive deterioration leading to a dramatic crisis in February 1784, this crisis itself, and a period of slow but steady progress toward recovery during the months of March and April.

We must now consider the testimony of Sir John Hawkins, our on-the-spot witness of these events (Boswell, in Scotland at the time, was not to

(3) Percy Scholes, the biographer of Sir John Hawkins, gives November or December of 1783 (*The Life and Activities of Sir John Hawkins* [London, 1953], pp. 166–168); J. M. Osborn, misinterpreting Boswell's report of the experience, gives May 1784 ("Dr. Johnson and the Contrary Converts," *New Light on Dr. Johnson*, ed. F.W. Hilles [New Haven, 1959], p. 305).

(4) Sir John Hawkins, *The Life of Samuel Johnson* (London, 1787), p. 561. Referred to hereafter as Hawkins.

(5) See letters 915, 916, 917.1 in *The Letters of Samuel Johnson*, ed. R.W. Chapman (Oxford, 1952), Vol. III of 3 vols. All letters of Johnson are cited from this edition and are referred to hereafter by number alone.

(6) 932; cf. 917.1, 918.1.

return to London until May). Hawkins and Johnson attended the first meeting of the revived Ivy Lane club on 3 December. "Johnson," says Hawkins,

> had proposed a meeting, like this, once a month, and we had one more; but, the time approaching for a third, he began to feel a return of some of his complaints, and signified a wish, that we would dine with him at his own house; and, accordingly, we met there, and were very chearfully entertained by him.(7)

Here Hawkins' memory played him false. Johnson had been confined to his house since 14 December (938); the second meeting, which took place on 7 January, was held, not at a tavern as Hawkins supposes, but at Johnson's house.(8) There is no record of a third meeting before the crisis in Johnson's illness, although it is by no means impossible that such a meeting was held. In any case, Hawkins' chronology of the Ivy Lane club meetings, however inaccurate, is quite "correct" in the sense that it gives February as the month of crisis. If precedent had been followed, Hawkins' supposed third meeting would have occurred sometime in early February, a date which agrees perfectly with Hawkins' day-to-day account of Johnson's crisis. "A few days after" this supposed third meeting Johnson sent for Hawkins, and "informed me," says the knight, "that he had discovered in himself the symptoms of a dropsy, and, indeed, his very much increased bulk, and the swoln appearance of his legs, seemed to indicate no less." Johnson told Hawkins that he wanted to make his will and asked Hawkins to be one of his executors.(9) This was ominous enough, but worse was to follow. On Tuesday, 17 February, Johnson wrote three letters: a letter to arrange for the care of his dependent Elizabeth Herne in the event of his death (934), a one-sentence note to a friend stating that he was too much "disordered" to write more (934.1), and a note indicating that an "issue" was to be made in his thigh "to drain away the water" (934.2).

On a Thursday "a few days" after the interview in which Johnson asked him to be an executor of his will, Hawkins, in consequence of "a very press-

---

(7) Hawkins, p. 562.

(8) See Appendix C, Boswell's *Life of Johnson*, ed. Hill-Powell (Oxford, 1934-50), IV, 435–436. All references to Boswell's *Life of Johnson* are to this edition, referred to hereafter as *Life*.

(9) Hawkins, p. 563.

ing request," hurried to Johnson's house where he found his friend "labouring under great dejection of mind." Johnson said "that he had the prospect of death before him, and that he dreaded to meet his Saviour," at one point exclaiming passionately, "Shall I, who have been the teacher of others, myself be a castaway ?" In the course of further conversation Johnson "declared his intention to devote the whole of the next day to fasting, humiliation, and such other devotional exercises as became a man in his situation"([10]). Johnson, preparing for death, was determined to make a last struggle for life. All that medicine and religion could do would be done; nothing would then remain but to await the event.

Hawkins, visiting Johnson "on the Saturday following," was struck by a remarkable change in his friend. The operation on Johnson's thigh had been completely successful. Johnson had "emitted in about twenty hours, full twenty pints of urine," and the "tumour" of his body had been "very much lessened" (935.1). A letter to Lucy Porter of Monday, 23 February, gives Thursday the 19th as the date of the operation: "I have been extremely ill of an Asthma and dropsy," writes Johnson, "but received by the mercy of God sudden and unexpected relief last thursday by the discharge of twenty pints of water" (935). We can now reconstruct a rather precise chronology of events. The Thursday of Hawkins' distressing interview with Johnson is the 19th; presumably later in the day, after Hawkins has left, the operation on Johnson's thigh takes place. Johnson spends the whole of Friday in devotional exercises while awaiting the final results of the operation. By Saturday, when Hawkins returns, the "twenty hours" and the "twenty pints" have passed, the operation has proved strikingly successful, and both Hawkins and Johnson agree that something in the nature of a miracle has occurred.

Hawkins, observing in Johnson's countenance on Saturday "such a serenity, as indicated that some remarkable crisis of his disorder had produced a change in his feelings," learned that Johnson during the course of his religious devotions the preceding day had "found himself relieved ... by a gradual evacuation of water to the amount of twenty pints, a like instance whereof he had never before experienced ...." Asked by Johnson what he thought of this occurrence, Hawkins, the cautious lawyer, does not hesitate to ascribe Johnson's relief to an act of God:

---

(10) *Ibid.*, pp. 563–564.

> I thought it would be little less than criminal, to ascribe his
> late relief to causes merely natural, and that the safer opinion
> was, that he had not in vain humbled himself before his Maker.
> He [Johnson] seemed to acquiesce in all that I said on this
> important subject, and, several times, while I was discoursing
> with him, cried out, "It is wonderful, very wonderful !"[11]

Johnson's letters immediately following his operation are cautiously
optimistic; he praises God for his relief but is fearful lest the water "gather
again" (935.1). By March, less fearful of a relapse, he is beginning to emphasize the "wonderful" quality of his experience: "The water passed naturally by God's mercy in a manner of which Dr Heberden has seen but four
examples" (938); "my Dropsy has run itself almost away, in a manner which
my Physician says is very uncommon" (939); "my deliverance has been very
extraordinary" (941); "I am, by the blessing of God, wonderfully relieved"
(946). Johnson's letters throughout April resound with similar expressions.
When on 21 April he at last found himself well enough to leave his house for
the first time since December, he re-emphasizes, in heartfelt tones, the
remarkable quality of his experience:

> I this day returned thanks to God in St. Clement's Church
> for my recovery, a recovery in my seventy fifth year from a
> distemper which few in the vigour of youth are known to
> surmount; a recovery of which neither myself, my friends,
> nor my physicians had any hope, for though they flattered
> me with some continuance of life, they never supposed that
> I would cease to be dropsical (955).

Saturday, 24 April was the *dies mirabilis* of this period, reflecting "the greatest degree of health" which Johnson was to reach before the gradual decline
which, setting in during the summer, led finally to his death the following
December (1022). "On Saturday," writes Johnson, "I shewed myself again
to the living world at the Exhibition; much and splendid was the company:
but like the Doge of Genoa at Paris, I admired nothing but myself. I went
up all the stairs to the pictures without stopping to rest or to breathe, 'In
all the madness of superfluous health' " (956).

---

(11) *Ibid.*, pp. 564–565.

On 5 May Boswell returned to London after a year's absence in Scotland. Visiting Johnson a few days later, he learned of the latter's remarkable experience, which he reports in the *Life* as follows:

> One morning afterwards, when I found him alone, he communicated to me, with solemn earnestness, a very remarkable circumstance which had happened in the course of his illness, when he was much distressed by the dropsy. He had shut himself up, and employed a day in particular exercises of religion,—fasting, humiliation, and prayer. On a sudden he obtained extraordinary relief, for which he looked up to Heaven with grateful devotion. He made no direct inference from this fact; but from his manner of telling it, I could perceive that it appeared to him as something more than an incident in the common course of events.

Boswell goes on to express his own view that Johnson owed his sudden relief to "an intermediate interposition of divine Providence."[12]

Although Johnson made "no direct inference" from the fact of his extraordinary deliverance, it seems clear that he regarded it as a special act of divine mercy, in the class of those acts which constitute supernatural intervention in the lives of men. I find no evidence that Johnson at any other time in his life ever felt himself the object of such intervention. Indeed, he seems to have spent a good deal of time and energy in search of authenticated instances of its occurrence in the lives of other people. Every reader of Boswell is aware of Johnson's earnest search "for more and more evidence

---

(12) *Life*, IV, 271–272. John Wilson Croker, believing the term "intermediate" not "quite clear," suggested that Boswell may have meant "immediate" (Boswell's *Life of Johnson*, ed. Croker [New York, 1843], II, 375, n. 2). But Boswell, I think, was choosing his terms with care, and Johnson, I believe, would have agreed with his choice of "intermediate." The "immediate" agent of Johnson's relief was the operation on his thigh. God had intervened *through* the operation, hence "intermediately." Johnson in his *Dictionary* defines "intermediate" as "Intervening; interposed; holding the middle place or degree between two extremes." Johnson's experience held the "middle place" between the extremes of miracle on the one hand (if relief had come without the operation having taken place) and ascription merely to natural causes on the other (if Johnson's relief had been ascribed to the effects of the operation *alone*.) Hence, I believe, the rather careful avoidance by Hawkins, Boswell, and Johnson himself of the term "miracle."

for spirit"[13]. He was "willing to believe" in the existence of the Lyttleton ghost because he was "so glad to have every evidence of the spiritual world."[14] Clearly, Johnson was not entirely satisfied with the usual "Christian evidences," based as they largely were upon events which had occurred in the past. He wanted, for the strengthening and confirmation of his faith, some clear evidence *here and now* of "contact" between the natural and the supernatural worlds. Such contact, proving the existence of the latter world, would do much, Johnson felt, to place the supernatural doctrines of orthodox Christianity beyond all serious possibility of doubt. Is it going too far to see in Johnson's "wonderful" experience something of that "contact" with "the spiritual world" which he had long so earnestly sought ? Although he believed, no doubt, with Hawkins that it might "savour of presumption" to call what God had wrought a "miracle,"[15] still it seems clear that Johnson felt there had been "contact" of a sort. He had prayed and had received, suddenly and unexpectedly, precisely what he had prayed for.

One thing seems obvious. His reaction to this experience would seem to cast doubt upon the theory that Johnson was at heart a religious sceptic — that he feared to have his faith questioned because he was only too conscious of its irrational foundations[16]. It should be clear, at least, that Johnson's February experience would have banished any lingering sceptical doubts he may have had prior to that time. An orthodox Christian praying to his God, he had experienced, he believed, a special act of divine intervention in his behalf; could he entertain doubts, after that, concerning the central dogmas of orthodoxy ? He died not only utterly committed to the moral teachings of Christian orthodoxy, but utterly convinced as well, it would seem, of the validity of its "supernaturalist" claims.

That Johnson regarded his deliverance as a reprieve, a chance, possibly his last, in which to repent of his sins is only what we should expect, given our knowledge of his religious attitudes. Orthodoxy demanded of its adherents two things: a Christian life ("good works") and trust in the merits of Christ the Redeemer. But Johnson, never able to convince himself that he had fulfilled the demands of the first requirement, found his strongest, perhaps his

---

(13) *Life*, II, 150.
(14) *Life*, IV, 298–299.
(15) Hawkins, p. 565.
(16) See E.C. Mossner, *The Forgotten Hume* (New York, 1943), p. 207.

only, hope in Christ's promise of salvation to those, whatever their sins, who had truly repented. And repentance, to be acceptable in the sight of God, had to be "felt on the heart." Repentance was much more to Johnson than a matter of cool assent to the proposition that one had sinned, followed by prayers for forgiveness. A passage from Johnson's Easter Day prayer of 11 April, in which he thanks God for his "late deliverance from imminent death," makes this very clear:

> Enable me, O Lord, to glorify thee for that knowledge of my Corruption, and that sense of thy wrath which my disease and weakness, and danger awakened in my mind. Give me such sorrow as may purify my heart, such indignation as may quench all confidence in my self, and such repentance as may by the intercession of my Redeemer obtain pardon.[17]

Johnson welcomed that knowledge of his "corruption" and that sense of God's wrath which the prospect of imminent death had awakened in him. Such feelings he regarded as the necessary accompaniments of any sincere, heartfelt repentance, and it was only through such repentance that he felt he could hope to "obtain pardon" at the Last Day. Thus, the unusually deep sense of his own unworthiness which had accompanied his prayers for recovery in February, far from plunging Johnson into gloom, was rather a cause for hope. His remarkable recovery he could not but regard as a sign that this hope had not been altogether vain — that his repentance had been of such depth and sincerity as to have found favor in the sight of God.

We need not be surprised, then, to find his Easter Day prayer "marked with unusual serenity and perhaps even confidence." And a diary entry, apparently written within a few days of his report to Boswell concerning his February experience, is marked by a degree of serenity not often found in the Diary at any period of his life: "Afternoon spent cheerfully and elegantly, I hope without offence to GOD or man; though in no holy duty, yet in the general exercise and cultivation of benevolence."[18] Critics have placed much emphasis upon the element of fearful anxiety which is so obvious and important a component of Johnson's religious experience. Johnson, it

---

(17) Samuel Johnson, *Diaries, Prayers, and Annals*, ed. E.L. McAdam, Jr. with Donald and Mary Hyde (New Haven, 1958), pp. 368-369.

(18) *Ibid.*

has been said, "knew little of the *comforts* of religion."[19] But it seems clear that during the spring of 1784 (and even later, as I shall show) Johnson's religion, always a source of anxiety, was also a source of hope.

We come now to the closing scenes of Johnson's life. Despite the return of his ailments during the summer of 1784, Johnson could write on 6 October: "My mind . . . is calmer than in the beginning of the year, and I comfort myself with hopes of every kind, neither despairing of ease in this world, nor of happiness in another" (1021). But Johnson's most revealing comment on what the February experience meant to him was made on 28 November, when he could no longer entertain much hope for "ease in this world." "I had", he told Hawkins

> very early in my life, the seeds of goodness in me: I had a love of virtue, and a reverence for religion; and these, I trust, have brought forth in me fruits meet for repentance; and, if I have repented as I ought, I am forgiven. I have, at times, entertained a loathing of sin and of myself, particularly at the beginning of this year, when I had the prospect of death before me; and this has not abated when my fears of death have been less; and, at these times, I have had such rays of hope shot into my soul, as have almost persuaded me, that I am in a state of reconciliation with God.[20]

This, for Johnson, is a remarkable statement. For Johnson to be even "almost" persuaded of his being in a state of reconciliation with God is unusual, to say the least. We see, furthermore, the lasting effects of the February "deliverance." The truly repentant spirit which he believed had accompanied his successful prayers for recovery had not vanished with renewed health, and this consideration leads Johnson to a degree of religious optimism two weeks before his death which we should find difficult to ascribe to him at most former periods of his life. If Johnson, as almost all the contemporary accounts maintain, died finally confident, or at least hopeful, we may ascribe this in considerable part to the continuing effects of his "wonderful" experience the preceding February—an experience which brought to Johnson the comforting implication that, after nearly a lifetime of search, he had at last found the way to acts of true and acceptable repentance.

---

(19) J.W. Krutch, *Samuel Johnson* (New York, 1945), p. 549.
(20) Hawkins, p. 582.

At eleven o'clock on the night of 13 December, some four hours after Johnson had drawn his last breath, Bennet Langton, "in an agony of mind," told Hawkins of a shocking discovery he had just made. It appeared that on the morning of the 13th Johnson, disregarding the protests of his servant Frank, had stabbed himself with a lancet and later with a pair of scissors. Hawkins soon satisfied himself that Johnson had not attempted suicide as Langton had thought, but had sought rather to prolong his life by making incisions which he hoped would "discharge the water that he conceived to be in him." Although the dying Johnson had expressed irritation with his physicians on a number of occasions, believing they had not probed deeply enough with the lancet in their efforts to relieve his dropsical condition, Hawkins nevertheless arrives at the conclusion that Johnson's self-stabbing was the act of a man "disturbed with terror at the prospect of the grave".[21] It may be so, but it is possible to believe that Johnson's act was less the product of his terror than of his hope. Johnson's situation was, after all, a replica of the one in which he had found himself the preceding February. His disease was the same; the means of relieving it were the same. A few days before his death Johnson had seemed to acquiesce in the opinion of his friend and physician Dr. Brocklesby that he could not recover without a "miracle"; yet a near-miracle had been responsible, he believed, for his reprieve in February — and Johnson believed that with God all things are possible.[22] Johnson's act, desperate as it appears, may have had its origin in what would have been for him a slim but not an irrational hope. It was too late of course, but according to William Windham, although one of the self-inflicted incisions "was a deep and ugly wound," the others "were not unskilfully made."[23]

UNIVERSITY OF MICHIGAN

---

(21) *Ibid.*, pp. 588–589.

(22) *Life*, IV, 415. "God, who has so wonderfully restored me," wrote Johnson during the spring, "can preserve me in all seasons" (952).

(23) *Johnsonian Miscellanies*, ed. G.B. Hill (Oxford, 1897), II, 386.

DONALD J. GREENE

Dr. Johnson's "Late Conversion": A Reconsideration

I

Almighty and most merciful Father, I am now, as to human eyes it seems, about to commemorate for the last time the death of thy son Jesus Christ, our Saviour and Redeemer. Grant, O Lord, that my whole hope and confidence may be in his merits and in thy mercy: forgive and accept my late conversion, enforce and accept my imperfect repentance; make this commemoration of him available to the confirmation of my Faith, the establishment of my Hope, and the enlargement of my Charity, and make the Death of thy son Jesus effectual to my redemption. Have mercy upon me and pardon the multitude of my offences. Bless my Friends, have mercy upon all men. Support me by the Grace of thy Holy Spirit in the days of weakness, and at the hour of death, and receive me, at my death, to everlasting happiness, for the Sake of Jesus Christ. Amen.[1]

Such was the prayer which that very great Christian, Samuel Johnson, composed and uttered — "with a degree of fervour that I had never been witness to before," says Hawkins — eight days before his death, when, in his sick room, he, with a few friends, received his last communion at the hands of

---

(1) Samuel Johnson, *Diaries, Prayers, and Annals*, ed. E.L. McAdam, Jr., with Donald and Mary Hyde [*The Yale Edition of the Works of Samuel Johnson*, Vol. I], (New Haven, 1958), 417–18 (to be cited as *Works* [1958], I). Strictly speaking, this may not be Johnson's "last prayer." He composed another prayer, also dated December 5, 1784 (the day of his last communion), in Latin verse (*Poems of Samuel Johnson*, ed. D. Nichol Smith and E.L. McAdam, Jr., 1941, p. 232). As the communion service was no doubt held in the morning, there seems a likelihood of the verse prayer's being the later.

the Reverend George Strahan. Strahan, Vicar of Islington, was the son of Johnson's old friend, the wealthy printer William Strahan. Johnson had befriended George, as a boy and a young man: many of his charming letters of advice and encouragement to him at school and university survive, as do a number of later ones, not so pleasant, when George had quarreled with his father, and Johnson was attempting to bring about a reconciliation.(2)

The transmission of the text of this prayer has had a curious history, involving very important questions concerning the nature of Johnson's fundamental religious beliefs. Eight months after Johnson's death, George Strahan became one of the first to publish in the field of competing Johnsonian biographers and editors, bringing out a book which he called *Prayers and Meditations, composed by Samuel Johnson, LL.D., and published from his manuscripts.* In this volume, heavily edited throughout, Strahan printed the prayer composed for Johnson's last communion — with silent alterations. The most drastic of these was the deletion of its second petition, "Forgive and accept my late conversion"(3). Hawkins later published, both in his *Life*

---

(2) Some of these latter make curious reading: for instance, *Letters of Samuel Johnson* (ed. R.W. Chapman, 1952), No. 800, August 19, 1782: "[I represented to your father] that discontent of which he complained so much, not as any personal disrespect to him but as a cast of mind which you had always had. Your discontent on many occasions has appeared to me little short of madness, which however I did not tell him. ... You may well be at a loss to conjecture why I should injure you, whom certainly I have no reason to injure." These are strange words for his old friend and helper to feel compelled to address to a man now thirty-eight, an ordained priest with a cure of souls. The psychologist with an interest in father-figures and their effects might find the correspondence useful in trying to explain Strahan's penchant for mutilating Johnson's diaries. See [E.L. McAdam, Jr., Donald and Mary Hyde, and George Milne,] *The Johnsons Photographed* (privately printed, 1956), p. [1]: "Strahan, it now appears, was more interested in creating and preserving a conventional pattern of Johnson's religion and marriage than in editing out all personal material. ... In ... instances where Johnson is talking about his relations with Tetty or about his religious doubts and scruples, Strahan, with an eye to posterity, has crosshatched Johnson's words so thoroughly that they cannot be read by ordinary means."

(3) Strahan made other revisions to the prayer, the most notable being to change the beginning of its last sentence, "Support me by the Grace of thy Holy Spirit," to "Support me by thy Holy Spirit." I do not know whether Strahan had a tendentious purpose in eliminating the mention of "Grace," or whether this was merely a slip. At any rate, the end result is an elementary theological solecism ("Support me by the Third Person of the Trinity").

of Johnson and in Volume XI of the collected *Works* of Johnson, the full text of the prayer. But Boswell, in his *Life*, chose to reproduce the version emended by Strahan, and it is this which appears in most modern collections of Johnson's devotional writings.

It seems likely that Strahan's motive in falsifying this important document (and Boswell's in perpetuating the falsification) was a wish to suppress evidence that might indicate Johnson's sympathy with the "Evangelical movement" in the Church of England and outside it. The action would seem quite indefensible by any criterion of either scholarly or religious ethics. But the latest editors of Johnson's prayers append a commentary that sounds like an attempt to defend it: "His last prayer was printed in full by Hawkins, copied by Strahan(4), who then deleted the clause 'forgive and accept my late conversion,' no doubt fearing that 'late conversion' might be misinterpreted, as indeed it has been, forgetting that one of the definitions in Johnson's *Dictionary* is 'Change from reprobation to grace, from a bad to a holy life.' "(5) This note, obscure in itself, must be referred for its interpretation to the essay from which it clearly derives, Maurice J. Quinlan's "The Rumor of Dr. Johnson's Conversion."(6) So too must a similar note in J.M. Osborn's "Dr. Johnson and the Contrary Converts" : "Much speculation has been based on the phrase in Dr. Johnson's last prayer, written a week before his death, which asked 'forgive and accept my late conversion' ...; Boswell omitted it when printing the prayer. But a glance at Johnson's *Dictionary* would have saved much ink, for his first two definitions of 'conversion' read: '1. Change from one state to another; transmutation .... 2. Change from reprobation to grace, from a bad to a holy life' (Quinlan, p. 259)."(7)

The main purpose of the present essay is to re-examine Mr. Quinlan's view of the matter, which clearly has come to be regarded as authoritative. Before we look at what Mr. Quinlan has to say, however, let us, for clarity,

---

(4) This is a strange mistake, if it means what it seems to. The prayer appeared in the first edition of Strahan's *Prayers and Meditations*, published in 1785. Hawkins' *Life* and his edition of the *Works* did not appear until 1787.

(5) *Works* (1958), I, 417–18. "Forgetting" is presumably to be construed, not with "Strahan," but with the implied "misinterpreters."

(6) *Review of Religion*, XII (March, 1948), 243–61. Mr. Quinlan is Professor of English in Boston College, an institution operated by the Jesuit order.

(7) *New Light on Dr. Johnson*, ed. F.W. Hilles (New Haven, 1959), p. 305, n. 5. The essay was earlier privately printed, 1954.

review the outward circumstances of the matter, which are little, if at all, in dispute. Most of the following incidents are noted by Quinlan, although I have added a few details to his list.

II

In 1783, Johnson's health, long basically robust in spite of his hypochondriac tendencies, began to break down seriously; he was now in his seventy-fourth year. In June he suffered a stroke, that deprived him temporarily of speech. This aphasia shocked and frightened him; but he presently recovered. In September a painful condition, which Johnson had imagined to be a hydrocele (a dropsical condition in the scrotum), was diagnosed by his medical advisers as a sarcocele (a tumour, possibly cancerous)[8]. They recommended immediate surgical excision — the use of "fire and sword" Johnson quotes one of them putting it poetically : a terrible prospect in the days before anaesthesia and antisepsis. Otherwise, gangrene was threatened. Fortunately the doctors were mistaken: the condition relieved itself by spontaneous discharge through an exploratory puncture that had been made. Both these incidents, though in the end they turned out to be not very important in themselves, were understandably terrifying to Johnson at the time, and must have made him face seriously, if he had not done so before, the prospect of imminent death. With the winter came his recurrent spasmodic asthma, coupled with the sufferings of gout and arthritis, and the appearance of a dropsical condition in his legs; for four months he was confined to his house, and during December, and January and early February, 1784, his letters breathe profound depression. "Gloomy," "cheerless," "dejection" occur again and again in them. His doctors prescribed opiates to relieve his pain and insomnia: their effect on his strong mind distressed and alarmed him[9].

------

(8) Although the condition continues to be referred to by Johnsonian students as a sarcocele, I gather Johnson's diagnosis was right and that of his doctors was wrong. See H.S. Carter, M.D., D.P.H.,"Samuel Johnson and Some Eighteenth-Century Doctors," *Glasgow Medical Journal*, XXXII (July, 1951), 223-24: "When Johnson was about seventy-four, he suffered from a hydrocele, like John Wesley and Gibbon. His advisers ... evidently got a dry puncture, suspected a solid tumour, and diagnosed sarcocele. They recommended excision.... While he was awaiting this operation with stoicism the puncture began to leak and the hydrocele drained."

(9) *Letters*, especially Nos. 848 to 855; 874(1) to 894.2; 917 to 932.

On January 6, 1784, he wrote to the bookseller Charles Dilly, asking him to send him "the best printed edition of Baxter's *Call to the Unconverted.*"(10)

On Thursday, February 19, in consequence of "a very pressing request," Hawkins called on him and "found him labouring under great dejection of mind." "He bade me draw near him," Hawkins continues, "and said he wanted to enter into a serious conversation with me; and, upon my expressing a willingness to join in it, he, with a look that cut me to the heart, told me, that he had the prospect of death before him, and that he dreaded to meet his Saviour. I ... advised him, as I had done once before, to reflect on the course of his life, and the services he had rendered to the cause of religion and virtue, as well by his example, as his writings; to which he answered, that he had written as a philosopher, but had not lived like one." "Every man knows his own sins," Johnson told Hawkins, "and also what grace he has resisted. ... " "At the conclusion of this argument, which he strongly enforced," says Hawkins, "he uttered this passionate exclamation, 'Shall I, who have been a teacher of others, myself be a castaway?' "(11) Hawkins, wondering "as much at the freedom with which he opened his mind, and the compunction he seemed to feel for the errors of his past life, as I did at his making choice of me for his confessor, knowing full well how meanly qualified I was for such an office," gave him what ineffectual consolation he could. Johnson then "declared his intention to devote the whole of the next day to fasting, humiliation, and such other devotional exercises as became a man in his situation," and Hawkins went away.

On Saturday, February 21, Hawkins called again, and "upon entering the room, observed in his countenance such a serenity as indicated that some

---

(10) *Letters* 924.

(11) One thinks immediately of Cowper's magnificent poem, "The Castaway," with its terrible concluding lines — "But I beneath a rougher sea,/And whelm'd in deeper gulphs than he." It was written in 1799, not many months before his own death, and long after he had been pronounced insane. The common source for both Johnson and Cowper was I Corinthians ix, 27. But one speculates to what extent these moving pages of Hawkins, which Cowper (as we shall see) would have read with the greatest care, were responsible for the idea of the poem. One thinks, too, of Virginia Woolf's wonderful use of the poem in *To the Lighthouse*, and of her own tragic end, and of the inheritance of the Stephens from the "Evangelical" milieu with which Cowper was associated.

remarkable crisis of his disorder had produced a change in his feelings."
Johnson reported that on Friday he had done as he had said he would, telling
Frank to admit no visitors, "For your master is preparing himself to die."
Then, in the course of his devotions, the dropsical condition of his legs had
relieved itself "by a gradual evacuation of water to the amount of twenty
pints, a like instance of which he had never before experienced." Hawkins
gave it as his opinion that "it would be little less than criminal to ascribe his
late relief to causes merely natural, and that the safer opinion was that he
had not in vain humbled himself before his Maker. He seemed to acquiesce
in all that I said on this important subject, and, several times, while I was
discoursing with him, cried out, 'It is wonderful, very wonderful !' "[12]
In all this, we could hardly ask for a better witness than the crusty and
"realistic" Hawkins, who, though a sincere and orthodox Anglican, was about
as far as possible from being a lover or devotee of facile emotionality, of
"enthusiasm," as much in his *Life*, as well as the testimony of his friends
(and enemies), makes clear.

From this time until his death, ten months later, Johnson's letters and
prayers provide copious evidence of his own conviction of the immense importance of what had happened on February 20. The following Monday, February
23, he wrote to the nearest relation he had left, Lucy Porter, to tell her of it:
"My dearest Love: I have been extremely ill of Asthma and dropsy, but received by the mercy of God sudden and unexpected relief last Thursday[13].
. . . Death my dear is very dreadful, let us think nothing worth our care but

---

(12) Sir John Hawkins, *Life of Johnson* (1787), pp. 563-65. Hawkins'
earlier account, pp. 540-47, of Johnson's religious attitudes in the latter part
of his life is also of great interest, and strikes me as probably more authentic
than many later accounts. He seems to record (pp. 545-46) an earlier "imperfect" conversion, the date of which, however, is extremely vague. (I attempt
to show, in section V below, that such "backslidings" are not inconsistent with
the Anglican and Methodist doctrine of "assurance" in conversion.) Hawkins'
motive for treating Johnson's religious life as fully as he does should be noted
(pp. 546-47) — it is "to refute the objections of many infidels, who, desirous
of having him thought to be of their party, endeavoured to make it believed
that he was a *mere moralist* [my italics]."

(13) Presumably Hawkins' circumstantial dating of the incident, Friday,
February 20, is to be preferred. Yet in *Letters* 943 Johnson again gives the
date as the 19th.

how to prepare for it, what we know amiss in ourselves let us make haste to amend, and put our trust in the mercy of God, and the intercession of our Saviour." On March 20, he wrote to Mrs. Thrale, exhorting her to take death and the preparation for it seriously: "You know all this, and I thought that I knew it too, but I know it now with a new conviction." On May 5, Boswell arrived in London from Scotland; the first time they were alone together, Johnson "communicated to me, with solemn earnestness, a very remarkable circumstance which had happened in the course of his illness, when he was much distressed by the dropsy. He had shut himself up, and employed a day in particular exercises of religion — fasting humiliation, and prayer. On a sudden he obtained extraordinary relief, for which he looked up to Heaven with grateful devotion. He made no direct inference from this fact; but from his manner of telling it, I could perceive that it appeared to him as something more than an incident in the common course of events.... I think even men of dry rationality may believe that there was an immediate interposition of divine Providence, and that 'the fervent prayer of this righteous man' availed." No doubt Boswell owed details of this description to Hawkins' earlier published account; it is, however, one of the rare occasions on which the two rival biographers concur fully not only in their report of factual details but in their interpretation of an incident on which disagreement in interpretation (it seems to us) would be so easy. On September 5, Johnson thanked God for "the awakening of my mind," and on September 18, his birthday, for "the great mercies of the last year ... and, O my gracious God, make me truly thankful for the call by which thou hast awakened my conscience and summoned me to Repentance." On November 28, when death again approached, he confided to Hawkins some "mental distraction," but added, "I had, very early in my life, the seeds of goodness in me ... these, I trust, have brought forth in me fruits meet for repentance; and, if I have repented as I ought, I am forgiven ... I have had such rays of hope shot into my soul, as have almost persuaded me that I am in a state of reconciliation with God." In their accounts of his last days, his biographers testify to the "serenity of mind" with which he met his end, unlike the terror of the previous winter, and to the frequency with which he exhorted those around him to religious seriousness. Dr. Brocklesby, his attending physician, reported, "For some time before his death, all his fears were calmed and absorbed by the prevalence of his faith, and his trust in the merits and propitiation of Jesus Christ. He talked often to me about the necessity of faith in the sacrifice of Jesus, as necessary beyond all good works whatever, for the salvation of mankind."[14]

The fact that Johnson had undergone a significant religious experience soon became more widely known. Before long, religiously-minded men outside the immediate Johnson circle were discussing it with interest. On May 11, 1784, William Cowper wrote to his friend, the "Evangelical" leader John Newton, then Rector of St. Mary Woolnoth, "We rejoice in the account you give us of Dr. Johnson. His conversion will indeed be a singular proof of the omnipotence of Grace."[15] In 1785, the Reverend James Fordyce, an eminent Presbyterian minister in London and an old acquaintance of Johnson's, devoted one of his six *Addresses to the Deity* to an account of Johnson's end:

> When trouble and anguish came upon thy aged servant, when "his sleep went from him," when in solemn recollection he "communed with his own heart upon his bed," and examined himself in the view of his last and great account, he saw wherein he had offended .... Let it be known that this man, after considering the uncertainty of life, after studying the sanctity of thy law, after discovering more clearly *the utter insufficiency of human attainments* [my italics], and contemplating with ardent solicitude the stupendous and unspeakable

---

(14) *Letters* 933, 593; Boswell, *Life,* ed. Hill-Powell (194-50), IV, 271-72; *Works* (1958), I, 393, 396-97; Hawkins, *Life,* p. 582; Boswell, *Life,* IV, 416. Professor Quinlan glosses the last sentence thus: "According to Brocklesby, Johnson had simply remarked that faith was more important than good works for salvation" (p. 286). But "necessity of" and "necessary beyond all good works whatever" mean something very different from "simply ... more important than".

(15) Quoted by Quinlan (pp. 244-45) from *The Correspondence of William Cowper,* ed. Thomas Wright (New York, 1904), II, 205. Cowper goes on to speak of Johnson's "doing honour to the cause to which he becomes a convert." Perhaps this expression is partly responsible for Professor Quinlan's misconception that by "conversion" Cowper meant "adopting Evangelical beliefs" (whatever, beyond Anglican beliefs, these might be). But the "cause" to which Cowper refers is made clear later on in the same passage — it is the cause of "the gospel."

importance of salvation, did with all the humility of faith cast himself on thine infinite mercy through Jesus Christ.(16)

Many years later, the son of Benjamin Latrobe, a Moravian clergyman, reported "the testimony of my late reverend father, who knew Dr. Johnson intimately, and always spoke of him as having become truly, before his death, 'a child of God by faith in Christ Jesus.' ... 'The great Dr. Johnson' ... did not, in his closing years, live, and certainly did not die, a formalist or a pharisee, trusting either wholly or in part to his own merits: .... his 'conversion' to God, to use his own expression, though 'late' — yet not so late, I feel assured as his last illness — was true."(17) Hannah More told a circumstantial story of Johnson's applying, shortly before his death, to the Reverend Thomas Winstanley, Rector of St. Dunstan's-in-the-East, for spiritual aid, and of Winstanley's writing to him on the subject of repentance: "these communications, together with the conversation of the late Mr. Latrobe, who was a particular friend of Dr. Johnson, appear to have been blessed by God in bringing this great man to the renunciation of self, and a simple reliance on Jesus as his Saviour...."(18)

To the validity of all this evidence in establishing that some important religious experience occurred to Johnson early in 1784, and that it was to this experience that Johnson referred in the prayer before his last communion, Professor Quinlan seems to assent. It is the question of what that experience is to be called that worries him. We might wonder why the word that Johnson

---

(16) *Johnsoniana, or Supplement to Boswell* [ed. J.W. Croker] (London, 1836), p. 445. Quinlan does not note this (very early) piece of testimony, which, although it does not use the word "conversion," says essentially what the passage next quoted, from Latrobe, does. I do not know whether Professor Quinlan would classify a clergyman of the established Church of Scotland, D.D. of Glasgow University, as an "Evangelical" or not.

(17) Quoted by Quinlan (p. 247) from C.I. Latrobe, "The Last Hours of Dr. Johnson," *Christian Observer*, XXVIII (January, 1828), 32.

(18) *Johnsonian Miscellanies*, ed. G.B. Hill (Oxford, 1897), II, 203-05, from William Roberts, ed., *Memoirs of the Life and Correspondence of Mrs. Hannah More* (1834), I, 376. Hannah More had the account from the Rev. Mr. Storry of Colchester. Writing in December, 1784, when Johnson was "past all hope," Hannah More reports that "his dread of dying is in a great measure subdued; and now he says 'the bitterness of death is past.' ... How delighted should I be to hear the dying discourse of this great and good man, especially now that faith has subdued his fears."

himself used to designate that experience, "conversion," should not be
thought to suffice for us, his readers, and why reports of it under that name
should be stigmatized as "rumor." Quinlan's conclusion, however, is that

> There is no clear evidence that Johnson was converted in the
> Evangelical sense, despite the fact that a rumor to that effect
> circulated for several decades. Although he included the peti-
> tion "forgive and accept my late conversion" in a prayer uttered
> shortly before his death, when he employed the term he pro-
> bably did not use it in the currently popular meaning. More
> likely he was referring to a change that had led to his turning
> to God and a general strengthening of his religious convictions.
> There is no indication that he adopted the belief that man is
> saved by faith alone, nor any evidence that he arrived at the
> typical Evangelical convert's ecstatic assurance of salvation.
> Even at the end, perhaps because of his essential humility,
> he seems never to have felt with certainty that he was among
> the *elect*.[19]

Earlier in his article he contends,

> In the popular language of the day "conversion" had come to
> mean adopting Evangelical beliefs .... [To an Evangelical]
> the specific reference to a "late conversion" could mean only
> one thing, that the great man had experienced a change that
> brought with it belief in justification by faith and assurance
> of salvation .... The fact that many people employed "con-
> version" in the particular Evangelical connotation, however,
> does not prove that Johnson intended to convey that meaning
> in his prayer. In his dictionary he lists three definitions of the
> term: (1) "change from one state into another; transmutation."
> (2) "change from reprobation to grace, from a bad to a holy
> life." and (3) "change from one religion to another." When he
> incorporated the word in his prayer, he probably meant it in
> the second sense, a change from reprobation to grace. But he
> probably did not mean reprobation in the Calvinistic sense,
> nor grace in the Evangelical meaning of justification by faith
> alone.[20]

---

(19) P. 261.
(20) P. 259.

There are many things in this commentary that are puzzling. What, for instance, can be meant by saying that Johnson, in his definition of conversion, "probably did not mean reprobation in the Calvinistic sense"? What other theological sense of the word was available to him than the "Calvinistic" one — the sense in which it was used by Augustine and Thomas Aquinas and Luther and by their followers and opponents in the great controversies over predestination in patristic, mediaeval, and Renaissance times; the sense in which it is still unanimously used in theological discourse; the sense which Johnson gives in his *Dictionary*, "The act of abandoning, or state of being abandoned, to eternal destruction: the contrary to election" ? The reasoning seems to be that Johnson, *a priori*, could not have had anything to do with Calvinism; therefore if he uses a word so much used in Calvinist theology, he must be using it in a non-Calvinistic sense. But theological dictionaries and encyclopaedias will be searched in vain for any sense differing essentially from Johnson's own definition. And what can be meant by saying that Johnson did not understand "grace in the Evangelical meaning of justification by faith alone" ? "Justification" is an act or process, "grace" is a spiritual quality or state: it is hard to imagine any Evangelical, indeed anyone familiar with theological discussion, equating them. The relevant definitions of "grace" in Johnson's *Dictionary* are "Favourable influence of God on the human mind" and "Virtue, the effect of God's influence." Substituting these periphrases in Johnson's second definition of "conversion," we arrive at something like "Change from imminent damnation to salvation, through God's influence on the mind." This is, in fact, the classic theological sense of "conversion," from the time of Augustine, and earlier, to the present, the sense in which it is normally used in serious theological discussion, Catholic or "Evangelical"; and it is unquestionably the sense in which Johnson used it in his prayer.

III

The concept of conversion is very old and very central in Christian theology. "Convertere" means literally "to turn around, to turn from one direction toward another"; the word and its derivatives frequently occur in the Vulgate, often in the simple, physical meaning, but sometimes in the higher, metaphorical sense of the turning of the human soul from wickedness and unbelief and error toward God. It is used, of course, of the great experience on the Damascus road when the persecutor Saul was changed into the apostle Paul; though the leading text is probably Acts III, 19, where Peter, preaching to the people of Jerusalem, chides them for their denial of Christ and exhorts them, "Repent ye, therefore, and be converted" (King James version; in the Vulgate, *Paenitemini, igitur, et convertimini*; μετανοήσατε οὖν καὶ ἐπιστρέψατε in the Greek). The concepts of repentance (μετάνοια—an "afterthought", a "change of mind upon reflection", as Liddell and Scott put it) and conversion (ἐπιστροφή — a turning about, a turning toward) have ever since been closely linked, sometimes virtually equated. Thus Johnson, to illustrate the second definition of "repentance" in his *Dictionary*, quotes from one of his favourite Anglican theologians, Henry Hammond: "*Repentance* is a change of mind, or a *conversion* [my italics] from sin to God: not some one bare act of change, but a lasting durable state of new life, which is called regeneration." But it was Augustine's classic auto-biographical account, written with all Augustine's poetic skill, that perhaps chiefly accounts for the later connotations of the word — the sudden moment of inner, spiritual enlightenment which is the great turning point of a man's life; as well as the tradition of "the typical Evangelical convert's ecstatic assurance of salvation." Seated under a fig tree near Milan, in great spiritual distress, he hears a child's voice chanting "Take and read, take and read !" He remembers that Saint Antony, reading the text in the Gospel *Go, sell what thou hast, and give to the poor*, "had been in that instant converted to Thee." He opens Saint Paul at random, and his eyes fall on Romans XIII, 13:

> As I finished the sentence, as though the light of assurance had been poured into my heart, all the shadows of doubt at once dispersed .... For Thou didst convert me to Thee. (*Statim quippe cum fine huiusce sententiae quasi luce securitatis infusa cordi meo omnes dubitationis tenebrae diffugerunt .... Convertisti enim me ad te.*)(21)

----

(21) *Confessiones*, VIII, xii, 30. Earlier, Augustine had gone, as a connoisseur of rhetoric, to hear Ambrose preach, had been gripped by his words, and formally enrolled himself as a Christian catechumen (V, xiii-xiv). But though "Ambrose taught the doctrine of salvation most profitably," "salvation is far from sinners such as I then was"; and some three years of bitter spiritual struggle were to follow this outward profession of adherence to Christianity and renunciation of Manichaeism before the inner awakening described here, which alone Augustine calls "conversion."

One might almost say that the history of western Christianity can be traced in a series of great conversions — Paul, Augustine, Francis after the revel in Assisi, Ignatius in his sick-room in the castle of Loyola, Luther in the Augustinian cloister at Wittenberg, Wesley in Aldersgate Street. If the delicacy of small men like the Reverend George Strahan was wounded by the unfashionable "Evangelical" connotations of the word "conversion," to men of larger minds and greater learning, like Johnson, Cowper, and Fordyce, it was nothing to be ashamed of.

The homiletic literature dealing with conversion is immense. It is common to all the major branches of western Christianity, Anglican, Methodist, Lutheran, Roman Catholic; and it is common to every period in the history of Christianity, from the earliest to the present. "Repent ye, and be converted"; "I am not come to call the righteous but sinners to repentance"; "Repent ye, for the kingdom of heaven is at hand" have been the texts of a million sermons, from Ambrose and Chrysostom, through Savonarola and Calvin, through Donne and Bossuet and Wesley, to Bishop Fulton Sheen and the Reverend Billy Graham. There have been doctrinal controversies about the extent to which the free will of unregenerated man can be effectual to conversion, about the degree of distinction to be made between the concepts of conversion and regeneration; but the central doctrine, that *a* conversion, an inward and spiritual change, a turning away of the soul from evil to good, from godlessness to God, is essential to salvation, and that the, chief task of the Christian preacher is to exhort and and facilitate such change has never been subjected to any serious challenge in western Christianity.

To document the contention that this is what the word "conversion" meant to Johnson (and Cowper and Newton and Fordyce), and that it could have meant only this, involves one in an embarrassment of riches. The works

------

=   Johnson, as might be expected, had no difficulty in distinguishing between the various senses of the word. He properly classifies the earlier of these two experiences of Augustine under the first of the two theological meanings of the verb "to convert" that he gives in his *Dictionary*: "2. To change from one religion to another. 'Augustine is *converted* by St. Ambrose's sermon, when he came to it on no such design.' *Hammond*." The second, and more important, meaning, "3. To turn from a bad to a good life," he illustrates from James v, 20 and Psalm li, 13 — "Then will I teach transgressors thy ways, and sinners shall be *converted* unto thee."

of the great Anglican homiletic writers of the sixteenth to eighteenth centuries — Latimer, Andrewes, Donne, South, Tillotson, Wake, Sherlock — as well as the humbler manuals of devotion could be drawn on to provide such documentation. The theologian I wish chiefly to cite, Henry Hammond (1605–1660), I choose, first, because as far as one can tell from a cursory inspection, Johnson seems to draw on him more heavily than on any other writer for illustrations of his definitions of theological terms in the *Dictionary* (though Robert South must run him a close second; and, interestingly, Milton is also used a good deal); second, because Hammond, as one of the great "Caroline divines" — he was chaplain to King Charles I, and attendant on him during the Civil War; if not directly a protégé of Laud, at least the recipient of patronage during Laud's ascendancy — is usually thought of as "High Church," and thus at the opposite pole from "Evangelicalism" (though how little use these partisan labels are to the serious study of the history of doctrine will perhaps become apparent): the standard edition of his works, from which I quote, is part of a series entitled *The Library of Anglo-Catholic Theology.* Johnson "was extremely fond of Dr. Hammond's Works, and sometimes gave them as a present to young men going into orders: he also bought them for the library at Streatham".(22) Here is a catena from Hammond; to it may be added the two passages quoted in the *Dictionary* that have been mentioned. I have italicized "conversion" and "convert" throughout:

> Repentance, whatever that word signifies — and that is certainly a sincere change and renovation of mind, a *conversion* of the sinner to God in a new life, "repentance from dead works" — is questionless it to which, on purpose, Christ came to call sinners. His whole embassy from His Father's bosom was projected and designed for this grand work.
>
> If there be any that mistake sorrow for sin, μεταμέλεια … and confound it with repentance, μετάνοια, which is never less than a *conversion* and change of mind, these by obtruding an insufficient part for the whole, the beginning of a change for the entire work of new life, will fall under the former guilt of obstructing this superstructure.
>
> No other use is sufficient [to avoid damnation] but repentance; and … no repentance is sufficient but the μετάνοια, "the change," which is here defined.

---

(22) *Johnsonian Miscellanies,* II, 19.

> A strange disorder hath most times accompanied this extra-
> ordinary *conversion* of more violent outrageous sinners .... We
> are not to be mistaken, as if we thought God's purposes tied
> to man's good behaviour, or man's moral goodness to woo and
> allure God's Spirit, as that the Almighty is not equally able
> to sanctify the foulest soul by His *converting* grace. .... When
> in hope to mend himself, and ease his fears, he shall fly to the
> comfort of his present *converted* state, and yet there espy
> many thorns of temptation, how can he but be frighted out cf
> himself ? .... Unless a man have been in some spiritual danger,
> and by the *converting* spirit be instructed into a sense and
> apprehension of it, he will not sufficiently observe the benefit
> and use of a deliverer .... How to distinguish a true *convert*
> from a false .... If the *conversion* of an inordinate sinner be
> not accompanied with unwonted joy .... How a great sinner
> may judge of his sincere certain *conversion* ....(23)

In short, Hammond, so far as I can see, uses the words "convert" and "conversion" as freely, and in the same doctrinal sense, and with as great emphasis, as any eighteenth-century "Evangelical," or nineteenth-century
Methodist, or twentieth-century Salvation Army preacher — or indeed any
barefooted friar of the middle ages.

A few more illustrations, from Anglican divines well known to Johnson.
From Robert South:

> The third and last sort [of faith], and which here only is intend-
> ed, is a saving, effectual faith, wrought in the soul by a sound
> and real work of *conversion*.(24)

From Bishop Jeremy Taylor:

> The *conversion* and repentance of every sinner is part of Christ's
> glorification.(25)

---

(23) *Miscellaneous Theological Works*, ed. N. Pocock, 3 vols. (Oxford,
1847-50), II, 169, 173 ("Of Fundamentals"); III, 73 (Sermon IV, "Repent,
for the kingdom of heaven is at hand"); III, 636-47 (Sermon XXX, "Of whom
I am the chief"). The definition of "repentance" that Johnson quotes in the
Dictionary is adapted from the *Practical Catechism* (I, 56).

(24) *Sermons*, 5 vols. (New York, 1871), IV, 225 (Sermon XVII, "For by
faith ye stand").

(25) *The Rules and Exercises of Holy Living*, Chap. IV, Sec. 9.

From William Law:

> There is no true and real *Conversion,* whether it be from infi-
> delity, or any other life of sin, till a man comes to know and
> feel that nothing less than his whole nature is to be parted
> with, and yet finds in himself no possibility of doing it.[26]

The manual for which Johnson sent in January, 1784, Richard Baxter's
A Call to the Unconverted, was a very famous and widely read "populari-
zation" of the standard doctrine of conversion. It was written, Baxter tells
us, in 1657, as a result of Archbishop Ussher's instigation. "In a little more
than a year there were about twenty thousand of them printed by my own
consent, and about ten thousand since, besides many thousands by stolen
impression .... Through God's mercy I have information of almost whole
households converted by this small book."[27] He goes on to mention translations into French and German, and tells us with pride that it was the first
book, after the Bible, that John Eliot translated into the language of the
Massachusetts Indians. The number of editions published during the eight-
teenth and early nineteenth centuries must be quite incalculable, as a glance
at the shelves of an older public library will show.[28] It "calls" to conversion,
as Baxter says, with "vehement persuasions" rather than mere "directions,"
and its rhetoric is scarcely distinguishable from that of a Dwight L. Moody
or a General Booth. "If you will believe God," it begins, "believe this: there
is but one of two ways for every wicked man, either conversion or damnation."
"You are but dead and damned men, except you will be converted"; "Hell
would not be so full, if people were but willing .... to enter in at the strait
gate of conversion"; "Thou must be converted or condemned: turn or die";
and so forth. Baxter, to be sure, was a "Puritan," and later became a Dissenter;
yet Charles II and Clarendon thought highly enough of him to offer to make
him Bishop of Hereford; and Johnson never speaks of him without
deep affection. Baxter's, it has been remarked, was one of the two great
"Calls" so widely read in the eighteenth century — the other, of course,

---

(26) *The Pocket William Law,* ed. A.W. Hopkinson (London, 1950),
p. 150 (*The Spirit of Prayer: Part the Second*).

(27) "Advertisement" prefixed to the edition I am using, an undated one
(ca. 1870 ?), published by the American Tract Society, New York. The full
title of the work is *A Call to the Unconverted to Turn and Live.*

(28) The British Museum catalogue lists a "69th ed., 1728."

was William Law's. It is interesting, and important, that both played a part in Johnson's religious life, Law's near the beginning, Baxter's near the end of it. The significance of Law's book — the source of the Evangelical movement — for Johnson's religion has long been recognized. Thanks to the efforts of Strahan and Boswell, that of Baxter's has not.

Two further points: in the literature of repentance and conversion, going back to Augustine himself, it became customary to recognize a series of normal "stages" in the process. The Church of England's Homily of Repentance (like many other such treatises) notes four "parts of repentance.... The first is the contrition of the heart....The second is an unfeigned confession, and acknowledging of our sins unto God .... It may also be thus taken, that we ought to confess our weakness and infirmities one to another .... The third part of repentance is faith .... The fourth is an amendment of life, or a new life, in bringing forth fruits worthy of repentance."[29] It is interesting that Johnson's spiritual history between January and December, 1784, seems to follow this pattern. The numerous declarations of his inadequacies found in his conversations of this period, like those found in his *Diaries* at all times, which puzzled his contemporaries and which modern students have characterized under such terms as "pessimism" and even "masochism," take on a somewhat different aspect when viewed as acts of contrition and confession. Hawkins's role as "confessor" in February becomes clearer when we consider the advice of the Homily regarding the second "stage" of conversion. So, too, do Johnson's activities in the summer and autumn of 1784 in providing tombstones for his wife, parents, and brother, inquiring into the welfare of distant relations and making provision for those who were poverty-stricken, sending expressions of his regard to neglected acquaintances, and the like.[30] True, one may well believe that Johnson, knowing death was approaching, would have done so without exhortation. Yet the activity fits in well enough with the fourth "stage" of repentance, the amendment of life. Johnson, in his own sermon on repentance (Sermon II), emphasizes the primacy of making "reparation and restitution" for harm done, directly or by neglect[31].

_____

(29) *Sermons or Homilies Appointed To Be Read in Churches* (London: S.P.C.K. [n.d.; ca. 1830], pp. 587-94.

(30) See., e.g., *Letters* 975, 977, 991. 992.1, 1018.1, 1024, 1037.1, 1039, 1040.

(31) Johnson, *Works* (Oxford, 1825), IX, 306.

Finally, in seventeenth- and eighteenth-century Anglican treatises and sermons on repentance and conversion, the importance of an *early* repentance is made much of. Sometimes this is consciously by way of challenge to what is declared to be the Roman doctrine of the sufficiency of a death-bed repentance. Thus Hammond:

> That frequent practice ... of the many, of secure spending in sin the youth, and riper age ... till forerunners of death and hell make their close approaches to them ... what do these but evacuate the whole force of the Christian faith, and absolutely resolve against building of Christian life upon it ? The unreasonableness and presumption, the danger and desperate insecurity of those that thus project ... is ... never sufficiently lamented, being that which is the debauching all parts of the world ... and hath the luck among all professions of Christians to have aids and offices diligent to offer it encouragements; the Romanists have many, formerly named, and their extreme unction, administered as the dying man's viaticum ... may be added to the catalogue.(32)

So South, who, though devoting a sermon to arguing against the contention that a death-bed conversion can *never* be efficacious, nevertheless concludes:

> I affirm, that it is more than ten to one but that all the pomp of a death-bed repentance, in its highest and most angelical resolutions, in its most sorrowful, mournful, and affectionate discoveries, moves wholly upon this false spring of fear .... It is highly probable that there is scarce one of a hundred in this condition but goes off with the forced sorrows of fear instead of repentance; and so dies terrified rather than sanctified.(33)

So indeed Johnson himself, in his Sermon II, the second "point" of which is "What are the obligations to an early repentance."(34) Thus, Johnson's expression of regret for his "late" conversion was, according to standard Anglican homiletics, perfectly proper.

---

(32) *Works*, II, 172 ("Of Fundamentals").

(33) *Sermons* (1871), IV, 595 (Sermon XXXVI, "Repent; or else I will come unto thee quickly").

(34) *Works* (1825), IX, 302.

To sum up: that a man must experience a "true and real Conversion" before salvation is possible was emphatically orthodox Anglican teaching as Johnson knew it; Johnson believed that he underwent this experience, or the essential beginning of it (regrettably late in life) on Friday, February 20, 1784; the pattern of Johnson's conversion follows the pattern suggested in Anglican (and other) treatises on the subject; and there can be no question that it was this experience to which Johnson referred in his prayer for his last communion, as he did in his prayer on his last birthday, September 18, where he returned thanks "for the great mercies of the last year ... and O my gracious God, make me truly thankful for the call by which thou hast awakened my conscience and summoned me to Repentance"(35). Again, Hammond's equation, "Repentance is a change of mind, or a conversion," should be noted. It was not by accident that in the prayer of December 5 Johnson carefully balanced the two words — "*accept* my *conversion*, and forgive its *lateness*; *accept* my *repentance*, and 'enforce' [*i.e.*, reinforce] its *imperfection*." It is sobering to reflect how little sensitive to the nuances of Johnson's style even the most assiduous Johnsonian students have been, when it has not hitherto been pointed out what violence Strahan's and Boswell's mangling of the prayer does to this elaborate rhetoric.

IV

But the crux of Professor Quinlan's argument is his contention that to "Evangelicals" like Cowper, Newton, and Latrobe, the word "conversion" meant something essentially different from this classic meaning of Christian theology — that "in the popular language of the day 'conversion' had come to mean adopting Evangelical beliefs." To this statement, three objections must be entered. First, Professor Quinlan gives no evidence and cites no authority for this important factual proposition — we have only the bare assertion. In the circumstances, one can only make the counter-assertion: it seems quite improbable that the word was used in serious religious discourse, however "Evangelical" and however "popular," in the late eighteenth and early nineteenth centuries, in any but the classic Augustinian sense, firmly established by so many centuries and so many millions of words of homiletics — that of an inward change, a turning of the individual human

---

(35) *Works* (1958), I, 396.

soul from evil, from the world, the flesh, and the devil, to God. If anyone
believes that when a "popular" evangelist shouts "Be converted or burn
everlastingly !" he is merely exhorting his hearers to abandon their memberships in one denomination and take out memberships in another, a quarter
of an hour's listening to a Salvation Army preacher on a street corner should
convince him that he is talking about nothing of the sort.

Second, even if such a "popular" sense were current, it would be hard
to believe that men so well read in Christian theology as Cowper, Newton,
and Latrobe would choose to use the term, in serious discussion among themselves, in this rather than the established theological sense.

Third, and most important, if such a popular sense were postulated,
we should still have to ask, "What could that sense — 'adopting Evangelical
beliefs' — possibly signify ?" For there were, and are, no "Evangelical beliefs"
apart from general Anglican beliefs. Evangelicalism is not, as Professor
Quinlan seems to think, a set of doctrines outside those of the Church of
England. Cowper, Newton (Rector of St. Mary Woolnoth), and John Wesley
were loyal Anglicans, who subscribed to the Thirty-Nine Articles, to all
the orthodox theological teaching of their church, and never wavered from
it or went beyond it. Even when Wesley's followers later separated from
the Church it was on the one point of discipline — the question of episcopal
ordination; apart from this, the basic documents of Methodist doctrine are
identical with those of the Church of England. The most one can say of
"Evangelicalism" as against non-"Evangelicalism" in the Church of England
is that the word stands for a very vaguely defined difference of emphasis
in promulgating orthodox teaching. Many bishops and even archbishops of
that Church, from Johnson's time to the present, have been described as
"Evangelicals" or sympathetic to "Evangelicalism" — for instance, Johnson's
friend, Beilby Porteus, Bishop of London (whose social life Johnson felt
was too frivolous). The point was, of course, emphatically made not long ago,
by the Archbishop of Canterbury's appearing on the platform of the Baptist
evangelist, Billy Graham, and Graham's being invited to preach before the
Queen in St. George's Chapel, Windsor.

Professor Quinlan implies that on two matters there were doctrinal
differences between "Evangelicals" and other Anglicans. Conversion in
"the Evangelical sense," he tells us, "brought with it belief in justification
by faith and assurance of salvation" — the clear implication being that
these were doctrines held by Cowper and other Evangelicals, but not

by Johnson and other presumed non-Evangelicals. On both these matters Professor Quinlan is mistaken: the first is general Anglican doctrine (or was in 1784: there is no need to extend our investigations beyond that date); the second, at least as Professor Quinlan interprets it, is not necessarily "Evangelical" doctrine.

First, the matter of "justification by faith alone." There has been a certain amount of allusion to this doctrine in recent literary studies of the eighteenth century, sometimes demonstrating considerable confusion about it on the part of the writers. Such confusion should not be necessary: the Anglican position between the sixteenth and eighteenth centuries — which is also the general Protestant position — is not really difficult to comprehend. Faith, and faith alone, *is* the one essential, on the part of the human individual, to justification; works without faith are useless, or worse than useless. Nevertheless, true faith *will* necessarily bring forth good works; a profession of faith which is not followed by good works is necessarily a false one — "faith" without works cannot be faith. More briefly, the performance of seemingly "good" works does not necessarily testify to the possession of justifying faith; though justifying faith must necessarily manifest itself in good works. But that it is faith which is essential to justification, works only incidental, though necessarily incidental, is the kernel of the doctrine, which goes back, of course, through Luther and others, to Augustine and Paul.

Starting with this, the orthodox position, it is possible for the professing Christian to fall into error, into hypocrisy, in either of two opposite directions. It is possible to err on the side of formalism — to think that by the mere outward performance of "acceptable" works, by "virtuous" modes of behavior, the individual can "merit" salvation, whatever the condition of his heart. On the other hand, by convincing himself and others that he has attained to a sufficient inward "faith," he may relieve himself of the trouble of having to maintain decent outward behavior — roughly, "antinomianism." Throughout the course of Christian history, there have been pendulum-swings from one side to the other of this range of possible positions. Jesus condemned the formalistic Pharisee; Saint Paul condemned the whole formalistic Jewish law. Seeing the alternative danger, however, Saint James pronounced, "Faith, if it hath not works, is dead ... shew me thy faith without thy works, and I will shew thee my faith by my works." As everyone knows, it was Luther's arriving at the conviction that the Roman church had degenerated into a mere clearing-house for indulgences and other formalities that brought about the Reformation, and a renewal of the Pauline and Augustinian emphasis on the inner rather than the outer man; presently the Anabaptists of Münster, extremist disciples of the Reformation, outraged Europe with their "antinomian" excesses. (36)

But the orthodox position, in sixteenth- to eighteenth-century Anglicanism, remained in the middle: without exception, the great preachers of the Church, like South and Hammond, reject formalism and antinomianism equally; and there can be no question that this is where Johnson stood on the matter of faith and works. This position, however, seems hard for some modern literary students to grasp, who appear to feel, whenever they encounter an expression by Johnson or South condemning antinomian tendencies, that they have obtained evidence of South's or Johnson's adherence to some sort of formalistic doctrine. Thus an influential essay published some years ago, expounding the theological point of view found in Fielding's *Shamela* and *Joseph Andrews*, makes much of a sermon of South's:

> The most serious fault found in the Methodists by the author of each of these works seems to have been, as Parson Adams phrases it, their setting up "the detestable Doctrine of Faith against Good Works." This is identical with "the useful and truly religious Doctrine of *Grace*" that Tickletext sees everywhere inculcated in Richardson's novel .... John Wesley was rather more polite but just as insistent on the necessity of salvation by faith: "Wherewith then shall a sinful man atone for any the least of his sins ? with his own works ? No .... Grace is the source, faith the condition of salvation." ... It is probably significant that one of Fielding's favorite clerical writers, the Restoration divine, Dr. Robert South, was a sardonic critic of Antinomians: "Some hope to be saved by *believing* well .... and shedding a few insipid tears. .... Therefore they will not think themselves hardly dealt with

(36) The exegesis of the Epistle of James is of course more complex than I have suggested here. But no qualified Biblical scholar or theologian would support such a view as that illustrated by the following quotation from a recent work of eighteenth-century literary scholarship: "These... [Anglican] divines stood staunchly with St. James *against* [my italics] St. Paul; 'Faith without works is dead,'" The fact that lessons from St. James and St. Paul alternate in the Anglican lectionary should cause the student at least to hesitate before pronouncing that their teaching were regarded as contradictory.

> though you require *Faith* of them if you will but dispense
> with *Good Works*."[37]

Anyone unfamiliar with the background of doctrinal history might
infer from this account (as indeed some students seem to have done) that
South is arguing *against* the sufficiency of true faith for salvation.
Of course, a careful reading of the quotation from South will show
that such an inference is unwarranted: he is arguing against those
who use the undoubted fact of the primacy of that requirement to
avoid the duty of leading truly Christian lives — and, of course, in doing so
demonstrate their own lack of true faith and grace, and convict themselves
of hypocrisy. (This, too, is undoubtedly the position of Fielding, who did
not pass through Eton without becoming aware of the elements of Anglican
doctrine in the matter.) In fact, further exploration of South's sermons will
reveal a great deal in the very vein of the remarks attributed to Wesley,
Tickletext, and Parson Adams' opponents. Here, for instance, is the opening
of his Sermon XVII, on the text "For by faith ye stand":

> There can be none here ignorant that the great evangelical
> virtue so frequently spoken of, so highly commended, and
> upon which the *whole* [my italics] weight of man's salvation
> leans and depends, is faith.

Having emphatically affirmed this, he goes on to make clear how this position
is compatible with anti-antinomianism (not that much clarification should
really be necessary):

> For it being the great and glorious badge of the citizens of
> heaven, the sons of God, and heirs of immortality, it is no
> wonder if every man has his mouth open to profess and boast
> of his faith: and those possibly the most loudly of all others,
> who entertain it only in opposition to good works.

After propounding two inferior definitions of faith, South continues,

> The third and last sort, and which here only is intended, is
> a saving, effectual faith, wrought in the soul by a sound and
> real work of conversion. It takes in both the former kinds, and

(37) Charles B. Woods, "Fielding and the Authorship of *Shamela*," *Philological Quarterly*, XXV (July, 1946), 262-66.

> superadds its own peculiar perfection besides .... It is a
> durable, fixed disposition of holiness, immediately infused
> by God into the soul, whereby the soul in all its faculties is
> changed, renewed, sanctified, and withal powerfully inclined
> to exert itself in all the actions of a pious life.[38]

This is pure Wesley: "Grace is the source, faith the condition of salvation."
It is also pure Augustine; and, if a recent analysis of his teaching is accurate, pure Thomas Aquinas. "Dans la *Somme Théologique* ... la conversion à Dieu commence strictement avec la foi; et la foi est à tous égards
une grâce prévenante, un don absolument gratuit de Dieu."[39] So South;
so Paul, Augustine, Aquinas, and Luther; so the Prayer Book, the Thirty-
Nine Articles, the Homilies; so Andrewes, Donne, Hammond; so Wesley,
Cowper, Newton. So Johnson, as we shall presently see.

If South was a sardonic critic of antinomianism, he was an at least
equally caustic critic of formalism, of any suspicion of a belief that any
man's "works" can in themselves contribute an iota toward his salvation.
His attacks on the notion inspire some of his highest flights of rhetoric:
here is the opening of his Sermon XVI ("But all their works they do for to
be seen of men"):

> It is strange to consider the great difference both of the prin-
> ciple and quality of most of those actions that in the world
> carry the same reputations. Of this we have here a notable
> instance in a sect of men among the Jews called the Pharisees;
> who made as glorious an appearance, and had as high a vogue
> for piety as the best. Their righteousness and good works so
> glistered that they even dashed the judging faculties of those
> who judged more by seeing than by weighing: and doubtless
> they were in show so exactly good that no argument from
> appearance could decide the difference.
>
> And yet, like those trees which are fair and flourishing at the
> top from the dung that lies at the root, the principle of all
> those good works was a sinful appetite, an appetite of glory,
> an ambitious desire.[40]

---

(38) *Sermons* (1871), IV, 224-25.

(39) Henri Bouillard, *Conversion et Grâce chez S. Thomas d'Aquin* (Paris,
1944), p. 194 [*Etudes publiées sous la direction de la Faculté de Théologie S.J.
de Lyon-Fourvière*]. Published with the imprimatur of the archdiocese of Lyons.

(40) *Sermons* (1871), IV, 203.

Even more forceful and pointed is his Sermon XXV, "The Doctrine of Merit Stated, and the Impossibility of Man's Meriting of God," on the great text in Job xxii, 19, "Can a man be profitable to God ?" South's answer is the simple Augustinian (and Calvinist) one — he cannot. After condemning Pelagianism, and the Roman doctrines of merit *de condigno* and *de congruo*, he launches into a whirlwind attack on Rome itself, in a manner which Luther could hardly have improved on:

> To proceed to another sort of men famous for corrupting Christianity more ways than one; to wit, those of the church of Rome. We shall find, that this doctrine of man's being able to merit of God is one of the chief foundations of Popery also: even the great Diana, which some of the most experienced craftsmen in the world do with so much zeal sacrifice to and make shrines for; and by so doing get their living, and that a very plentiful and splendid one too; as knowing full well, that without it the grandeur of their church (which is all their religion) would quickly fall to the ground. For if there be no merit of good works, then no supererogation; and if no super-erogation, no indulgences; and if no indulgences, then it is to be feared that the silversmith's trade will run low, and the credit of the pontifical bank begin to fail. So that the very marrow, the life and spirit of Popery lies in a stiff adherence to this doctrine: the grand question still insisted upon by these merchants being *Quid dabitis* ? and the great commodity set to sale by them being merit.

And much more abuse of the Pope and cardinals, which I omit. Finally,

> In a word, take away the foundation, and the house must fall; and, in like manner, beat down merit, and down goes Popery too.[41]

"God doth not need/Either man's work or his own gifts," as Milton put it. I have quoted from South because he has been mistakenly used to give color to the suggestion that orthodox Anglican teaching in the seventeenth and eighteenth centuries at least allowed the notion to be entertained that human "works" in themselves may bring with them some degree of merit. But any other reputable Anglican divine of the period could be cited equally to prove that it refused to tolerate the least hint of any such notion. William Law

---

(41) *Sermons Preached upon Several Occasions* (Oxford, 1842), **II**, 90-91.

puts it with succinctness, bluntness, and finality — "Christianity is not a
school for the teaching of moral virtue."(42) If the modern student, even
the modern student who thinks he is a Christian, starts back from this pronouncement in blank amaze, he is advised to begin the study of William
Law, as Johnson did, and he may in time find out what Christianity meant
to these men, and to South, Hammond, Cowper, Newton, and the rest.

Finally, Johnson himself may be allowed to answer Professor Quinlan's
contention that "there is no indication that he adopted the belief that man
is saved by faith alone." In his fine Sermon XIII, on the text 2 Timothy
iii, 5, "Having a form of godliness, but denying the power thereof," he
treats the question of faith and works from the orthodox Anglican point
of view — the same point of view from which we have just seen South treating it. After discussing and condemning Jewish and Roman Catholic emphasis
on ceremonies and other "works," Johnson declares,

> Nothing can be more repugnant to the general tenour of the
> evangelical revelation than an opinion that pardon may be
> bought, and guilt effaced, by a stipulated expiation .... But
> ... to give the heart to God, and to give the whole heart,
> is very difficult; the last, the great effort of long labour, fer-
> vent prayer, and diligent meditation. Many resolutions are
> made, and many relapses lamented, and many conflicts with
> our own desires, with the powers of the world, and the powers
> of darkness, must be sustained, before the will of man is made
> wholly obedient to the will of God.

To Johnson, as to Augustine, to Luther, to South, to Law, Wesley, and
Cowper, Christianity is a matter of the heart, or it is nothing. He goes on
to speak of those who "please themselves with a constant regularity of life,
and decency of behaviour" — like Johnson himself:

> Some are punctual in the attendance on public worship, and
> perhaps in the performance of private devotion .... Their
> religion is sincere; what is reprehensible is that it is partial,
> that the heart is not yet purified .... In condemnation of

---

(42) *The Pocket William Law* (1950), p. 33 (*A Practical Treatise upon
Christian Perfection*, Chap. 3). Note also Hammond's remark (p. 75 above) :
"We are not to be mistaken, as if we thought God's purposes tied to man's
good behaviour, or man's moral goodness to woo and allure God's spirit. ..."

those who presume to hope that the performance of one duty will obtain excuse for the violation of others, it is affirmed by St. James that he who breaks one commandment is guilty of all.(43)

Indeed, the doctrine of justification by faith alone is the foundation of the whole edifice of Johnson's religion, as it was of eighteenth-century Anglicanism, and of Protestantism generally. It was on this point that Luther broke with Rome; and it was because he fervently believed that doctrine that Johnson, throughout his life, suffered from the same agonies as did Luther. He knew that he had amply bestowed his intellectual and artistic gifts to the greater glory of God; he had made his life an example of piety; he had fasted and given of his substance to the poor; he was not as other men are, extortioners, unjust, adulterers. So had the Pharisee done, and it had profited him nothing. Was his proud and skeptical mind completely humbled (through the divine Grace) to perfect love of God and faith in Christ ? Was the element of self — self-will, self-display, self-congratulation — completely eradicated from those "good works" with the mention of which Hawkins had in vain tried to console him ? That was the great, the terrible question; and it was not until the experience of the twentieth of February, 1784, that Johnson began to feel any confidence that this essential internal transformation had begun to take place.

There is nothing strange or aberrant in all this, nothing that needs to be explained away or to have an eyebrow lifted over. It is simple and basic Protestantism, to be found in a thousand prayers, hymns, and sermons since the time of Luther; nor is it merely or exclusively Protestantism. The only difficulty for the modern student arises from the fact that Johnson (like Cowper) took it seriously, and that many of his contemporaries and most of his later commentators have been unable to comprehend that he did. Were it not for that difficulty, the question could be briefly disposed of by directing attention to the first petition in Johnson's prayer for his last communion, the petition preceding the one which Strahan took it on himself to delete: "Grant, O Lord, that my *whole* hope and confidence may be in Christ's merits and in Thy mercy" — and no particle of it in "regularity of life, and decency of behaviour," in any works of self-willed man, which are

---

(43) *Works* (1825), IX, 408-10.

incapable of "meriting of God." It was not an occasion on which Johnson was likely to express himself loosely.

V

Finally, the matter of "assurance of salvation." Professor Quinlan mentions this twice as a criterion of conversion "in the Evangelical sense": he speaks of the "typical Evangelical convert's ecstatic assurance of salvation," and remarks (what is quite true) that after Johnson's experience in February, 1784, he still did not feel "with certainty that he was among the *elect*."

Now it is true that the word and the concept "assurance" were much used by Wesley and his followers, and that there have been varying interpretations of this complex and subtle doctrine. But that the "assurance" to be expected by one who had experienced conversion was necessarily anything so crude as certainty of being one of the elect, Wesley himself, and others, took great pains to deny. As competent a piece of evidence as any on this point (as well as on the point discussed in the preceding section of this paper) is Charles Wesley's account of his and his brother's interview with their diocesan, the great Edmund Gibson, Bishop of London, on October 20, 1738:

> I waited with my brother on the Bishop of London, to answer the complaint he had heard against us, that we preached an absolute assurance of salvation. Some of his words were, "If by 'assurance' you mean an inward persuasion, whereby a man is conscious in himself, after examining his life by the law of God, and weighing his own sincerity, that he is in a state of salvation I don't see how any good Christian can be without such an assurance."
>
> "This," we answered, "is what we contend for: but we have been charged as Antinomians for preaching justification by faith only."

And the reply of the prelate, the most powerful figure in the Anglican hierarchy of his time, and perhaps of the century, the very personification of / that was official and orthodox in the Church, was, "Can any one preach otherwise who agrees to our Church and the Scriptures?"[44]

---

(44) *The Journal of John Wesley*, ed. N. Curnock (London, 1938), II, n.93, 1.

John Wesley's own conversion, on May 24, 1738, was without "ecstatic assurance": in his account of it he says,

> But it was not long before the enemy suggested, "This cannot be faith; for where is thy joy ?" Then was I taught that peace and victory over sin are essential to faith in the Captain of our salvation: but that, as to the transports of joy that usually attend the beginning of it, especially in those who have mourned deeply, God sometimes giveth, sometimes withholdeth them, according to the counsels of His own will.(45)

"Peace and victory over sin," though without the "transports of joy" that absolute certainty of salvation would bring, adequately describes Johnson's state of mind after February, 1784. *Absolute* assurance, a never-failing conviction of election, as a necessary concomitant of conversion, was never a doctrine of the Wesleys.(46) Indeed, Henry Hammond, the seventeenth-century "High Church" divine, on whom Johnson relies so frequently, gives an exposition of "the comfortable doctrine of assurance" which seems closer to that which Professor Quinlan postulates of the "Evangelicals" than does Wesley's own account:

> He that by God's inward effectual working is come to a clear sight and accurate feeling of his sins .... may be as sure that he shall die the death, and reign the life of a saint, as he is re-solved that God is faithful in his promises: then he may live with the syllogism of confidence, not presumption, in his mouth, "it is a faithful saying that Christ came into the world" to justify, sanctify, and "save believing humble sinners".... I will not discuss the nature of this assurance, whether it be an act of faith or hope, only thus much, it seems to be derived or bestowed upon hope by faith, an expectation of the per-formances of the promises grounded upon a firm faith in them, and so to be either an eminent degree of faith, or a confirmed hope. The use of this point is, not to be content with this bare assurance, but to labour to confirm it to us by those effects which do ordinarily and naturally spring from it. Such are, first, joy, or glorying ...; second, a delight in God ... [and four more].(47)

---

(45) Wesley, *Journal*, I, 476.

(46) See *The New Schaff-Herzog Encyclopedia of Religious Knowledge*, art. "assurance": "full confidence of present, *not eternal*, salvation (Methodism)" [my italics].

(47) *Miscellaneous Theological Works*, III, 662-63.

But a careful reading makes it clear that Hammond and Wesley agree in distinguishing between their "assurance," which brings with it a greater or less degree of temporary and conditional, not necessarily permanent, confidence, and, what they both reject, "presumption," *certainty* that one is among the elect. Whether there were or are sects or individuals which hold the doctrine that such certainty follows conversion, I do not know; but it is clear that such doctrine is the doctrine of neither Hammond nor Wesley, Anglicanism nor Methodism.

To recapitulate: when Johnson in his solemn death-bed prayer wrote "forgive and accept my late conversion," there is no reason for doubting that he meant the word "conversion" in its classic theological sense, the sense in which it is used in the Authorized Version, the sense in which Saint Augustine used it, and in which it was used in the Anglican theological writing with which Johnson was familiar.[48] It is still used in that sense today: the desirability of conversion, as Augustine understood it, is still sound Anglican, Protestant, for that matter Roman Catholic[49] doctrine. There is no reason to believe that this was not the sense in which Wesley, Cowper, Newton, and the other "Evangelicals" used it. The statement "In the popular language of the day, 'conversion' had come to mean adopting Evangelical beliefs" is meaningless — there were no Evangelical beliefs different from

---

(48) Another suggested interpretation of the expression, that it refers to the time when, as an Oxford undergraduate, Johnson "took up 'Law's Serious Call to a Holy Life' ... this was the first occasion of my thinking in earnest of religion, after I became capable of rational inquiry," cannot be entertained. Johnson well knew the difference between beginning to think in earnest of religion, in a spirit of rational inquiry, and conversion.

(49) See Bishop Fulton Sheen, *Peace of Soul* (New York, 1950; published with the imprimatur of Cardinal Spellman, Archbishop of New York). Its three concluding chapters are entitled "The Psychology of Conversion," "The Theology of Conversion," and "The Effects of Conversion." As far as I can see, Bishop Sheen describes and recommends conversion in a way not essentially different from that in which Wesley and Billy Graham describe and recommend it. One remark (p. 268), "The refusal of God's supernatural gift [of grace] is the most tragic mistake a man can make. Its acceptance is called conversion," provides a useful gloss to Johnson's remark to Hawkins, during the conversation that preceded the experience of February 20, 1784, "Every man knows his own sins, and also, what grace he has resisted" (Hawkins, *Life*, p. 563).

those of general Anglican doctrine. The doctrine of "assurance of salvation" is not to be interpreted, so far as Wesley and many other Evangelicals are concerned, as meaning that "certainty of election" is a criterion of conversion. Above all, the declaration "There is no indication that he [Johnson] adopted the belief that man is saved by faith alone" must be utterly rejected. To assert this is to reduce the whole of Johnson's rich religious life to nonsense: the belief was the indspensable keystone of the whole structure, the heart of Johnson's personal religious problem. That a professed "faith" which brought forth no works was no faith, he held, of course. But that "We are accounted righteous before God only for the merit of our Lord and Saviour Jesus Christ by Faith, and not for our own works or deservings: wherefore, that we are justified by Faith only is a most wholesome doctrine" (50) he believed, and asserted in his Sermon XIII, as emphatically as every other orthodox Anglican theological writer from the Reformation to his own day had asserted it (51).

---

(50) Articles of Religion of the Church of England; Article XI.

(51) In Professor Quinlan's *William Cowper: A Critical Life* (Minneapolis, 1953), he makes the statement, about eighteenth-century England, "There was a common assumption that, if an after life exists, one could best be assured of eternity by performing good works in this world" (p. 49). One wonders what the source of this amazing legend about the century was — I have encountered other versions of it in literary and social histories. The Book of Common Prayer, read to a vast majority of the population of England every Sunday or oftener, is dedicated to the rebuttal of any such proposition ("Rend your heart and not your garments"; "The sacrifices of God are a broken spirit"); so are the Westminster Confession and other statements of belief of the dissenting bodies that comprised most of the remainder of the population; it is safe to say that any clergyman of the Established or Dissenting churches who insisted on promulgating this doctrine would very soon have been unfrocked.

If, of course, the statement merely means that in spite of all official precept to the contrary, this was the principle in accordance with which the ordinary citizen, in practice, behaved, I do not know how it could be shown that it was more widespread in the eighteenth than in any other century. As a legend of literary history, of course, it fits in well enough with the propaganda of romanticists that the eighteenth century was an "unemotional" age; just as the particular application of it to Johnson fits in with the myth of Johnson's "sturdy common sense," "rationality," and so on. But before passing it on, students really should take the trouble to see what Johnson actually said on the matter.

Better arguments than this are needed to vindicate Strahan's scandalous emendation of Johnson's beautiful and moving prayer before his last communion. There is no evidence that Johnson's phrase "my late conversion" was misinterpreted by his contemporaries (unless by Strahan himself). Johnson knew very well what he meant by the expression, and so did Cowper, Newton, and the others who rejoiced at the news of it.

F . N . DOUBLEDAY

The Religion of Dr. Samuel Johnson

From the earliest known periods of history some form of religion has been practised by mankind. The form of religion is not the same among all peoples but in the human mind there has always been a search for something deeper and more permanent than the daily routine of men's lives.

Dr. Johnson was a truly religious man, he is sometimes accused of pessimism, and that his religion sprang from that source, but from his earliest youth to his death there is no doubt as to the value which he placed upon the practise of religion.

Johnson saw clearly the distinction between right and wrong. In his "Review of a Free Enquiry"[1] he writes, "To this account of the essence of vice and virtue, it is only necessary to add, that the consequences of human actions being sometimes uncertain and sometimes remote, it is not possible in many cases for most men, nor in all cases for any man to determine what actions will ultimately produce happiness, and therefore it was proper that Revelation should lay down a rule to be followed invariably in opposition to appearances, and in every change of circumstances, by which we may be certain to promote the general felicity, and be set free from the dangerous temptation of doing evil that good may come.

Because it may easily happen, and in effect will happen very frequently, that our own private happiness may be promoted by an act injurious to others, when yet no man can be obliged by nature to prefer ultimately the happiness of others to his own; therefore, to the instructions of infinite wisdom it was necessary that infinite power should add penal sanctions. That every man

---

(1) Wilson, Mona, *Johnson, Prose and Poetry* p. 371. London. Rupert Hart - Davis. (1950)

to whom these instructions shall be imparted may know, that he can never ultimately injure himself by benefitting others, or ultimately by injuring others benefit himself; but that however the lot of the good and bad may be huddled together in the seeming confusion of our present state, the time shall undoubtedly come, when the most virtuous will be most happy."

And again in the same paper(2), he makes these observations, "Such wisdom arising from the comparison of a part with the whole of our existence, those that want it most cannot possibly obtain from philosophy, nor unless the method of education, and the general tenour of life are changed, will very easily receive it from religion. The bulk of mankind is not likely to be very wise or very good: and I know not whether there are not many states of life, in which all knowledge less than the highest wisdom, will produce discontent and danger. But such is the condition of humanity, that we easily see, or quickly feel the wrong, but cannot always distinguish the right." The religion of Samuel Johnson was shown in these characteristics; humility, in the presence of a higher power, God; worship, the knowledge that life is at its best when the soul is lifted up to its maker, God: a sense of his own shortcomings, sin: charity, Johnson was a generous man towards the poor and unknown. How much the inner life of man is dependant upon his outlook is shown by some lines which Johnson contributed to Oliver Goldsmith's poem, "The Traveller",

> How small, of all that human hearts endure,
> That part which laws or kings can cause or cure,
> Still to ourselves in every place consign'd,
> Our own felicity we make or find:

In No. 41 of the *Idler*, Johnson writes thus of the need of religion. "These are the great occasions which force the mind to take refuge in the presence of death in religion; when we have no help in ourselves, what can remain but that we look up to a higher and a greater Power ? and to what hope may we not raise our eyes and hearts, when we consider that the greatest power is the best ? — The precepts of Epicurus, who teaches us to endure what the Laws of the Universe make necessary, may silence, but not content us. The dictates of Zeno, who commands us to look with indifference on external things, may dispose us to conceal our sorrow, but cannot assuage it. Real alleviation of the loss of friends, and rational tranquility in the prospect of

(2) Locus cit. p. 358.

our own dissolution, can be received only from the promises of Him in whose hands are life and death, and from the assurance of another and better state, in which all tears will be wiped from the eyes, and the whole soul shall be filled with joy. Philosophy may infuse stubborness, but religion only can give Patience".

During his life Johnson paid great attention to prayer and to meditation. It may be well to define the terms. In his dictionary Johnson defines "to Pray" to make petition to heaven to entreat, to ask submissively; to entreat in ceremony or form. Meditation is defined as deep thought, close attention; contemplation; thought employed upon sacred objects; a series of thoughts, occasioned by any object or occurrence".

Among all peoples prayer is something which comes naturally to men. The act of prayer concentrates the mind on certain essential things; its performance lifts them out of themselves onto a broader plane. Dom Butler observes(3) "St. Benedict lays down that private prayer should be short, unless it be prolonged by devotion due to the inspiration of divine grace, so that its duration is to be determined by the enablement received from the Holy Ghost".

The published prayers of Samuel Johnson are meditative. In studying them one must consider the nature of prayer in general. From the earliest recorded time men of all religions and of all races have made use of prayer; not only do the humble seek help but also the greatest men have acknowledged that in times of crisis they have prayed for the guidance of a higher power. Perhaps the most helpful prayers are those of the Collects of the English Book of Common Prayer, which are concise, and which sum up the thought of the Epistle or Gospel for the Day. Here is such an example from the Collect for the 4th Sunday after Easter, as given in the Gelasian Sacramentary, and the translation in the Book of Common Prayer, which contains a verbal modification made by Bishop Cosin in 1661. The Collect of Pope Gelasius reads, "Deus, qui fidelium mentes unius efficis voluntatis; da populis tuis in amare quod praecipis, id desiderare quod promittis; ut inter mundamus varietates ibi nostra fixa sint corda ubi vera sunt gaudia. Per Dominum nostrum, Christum Jesus. Amen" The English version of the Book of Common Prayer is as follows, "O Almighty God, who alone canst order the unruly wills and affections of sinful men; Grant unto thy people,

(3) Butler, The Right Rev. Cuthbert, *Benedictine Monachism*, London, Longmans, Green & Co. 1919.

that they may love the thing which thou commandest and desire that which thou dost promise, that so, among the sundry and manifold changes of the world, our hearts may surely there be fixed, where true joys are to be found; through Jesus Christ our Lord. Amen" Or again, there is the beautiful Constant Collect, contained in the Missal presented by Bishop Leofric to Exeter Cathedral, in 1050, and translated by Archbishop Thomas Cranmer, for the Book of Common Prayer of 1549. After the Priest has completed the Psalms and Prayers, which constitute his own preparation, he stands before the Altar, and repeats for himself, the Pater Noster, and then begins the public recital of the Office, 'Almighty God unto whom all hearts be open, all desires known, and from whom no secrets are hid; Cleanse the thoughts of our hearts by the inspiration of thy Holy Spirit, that we may perfectly love Thee, and worthily magnify thy Holy Name; Through Christ, our Lord. Amen.'

Johnson wrote out his own prayers to meet the requirements of his life. This is one dated January 1st, 1744, "Almighty and everlasting God, in whose hands are Life and Death, by whose Will all things were created and by whose Providence they were sustained, I return Thee thanks that Thou hast given me Life, and that Thou hast continued it to this time; that Thou hast hitherto forborn to snatch me away in the midst of Sin and Folly, and hast permitted me still to enjoy the means of Grace, and vouchsafed to call me yet again to Repentance. Grant, O merciful Lord, that Thy Call may not be in vain: that my Life may not be continued to increase my Guilt and that Thy gracious Forbearance may not harden my heart in wickedness. Let me remember, O my God, that as Days and Years pass over me, I approach nearer to the grave where there is no repentance; and grant, that by the assistance of Thy Holy Spirit, I may so pass through this Life, that I may obtain Life everlasting, for the sake of our Lord Jesus Christ Amen".

One of the characteristics of a truly religious man is the power of concentrated meditation. The hermits of Egypt in the first century of the Christian era, retired to solitary places in the desert, where they might meditate undisturbed. This necessity for meditation is felt by the religious regardless of the outward form of religion to which they may adhere; it was deeply felt by Samuel Johnson. In the *Rambler* of April 10th, 1750, Johnson writes thus "But there is an universal reason for some stated intervals of solitude, which the institutions of the church call upon me now especially to mention; a reason which extends as wide as moral duty, or the hopes of divine favour in a future state; and which ought to influence all ranks of life, and all degrees of intellect; since none can imagine themselves not comprehended in its obligation, but such as determine to set their Maker at defiance by obstinate wickedness, or whose enthusiastick security of his approbation places them above external ordinances, and all human means of improvement".

Dr. Johnson was a mystic[4]. The solitude of the desert, the wonderful changing lights of Egypt have influenced many of its inhabitants to a study of the intangible considerations which lie behind all life. Dr. Arberry[5] writes, "To the mystical side of Islam, Egypt has made a full and worthy contribution — worthy of the land in which mysticism appears to be indigenous. It may be justly conjectured, though it cannot with certainty be proved, that the early Muslims were profoundly influenced by the example of the Christian monks and anchorites living in the deserts of Egypt and Sinai, and it is at least feasible that the rise of the ascetic movement in Islam during the seventh and eighth centuries may have been largely inspired by contact with such men".

On May 12th, 1778, Boswell records[6] "we were soon engaged in very different speculation; humbly and reverently considering and wondering at the universal mystery of all things, as our imperfect faculties can now judge of them". "There are", said Johnson, "innumerable questions to which the inquisitive mind can in this state receive no answer: why do you and I exist ? Why was this world created ? Since it was created, why was it not created sooner ?."

In one number of the *Rambler* (No. 48) Johnson uses this heading

"Non est vivere, sed valere, vita"
"For life is not to live, but to be well".

---

(4) O.E.D. 2. "One who seeks by contemplation and self-surrender to obtain union with or absorption into the Deity, or who believes in spiritual apprehension of truths beyond the understanding".

(5) Arberry, A.J. "The Contribution to Islam". *The Legacy of Egypt*, London. O.U.P. 1942, p. 351.

(6) Powell, L. F. Vol. 3 p. 342. *Boswell's Life of Johnson*. Oxford, at the Clarendon Press. 1934.

Johnson had a real sense of the devotional life. On September 8th 1783(⁷) he had been reading a book entitled "Golden Remains" by the Rev. John Hales, a Prebendary of Windsor, and a Fellow of Eton College. From it he notes a reference to the Blessed Thomas Aquinas as follows, "He that doth God the greatest service, and receives from him the least reward, is the happiest man in the world." There goes a story of Aquinas, that praying once before the Crucifix, the Crucifix miraculously speaks thus unto him. "Bene de me scripsisti Thoma, quam ergo mercedem accipies ? Thou hast written well of me, Thomas, what reward dost thou desire ?". To whom Thomas is made to answer, "Nullam, Domine, praeter Teipsum; no reward, Lord, but thyself". The comment upon this is "Tis great pity this tale is not true, it doth so excellently teach, what to ask of God for our reward in his service". Johnson also had a keen appreciation of the value of solitary meditation. This is clearly expressed in the *Rambler* of April 10th, 1750. "But there is an universal reason for some stated intervals of solitude, which the institutions of the Church call upon me now especially to mention; a reason which extends as wide as moral duty, or the hopes of divine favour in a future state; and which ought to influence all ranks of life, and all degrees of intellect; since none can imagine themselves not comprehended in its obligation, but such as determine to set their maker at defiance by obstinate wickedness, or whose enthusiastic security of his approbation places them above external ordinances, and all human means of improvement". Another example of the deeper religious experience of Samuel Johnson is seen in a record made by Boswell on May 5th, 1784,(⁸) "One morning afterwards when I found him alone, he communicated to me with solemn earnestness, a very remarkable circumstance which had happened in the course of his illness, when he was much distressed by the dropsy. He had shut himself up, and employed a day in particular exercises of religion, — fasting, humiliation, and prayer. On a sudden he obtained extraordinary relief, for which he looked up to heaven with grateful devotion. He made no direct inference from this fact; but from his manner of telling it, I could perceive that it appeared to him as something more than an incident in the common course of events."

Johnson was very conscious of his ineffectual efforts to maintain continuous religious observance. In his Journal of April 6th, 1777, he records "At the beginning of the year I proposed to myself a scheme of life, and a plan of study, but neither has life been rectified or study followed. Days

(7) *Diaries, Prayers, and Annals.* p. 365 note.
(8) locus cit. Vol. IV, p. 271.

and months pass as in a dream, and I am afraid that my memory grows less tenacious, and my observations less attentive. If I am decaying it is time to make haste. My nights are restless and tedious, and my days drowsy. The flatulence which torments me, has sometimes so obstructed my breath that the act of respiration became not only voluntary but laborius in a decumbent posture. By copious bleeding I was relieved but not cured. I have this year omitted church on most Sundays, intending to supply the deficiency in the week. So that I owe twelve attendances on worship. I will make no more superstitious sitpulations which entangle the mind with unbidden obligations. My purpose once more, O Thou merciful Creator, that governest all our hearts and actions — let not my purpose be vain. My purpose once more is 1. To rise at eight, to keep a journal. 2. To read the whole Bible in some language before Easter. 3. To gather the arguments for Christianity. 4. To worship God more frequently in publick".

Johnson wrote in the *Rambler* "The great remedy which heaven put into our hands is patience, by which, though we cannot lessen the torments of the body, we can in great measure preserve the peace of the mind, and shall suffer only the natural and genuine force of an evil, without heightening its acrimony, or prolonging its effects". Johnson had a great belief in the necessity of quietness of mind, Boswell quotes Dr. Johnson as saying "He told us that whatever a man's distemper was Dr. Nichols would not attend him, as a physician, if his mind was not at ease; for he believed that no medicines would have any influence. He once attended a man in trade, upon whom he found that none of the medicines he prescribed had any effect; he asked the man's wife privately whether his affairs were not in a bad way. She said no. He continued his attendance some time still without success. At length the man's wife told him she had discovered that her husband's affairs were in a bad way".

In his earlier years Samuel Johnson lived in real poverty, this probably accentuated a natural disposition to be charitable to others. It is recorded that at a time when Johnson had scarcely enough money to buy food for himself he would often slip pennies into the hands of outcaste children, who were sleeping in the doorways in the Strand, in London. One of the numbers of the *Rambler* he headed with a quotation from Antiphilus,

> "Young was I once and poor, now rich and old,
> A harder case than mine was never told.
> Blest with the power to use them — I had none,
> Loaded with riches now, the power is gone".

Johnson's charity was also shown in the treatment of three poor people who were dependent upon him. Anna Williams had been a friend of Johnson's wife, she was the daughter of a Welsh physician. After the death of Mrs. Johnson, Anna Williams was found to be nearly blind and with very scanty resources; Johnson took her into his home, and she kept house for him until she died only a short time before his own death. Another dependant who lived in Johnson's house for many years was "Dr." Levett. He was a Yorkshireman, who served as a waiter in London and in Paris and picked up a good deal of medical knowledge from his customers and may perhaps have attended some lectures in Paris. On his return to London he developed an extensive practice among poor people. Johnson who is believed to have become acquainted with Levett through meeting him in coffee houses, took a liking to him and invited him to occupy a room in Johnson's house, which he did for many years. Johnson had great faith in his skill and said that though he himself was attended by the whole of the Royal College of Physicians he would not be content unless Levett also cared for him. Another protégé who lived in his house was Francis Barber. He was a native of Jamaica who was brought to England as a slave and there freed. When his wife died Johnson took the boy into his house as his personal attendant but he treated him more like a son. At Johnson's expense Barber was educated at the Grammar School in Bishops Stortford, he married an English wife, and, when Johnson died, he left to Barber the residue of his estate.

Dr. Cairns[9] has observed that as we read the various contemporary accounts of Samuel Johnson they differ greatly but all of them have this common characteristic, his sincere profession and practice of religion; this was founded on extensive reading and rational enquiry, and was confirmed by the active practice of its precepts. The influence of Johnson on the 18th century was largely due to his conversation and upon his insistence that all who were in his company must maintain Christian standards of conduct. Boswell writing on October, 1769 says that 'to my question whether we might not fortify our minds for the approach of death, he answered in a passion, 'No, Sir, let it alone. It matters not how a man dies, but how he lives.'

---

(9) Cairns, W.T. *The Religion of Dr. Johnson*, London at the Oxford University Press. 1945.

R . K . K A U L

Dr. Johnson On Matter and Mind

In this article it is proposed to consider Dr. Johnson's position on the most basic metaphysical question of his time viz. the relationship of matter and mind or body and soul[1]. Johnson's view of matter emerges quite clearly from his discussion of the contemporary views about the nature of matter. Johnson definitely rejected Bishop Berkeley's idealism:

> After we came out of the church, we stood talking for some time together of Bishop Berkeley's ingenious sophistry to prove the non-existence of matter, and that every thing in the universe is merely ideal. I observed, that though we are satisfied his doctrine is not true, it is impossible to refute it. I never shall forget the alacrity with which Johnson answered, striking his foot with mighty force against a large stone, till he rebounded from it, 'I refute it *thus.*' This was a stout exemplification of the *first truths* of Pere Bouffier, or the *original principles* of Reid and Beattie;...[2]

Until Mr. Hallett published his article, "Dr. Johnson's Refutation of Bishop Berkeley", this was taken as an example of the Great Cham's failure to grasp the subtlety of Bishop Berkeley's speculation. But thanks to Mr. Hallett we now know better. Clearly, Johnson understood that the pain he suffered was not in the stone. Further, he saw that the sensations of hardness and solidity in themselves proved no independent existence:

---

(1) In the philosophical sense they were interchangeable. See Johnson's *Dictionary of the English Language*, 2 vols., 1773, s.v. "Matter", "Mind", "Soul", and "Spirit".

(2) See Boswell's *Life of S. Johnson*, ed. G.B. Hill, & L.F. Powell, 1934-50, I. 471.

> But what is not sensational is the "kicking" and the "rebound-
> ing" from the stone that *kicks back*. It was not that he *felt*
> the stone, but that there was "action and reaction" between
> his body and the stone; and he argued that it is absurd to say
> that the stone is a collection of passive "ideas", "ideal contents",
> or "sense data", when "action and reaction" takes place between
> body and stone. .... Bodies are not collections of "ideas",
> "ideal contents" or "sense data", but the physical agents which
> thus make objective *appearance*.[3]

Johnson then was unwilling to dispose of matter in the Berkeleyan
fashion. He would not let the domain of spirit extend to matter. Equally,
he avoided the other extreme of allowing matter to encroach on the domain
of spirit. He kept a steady middle course.

The materialist challenge was more formidable because it emanated from
Locke. Since Johnson makes frequent protests against the view that thought
may inhere in matter, I have provided a summary of the controversy that
gave rise to these protests. This will serve as a background to Johnson's
contribution to the subject.

Locke had somewhat charily illustrated the uncertainty and narrowness of human knowledge with the following example:

> We have the ideas of *matter* and *thinking*, but possibly shall
> never be able to know whether any mere material being thinks
> or no; it being impossible for us, by the contemplation of our
> own ideas, without revelation, to discover whether Omni-
> potency has not given to some systems of matter, fitly disposed,
> a power to perceive and think, or else joined and fixed to
> matter, so disposed, a thinking immaterial substance: ... [4]

Very cautiously, he offers the hypothesis that:

> For I see no contradiction in it, that the first Eternal thinking
> Being, or Omnipotent Spirit, should, if he pleased, give to
> certain systems of created senseless matter, put together as he
> thinks fit, some degrees of sense, perception, and thought: ...[5]

---

(3) See *Mind*, LVI, 1947, pp. 138-39.

(4) See J. Locke, *An Essay Concerning Human Understanding*, IV, iii, 6, ed.
A.C. Fraser, 1894.

(5) ibid, IV, iii, 6.

Even this tentative manner of propounding his hypothesis, however, caused offence to Bishop Stillingfleet. In *A Discourse in Vindication of the Doctrine of Trinity* (1697), the Bishop took exception to Locke's test of the certainty of knowledge, whereby the appropriation of thinking to the soul was questioned. The orthodox argument ran roughly like this: In the nature of things, thought could not inhere in matter. There must therefore be an immaterial subject in which thought inheres. That immaterial subject must be the soul[6]. By questioning the first premise Locke put the inference in doubt. If thinking could be an attribute of matter, the soul must be redundant or non-existent...

After quoting the above passage from Locke Stillingfleet comments :

> Whoever asserts this, can never prove a *Spiritual Substance* in us, from a *Faculty of Thinking*; because he cannot know from *the Idea of Matter and Thinking*, that Matter so disposed cannot Think. And he cannot be certain that God hath not framed the Matter of our Bodies, so as to be capable of it.[7]

Locke in his *Letter to Edward Lord Bishop of Worcester* (1697) maintained his original position but contended that immateriality was not essential for the spirit:

> .... That the general Idea of Substance being the same every where, the Modification of *Thinking*, or the Power of *Thinking* joined to it, makes it a *Spirit*, without considering what other Modifications it has, as, whether it has the Modification of *Solidity* or no.[8]

He admitted that by his test of certainty, the *immateriality* of the spirit could not be proved. Nevertheless he considered it probable that "the thinking Substance in us is immaterial".[9]

Bishop Stillingfleet, however, not sharing Locke's prudence in philosophical matters, refused to be satisfied with mere probabilities. He wanted to be certain of whether matter, modified by the power of thinking, was still matter. In fact the difference came from the blurring of the neat dualism of

---

(6) I owe this summary to Leslie Stephen's *History of English Thought in the Eighteenth Century*, 1927, I. 283-84.

(7) *A discourse in Vindication of the Doctrine of Trinity*, 1697, p. 242.

(8) *Letter to Edward Lord Bishop of Worcester*, 1697, p. 66.

(9) ibid, p. 67.

body and spirit that had been customary in philosophy([10]). Upon the assumption of the immateriality of the spirit rested the belief in its immortality:

> For if the *Soul* be a *material Substance* it is really nothing but *Life*; or Matter put into Motion with such Organs and Parts as are necessary to hold them together; and when Death comes, then this *Material Substance* so modified is lost([11]).

The controversy did not end there but our concern is not with the wider question of whether or not certainty lies in the perception of the agreement or disagreement of ideas. With reference to Johnson the question most relevant is the dualism of matter and mind because it affects the immortality of the soul and the resurrection of the dead. The following quotation from Stillingfleet concludes the relevant part of the controversy quite effectively:

> And if the *Personal Identity* consists in a *Self-consciousness* depending on such a Substance as cannot be preserved without an Organiz'd Body, then there is no Subsistence of it separate from the Body, and the Resurrection must be giving a new Life. To whom ? To a Material Substance which wholly lost its Personal Identity by Death([12]).

Locke's speculation then had put both the immortality of the soul and the resurrection of the body in doubt.

Johnson's references to this controversy are persistent. And from his references, serious or casual, it is possible to infer Johnson's classification of the orders of reality. The philosophical antics of the Sceptic in *Rambler* No. 95 included a wilful attempt to confuse the orders of being, "I sometimes exalted vegetables to sense, and sometimes degraded animals to mechanism." According to Johnson then, there are three kinds of creation, in the ascending order, the mechanical([13]), the sensitive and the rational.

---

(10) We have good reason to believe that Descartes's position on the subject had acquired the status of orthodoxy. See L. Stephens, *History of English Thought* etc., I. 25

(11) *The Bishop of Worcester's Answer to Mr. Locke's Letter*, 1697, p. 55.

(12) *The Bishop of Worcester's Answer to Mr. Locke's Second Letter*, 1698, p. 36.

(13) See Johnson's *Dictionary*, s.v. "Mechanism". Sense 2 is defined as "Construction of parts depending on each other in any complicated fabrick."

The animals have sensitive faculties in addition to the "mechanical", and the humans have rational faculties as well as sensitive[14] and mechanical.

Matter (or body) and mind (or soul) were, in Johnson's view, two distinct orders of reality. The characteristics of matter, according to Johnson were those that he quoted from Watts's *Logick*:

> Some have dimensions of length, breadth, and depth, and have also a power of resistance, or exclude every thing of the same kind from being in the same place; this is the proper character of matter or body.[15]

The one quality he was not willing to grant to matter was thought, because that would have blurred the distinction between it and mind or spirit. It will be remembered that he criticized Milton's *Paradise Lost* for attributing body to the angels[16]. In *Rasselas* XLVIII Imlac asserts, "the unconsciousness of matter" with philosophical gravity and possibly with the Locke-Stillingfleet controversy in mind. To credit matter with consciousness was to efface the *differentia* of the spirit, thereby making it subject to the laws of motion and ultimately depriving it of free will. Johnson found this view abhorrent not olny because it was unorthodox and contrary to experience but also because it was debasing to human dignity. Having surrendered the physical universe to the irrevocable laws of motion,[17] it was necessary to guard the soul from their encroachment.

Johnson consequently sided with Stillingfleet in the Bishop's controversy with Locke:

> "It was never supposed that cogitation is inherent in matter, or that every particle is a thinking being. Yet, if any part of

---

(14) Vide "I could do all which they delighted in doing by powers merely *sensitive*, while my *intellectual* faculties were flown to Cairo." (Italics mine) *Rasselas*, XXXIX.

(15) Vide *Dictionary*, s.v. "Matter", sense 1. It might be noted that matter has been stripped of all its "secondary" qualities, for example, colour, taste, smell and sound. Locke included only solidity, extension, figure, mobility and number amongst the "primary" qualities. See *Essay*, II, viii, 9.

(16) See *Lives of the English Poets*, ed. G.B. Hill, 1905, I. 184-85.

(17) It may be pointed out that Johnson, like Crousaz, criticized Pope for representing "the whole course of things as a necessary concatenation of indissoluble fatality ..." *Lives*, III. 165.

> matter be devoid of thought, what part can we suppose to
> think ? Matter can differ from matter only in form, density,
> bulk, motion, and direction of motion: to which of these,
> however varied or combined, can consciousness be annexed ?
> To be round or square, to be solid or fluid, to be great or little,
> to be mo,ed slowly or swiftly one way or another, are modes
> of material existence, all equally alien from the nature of
> cogitation. If matter be once without thought, it can only be
> made to think by some new modification, but all the modi-
> fications which it can admit are equally unconnected with
> cogitative powers."[18]

Not only did Johnson refuse to credit matter with the power of cogit-
ation he even refused to grant it active motion. It was, according to him,
passive and urged on by an agency outside itself (*i.e.*, God), "All that we
know of matter is, that matter is inert, senseless, and lifeless;..."[19]

This position is stated more emphatically in his review of Newton's
letters to Bentley:

> Turn matter on all sides, make it eternal, or of late production,
> finite or infinite, there can be no regular system produced but
> by a voluntary and meaning agent.[20]

Similarly in the very solemn *Sermon* XXV which he wrote on his wife's death,
he affirmed the inertness of matter:

> .... continual contemplation of matter will, I believe, show it,
> at length, wholly incapable of motion, sensation, or order,
> by any powers of its own, and, therefore, necessarily establish
> the immateriality, and probably, the immortality of the soul...[21]

In contrast to matter, the nature of the soul was such as to free it
from "the course of nature". Because none of the properties of matter viz.
solidity, extension and figure was applicable to it, it was also immune to divi-
sibility and corruption which matter is heir to. Johnson would have found
Bishop Berkeley's account of the soul acceptable:

---

(18) *Rasselas*, XLVIII.

(19) ibid.

(20) See *The Works of S. Johnson*, ed. A. Murphy, 1823, XI. 238.

(21) See *The Works*, Oxford, 1825, IX. 519.

We have shewn that the soul is indivisible, incorporeal, un-extended, and it is consequently incorruptible. Nothing can be plainer than that the motions, changes, decays and dis-solutions which we hourly see befal natural bodies (and which is what we mean by the *course of nature*) cannot possibly affect an active, simple, uncompounded substance: nature; that is to say, 'the soul of man is naturally immortal'[22].

For the sharp distinction that Johnson, with all the orthodox Christian thinkers, accepted between matter and soul there was scientific authority. There was the authority of the one man whose position was unquestioned in both the camps[23]. The very scientist whose discovery of the laws of gravitation had given birth to the new concept of nature confessed towards the end of his career that gravity was not innate in matter:

"In my former (*i.e.*, letter) I represented that the diurnal rotations of the planets could not be derived from gravity, but required a divine arm to impress them.... I would now add, that the hypothesis of matter's being at first evenly spread through the heavens, is, in my opinion, inconsistent with the hypothesis of innate gravity, without a supernatural power to reconcile them, and therefore it infers a Deity".[24]

If matter was physically inert, according to Newton, it seemed rash to suggest that it might possess the power of intellectual activity. Johnson felt no hesitation therefore in questioning the propriety of Locke's challenge to Descartes. From Johnson's appreciative references to Malebranche, it appears likely that the Cartesian views on this matter were transmitted to him through Malebranche:

The fundamental principles of Malebranche's theory of know-ledge are undoubtedly Cartesian in character. He starts from the view that soul and body are substances whose positive at-tributes are mutually exclusive. The essence of body or corporeal reality is extension, and its properties can consist only in spatial

---

(22) See *A Treatise concerning the Principles of Human Knowledge*, CXLI, ed. A.C. Fraser, 1871.

(23) Not only physical scientists but also biological scientists accepted the dualism. Boerhaave, for example, is praised by Johnson for maintaining "the distinct nature of the soul and body." See Murphy, IX. 15.

(24) Quoted in Johnson's Review. See Murphy, XI. 239.

relations, rest, movement and figure. The essence of mind, on the other hand, is thought or consciousness[25].

In fact, as Leslie Stephen explains, the imputation of atheism to Spinoza was owing to his monistic position on this question[26]. We have the evidence of Hume to that effect:

> The fundamental principle of the atheism of Spinoza is the doctrine of the simplicity of the universe, and the unity of that substance, in which he supposes both thought and matter to inhere[27].

The belief in the immortality of the soul depended on its immateriality. The least suggestion that the thinking substance in man might be material cast doubts on its immortality.

In *Rambler* No. 78, Johnson defines death as "the disruption of man's union with visible nature" Here Johnson, like Bishop Butler, regards the body as detachable from "man" who is thereby equated with the soul:

> .... it follows, that our organized bodies are no more ourselves, or part of ourselves, than any other matter around us .... It is as easy to conceive, that we may exist out of bodies, as in them...[28]

---

(25) See N. Malebranche, *Dialogues on Metaphysics and on Religion*, 1923, trans. M. Ginsberg, Introduction, p. 21.

(26) See *History of English Thought*, I. 31.

(27) See D. Hume, *A Treatise on Human Nature*, I, iv, 5, ed. Green and Grose, 1874,

(28) See *The Analogy of Religion*, I, i, 8. ed. J.H. Bernard, 1900.

J . D . F L E E M A N

Johnson and the Truth

As far as Johnson was concerned, "the basis of *all* excellence is truth."[1]
His insistence upon truthfulness, and his abhorrence of all forms of deception, are primary features of all his writings. In his works veracity is repeatedly
and steadily inculcated:

> "No private views or personal regard can discharge any man
> from his general obligations to virtue and to truth."[2]

His reasons for this were practical. He quoted Aristotle with approval:

> "When Aristotle was once asked what a man could gain by
> uttering falsehoods ? he replied, 'not to be credited when he
> shall tell the truth.' "[3]

Untruthfulness was the basis of deception, and deception was the foundation of crime and folly: allied with self-interest it resulted in crime and
hypocrisy; joined with vanity it produced folly and affectation. Though
affectation was harmless in itself, it was visible proof that a sense of true
values had been vitiated, and that a tendency towards deception had become

---

(1) Life of Cowley, [*Lives of the Poets*, ed. Hill.] §14, *Works* (1825) vii,4.
[My italics.] He applied this standard to portraiture: *Life* [ed. Hill-Powell].
v, 219. It was the foundation of his denigration of the professional 'deception'
of actors (*Life*, ii, 404), and led him to deny the Dramatic Illusion in the Preface to Shakespeare §54, (*Works*, v, 121). It will generally be found that there
is some form of falsehood or deception behind the object of Johnson's censure.
Cf. Anecdotes by Mr Wickins, *Johnsonian Miscellanies* [ed. Hill], ii, 427-28.

(2) *Rambler* 136 §10 (*Works*, iii, 147). The 1825 text erroneously reads
"of" for "or".

(3) *Adventurer* 50 §1 (*Works*, iv, 21).

established in the character; from the deceptions of vanity it was but a step to the deceptions of crime. Vanity and affectation were also signs that others had encouraged by flattery the false values upon which they were based:

> "In every instance of vanity it will be found that the blame ought to be shared among more than it generally reaches; all who exalt trifles by immoderate praise, or instigate needless emulation by invidious incitements, are to be considered as perverters of reason and corrupters of the world: and since every man is obliged to promote happiness and virtue, he should be careful not to mislead unwary minds by appearing to set too high a value upon things by which no real excellence is conferred."(4)

The reasons for Johnson's insistence upon veracity are to be found in his views on the nature of society. His idea of the structure of society was fairly simple:

> "The great community of mankind is therefore necessarily broken into smaller independent societies;...
>
> Such unions are again separated into subordinate classes and combinations, and social life is perpetually branched out into minuter subdivisions, till it terminates in the last ramifications of private friendship."(5)

and on friendship he goes yet further:

> " ... marriage is the strictest tie of perpetual friendship, ... there can be no friendship without confidence, and no confidence without integrity ..." (6)

The last quotation shows why Johnson held truth to be important in society: it generated confidence, and without confidence society would collapse:

> "It is apparent that men can be social beings no longer than they believe each other. When speech is employed only as the

---

(4) *Rambler* 66 §12 (*Works*, ii, 317).

(5) *Rambler* 99 §§7-8 (*Works*, ii, 470). Johnson's Social Contract was built upon small combinations united by reasonable self-interest. Cf. also *Taxation no Tyranny* §35 (*Works*, vi, 232), and *Rambler* 104 §1 (*Works*, ii, 491).

(6) *Rambler* 18 §13 (*Works*, ii, 92). It should not be thought that Johnson had any illusions about friendship. Cp. Life of Pope §274 (*Works*, viii, 314-15), and *Idler* 23 (*Works*, iv, 216-18).

vehicle of falsehood every man must disunite himself from others, inhabit his own cave, and seek prey only for himself."[7]

Hence the violence of his attacks upon those who by their carelessness, vanity, folly or malice, weaken the influence of truth and so undermine society. Johnson knew what anarchy could mean: stories and memories of the Civil War which he could have heard in his youth in Lichfield, had a strong influence upon his political thought.[8] He longed for stability and the tranquillity of mind which he associated with political security, and he was not the man to allow the liars to deprive him of it:

> "Whoever commits a fraud is guilty not only of the particular injury to him whom he deceives, but of the diminution of that confidence which constitutes not only the ease, but the existence of society."[9]

Veracity was essential for confidence. Johnson twice refers to Sir Thomas Browne as the author of the remark:

> "The devils do not tell lies to one another; for truth is necessary to all societies; nor can the society of hell subsist without it."[10]

The conviction of the practical necessity of veracity led Johnson to make strenuous efforts to ensure that his own practice was not at variance with his words:

> "A strict adherence to truth he considered as a sacred obligation insomuch that in relating the most minute anecdote he would not allow himself the smallest addition to embellish his story. The late Mr Tyers who knew Johnson intimately observed,'that he always talked as if he was talking on oath.' "[11]

---

(7) *Idler* 20 §1 (*Works*, iv, 206). Cf. also *Dictionary* (1773), s.v. CONFIDENCE.

(8) Cf. J.L. Clifford: *Young Samuel Johnson*, (1955), pp. 33-35.

(9) *Rambler* 79 §13 (*Works*, ii, 374). Cf. also Life of Browne §11 (*Works*, vi, 478), and Life of Thomson §26 (*Works*, viii, 371). The reason for the violence of his reactions is illustrated in *Life*, iii, 10-12.

(10) *Adventurer* 50 §3 (*Works*, iv, 21); also *Life*, iii, 293.

(11) Murphy: *An Essay on the Life and Genius* &c., (1792), p. 147. (*Works*, i, lxvii); also in *Johnsonian Miscellanies*, i, 458, Johnson's practical concern is illustrated in *Life*, i, 436.

Johnson was well aware that rigid veracity demanded constant effort:

> " [Mrs Thrale] .... but little variations in narrative must
> happen a thousand times a day, if one is not perpetually wat-
> ching. JOHNSON. Well, Madam, and you *ought* to be per-
> petually watching. It is more from carelessness about truth,
> than from intentional lying that there is so much falsehood
> in the world."[12]

This opinion enabled him to take a liberal view of the laxity of the High-
landers in answering his and Boswell's questions:

> " .... yet I do not say that they deliberately speak studied
> falsehood, or have a settled purpose to deceive. They have
> inquired and considered little, and do not always feel their
> own ignorance. They are not much accustomed to be interro-
> gated by others, and seem never to have thought upon inter-
> rogating themselves; so that if they do not know what they
> tell to be true, they likewise do not distinctly perceive it to be
> false."[13]

His belief in the frequency of falsehood accounts for his notorious scepticism.
Boswell says:

> "He was indeed so much impressed with the prevalence of false-
> hood, voluntary or unintentional, that I never knew any person
> who upon hearing an extraordinary circumstance told, dis-
> covered more of the *incredulus odi*."[14]

The Cock-Lane ghost, the Lisbon earthquake, and Macpherson's *Ossian*
were all objects upon which he exercised his incredulity. But it is noteworthy

---

(12) *Life*, iii, 228-29. Cf. also Boswell's ostentatious discipleship: *Life*,
iv, 83-4.

(13) *Journey to the Western Islands* §443 [*sub*. Ostig in Skye], ed. R.W.
Chapman, (1924), p. 106 (*Works*, ix, 114). Despite his liberality in practice,
Johnson was, in theory, prepared to punish the same offence with some
severity: *Adventurer* 50 §13 (*Works*, iv, 25).

(14) *Life*, iii, 229. Cp. also Review of Warton's *Essay on Pope* § 16 (*Works*,
vi, 42); *Rambler* 96 §3 (*Works*, ii, 454); Life of Congreve §3 (*Works*, viii, 23).
Johnson's censure of carelessness about truth does not mean that he was unaware of the fact that such care was not always easy or possible: Life of
Collins §10 (*Works*, viii, 402).

that he is only sceptical about verifiable matters: he disapproved of scepticism about things which were less susceptible of empirical proof:

> "It had been happy for me could I have confined my scepticism to historical controversies and philosophical disquisitions; but having now violated my reason, and accustomed myself to enquire not after proofs but objections, I had perplexed truth with falsehood till my ideas were confused, my judgment embarrassed, and my intellects distorted."[15]

Johnson's personal and emotional desire for intellectual and religious certainty and stability, (of which political and social stability was merely the visible expression), led him consistently to stress the importance of veracity about facts, so that from these facts reason[16] could proceed to knowledge of universal and immutable truth.[17] This ultimate truth[18] was the psychological sheet-anchor which could afford him respite from the mental and emotional turbulences of his doubts, scruples, and recurrent fears of damnation.[19]

---

(15) *Rambler* 95 §18 (*Works*, ii, 452). Cf. also *Idler* 87 §2 (*Works*, iv, 406). On the ghost cf. *Life*, i, 22 and 407; the earthquake — Mrs Piozzi, Anecdotes, *Johnsonian Miscellanies*, i, 244; and *Ossian*, cf. Index to *Life*, vi, 263, and refs.

(16) Reason is defined in the *Dictionary* (1773), as "The power by which man deduces one proposition from another, or proceeds from premises to consequences." Reason had access to truth in literature — cf. *Rambler* 96 §18 (*Works*, ii, 457), — and in ratiocination the facts with which veracity was concerned were the premises from which reason was able to proceed to the consequence of the ultimate truth. Cf. also *Rambler* 96 §9 (*Works*, ii, 455).

(17) " .... external things are naturally variable, but truth and reason are always the same." — *Rasselas*, xviii, §8 (*Works*, i, 241). Cf. also Life of Cowley §182 (*Works*, vii, 51); and *Idler* 52 §4 (*Works*, iv, 303).

(18) Johnson frequently identified truth in this sense with religion. Cf. Introduction to the *Proceedings of the Committee for the Cloathing of French Prisoners of War* §8 (*Works*, vi, 149); Life of Blackmore §34 (*Works*, viii, 46-47); and Life of Milton §183 (*Works*, vii, 120).

(19) Cf. *Diaries Prayers and Annals*, ed. McAdam-Hyde, Yale, 1958, refs. index: s.v. JOHNSON, Samuel, III, 'scruples' p. 440; *Rambler* 29 (*Works*, ii, 142-6); *Rambler* 110 §1 (*Works*, iii, 20-21); *Life*, index. svv: 'Death' (vi, 98). JOHNSON, I, 'death' (vi, 198), 'madness' and 'melancholy' (vi, 204). Cf. also Hagstrum, J.H.: "On Dr Johnson's Fear of Death." – *Journal of English Literary History*, (1947), xiv, 308 ff.

ANTHONY J. TILLINGHAST

The Moral and Philosophical Basis of Johnson's and Boswell's Idea of Biography

Bergen Evans has shown that there is a sufficient consistency in Johnson's scattered statements on biography for us to talk usefully about Johnson's biographical *theory*(1). Evans, however, does not always observe the chronology of Johnson's remarks which fact, among other things, prevents him from observing the significance of the difference between *Rambler* 60 and *Idler* 84(2). The main emphasis of this essay will be upon these two papers which, while only amounting to a small part of Johnson's total statements on biography, are different in status from the rest. By their appearance in printed form we must look upon them as considered statements of Johnson's views whereas much of the other relevant materials, from his conversation and letters and elsewhere, were products of the moment. This latter material I will use as ramifications and illustrations of the main thesis outlined in Johnson's two essays.

It is commonly assumed that the growth of philosophy in the eighteenth century had some effect upon the evolution of biographical theory and practice(3). Certainly, a philosophy almost wholly concerned with the empi-

---

(1) "Dr. Johnson's Theory of Biography', *Review of English Studies,* (1934), Vol. X, 301-310.

(2) An example of this is Evan's use of the *Life of Sir Thomas Browne* and *Rambler* 28 as qualifications of an argument found in *Idler* 84. In fact both of these works *antedate Idler* 84.

(3) Particularly philosophy is thought to have had some effect upon the biographical orientation of the English novel in the Eighteenth century. This is best argued in Ian Watt's chap. on 'Realism and the Novel Form' in *The Rise of the Novel*, (London, 1960), pp. 9-34.

rical study of man must have had an influence upon the biographer. But in an age so thoroughly eclectic as the Eighteenth century, influences are hard to pin-point and we must be cautious in attributing any given idea of a writer to a particular source. I shall not therefore propose any specific philosophical influences upon Johnson and Boswell but rather examine the relationship between their ideas and those of the philosophers.

Rambler 60 begins :

> All joy and sorrow for the happiness or calamities of others is produced by an act of imagination, that realizes the event however fictitious, or approximates it however remote, by placing us, for a time, in the condition of him whose fortune we contemplate; so that we feel, while this deception lasts, whatever motions would be excited by the same good or evil happening to ourselves.(4)

Some nine years after this was written, Adam Smith wrote:

> By the imagination we place ourselves in [another's] situation, we conceive ourselves enduring all the same torments, we enter as it were into his body, and become in some measure the same person with him, and thence form some idea of his sensations, and even feel something which, though weaker in degree, is not altogether unlike them.(5)

The doctrine of the Sympathetic Imagination was axiomatic for both Johnson and Adam Smith. It had great utility for the biographer too, for by merely presenting human actions and situations he was assured of a response by the reader through the almost automatic workings of Sympathy(6). In particular the theory would appeal to those interested in biography as a didactic medium(7). There was, however, a slight qualification to the theory, for as Johnson observed in *Rambler* 60, sympathy was more easily evoked the nearer the reader's situation was to the subject:

---

(4) Johnson, *Works*, Ed. Arthur Murphy, (London, 1816) IV, 381.

(5) *The Theory of Moral Sentiments*, (London, 1797) I, 3.

(6) Donald A. Stauffer has remarked upon the relevance for the biographer of Adam Smith's theory. See, *The Art of Biography in Eighteenth Century England*, (Princeton, 1941), pp. 351-2.

(7) The theory was, of course, used to show the didactic value of other kinds of literature. See, for example, Adam Ferguson's *The Morality of Stage Plays Seriously Considered* (1751); Kames' *Essays on the Principles of Morality and Natural Religion* (Edinburgh, 1751) pp. 17-18.

Our passions are therefore more strongly moved, in proportion as we can more readily adopt the pains or pleasure proposed to our minds, by recognising them as our own, or considering them as naturally incident to our state of life.... Histories of the downfall of kingdoms, and revolutions of empires, are read with great tranquillity.... Those parallel circumstances and kindred images, to which we readily conform our minds, are, above all other writings, to be found in the narratives of the lives of particular persons; and therefore no species of writing seems more worthy of cultivation than biography, since none can more certainly enchain the heart by irresistible interest, or more widely diffuse instruction to every diversity of condition.(8)

Hume, writing on a similar subject expressed a view essentially the same as Johnson's:

There is no necessity that a generous action, barely mentioned in an old history or remote gazette, should communicate any strong feelings of applause and admiration .... Bring this virtue nearer, by either our acquaintance or connection with the persons, or even by an eloquent recital of the case; our hearts are immediately caught, our sympathy enlivened ...(9)

Underlying the principle of sympathy, of course, was the assumption of a uniformity in human nature:

but there is such a uniformity in the state of man .... that there is scarce any possibility of good or ill, but is common to human kind.(10) (*Rambler* 60)

This belief was at the heart of neoclassicism(11) and also found great support among the Scottish philosophers. Kames, for example, stated that:

With respect to the common nature of man in particular we have a conviction that it is invariable not less than universal;

---

(8) *Works*, IV, 381-2.

(9) Hume, *Enquiry Concerning the Principles of Morals*, Ed. Selby-Bigge, (Oxford, 1957), p. 12.

(10) *Works*, IV, 383.

(11) See René Wellek, *A History of Modern Criticism: The Later Eighteenth Century*, (London, 1955), p. 12.

that it will be the same hereafter as at present, and as it was
in time past; the same among all nations and in all corners of
the earth.(12)

Virtually the same point is made by Hume in his *Enquiry*(13). For the writer
such a view was necessary so that "that uniformity of sentiment" could enable
him "to conceive and to excite the pains and pleasure of other minds"(14).
For the philosopher:

> .... were there no uniformity in human actions, and were
> every experiment which we could form of this kind irregular
> and anomalous, it were impossible to collect any general
> observations concerning mankind; and no experience, how-
> ever accurately digested by reflection, would ever serve to
> any purpose.(15)

Johnson's position can usefully be shown by observing that he found these
views necessary both in a literary and a philosophical sense since experience
for Johnson had the same status as it did for Hume: experience like an
experiment had to be repeatable to have any use. The individual, like man
in general, had to be able to remember and learn from error, otherwise his
experience had no value(16). I return to this point later but it is important
to remember that the philosopher and biographer alike had to assume certain
'common denominators' among human beings or their observations would
not be useful but merely interesting.

It was characteristic of Eighteenth century philosophy that it was
mainly utilitarian in intention. Locke, we know, intended his *Conduct of
the Understanding* as a final section to his *Essay* where he stated "Our business
here is not to know all things but those which concern our conduct".(17)
The Scottish philosophers, too, were principally concerned with human
conduct; for them, understanding human behaviour was a necessary task

---

(12) *Elements of Criticism*, (Edinburgh, 1788) II, 491.

(13) *An Enquiry Concerning Human Understanding*, (Oxford 1957), p. 85.

(14) Johnson, *Lives of the Poets*, Ed. Hill, (Oxford, 1905), Vol. I, 'Life
of Cowley' par. 57.

(15) Hume, *An Enquiry Concerning Human Understanding*, p. 85.

(16) See below, pp. 125-6.

(17) Ed. Alexander Campbell Fraser, (London, 1894), I, 31.

before ways of achieving the proper conduct of individuals and institutions could be proposed. Before human nature could be understood, honest and precise observations were needed: this was equally the case for the biographer before biography could play the utilitarian rôle which Johnson expected of it. Johnson's concern for honesty is characteristically expressed in this extract from the *Life of Boerhaave*:

> We could have made it much larger, by adopting flying reports, and inserting unattested facts; a close adherence to certainty has contracted our narrative, and hindered it from swelling to that bulk, at which modern histories generally arrive.[18]

Another aspect of Johnson's view of biography which closely associates him with the philosophers was expressed in a conversation with Monboddo:

> *Monboddo*. 'The history of manners is the most valuable. I never set a high value on any other history.' *Johnson*. 'Nor I; and therefore I esteem biography, as giving us what comes near to ourselves, what we can turn to use.' *Boswell*. 'But in the course of general history, we find manners. In wars we see the disposition of people, their degrees of humanity and other particulars.' — *Johnson*. 'Yes; but then you must take all the facts to get this; and it is but little you get.'[19]

This discussion, read in the light of Carl Becker's argument in his chapter[20] on the philosophers' awareness of the educational value of history, further underlines Johnson's affinities with the philosophical thought of the age. A great deal in fact lies behind Johnson's remark in *Rambler* 60 "If we owe regard to the memory of the dead, there is more respect to be paid to knowledge, to virtue, and to truth"[21].

The similarity between the techniques of the biographer and the philosopher is hinted at in *Rambler* 60:

---

(18) *Works*, XII, 11. Elsewhere too, Johnson emphasized his concern for truth. E.g. *Life*, (Ed. Hill & Powell, Oxford, 1950), IV, 53, 369, V, 255.

(19) Boswell, *Journal of a Tour to the Hebrides*, (Ed. Pottle & Bennett, London, 1936), p. 55.

(20) In Carl Becker's *The Heavenly City of the Eighteenth Century Philosopher*, (Yale, 1932), pp. 71-118.

(21) *Works*, IV, 386.

> There are many invisible circumstances ¡which, whether we
> read as enquirers after natural or moral knowledge, whether
> we intend to enlarge our science, or increase our virtue, are
> more important than public occurrences.(22)

In Johnson's experiential theory of knowledge, biography had a specific
status, since biography was *knowledge*, provided it satisfied his strict standards. This can be seen if we consider Johnson's remark:

> I have often thought that there has rarely passed a life of
> which a judicious and faithful narrative would not be useful.(23)

Kenneth MacLean has observed that Locke's "philosophy was a levelling force
and fostered intellectual democracy. The process of equalization begins, it
appears, with the denial of innate ideas."(24) Johnson's remarks upon the
importance of the ordinary life are perhaps one ramification of this democ-
ratization. Once it was realized that *any* individual's ¡experience was illustrative of the universal nature of the sensations and passions, in fact of man's
whole psychological make-up, social and occupational distinctions became
relatively unimportant. The biographer was asked "to pass slightly over
those performances and incidents, which produce vulgar greatness... and
to display the minute details of daily life, where exterior appendages are cast
aside."(25) The "decorations and disguises"(25) needed to be removed before
what was fundamental and therefore common to all men could be discovered — before what was particular could be assumed to be general.

These general remarks on Johnson's view of biography are equally applicable to Boswell. The broad principles laid down in *Rambler* 60 met sufficiently with Boswell's approval for him to give an important place to *Rambler*
60 in the Introduction to the *Life* and it is clear that throughout the *Life*
he worked from Johnson's example. Boswell went to great pains to ascertain
the accuracy of his information; he collected material while Johnson was
alive to avoid the ravages of falling memory and, of course, he endeavoured

---

(22) *Ibid*, p. 384.

(23) *Ibid*, p. 382.

(24) *John Locke and English Literature of the Eighteenth Century*, (Yale,
1936), p. 39.

(25) *Works*, IV, 384.

(26) *Ibid*, p. 383.

to maintain his "sacred love of truth".(27) Fortunately, however, he brought literary and dramatic skill to the bare bones of the material giving his work, among other things, the dimensions of action and time. But whatever he added, he left nothing of the Johnsonian formula *out*.

In attempting to establish a relationship between Johnson's idea of biography and contemporary philosophy I do not want to suggest too close a relationship nor a thoroughly consistent one. Johnson was not a philosopher, nor was he much interested in the intricacies of Eighteenth century philosophical controversy. The relationship exists at the more fundamental level at which there was considerable agreement among philosophers; their belief in the study of man and his conduct as being of primary importance, their assumption of a sameness in human nature and their demand for an accurate documentation of human lives. Johnson often imported many of his critical standards from outside the genres he criticized and with biography the consistency of his criticism arises, I think, from his use of basic philosophical values. He was able to import this framework the more easily because the biographer and the philosopher were concerned with the same broad field of study, man.

The philosophers though were not happy about the *kind* of knowledge provided by observation of other people since observation could be affected by all kinds of non-empirical considerations and had at least one serious philosophical flaw. The general difficulties are mentioned everywhere in Johnson's work. The reasons for writing a biography, for example, might prevent a detached view of a life and however honest the biographer was merely unimportant facts might be recorded(28); according to Johnson, Tickell was guilty in this respect in his life of Addison.(29) Thus, for a number of psychological and intellectual reasons, biography often could, and did fail to provide a sufficiently useful narrative.

---

(27) *Life*, IV, 397. With reference to Boswell's observation of the Johnsonian formula, it is interesting to note Boswell's remark, "preserving at once my regard to truth, — to my friend, — and to the interests of virtue and religion." *Life*, IV, 398. This is close to Johnson's criterion, see above, n. 22.

(28) It is worth mentioning that Carl Becker suggests that Eighteenth century philosophers were making the same complaint about historians. *op. cit.* p. 92, *et. seq.*

(29) *Works*, IV, 385.

While *Idler* 84 continued the arguments of *Rambler* 60 for the utility of honest and detailed biography and while Johnson continued to adhere to the doctrine of Sympathy, his preference was now for Autobiography rather than Biography. Significantly the change was for empirical reasons:

> What we collect by conjecture only, and by conjecture only, can one man judge of another's motives or sentiments, is easily modified by fancy or desire; as objects imperfectly discerned take forms from the hope or fear of the beholder.[30]

In the same year that this was written, Adam Smith's *Theory of Moral Sentiments* was published. Smith made almost exactly the same qualification to the theory as Johnson:

> As we have no immediate experience of what other men feel, we form no idea of the manner in which they are affected, by conceiving what we ourselves should feel in the like situation .... our senses .... never did, and never can, carry us beyond our own person, and it is by the imagination only that we can form any conception of what are his [another's] sensations.[31]

This pin-points the philosophical flaw mentioned above. It was impossible to *know* "another's motives or sentiments" in a thoroughly empirical way. The workings of the mind only manifested themselves through external actions and the observer of these was thrown upon interpretation (Johnson's 'conjecture') which could be influenced by his own biases and any feelings he had about the observed person. Johnson had already suggested the way in which personal considerations could affect the accuracy of biography but this new consideration of 'conjecture' indicates that Johnson's preference for autobiography rested on empirical arguments: *no* biography could be as sound as autobiography on principle, for the distinction between them was that between first and second-hand knowledge.

It was because some forms of autobiography provided "certainty of knowledge" that Johnson preferred it. Johnson was perfectly aware that autobiography like biography could be written for the wrong reasons[32]

---

(30) *Works*, VII, 341. A midway view can be found in *Adventurer* 138, *Works*, III, 295.

(31) Adam Smith, *op. cit.*, pp. 2-3.

(32) *Works*, VII, 342.

and be inaccurate but theoretically autobiography had more chance of revealing the truth:

> The writer of his own life has at least the first qualification of
> an historian, the knowledge of the truth;[33]

(Idler 84)

Johnson's empirical foundation for stating this can be found in the
philosophers. For example, Thomas Reid observed,

> But the anatomist of the mind cannot have the same advan-
> tage. It is his own mind only that he can examine with any
> degree of accuracy and distinctness. This is the only subject
> that he can look into.[34]

philosophers frequently referred their reader to his own experience for
proof of their arguments. Self-analysis was claimed to be the main method
of investigation by most of the philosophers; it was the basis of Locke's
"plain historical method" and the source of certainty for Hutcheson[35]
and many others. Philosophers in fact stressed the primacy of *individual*
experience in their quest for knowledge.

But it is more than simply the "certainty of knowledge" which concerned
Johnson for when we discuss autobiography in the light of *Idler* 84, we
must take into account a number of acts which come within Johnson's vague
framework of autobiography. At the end of *Idler* 84 Johnson remarked:

> .... but he that sits down calmly and voluntarily to review
> his life for the admonition of posterity, or to amuse himself,
> and leaves his account unpublished, may be commonly
> presumed to tell the truth, since falsehood cannot appease
> his own mind, and fame will not be heard beneath the tomb. [36]

----

(33) *Ibid*, p. 341.

(34) Thomas Reid, *An Enquiry into the Human Mind*, (London, 1785),
p. 5.

(35) Francis Hutcheson, *An Essay on the Nature and Conduct of the Passions and Affections*, (London, 1728) p. 2.

(36) *Works*, VII, 346. Gibbon's statement about his *Autobiography* is,
presumably, close to Johnson's ideal (*The Autobiographies*, London, 1896,
p. 353) and so were some of Goldsmith's views (see Stauffer, *op. cit.*, p. 384).
Also it should be remembered that Johnson was prepared to allow his own
to private writings be published after his death.

It is clear that ideally for Johnson, the review should be written with detached objectivity but he remained indefinite as to the precise form and technique the reviewer should pursue. By going outside *Idler* 84 we can discover that when Johnson refers to the 'review' we are in fact introduced to an idea which occurs in a variety of forms in his other writing. Indeed the review had an important place in the fabric of Johnson's morality and in his concern for self-knowledge. First we may look at Johnson's opinion on a kindred subject in a letter to Mrs Thrale:

> In a man's letters you know, Madam, his soul lies naked, his letters are only the mirrour of his breast, whatever passes within him is shown undisguised in its natural process. Nothing is inverted, nothing is distorted, you see systems in their elements, you discover actions in their motives.[37]

And a passage from the *Life of Pope:*

> It has so long been said as to be commonly believed, that the true characters of men may be found in their Letters, and that he that writes to his friend lays his heart open before him. But the truth is, that such were the simple friendships of the *Golden Age*, and are now the friendships only of children. Very few can boast of hearts which they dare lay open to themselves, and of which, by whatever accident exposed, they do not shun a distinct and continued view; and, certainly, what we hide from ourselves we do not show to our friends.[38]

Apart from incidentally indicating the pitfalls in using scattered statements as evidence of Johnson's beliefs, these remarks show a consistency beneath their apparent contradiction. As elsewhere, Johnson was concerned with truth and he is consistent in his attempt to discover what kind of information was psychologically valid. He varies here for the same reason that he was prepared to accept autobiography as more valid than biography: his rejection of letters as valid testimony is made for the same reason that he was suspicious of autobiography which was not private. The letter has the same status in the latter passage as autobiography for the public eye. When writing to Mrs Thrale he possibly had Locke's remarks in mind:

> the writing of letters has so much to do in all the occurrences of human life, that no gentleman can avoid showing himself

---

(37) Johnson, *Letters*, Ed. R.W. Chapman, (Oxford, 1952), II, 228.

(38) Johnson, *Lives*, III, 'Life of Pope', par. 273.

> in this kind of writing: occasions will daily force him to make
> use of his pen, which .... always lays him open to a severer
> examination of his breeding, sense, and abilities than oral
> discourse ... [39]

This brief discussion of letters provides a rather illuminating parallel to
Johnson's concern with autobiography. We can approach the subject from
another side too by using Boswell:

> Mr. Samuel Johnson has often recommended to me to keep
> a Journal, of which he is so sensible of the utility that he has
> several times tried it, but never could persist. I have at diffe-
> rent periods of my life persisted a good time, ... I shall
> only put down hints of what I have thought, seen or heard
> every day .... and I shall from these, at certain periods, make
> up masses or larger views of my existence. Mr Johnson said
> that the great thing was to register the state of my mind. [40]

The 'larger views' to which Boswell refers are obviously akin to Johnson's
review. Elsewhere, in a letter to Mrs Thrale, Johnson comments "Why
you should suppose yourself not desirous hereafter to read the history of
your own mind I do not see".[41] And in conversation with Mrs Thrale he
remarked ".... a man loves to review his own mind. That is the use of a
diary or journal."[42] On the same occasion Boswell observed "as a lady
adjusts her dress before a mirror, a man adjusts his character by looking at
his journal."[43] These various observations are based, I think, on an idea
already partially referred to above:

> The serious and impartial retrospect of our conduct, is in-
> disputedly necessary to the confirmation or recovery of virtue,
> and is, therefore, recommended under the name of self-exami-
> nation, by divines as the first act previous to repentence. It is
> indeed, of so great a use, that without it we should always be
> [sic] to begin life, be seduced for ever by the same allurements,
> and misled by the same fallacies. (*Rambler* 60).[44]

---

(39) Locke, *Works*, (London, 1727) *Some Thoughts Concerning Education*,
Vol. III, 86.

(40) Boswell, *Private Papers*, IX, 127.

(41) *Letters*, II, 79.

(42) *Life*, III, 228.

(43) *Ibid.*, p. 228.

(44) *Works*, IV, 50.

As man is a being very sparingly furnished with the power
of prescience, he can provide for the future only by considering the past; and as futurity is all in which he has any real
interest, he ought very diligently to use the only means by
which he can be enabled to enjoy it, and frequently to revolve
the experiments which he has hitherto made upon life, that
he may gain wisdom from his mistakes and caution from his
miscarriages.

Though I do not so exactly conform to the precepts of PY-
THAGORAS, as to practise every night this solemn recollection, yet I am not so lost in dissipation as wholly to omit it;
nor can I forbear sometimes to enquire of myself, in what
employment my life has passed away. Much of my time has sunk
into nothing, and left no trace by which it can be distinguished;
and of this I now only know, that it was once in my power,
and might once have been improved.(45)

We can usefully, perhaps rather surprisingly, set these remarks alongside
a relevant comment from one of Sterne's sermons:

That, for this end, he must call his own ways to rememberance
and search out his spirit; — search his actions with the same
critical exactness and the same piercing curiosity, we are wont
to sit in judgement upon others; varnishing nothing and
disguising nothing. If he proceeds thus, and in every relation
of life takes a full view of himself without prejudice — traces
his actions to their principles without mercy, and looks into
the dark corners and recessess of his heart without fear —
and if upon such an inquiry — he acts consistent with his view
in it, by reforming his errors, separating the dross, and
purifying the whole mass with repentance; this will bid fair
for examining a man's works in the Apostle's sense; — (46)

Another divine, Isaac Watts, expresses virtually the same views in his
Improvement of the Mind(47) which was largely based on Locke's *Conduct*

---

(45) *Adventurer* 137, *Works*, III, pp. 228-9.

(46) Sterne, *Sermons*, (London, 1785) Vol. I, (Sermon XIV), p. 104 and
pp. 51-6, (Sermon IV), and also Vol. II, Sermon XXVII which also appears
in *Tristram Shandy*, Bk. II, Chap. 17.

(47) Published (London, 1810). See Pt.I, Chap. III, 'Rules Relating to
Observation', also the first paragraph of Pt.I, Chap.I.

of the Understanding(48). It is also worth recalling here Tristram's words on Locke's essay:

> I will tell you in three words what the book is. — It is a history ! of who ? what ? where ? when ? Don't hurry yourself — It is a history book, Sir, (which may possibly recommend it to the world) of what passes in a man's own mind.(49)

It is interesting that Sterne and Watts should have been influenced by Locke and that they seem to convert a philosophical technique (self-analysis) to Christian purposes. When Johnson mentions the review it is, in fact, part of a larger concern with conduct, supported by Christian and philosophical ideas which are inextricably mingled together as, indeed, they are in Sterne and Watts(50). Johnson's own attempts at reviewing his life and his keeping of a journal are an integral part of his concern with Christian morality :

> When I review the last year, I am unable to recollect so little done, that shame and sorrow, though perhaps too weakly, come upon me .... I have, I think, been less guilty of neglecting publick worship than formerly. I have commonly on Sunday gone once to church, and if I have missed, have reproached my self.(51)

On another occasion he wrote:

> My general resolution to which I humbly implore the help of God is to methodise my life; to resist sloth and to combat scruples. I hope from this time to keep a Journal.(52)

---

(48) Johnson, *Lives*, III, 'Life of Watts', par. 26.

(49) Sterne, *Tristram Shandy*, Bk. II, Chap. 2.

(50) It is important to remember here, as Jean H. Hagstrum has remarked, that Watts was 'Johnson's mentor and guide in matters relating to the human mind' (*Samuel Johnson's Literary Criticism*, p. 13). In this context it is worth mentioning a similarity between Johnson's remarks in *Adventurer* 137, (see above) and a passage where Watts commends the 'Pythagorean' method, *op. cit.* p. 20. Joseph Butler, incidentally, was another divine who appears to have been influenced by Locke. His use of the idea of 'reflection' for moral ends is an example. See, *Sermons*, in *Works*, Ed. Gladstone, (Oxford, 1896) II, Preface (Sec'ns. 18-21) and Sermon X.

(51) Johnson, *Works*, (Oxford, 1958), I, 146.

(52) *Ibid.*, p. 155.

The review then, was seen by Johnson as an aid to regulating conduct. It was a retrospective act based on a knowledge of one's past life and more effectively carried out if one had recorded, at least, the more important events of past life. When Johnson remarked in *Idler* 84 "The writer of his own life has at least the first qualification of an historian..." the Christian and philosophical interests were both present. Self-examination, if properly pursued, necessarily led to self-knowledge, which in turn could be used by the individual for correcting his conduct.

On turning to Boswell we can note his remarks at the beginning of the *London Journal:*

> The ancient philosopher certainly gave a wise counsel when he said "Know thyself". For surely this knowledge is of all the most important. ... A man cannot know himself better than by attending to the feelings of his heart and to his external actions, from which he may with tolerable certainty judge "what manner of person he is". I have therefore determined to keep a daily journal in which I shall set down my various sentiments and my various conduct, which will not only be useful but very agreeable .... if I should go wrong, it will assist me in resolutions of doing better.[53]

These remarks precede the personal influence of Johnson although Boswell had probably read the relevant Idlers. However, another source offers itself if we consider that Hutcheson, who had an enormous influence upon the Scottish philosophers, outlined the philosopher's task thus:

> We must therefore search accurately into the constitution of our nature, to see what sort of creatures we are; for what purposes nature has formed us; what character God our Creator requires us to maintain .... In this inquiry we shall lightly pass over such natural powers as are treated in other arts, dwelling chiefly upon those which are of consequence in regulating our morals.[54]

Accepting the obvious differences between the two passages, and realizing that one is taken from a journal, the other from a philosophical treatise, there remains a close parallel between their attitudes, intentions and techniques.

---

(53) *London Journal*, Ed. F.A. Pottle, (London, 1952), p. 39.

(54) *A Short Introduction to Moral Philosophy*, (Glasgow 1748), p. 2.

It is not claimed, of course, that Boswell is something of a philosopher in disguise[55] but rather that his concern with self-knowledge had firm roots in the work and thought of his contemporaries, the Scottish philosophers. Indeed, a likely source for these ideas presents itself if we consider Boswell's education and his friendships[56] with many of the brilliant men in Scotland of the 1760's, and that he attended the lectures of Adam Smith on Moral Philosophy[57]. It is interesting, therefore, that Boswell's most intensive period of journalizing followed fairly closely upon the publication of Hume's *Enquiry Concerning the Principles of Morals*, Lord Kames' *Essays on the Principles of Morality and Natural Religion* (both in 1751), Hutcheson's *A Short Introduction to Moral Philosophy* (1747) and Adam Smith's *Theory of Moral Sentiments* (1759). That all of these titles indicate a concern with morality is important, for, while these philosophers often diverged on even fundamental issues, their concern with morality and conduct remained a unifying theme, and self-examination a unifying technique.

An examination of another passage indicates in even closer link between Boswell and the philosophers:

> The ancient precept "γνῶθι σεαυτόν" — "Know thyself," ... cannot be so perfectly obeyed without the assistance of a register of one's life. For memory is so frail and variable and so apt to be disturbed and confused by the perpetual succession of external objects and mental operations, that if our situation be not limited indeed, it is very necessary to have our thoughts and actions preserved in a mode not subject to change, if we would have a fair and distinct view of our character.[58]

Johnson, we know, constantly advised Boswell and others to keep a journal, recording "while the impression is fresh, for it will not be the same a week

---

(55) Much of Boswell's writing, however, *is* closely related to philosophy. A good example is his second essay, *On the Profession of a Player*. His writings abound in quasi - philosophical thought of the kind to be found in this essay.

(56) See *The Literary Career of James Boswell, Esq.*, Ed. F.A. Pottle, (Oxford, 1929), p. xxxii.

(57) *Ibid.*, p. xxx. Of Smith's lectures he always spoke very highly and they seem to have been a very influential part of his university education.

(58) *Boswell's Column*, Ed. Margery Bailey, p. 330. Another of his essays 'On Conscience' can usefully be compared with the religious writers mentioned above, esp. Sterne, Sermon, XXVII and Butler's work.

afterwards". No doubt the above remarks were influenced by Johnson's advice but also they accorded with contemporary philosophy. Boswell's awareness of the weakness of memory, of the complexity and variety of 'mental operations' and the changeability of the individual, all have their parallels in the philosophical thought of the period. Boswell was well aware of the common assumption that personal identity could only be discovered by way of memory,[59] but for memory, he substituted the journal[60]. It is worth remarking here that when dealing with the frailty of memory both Locke and Watts write in an unusually impassioned manner[61]. Both see man without memory as isolated and static and Boswell's reference to them in his essay *On Memory*[62] is therefore interesting.

Many modern critics and reviewers have been baffled by the honesty of Boswell's self-analysis and have relied, perhaps a little too much, on psychological traits as an explanation rather than on an examination of his intellectual environment. But, if we remember that for the eighteenth century philosopher it was apparent that before human conduct could be remoulded and redirected it had to be accurately and minutely analysed, it is reasonable to suggest that Boswell was of the same opinion. He always found the tender considerations of propriety a baffling thing in his published work and, like Johnson, was astonished that anyone should not want to know *facts*, but in his journals he could indulge in unfettered honesty. Indeed, if Boswell wanted his life to "tell" and his record to be of use to himself, there was little point in recording a fabric of inaccuracies and falsifications.

The importance of relating Johnson's and Boswell's theorizing to contemporary philosophy is that it emphasizes their seriousness, their consistency and their moral preoccupations. Whatever failings Boswell had in practice he retained the belief in the efficacy of the journal and Johnson was equally consistent in trying to write one.

To underline the general argument it is useful to look at the remarks of another eighteenth century philosopher, Dugald Stewart, upon another

---

(59) See Hume's *A Treatise of Human Nature*, Pt. IV, Sec. IV, where he also refers to its popularity as a subject of enquiry. See also, Locke, *An Essay Concerning Human Understanding*, I, 464, and Addison, *Spectator*, 578.

(60) See *Journal of a Tour to the Hebrides*, p. 384.

(61) Locke, *Essay*, I, 196. Isaac Watts, *op. cit.*, pp. 163-4.

(62) *Boswell's Column*, p. 340.

autobiographer, Montaigne. He placed Montaigne among the first of modern French philosophers:

> He has accordingly produced a work, *unique* in its kind; valuable, in an eminent degree, as an authentic record of many interesting facts relative to human nature; but more valuable by far, as holding up a mirror in which every individual, if he does not see his own image, will at least occasionally perceive of resemblance to it, as can scarcely fail to invite his curiosity to a more careful review of himself.
>
> .... it may be fairly questioned, notwithstanding the scrupulous fidelity with which Montaigne has endeavoured to delineate his own portrait, if he has always been sufficiently aware of the secret folds and reduplications of the human heart .... but this consideration .... is one of the most instructive lessons they afford to those who, after the example of the author, may undertake the salutary but humiliating task of self-examination(.[63])

Dugald Stewart as a philosopher finds Montaigne's work notable for the same reasons that Johnson's ideal autobiography would have been useful to him and, we may fairly observe, Montaigne's achievement as stated here, must be very similar to Boswell's if examined in the same way. Also, bearing in mind Dugald Stewart's continuity with the Scottish Philosophers, his mention of "a more careful review" and the use of self-examination illustrates the philosophical relevance of these acts. In fact, Montaigne is given the combined rôle of philosopher and self-examiner for moral ends: the two rôles, indeed, are seen as virtually synonomous.

Johnson would probably have agreed with Stewart's observation that Montaigne had given "an authentic record of many interesting facts relative to human nature". Johnson's moral concern was always supported by a tough empirical sense:"There is something noble" Johnson once observed([64]), "in publishing truth, though it condemns one's self".

---

(63) Dugald Stewart, *Dissertation on Metaphysical, Ethical and Political Philosophy*, Ed. Sir W. Hamilton, (Edinburgh, 1854), p. 99.

(64) *Life*, IV, 396.

ARTHUR SHERBO

Samuel Johnson and
The *Gentleman's Magazine,* 1750-1755 [1]

A number of months ago, while looking for something entirely different, my eye caught a title in the list of publications in the *GM* for May, 1752. The title, number 51 in the list, appearing on p. 243, was "Remarks on Mr. Mason's *Elfrida*; in letters to a friend." I remembered Donald Greene's article (*RES*, 1952) on dramatic criticism in the *GM* in the early 1950's and remembered too that he had claimed a review of Mason's *Elfrida* for Samuel Johnson. And as I read the comments on the "Remarks on Mr. Mason's *Elfrida*" by the anonymous reviewer for the *GM* I was convinced that I was reading Johnson again. Since, of late, I have been accused of seeing Johnson where others cannot, I decided to examine all the reviews in the book lists for 1752 and then check my findings with Donald Greene. I will anticipate my later discussion of items in the 1752 *GM* only to the extent of saying that Green's verdict on the "Remarks" was that the review was "definitely" Johnson's. On other items we disagreed. In any event, encouraged and comforted by the fact that, if in error, I was not alone, I went through the *GM* for the years 1750 through 1755, paying particular attention to the comments on publications in the monthly list of books. In this study, I wish to give the results of my investigations. *While I shall heartily welcome concurrence in some or any of my opinions, I shall be almost equally content to be considered a raiser of questions.*

The statement that Johnson had much more to do with the *GM* than has commonly been accepted has been documented more than once of late, most recently by Donald Greene in *PMLA* for 1959. The importance of

---

(1) I use the abbreviation *GM* for the *Gentleman's Magazine* hereafter. References to Boswell's *Life of Johnson* are to the Hill —Powell edition. I thank my good friend Donald Greene for his interest and cooperation.

Edmund Cave and the *GM*, under himself and later editors, in Johnson's
life was great and lasting. In 1734, writing pseudonymously from Birmingham,
Johnson had offered his services to Cave, who, we know, answered the letter,
although nothing seems to have come of this brief correspondence. Soon
after arriving in London with David Garrick, Johnson wrote again to Cave,
this time offering to undertake a translation of Father Sarpi's *History of the
Council of Trent* for him; from this letter, Professor Clifford believes, came
the first meeting of the two men in July, 1737(²). Whenever their first meeting took place, in the March 1738 *GM* there appeared a Latin poem, *Ad
Urbanum*, "addressed to the editor in so happy a style of compliment, that
Cave must have been destitute both of taste and sensibility had he not felt
himself highly gratified" (*Life*, I, 113). The author was Samuel Johnson.
Almost fifty years later, in December, 1784, to be precise, the *GM*, now under
the editorship of John Nichols, printed a letter concerning the authorship
of the parts of several volumes of the *Ancient Universal History*. This, too,
was by Samuel Johnson, printed "by his express desire" and "perhaps the
last scrap he ever dictated for the press," says Nichols. In the period between
1738 and 1784 Johnson was to edit the *GM*, write the Preface to its first
collected index in 1753, write parliamentary debates for it, write prefaces
to individual volumes for a number of years, and to contribute to its pages
a variety of letters, poems, essays, and reviews.

Johnson's closest connection with, and dependence on, the *GM* came
in the years from 1738 to 1745 when, we learn from the Rev. John Hussey,
who was, he says, told by Johnson himself, Cave employed Johnson as editor
(*Life*, I, 532). Most of his own contributions to the periodical were written
in these years. With the publication of the *Miscellaneous Observations on the
Tragedy of Macbeth* in 1745, advertising an abortive edition of Shakespeare's
plays, and with the publication two years later of the *Plan of a Dictionary of
the English Language*, it may be supposed that Johnson was wearying of the
relative anonymity and lack of freedom that accompanied his position as
editor of the *GM* and was seeking some large and important literary-scholarly
project that would make him his own man. We find, hence, only one possible
piece by him in the 1745 *GM*, another doubtfully by him in 1746, and a group
of eight poems, none of which, in my opinion, is firmly established in the

---

(2) *Young Sam Johnson* (New York, 1955), p. 183.

canon, in 1747.(³) Johnson did, however, write the November installment of the *GM*'s "Foreign History" in 1747.(⁴) It is, incidentally, in 1747 that Johnson, according to John Nichols, "occasionally afforded his powerful assistance to the Magazine; and though many entire pieces cannot be ascertained to have come from his pen, he was frequently, if not constantly, employed to superintend the materials of the Magazine" (*Life*, I, 532). Efforts to find Johnson's hand in the 1747 volume have resulted in the following attributions by various scholars: a poem, "On Lord Lovat's Execution," p. 194; a letter signed "William Lauder," pp. 363-4; certain proposals for printing Lauder's translation of *Adamus Exsul*, p. 404 (this is by Johnson); another letter on the Lauder affair, pp. 530-1; and a possible part in "Sir Thomas DeVeil's Life," pp. 562-4. In 1748 the *GM* printed Johnson's *Life of the Earl of Roscommon*. Boswell, almost surely mistakenly, attributed the "Foreign History" for November to Johnson, and there are two poems which, while once attributed to Johnson, are, again almost surely, by John Hawkesworth. In 1749 a letter on fireworks appeared in the January number of the periodical; it was attributed to Johnson by Alexander Chalmers, and I concur in the attribution. C.L. Carlson, *The First Magazine*, 1938, pp. 22-3. has no doubt that the introduction to an abstract of Anson's *Voyages*, appearing in September, p. 393, was written by Johnson and suggests he may also have written the "abstract" itself; the latter appears in the September, October, and December numbers and in the February and March numbers in 1750. An introductory note (1749, p. 563) to Johnson's reprinted Postscript to Lauder's *Essay* on Milton is claimed for Johnson by Donald Greene in a work still in manuscript. The Courtney-Smith bibliography lists no further contributions by Johnson to the *GM* until 1754, when he wrote a life of Edward Cave, who had died on the tenth of January of that year. It would seem from this that Johnson had very little to do with the *GM* after, say, 1747. That this is not at all accurate will be demonstrated in what follows.

1750

Donald Greene has called attention (*PMLA*, 1959, 83-4) to a piece entitled "Some Account of the Present State of the Controversy Concerning

---

(3) See, however, D.N. Smith and E.L. McAdam, *Poems of Samuel Johnson* (London, 1940, pp. 116-126). I may some day record the reasons for my opinion.

(4) See *JEGP*, LII (1953), 543-8 and *PMLA*, LXXIV (1959), 81-3.

Milton's Imitation of the Moderns" in the *GM* for December 1750, which he claims for Johnson. The writer of the piece, if it was Johnson, as I believe and hope further to establish, seems to speak for the *GM* in some sort of official capacity. Two months earlier, the *GM* had reprinted *Rambler* 60 and had appended a note listing Johnson's early biographical contributions to its pages (Greene, p. 84). From these two facts it would seem that Johnson, active in the direction of the *GM* in 1747 (see above, p. 135), resumed a connection with the periodical that may have lapsed, entirely or in part, during 1748 and 1749. For, unless I am mistaken, Johnson wrote the "Remarks on the Tragedy called The Black Prince," the lead article in the *GM* for February, 1750 and probably also the preliminary "Account" of the same play in the January number. And, always under pain of possible correction, I am quite confident that Johnson wrote the "Foreign History" (see Greene, pp. 81-3) for the December number and a review of a book entitled "Harriot Stuart" in the same number. In the September *GM* (p. 432) there is an advertisement for Mrs. Williams' *Essays in Prose and Verse*, first attributed to Johnson by Chalmers, that has found a firm place in the canon. Let me elaborate on the criticism of *The Black Prince*, the "Foreign History," and the one book review.

Johnson's role as theatrical critic of the *GM* in the early 1750's was discussed by Donald Greene in 1952 (*RES*); the actual years in which reviews, possibly by Johnson, appeared were 1751-4. I would push the *terminus a quo* back a year to include the piece on William Shirley's *Black Prince*. The evidence for this attribution, other than the fact that Johnson almost surely wrote theatrical criticism for the *GM* from 1751 through 1754, is internal; the style, and the sentiments are Johnson's. Here are illustrations of what I mean:

> But to suppose that the spirit of his father was really present, cloathed in some vehicle that resembled his person, is to confirm the tales of the nurse, and realize the dreams of ignorance and superstition; and admitting the reality of an intercourse between departing spirits and surviving friends, by the miraculous interposition of providence, such event cannot be justly supposed in the present case, because it answers no end.

> That an assasin should imagine he sees the spectres of those whom he has murder'd, denouncing vengeance, and threating destruction, is natural, because terror is the effect of guilt,

and superstition and delirium are the effects of terror; but, on the contrary, peace of mind, pleasing hopes, and calm fortitude, are essential to a consciousness of virtue; especially if that virtue be of the heroic kind; nor can the imagination of such a person as Ribemont suggest the appearance of spectres that strike with terror or forbode calamity.

These are the blemishes that appear on the first view of this play; to particularise those which are of an inferior kind, and are discover'd only on a more attentive examination, would betray a propensity to blame, and a kind of industrious ill-nature, which has render'd criticism infamous.

As to the *language* of this piece, if it is not adorned with the most brilliant and striking beauties of poetry, it is not debased by groveling expressions, or forced conceit.

The *sentiments* throughout are not only virtuous but noble: the *Numbers*, for the most part, are easy and flowing: the distress of the Lovers is generally well painted; and the character of a kind master, a good general, and a wise and beneficent prince, is happily sustained in the hero of the poem. But, that the reader may judge of the piece, with respect to particular excellencies or defects, that are independent of the general plan and conduct of the drama, the following Extracts are added to these Remarks.

My chief reason for attributing the "Foreign History," in December, 1750 to Johnson, other than the fact that he is known to have written some and may have written or had a hand in many more "Foreign History's" for the *GM*, is again based on the style of the piece. There is, too, the cluster, or possible cluster if you will, in December of the review I shall discuss below, the piece on the Lauder controversy (see above, pp. 135-136), and the "Foreign History" now under examination. Readers may need to be reminded of the distinction between the general observations of the Johnsonian "Foreign History's" and the specific remarks of the non-Johnsonian. The "Foreign History" in the *GM* starts out with two paragraphs summing up occurences in foreign nations during the year and then, to some extent, particularizes what has transpired in each nation. In my opinion, the whole piece, not simply the two opening paragraphs, is Johnson's. For example here is the short paragraph on the Dutch:

> The Hollanders are still employed in settling their government, redressing grievances, detecting corruptions, and finding, what no politician has yet reached, methods of laying taxes on the people without provoking them.

Or, part of the paragraph on Germany:

> The negotiators are busy in adjusting contrary interests, and
> in palliating disputes which cannot be decided.

The whole piece ends with a short biographical account of Marshal Saxe,
capped by an anecdote. All this smacks of Johnson to me. And here, even
more powerful as evidence, are the two opening paragraphs:

> The year which we are now closing has not been made
> memorable by any great events. The European nations are
> employed in repairing the ruins of the late war, and settling
> themselves in tranquillity, after its concessions. — In Asia
> we hear the sound of remote commotions, but confused and
> indistinct, nor is there yet any knowledge to be gained of the
> designs or pretensions of either party. The Africans, indeed,
> might be said to be at war in the Mediterranean, but that they
> seem hitherto not to have been opposed, and there can be no
> war where there is no resistance.
>
> The Turks have for some time been looked on with suspi-
> cion by the bordering powers, of which each has been afraid
> of some sudden attack; not that either the Sultan or his ministers
> are supposed to desire a war for the sake of conquest, but be-
> cause the Janizaries are tumultuous, and there is no method of
> appeasing them so effectual as a busy life, and remote employ-
> ment. The alarm however begins to grow less, and there is
> reason to hope that mutual fear will continue peace.

The monthly "Register of Books" in the *GM* had been, up to 1748
when a few scattered summaries of or extracts from English books began
to appear, nothing but a bare list of books and pamphlets. In 1750, from
January through November, the same procedure had been followed: the
"Registers" occupied one page apiece and there were only thirteen summaries
in the eleven months. There were no *critical* remarks. But a new departure
was signalled in the very table of contents (p. 530) of the December *GM*,
for there the words "Books and Pamphlets with Remarks" took the place
of the usual "Register of Books." The section contains some seven or eight
summaries or remarks, the whole taking up two pages. Some of the summaries are quite long. What is more, and of great significance, I think, is the
presence for the first time in the *GM* indexes of books (for the individual
volumes) of asterisks beside those titles of which some account had been

given. Most interesting, however, is the presence of the first note of literary criticism:

> These volumes contain a series of love-affairs from 11 years of age [sic], attended with a number of her adventures and misfortunes, which were borne with the patience, and are penn'd with the purity of a Clarissa. No part of the history is short enough to be detached, nor can it be abridged without great injury to the original.

The book is "The Life of Harriot Stuart, written by herself. 2 vols. 12 mo. 5s bound. Payne"; the author, Mrs. Charlotte Lennox. It was in honor of the publication of Mrs. Lennox's book that Johnson organized an all-night party, staying up until five, at least, and achieving " a meridian splendour" about his face although he drank only lemonade (*Life*, I, 255n).

1751

If, as I suppose, Johnson resumed an interrupted editorial function in 1750, the evidence for its continuance the next year is slight. Alexander Chalmers attributed the Preface to this year's *GM* to Johnson; it is my own belief that if he did not write it, he touched it up here and there. The review of Edward Moore's *Gil Blas* in the February number has been confidently claimed for Johnson (Greene, *RES*, 1952); I have no doubt it is his(5). I find little else that may be his. While there are a number of summaries of books and pamphlets in the monthly lists of publications, there are almost no reviews, *i.e.*, critical examinations. One exception is the notice of a book entitled "An exposition of the uncertainties in the practice of physic," by Benito Geronimo Feijo, master general of the order of St. Benedict (Feb., p. 95). This may be Johnson's: he was interested in medicine; the style suggests his hand; and he singles out for comment Dr. Sydenham, whose life he himself had written for the 1742 *GM*. What is more, item 494 of the Sales Catalogue of his books is "Brett's works of Feyjoo, 4 vols." Only one other piece caught my attention, a short piece with a few remarks on, and three passages from, a mock-heroic poem called *The Scribleriad* (Jan., pp. 31-2). Although there is little to go on, there are two learned notes, one on the story of a petrified city in Africa and the other on Egyptian prophets,

---

(5) Richard Wright makes the same attribution in his *Account of the Life of Dr. Samuel Johnson*, 1805.

which bring Johnson to mind. One of the notes retells an anecdote from Shaw's *Travels*, a work which appears in the sales catalogue (No. 67) of Johnson's library; when he acquired the book, published in 1747, is of course not determinable. There is also one remark, comparing the use of a word or thought in the poem with its use in Rabelais, that adds a bit to my hesitant conjecture that it is by Johnson. The sentence reads, "Whoever will compare these passages will see a remarkable instance of the great difference there is in the same thought, thrown out as the flight of a wild imagination, or worked up with the art of a writer whose genius, though equally daring, is tempered with judgment." If this piece is Johnson's, there is the further possibility that the notice of the same work in the February list of books (p. 95) is also his. The decision on style is virtually impossible since the notice is a summary of the events of the poem.

I would add one note at this point. In this year and in 1753 — and once in 1752 — there are a number of notices of books, beginning inelegantly with "It" and referring to the book, poem, or pamphlet under discussion. There are also, as will be seen, in the years 1750-1755, a number of notices that suggest Johnson. And there are, finally, a number of notices by neither Johnson nor the infelicitous reviewer first mentioned. There were, then, for a period, at least three different men concerned with the notices of books in the monthly lists.

1752

It was, it may be remembered, a notice of some "Remarks on William Mason's *Elfrida*" (May, p. 243) that set me off on this investigation. Before reporting my own findings in this volume of the *GM*, let me quickly note other pieces that have already been attributed to Johnson. G.B. Hill believed a notice of Mrs. Lennox's *Female Quixote* in the March list (p. 146) of books Johnson's (*Life*, 1887, I, 367, n.1); I find no great difficulty in putting it down as probably by Johnson, since he had written the dedication for the novel and one of the last chapters also. The book list for August (p. 387) contains another notice that has been accepted by some as Johnson's. The notice is of a periodical called *The Impertinent*; the first attribution to Johnson I have found was by Professor Cross in his *History of Henry Fielding* (II, 414). I myself can see nothing Johnsonian about it. And there is, finally, the review of Mason's *Elfrida* which Greene (*RES*, 1952) and I feel sure is by Johnson. It might, further, be well to point out that extracts from two *Rambler* essays, full quotation of the last *Rambler*, and a number of "the Subjects, Mottoes, and other Citations in the Rambler" appeared in this year. The fact that Johnson had some part in Hawkesworth's *Adventurer*, although he wrote no essays for it until later, may possibly, though hardly necessarily, have something to do with the account of the first four essays in that series plus full quotation of numbers 5 and 10.

Since the notice of the "Remarks on Mr. Mason's *Elfrida*" started me off, I shall quote it in full:

> This piece, under the appearance of a criticism, is a most extravagant panegyrick on Elfrida. But little regard surely is due to his opinion of poetry, whose language is barbarous, and whose ideas are confused. The fable, he says, is so far domestic as to be *closely* interesting. And by a *domestic* fable, he means a fable taken from *common life;* not considering that persons who are most elevated above common life, may be involved in domestic distress and consequently be the subjects of a domestic fable. — By the following quotations, it will appear that the knowledge of grammar is not always attained by those who profess criticism in other sciences. — 'Whether we consider the characters of Elfrida in *any* of the foregoing lights, we shall find them unexceptionably excellent.'— 'The prospect darkens after his *having had a* clear and fair one, and *had* reason to think, &c.' — 'Athelwold's inward compunction and generous remorse cannot be too much admir'd, as *likewise* his alarm and confusion.' — But this writer, tho' he does not excel in grammar, is remarkably bold in his metaphors; for he has affirmed of *naked* and bare sentences, that if they are *stripped* they become as unpoetical as *scraps* that are to be met with *up* and *down* Diogenes Laertius. — — Among other beauties, he has pointed out an expression which he calls a Grecism. — 'A man that thinks such thoughts;' — a beauty of which he has himself attempted a distant imitation, by introducing several Gallicisms into his remarks, and particularly by using *trait* for stroke.

I think the style is Johnson's; I find familiar the concern with grammar, mixed metaphors, and Gallicisms; and I recall, in reading the remarks on "domestic fable," that Johnson called Shakespeare's *Timon of Athens* a "domestick Tragedy."

G.B. Hill's and Cross's "detection" of Johnson's hand in the notices of books in two different months and my own belief about his authorship

of a notice in a third monthly list made it imperative that I study closely
all the other notices in these, and indeed in all, lists. It was, hence, working
on the 1752 volume that prompted me to scrutinize the monthly lists of books
for the period 1750-1755. In the January (1752) number I found two pieces
that suggested Johnson's hand. The first (No. 29) is a notice of "Encyclo-
paedia No. 1," the Diderot-D'Alembert undertaking; I feel fairly confident
it is Johnson's. The second (No. 36), a few critical remarks on a poem, *On
the Abuse of Poetry*, may be his. One piece in February is probably by Johnson.
It is a notice of *Sparks, or, small poems morally turned*; part of the first sentence will show, I think, why I (and Donald Greene) believe it to be Johnson's: "The turns in these poems are generally ingenious and new, the sentiment is just, and the thoughts frequently poetical; but harmony is sometimes
wanting, and the verse, although intended to be that of 7 syllables, is often
rather that of 8 mutilated ... " The rest, the quoted part is roughly one-
third of the whole notice, is also in the same vein and style. In March I find
the notice of *The Oracle, a comedy of one act, translated from the French by
Mrs. Cibber* stylistically reminiscent of Johnson. Number 51, in May, is the
Remarks on Mr. Mason's Elfrida. And Number 52, first suggested as Johnson's to me by Greene, is on Zachary Grey's notes upon *Hudibras*, an attribution in which I am glad to concur. *An account of six years residence in
Hudson's Bay*, No. 6 in June, is the kind of book I think Johnson would
pick to review himself rather than give to another. While the notice is chiefly
a resumé it contains one sentence that suggests Johnson — possibly writing
hurriedly: "From the several particulars the curiosity of the naturalist will
be gratified, and the judgment of the politician enlightened; those who
read for amusement will find entertainment, and those who seek information will gain much useful knowledge." "In this piece," says the reviewer of
George Alexander Steevens' *Distress Upon Distress* in the July issue (No. 27),
"there is much true humour and just satire, and it is to be regretted that the
object of both is confined to the play house; there are however several inaccuracies which shew it to be rather the production of a wit than a scholar.
No judgment can be form'd of its merit by an epitome, or an extract. But it
cannot fail of entertaining those that are well acquainted with the theatrical
taste." I find it hard to account for my belief that this is Johnson's, but neither
I nor Greene had any doubts about it. Possibly Johnson's "wit-scholar" antithesis in a remark on Thomas Edwards and Benjamin Heath in the Preface
to Shakespeare influenced my decision. He says there, of the critics, that
"one is a wit, and one a scholar."

Donald Greene, in an independent examination of the notices in the *GM* for this year, agreed with four of my attributions.

1753

Edmund Cave, having successfully weathered the first twenty years of the *GM*, decided to publish an index to the contents of the first twenty volumes; whoever compiled the index, Johnson wrote the preface to it. The index was published in 1753. Alexander Chalmers attributes the Preface to the *GM* for this year to Johnson; I agree. A short notice of Cave's death appears on the last page of the index for the collected numbers of the *GM* in this year (the index was actually published in 1754); Chalmers thought it Johnson's, as do I. The lead article for the February number is devoted to an account and criticism of Edward Moore's *The Gamester*; this is by Johnson, and the similar examination of Edward Young's *The Brothers* is also very probably his (Greene, *RES*, 1952)(6). What is more, it is in this year that Cave employed the pages of the *GM* to advertise an edition of the works of Richard Savage. I have discussed this enterprise and Johnson's possible connection with it elsewhere (*N&Q*, 1952, pp. 51-4); I bring it up again further to strengthen my premise that Johnson was playing an important part in the operation of the periodical in these years.

If I am right, or even partially right, in what follows, it will be seen, in conjunction with what has already been said about Johnson and the 1753 *GM*, that this was one of the most fruitful years of his connection with Cave's periodical. First of all, the first paragraph of the "Foreign History" for November is surely Johnson's:

PERSIA

The intestine wars which have so longed ravaged this unhappy country, are revived with fresh fury, and, to complete its calamities, two other dreadful scourges, famine and pestilence, the usual consequences of civil wars, violently persued and long continued, begin to be felt. Yet vast armies list themselves under the banners of the respective competitors, obliged to it perhaps for protection, and chusing rather to espouse some party in the field, than by standing neuter to be plundered and murdered at home.

---

(6) But see Johnson's *Life of Young* where he says: "Of *The Brothers* I may be allowed to say nothing, since nothing was ever said of it by the Publick" (*Lives* ed. Hill, III, 397).

I find nothing else that resembles Johnson's style in the rest of this "Foreign History."

Whether or not Johnson wrote the Preface for the *GM* in this year, we can assume his familiarity with it. The Preface states, "that we might comprehend a greater variety of knowledge, we have added to those tracts which are originally published in our Miscellany, rot a list only, but some account of the books that have appeared as well in our own as in foreign countries." Now, Donald Greene (*PMLA*, 1959, p. 83) has suggested that Johnson probably "played an important role in the compilation of the scholarly and intelligent 'Foreign Books' section that began to appear in the *GM* in November 1741 and ceased in September 1743. (There are two isolated 'Foreign Literary Articles' in January and September 1744)." One would, hence, look for the recurrence of these sections of "Foreign Books" and be tempted, naturally, to link them with Johnson in some fashion. Coincidence may play a part in such a recurrence in 1753; the fact remains that the Supplement (pp. 624-26) contains a list of books "publish'd abroad in the Course of the Year 1753" and the expressed intention to provide "the like in each of our future Supplements". Johnsonians will have to decide for themselves what, if any, significance to attach to the brief accounts appended to many of the books in this list.

Johnson probably wrote the accounts and criticisms of two plays in the *GM* this year (see above, p. 143); there is a third account, identical in format with the other two, that has not been attributed to him. The play in question is *Boadicea*, by Richard Glover, of whose famous poem *Leonidas* Johnson said that one must *seek* for its good passages (*Life*, V. 116); the remark was made in 1773. Despite the complimentary reference to *Leonidas* in the last paragraph of the account, I think Johnson wrote the whole. I quote only the critical part of the account:

> Whatever general precept results from the action, or, in the usual phrase, whatever is called the moral of the plot, will be easily discover'd by this account; The particular precepts which are interwoven in the dialogue cannot be detached without great injury to the author, because they receive, not only their beauty, but their force, from the circumstances in which are delivered, and the characters which they sustain.
>
> This piece is written with sufficient regard to dramatic rules, and, in general, is such as a good critic might expect from the author of *Leonidas*. The 13th scene of the last act is extremely

tender, and many circumstances of the distress are new. The author seems to have been somewhat embarrassed by the under plot; for all that passes between the two Roman captives concerning their escape, and the love of Flaminius to the daughter of Boadicia is but slightly connected with the principal action, tho' the expectation of an English audience would scarce have been gratified without it.

The evidence, external and internal, it seems to me, demands that the piece be claimed for Johnson.

There remain only the book-lists to examine. In March (No. 28) Johnson may have written the notice of *The Carnation* by R. Dyer. The last of the three sentences reads, somewhat reminiscent of Johnson, "Upon this piece, therefore, criticism would surely be ill employ'd, and he who has the best heart will perhaps most wish to praise it." In May there are two accounts that may be Johnson's: No. 34, *Shakespear Illustrated*, is by Mrs. Lennox and has a Dedication written by Johnson; the contents of the two volumes (the third was not yet published) is given and the purpose of the work is explained. The account manages to be complimentary without examining the actual performance of its author. No. 59, *Employment for the Microscope*, by Henry Baker, may also be Johnson's; Johnson was acquainted with the workings of the microscope, as evidenced in his interview with George III (*Life*, II, 38-39), and the clarity and precision of the style suggest his hand. The June list contains but one account (No. 5) that I would suggest for further consideration, that of a book entitled *Moral and Religious Aphorisms*. Again it is the style, if such a word can be used of many of these brief accounts, and the subject matter of the work reviewed which incline me to think that Johnson may have written it.

There is one review, No. 26 in the November list, that deserves separate attention. I quote the whole, full title and all:

> 26. The history of Sir Charles Grandison, in a series of letters published from the originals. By the editor of *Pamela* and *Clarissa*, 4 vols, in 8vo. boards 17s. 12mo. 10s.6d. — In this work, of which 4 volumes only are published, the author has compleated a plan, of which *Pamela* and *Clarissa* are parts. In *Pamela* he intended to exhibit the beauty and superiority of virtue in an unpolished mind, with the temporary reward which it frequently obtains, and to render the character of a libertine contemptible. His chief design in *Clarissa*, was to shew the

excellence of virtue, tho' in this life it should not be rewarded, and to represent the life of a libertine, with every adventitious advantage, as an object not only of detestation, but of horror. In Sir Charles Grandison, he proposed to display the superiority of virtue in yet another light; and by exhibiting the character and actions of a man of true honour, to shew that every natural and accidental advantage, is improved by virtue and piety; that these polish elegance, heighten dignity, and produce universal love, esteem and veneration. How far this important design is effected, the world will soon be able to judge, as the last volume, will be published in the beginning of the year. The author's abilities are already sufficiently known, and as we cannot suppose the encomium of our correspondent (See p. 511) to have been written without a view of the whole, there is yet more reason to conclude that the expectation of the publick will not be disappointed.

There is no need to catalogue Johnson's opinions on Richardson's work as a novelist; they have been gathered together by Joseph Epes Brown in his *Critical Opinions of Samuel Johnson*. One need only remember that Richardson ranked very high indeed in Johnson's mind as a writer of fiction. If the review is Johnson's, as I very strongly believe it is, we have this brief resumé of what he feels Richardson was trying to do in his three novels. I might add that there is a concentration of various pieces possibly by Johnson in the November and December numbers.

The December *GM* contains two accounts that may be Johnson's. No. 31, *The Analysis of Beauty*, by Hogarth, may have been reviewed by Johnson; No. 35, a review of a work entitled *Some Few Reflections on the Tragedy of Boadicea*, is almost surely his. I quote the entire account:

> This is an attempt to recommend dramatic dialogue without incidents, and poetry without description, metaphor, or simile: Tragedies written on these principles, says the writer, approach nearest to perfection, because they approach nearest to nature; but if this be the rule, as nothing can be a more evident, or perpetual deviation from nature, than a dialogue in verse; verse should also be rejected as well as poetry and incidents, and it is to be wished this gentleman would oblige the world with a tragedy upon so excellent a plan.

Something should be said here that should probably have been said earlier : the accounts of books that I have been suggesting as possibly or probably by Johnson are largely only those which strike me *most* as his. That is, there are others which might equally well be his, but for which the argument would rest solely on his supposed presence as reviewer in these years and on his known interests in literature in certain fields and on certain topics. Often, as I have suggested above, the evidence of style cannot be invoked positively; one can only say, negatively, that certain of these accounts are so poorly written that they cannot be Johnson's. It may also be well to include here some statistics which are valuable both for what has gone before and what is to follow. Using the *GM's* yearly index to the lists of books published and counting those marked by asterisks, a device introduced in 1750 to call attention to those books of which some account was given, I found the following distribution of reviews or accounts of books from 1750-1755:

1750 (20) 1751 (40) 1752 (42) 1753 (76) 1754 (106) 1755 (64)

The statistics cannot be exact since a work would sometimes appear under two headings, and in a few instances the index listed works, usually plays, which were reviewed elsewhere than in the monthly register of books in the periodical. The figure for 1755 includes some ten titles of foreign books, a practice I did not observe in the previous lists. The figure for 1754, the highest of all, is significant, to anticipate, in the light of the heavy concentration of Johnsonian and possibly Johnsonian pieces in that year. Here, too, is a breakdown of the number of reviews in the monthly lists that I have assigned to Johnson with differing degrees of assurance:

1750 (1) 1751 (2) 1752 (8) 1753 (7) 1754 (15) 1755 (3)

Of 348 reviews (or accounts), I have selected 36 which I think have a right to be considered by Johnsonians.

1754

The *GM* for this year is exceeding rich in possible Johnsonian pieces. The Preface, claimed for Johnson by Chalmers, strikes me forcibly as his, although Nichols (*Literary Anecdotes*, IX, 592) says it was written by Hawkesworth. Johnson's *Life of Edmund Cave* was the first essay in the February number; Cave had died early in January. And the reviews of two plays, *Philoclea* (Feb.) and *Constantine* (April), are Johnson's, according to Greene

(*RES*, 1952). I might add, since Greene only refers to it in passing, that the account, and it is nothing more than that, of another play, *Virginia* (March), is very probably also by Johnson. The evidence for this supposition lies in a note at the end of the account of *Virginia*, "The account of Constantine must be deferr'd till our next, for want of room" (p. 129) and a request, at the head of the account of *Constantine* (p. 178) that the reader "See p. 128," *i.e.*, where the account of *Virginia* begins. What is more, the opening sentence of the account of *Virginia* begins, "Since our last two tragedies have been exhibited, but with different success." The very presence of some "Remarks" on William Whitehead's tragedy *Creusa* in the *GM* this year, while hardly strong evidence, makes it a possible candidate for the canon, and the concluding remarks sound like Johnson to me. I quote the whole of these:

> It has been objected to this tragedy, that Aletes is discovered to be Nicander, and Ilyssus his son by Creusa, too soon; but the tender solicitude which this discovery produces, is more than equivalent to the surprize of a discovery more sudden and longer delayed.
>
> Perhaps some incidents may be thought to exceed the bounds of probability, as the delivery of Creusa on the night Nicander was banished, without suspicion of such an incident, and his preserving the new born infant during his flight, who, as his birth was premature, stood in greater need of that assistance, which in such a situation could not be procured; this, however, is an objection which the mind is not at leisure to make when the passions are strongly excited, and curiosity is impatient for the catastrophe.
>
> Some faults indeed there are, which, if they are more obvious, are less important.
>
> The idiom is sometimes vulgar and sometimes barbarous; *unlucky fate* is not only a coarse, but an inaccurate expression; *please you* is a phrase of low civility, by which the stile of tragedy is debased; "*please you* — to taste some light refection," are words so ill sorted, as to have the appearance of burlesque; for either the address should have been more elevated than *please you*, or the term of the request more familiar than *refection*. Ilyssus, twice in one scene asks if it is the queen's pleasure that he should withdraw by the phrase, *please you, retire* ? *You* and *thee* are used promiscuously in the same speech; and absolute terms used in a comparative sense, as *so* totally exposed *so* totally transformed. *O God !* is a vulgar and a prophane exclamation:

O God ! I feel the truth of what thou utterest,

To *settle all*, is a phrase too common and too mercantile to become the priestess of Apollo; and the statesman talks like a rude provincial when he tells a lady "there is mischief *toward*." Synonima's are sometimes multiplied for the sake of measure, as *force* and *energy*, and a verb is unwarrantably changed to a noun, by substituting *feel* for *sensation*.

——— Thus sensibly alive
To glory's finest *feel*, ———

But though the language is not always sufficiently elevated or pure, yet the numbers are frequently such as suit rather with epic than dramatic poetry.

Comes she on pious purpose to adore
The mistic shrine oracular ? ———
The good king found ———
Th' audacious fraud, and drive the guilty youth
To banishment perpetual.

That cadence which constitutes an English verse is not always preserved, though the syllables are scrupulously numbered;

Under seal
Of firmest secresy told the king.

neither are the metaphors always unmixed.

I feel within
An heav'n-born impulse, and the seeds of truth
Are lab'ring in my breast.

Here is an *impulse* that is *born*, and *seeds* that *labour*. These blemishes, however, are so minute that they would not have been remarked if they had been found in a work less likely to be quoted as a precedent, and followed as an example.

And I would also very gingerly propose that the account of *Barbarossa* that heads the December number might also be Johnson's. There are no critical remarks, although an end-note promises that "some remarks upon this piece may, perhaps, be published in our next." The promise was never kept.

Another of the offerings this year may also be considered Johnson's. On pp. 293-4 (June) there is a "List of Foreign Books, continued from Vol. 23 [1753], p. 626"; similar lists, each marked as a continuation of the preceding one, occur at pp. 436-8 (September) and pp. 598-600 (Supplement). I think it eminently worth noting that only in this volume, out of those covering 1750-1755, is there a separate "Index to the Foreign Books." Again I invite

Johnsonians to study the books listed and the brief comments, summaries of contents, in these lists.

The presence of a poem by Anna Williams, *Verses to Mr. Richardson, on his History of Sir Charles Grandison*, later to be published in her *Miscellanies*. which Boswell (*Life*, II, 25-6) believed to have "evidently received additions from [Johnson's] superiour pen," may be additional evidence of his role as editor. The same, although conjecture here is weaker, may hold true for the publication of a number of poems by Christopher Smart. Smart had not previously published in the *GM*, possibly because first *The Student* and then *The Midwife* had precluded much outside and incidental writing. Johnson had contributed the *Life of Cheynel* to *The Student* and some of his *Rambler* essays were reprinted and praised in *The Midwife*. He may, hence, have opened the poetry columns of the *GM* to a friend who always stood in need of more money.

One other piece exerted a considerable attraction on me, partly because it was linked with something in the 1753 *GM*. I suggested above that Johnson may have reviewed Hogarth's *Analysis of Beauty* in the Dec. 1753, *GM*, (p. 593); in January, 1754, four and a half pages of the periodical were given over to "Some Account of the Principles of Beauty and Gracefulness, with respect to Colour, Figure, Proportion, Atttiude and Action From Mr. Hogarth's Analysis" (pp. 11-15). All except two concluding paragraphs is taken from Hogarth's work:

> Such are the principles which Mr. Hogarth has established, explained, and applied to practice in his analysis of beauty; a book, written with that precision and perspicuity, which can only result from a perfect knowledge of his subject in all its extent. His rules are illustrated by near two hundred figures, engraved by himself; the knowledge which it contains is universally useful, and as all terms of art are avoided, the language will be universally understood. The player and the dancing-master, whom others consider as patterns of just action and genteel deportment, are not less instructed than the statuary and the painter; nor is there any species cf beauty or elegance that is not here investigated and analysed.

> A bock, by which the author has discovered such superiority, could scarce fail of creating many enemies; those who admit this analysis to be just, are disposed to deny that it is new tho' in the year 1745, having drawn a serpentine line on a painter's pallet, with these words under it, "the line of beauty','

as a frontispiece to his prints, no Egyptian hyeroglyphic ever produced greater variety of speculation; both painters and sculptors then came to enquire the meaning of a symbol, which they so long pretended to have been their old acquaintance; tho' the account they could give of its properties was scarce so satisfactory as that of a day labourer, who constantly uses the lever, could give of that instrument, as a mechanical power. The work however will live when these cavils are forgotten; and except the originals, of which it is pretended to be a copy, are produced, there is no question but that the name of the author will descend to posterity with that honour which competitors only can wish to withhold.

Johnson does not, I believe, elsewhere record his opinion of Hogarth's work — if this is, indeed, his.

With all these out of the way, there remain a number of notices of books which, with varying degrees of probability, may be considered for the canon. One of these had been attributed to Johnson long ago by Chalmers; I made the attribution independently, not having checked previous attributions in the desire not to be overly influenced by the opinions of others. I refer to a notice of Lauder's *The Grand Impostor Detected*, appearing as number 26 in the February *GM*, pp. 97-8. Since at least one eminent Johnsonian has disagreed with Chalmers,[7] I intend here only a much belated seconding of the attribution, partly in the light of Johnson's close connection with the *GM* at this time. The notices of books, I might add, had come in for special attention in the Preface to the *GM* this year, the writer of the Preface, probably Johnson, according to Chalmers, stating that "we have continued to gratify Literary Curiosity with an impartial account of new Books: An article which we have occasionally enlarged, and to which we shall, perhaps, more frequently allot an extraordinary page than heretofore." I think this statement, with the fact of Johnson's presence looming large in the *GM* this year, and with Johnson's known connections with the whole Lauder business, make a second or third look at the notice in question necessary.

A notice, mostly a resumé of contents, of Saunders Welch's *Observations on the Office of a Constable*, March, pp. 144-5, may be Johnson's. He knew Welch as early as 1753 and, as Professor McAdam has pointed out, wrote the concluding three paragraphs of Welch's *Proposal.. to Remove the Nuisance*

---

(7) Allen Hazen, *Samuel Johnson's Prefaces and Dedications* (New Haven 1937), p. 80n.

of Common Prostitutes from the Streets, 1759 (*RES*, 1953). Professor McAdam notes that Welch's *Observations* were "favorably reviewed and extensively in the *GM*," but hazards no guess as to the identity of the reviewer (p. 339n). In the same monthly list there are three other reviews to which I should also like to draw attention. These are numbers 39, 46, and 47, reviews of *The Feminiad*, by John Duncombe, A.M.; *The Immortality of the Soul, from the Latin of Mr. Isaac Hawkins Brown*, by William Hay; and *Another translation of Mr. Browne's poem*, by Dr. Grey. Each of these has something that is reminiscent of Johnson, the third more strongly than the other two. Possibly, too, the review of number 42, a pastoral elegy in memory of the Rt. Hon. Henry Pelham, with its obvious sarcasm at the expense of the pastoral convention, will be thought worthy of consideration. While the author of this elegy on Pelham was anonymous, the author of "Verses to the memory of Mr. Pelham," reviewed in April (number 17, on p. 193), saw no reason not to acknowledge his hand. Colley Cibber, for it was he, had better left his name off this specimen of his powers, however, for the reviewer was terse and merciless: "The publick is too well acquainted with this writer to need a specimen of his performance, and to consider it as the subject of criticism would be to forget his age and his odes." There is an expertness of execution here that I would not put beyond Johnson.

Suspicion that one review is Johnson's sometimes necessitates further suspicion that a companion review is also his. This is true of numbers 42 and 43 in the April list. The first, a review of *The history of Pudica, a lady of N-rf-k*, reads: "This is a rhapsody of private scandal, too dull to excite mirth, and too obscure to gratify curiosity. It is not adapted to any passion but malice, and can neither please those who read for vicious or virtuous purposes." Despite the abruptness of the end, I think this close to Johnson's style. If it is his, the undistinguished one-sentence review of *A letter . . . . with observations on the history of Pudica* is probably his too.

The following month's list contains two reviews, numbers 15 and 21, which could be Johnson's. The first (p. 245) concerns itself with *Pomery Hill*, a poem with a preface which first attracts the reviewer:

> To these poems is prefixed a dissertation on the excellencies and defects of our language, and the structure of verse, which the author proposes to render more harmonious, by taking some liberties which he confesses are without precedent. What knowledge he has of propriety, and what ear for music may easily be determined from the quotations that follow.

Several infelicitous experiments are illustrated and, by their very selection and the tone of the introductory comments, criticized. The reviewer concludes in the same ironic vein:

> The quotation of these passages has made the article too long, but it would have been injurious to suppress what has been exhibited to improve and harmonize our language and versification, and elaborately defended with a great parade of critical knowledge and a fine ear.

The second review is largely a resumé of a piece, described earlier (April, p. 193) as "a dramatic tale," entitled *Narcissa and Eliza*. Even though there is no criticism, I think the review Johnson's.

Only the review of *The Day of Doom* catches the eye in the June list of books (p. 295). The reviewer opens with:

> The author tells us in his preface, that his motive to write a poem on the last day was to prevent further talk about Elizabeth Canning. It has been said, that in the productions of the worst writer there is something to commend, and in those of the best, something to blame; it will appear from the following extract, that this piece is not free from grammar faults, and yet, that it is not destitute of poetical sentiments, or harmony of numbers.

He then quotes twenty-odd lines of the poem and ends with a single sentence:

> In these verses, though the metaphors are pure, and the epithets in general well chosen, yet *a power* is called *vicegerents*, and expres'd by *they*; and locking up nations in *eternal* frost is represented as a repeated act.

All this I find Johnsonian.

In August (p. 390) the review of *The Day of Judgment*, "a poem, in two books", is almost certainly by Johnson. After an introductory sentence and quotation of some forty lines from the poem, the reviewer proceeds to the actual criticism:

> This extract is sufficient to shew that poetical imagination is not wanting, and that the versification is remarkably good: But the descriptions frequently become languid, meerly by their diffusion, and sometimes disgust by an anti-climax.

> After describing a deluge of fire swelling to the tops of the
> highest hills, the sea exhausted of water, the central fire burst-
> ing out, and the Alps and Andes in a blaze, the period is closed
> with this exclamation,
>
> ———— amazing change ! alike unknown
> Where Nassau fought, or godlike Marlb'rough shone.
>
> With respect to this subject, the poet is certainly under in-
> superable disadvantages, for it immediately fills the mind with
> ideas, of which his most labour'd descriptions must always
> fall short: Neither can his subject receive any dignity from
> these arts which dignify every other; Similies in particular
> must always rather degrade than elevate. Our idea of the
> shock of two armies is heightened by comparing it to thunder
> or an earthquake; but sure the contrary must happen, when
> the re-assemblage of all the scattered parts of the human
> race, from the earth, the air, and the sea, at the general resur-
> rection, is compared with Raphael Urbin's painting a picture;
> and the littleness of this incident becomes in some degree
> ridiculous, when the painter, upon this occasion, is called
> *great Raphael* and his picture a *vast* design.

The views on the treatment of religious subjects in poetry and on the folly
of trying to embellish such subjects with figurative language are those held
by Johnson.

There is a bare possibility that in September (p. 439) Johnson reviewed
Barbadoes, a poem by a Mr. Weekes, another of whose pieces, appearing
in the March *GM* this year, the reviewer mentions. The review of *Barbadoes*
is sarcastic in a manner of which Johnson is capable but to lengths which I
feel he might not have gone. Whoever reviewed *Barbadoes* also reviewed the
earlier piece, *The Choice of an Husband* (p. 146); the kind of sarcasm employed
is identical. The December number of the *GM* contains three reviews which,
largely by style, I would ascribe to Johnson in the following descending order
of assurance:

1. — Number 26, *A Dissertation upon Genius*, by W. Sharpe (pp. 581-2).
Although this is almost wholly a resumé of the work's contents, this conclusion struck me as Johnsonian: "Upon the whole, this work appears to be
the production of a busy mind, secluded from books and conversation; and
this indeed, which is the author's apology, will, upon his own principles,
account for the want of precision and perspicuity; for the singularity of
opinion, and inaccuracy of expression."

2. — Number 10, *A descriptive poem*, by Mr. Dalton. It will be remembered that in his *Life of Cowley* Johnson had said that "a coalpit has not *often* [my italics] found its poet." He may have remembered Mr. Dalton's poem when he was writing the *Life of Cowley*, for the sentence that smacked of Johnson to me was: "A coal mine is perhaps the only subject which descriptive poetry has not exhausted, and the difficulty of representing images, to which poetical words have not already been adapted, is abundantly compensated by the advantages which they derive from novelty, the curiosity which they excite, and the new knowledge which they communicate."

3. — Number 31, *Miscellanies in prose and verse*, by C. Hallifax (pp. 582-3). I hear, or think I hear, a clear echo of a Johnsonian phrase, which now eludes me, in the latter part of this sentence from the review: "The pretence of uttering 20 or 30 verses extempore, is always the pretence of a dunce, who does not know that he assumes a power which no man possesses." The next sentence, too, is one Johnson might have written: "It is the fraud of those whom folly has rendered arrogant, and ignorance has made fearless of detection" (p. 582).

1755

The possible traces of Johnson's presence in the *GM* for this year are few. I would suppose that at some period after the death of Cave, his brother-in-law, David Henry, took over the *GM* and hired John Hawkesworth as co-editor. There is at least one contemporary reference which implies that these two men were directing the periodical in 1756.[8] I suppose further that Johnson undertook the lion's share, if not all, of the handling of the *GM* in 1754 and then continued to help the new editors in the first three or four months of 1755, for I find nothing remotely Johnsonian beyond the April number for 1755, with the one exception discussed immediately below.

What little I would call attention to in this year, then, is the appearance of "An Account of the best foreign Books, continued from our Supplement to 1754" in the September number (p. 430) and a few notices in the regular monthly list of books published in England. Since the "Account of the best foreign Books" is a continuation of similar accounts in which I believe Johnson may have had a hand, it too must be considered with the

---

(8) C.L. Carlson, *The First Magazine* (Providence, R.I., 1938), p. 22n. Nichols, *Literary Anecdotes*, III, 423 says Henry first became a partner in the *GM* in 1754.

others. The notices of foreign books continue in 1756 (March, pp. 137-8)
and 1757 (Supplement, pp. 606-7); I have arbitrarily set 1757 as the *terminus
ad quem* of this aspect of my investigation as there seems little hope of establishing precisely Johnson's part in these lists. As far as the notices go, I find
it difficult, almost impossible, to see anybody but Johnson writing the following, which I quote in full:

> 30. Select epitaphs; collected by W. Toldervey. Dodsley,
> Millar. — In the preface to this collection it is said to have
> been undertaken principally, 'to rescue the names and accom-
> plishments of the great and good, who have gone before us
> from oblivion,' many of whose monuments are either mould-
> ring into ruin, or by their situation known but to few, or per-
> haps not inscribed at all. The editor, therefore, consistently
> with this view, has published only *translations* of those epi-
> taphs which are not in English, as English in this country is
> more generally understood: He has also published many
> epitaphs, which were only *intended* for the persons whom
> they celebrate, and not inscribed on any monuments erected
> to their memory. This collection is also recommended as an
> epitome of the history of great persons, and a specimen of the
> manner of writing in successive ages: But as writers of
> epitaphs have always supposed themselves at liberty to sup-
> press every failing, and generally to exaggerate every virtue,
> they must certainly be wretched materials for history, of which
> the very essence is truth; neither can the manner of writing be
> discerned thro' a translation, however accurate. But in this
> collection of memorials of the *great* and *good*, many are to be
> found of those whom neither rank, fortune, or virtue have
> distinguished; *children*, of whose parents posterity will know
> nothing but that they were human beings; and others, of whom
> the very name is not preserved with the epitaph; so that as
> they record nothing which is not common to all, except moral
> perfection, to which the dead have a prescriptive right, they
> may at any time be appropriated without alteration. There
> are, however, in these volumes, many elegant compositions,
> and most of the translations are such as do honour to our
> language.

The style is Johnson's; the sentiments on epitaphs and on history are his.

The list of books for January contains another notice (p. 47) which has
almost equal right as that on *Select Epitaphs* to be considered Johnson's.
The book is Zachariah Williams' *Account of an Attempt to Ascertain the
Longitude*, nominally by Miss Anna Williams' father, but actually written

by Johnson himself. Half the notice is original, half is quotation from the work. The work is praised, and praised in language reminiscent of Johnson's. In February, p. 93, the rather full account of *A New English Translation of the Psalms from the Original Hebrew* may be by Johnson. The discussion of metre in the Psalms is in language which renders a decision on authorship most hazardous. Only one notice in the April list may be by Johnson, that on *The History of Margaret of Anjou, Q. of England*, "a translation from the French of the Abbé Prévost." I quote in full:

> This is a narrative of events so extraordinary as to excite perpetual wonder, and so supported as almost to compel belief: The distress, tho' it is that of the great, is yet of the domestic kind, such as every man has felt, tho' not in the same degree, and such as every imagination therefore can so far realize as to pursue with the most interested curiosity, and participate with excess of pity.

The remark on "domestic fable" accords nicely with Johnson's views.

That last notice that demands scrutiny is of a work listed in March (p. 143); the full title is *An Essay towards a Translation of Homer's Work, in Blank Verse, with Notes*, by Joseph Nichol Scott, M.D. I have no hesitation about claiming this review for Johnson. The first sentence reads: "It appears by this performance that the author has not considered, that all translations are intended chiefly for those who cannot read the original; and therefore, that the relative beauty, which might be perceived upon a comparison of the English with the Greek resulting from the exact correspondence of the copy with the original, cannot be a general recommendation." Compare Johnson: "Translations are, in general, for people who cannot read the original" (*Life*, III, 256). "Besides," the reviewer continues, "if the Iliad and Odyssey had been written in prose, it is probable, that they would long since have been forgotten; and therefore, if they are not decorated with the same poetical ornaments in the translation, they will lose their power in awkwardness and insipidity, and the English reader, instead of reading the sentiments with the rapture that fired the translator, will wonder how the work on which he has bestowed so much labour came to be admired." Not only does this closely coincide with Johnson's views on translation, it also anticipates a remark he was to make in later years when somebody expressed a desire to see a translation of the *Iliad* in "poetical prose." "Sir," returned Johnson, "you could not read it without the pleasure of verse." (*Life* III, 333). The reviewer goes on to say that "the first care of a translator should be to give his work the air of an original, to divest it of all the peculiarities of the language in which it was first written, and recommend it by the beauties of his own." Again, all this is consonant with Johnson's views on translation, particularly with his statement that "the great difficulty of a translator is to preserve the native form of his language, and the unconstrained manner of an original writer" (*Works*, Oxford, 1825, VI, 78). The reviewer devotes a sentence to Pope's translation, "In this respect, Mr. Pope's version has left no room for another, and a thousand mistakes in the sense can never degrade it as an English poem, or much lessen the pleasure with which it is read by an English reader of quick sensation and a true taste," and then compares a passage in both Scott's and Pope's versions. Johnson's opinion of Pope's translation of Homer, expressed in his *Life of Pope*, is precisely that of the reviewer — as it should be, since, as I have confidently stated, he was the reviewer.

Johnson's close connection with the *GM* came to end with the 1754 volume, but he may, as I have indicated, have written a very few book notices up to April, 1755. A year later he undertook the direction of a new venture, the *Literary Magazine*, writing practically the whole contents of that periodical for several months, beginning with the first number, April 15 to May 15.(9) At some time in this period he must have been approached by the projectors of the new periodical and may even have done some preliminary work for it. Whatever his activities in this period from April 1755 to April 1756 and on to the end of that year, I am almost positive that he had no hand in the *GM*. Indeed, the *GM* for 1756 is a very messy affair, with the new editor, or editors, trying new arrangements of the contents and giving more emphasis to certain features than had been accorded them before. One of these was the book review section which, appearing in its usual place as the penultimate section in the periodical in January and February, was shifted to a more prominent place for the months of March through August (except July, when there was none), and then put back to its original place for the rest of the year. What is more, a great deal more space was devoted to the book review section in the first eight months of this year, the May list covering eight pages, for example, and some individual reviews taking up one or two whole pages. But when the section was

---

(9) See D.J. Greene, *RES*, 1956, on the whole question of the extent of Johnson's contributions to the *Literary Magazine*.

shifted back to its original position in September, and for the rest of the year, it was accorded precisely one page made up of virtually nothing but titles. The reviewer, or reviewers, favored opening expressions such as "This is," "The author," "These observations," etc., and one can observe a change in interest, with books on trade and on politics being given fuller treatment. Occasionally, a play is reviewed in this section and extracts are quoted.

One other feature of the *GM* suffered this year. This was the section on "Foreign History." It was in July that the first "Foreign History" section appeared; for some inexplicable reason there was none in the first six months. While there was a "Foreign History" in the September number the fact was somehow omitted in the table of contents for that month, an omission that was certainly exceedingly rare, if not unique. And then, too, as with the book review section, the editor had trouble deciding where he wanted the "Foreign History" to appear regularly, for its position was shifted about in this year. Finally, the July and August "Foreign Histories" were limited to a fairly straight-forward account covering one page each; in the remaining four months the section received a very generous and unchanging four pages, allowing the writer to expatiate rather freely. One conclusion seems inevitable: when Cave died at the beginning of 1754 Johnson took over the *GM* and ran it for about fifteen months until the new editors, Henry and Hawkesworth, replaced him. Presumably they were content to continue the periodical in its traditional format for the remainder of 1755 but began experimenting with it in 1756. If Johnson played the part of advisor in 1755, it is almost a certainty, from the evidence I have just presented, that he had entirely withdrawn from the *GM* in every capacity by the beginning of 1756. Although he was Hawkesworth's friend until the latter's death and also very friendly with John Nichols, the next editor of the *GM*, until his own death, he never again took a prominent part in the affairs of the periodical. (10)

MICHIGAN STATE UNIVERSITY.

---

(10) Jacob Leed's "Two Notes on Johnson and the *Gentleman's Magazine*, *PBSA*, 54 (1960), 101-110, appeared after I had completed this article, it strengthens the case for J's hand in the Foreign Books section of the *GM* in the 1740's. I add here, as afterthoughts, that Johnson revised his translation of Pope's *Messiah*, originally appearing in 1731, for the *GM* in 1752; that a poem, *The Vanity of Wealth*, in the *GM* for 1750 is thought by some to be J's; and that in October, 1750 issue of the *GM* there is what appears to be an attempt to list Johnson's biographical contributions to that periodical (see *PMLA*, 1959, p. 84, n. 4).

J. E. CONGLETON

James Thomson Callender, Johnson and Jefferson

Because of the uncertainty of the authorship of two of his early productions, the similarity between the early career of James Thomson Callender in Great Britain and his final career in America has usually been overlooked. In the early 1780's two anonymous pamphlets unrestrainedly and hilariously ridiculing Johnson were published — the *Deformities of Dr. Samuel Johnson. Selected from his Works*, 1782, and *A Critical Review of the Works of Dr. Samuel Johnson*, 1783. (¹) These pamphlets are now rare; and often, if not always, in library catalogs attributed to John Callander of Craigforth.

Not mentioned by Boswell, the second of these publications has attracted little consideration from the students of Johnson; nor have they been concerned about who wrote it. The *Deformities*, on the other hand, introduced by Boswell,(²) has often come under their view, and considerable

---

(1) There were two editions of the first of these pamphlets and three of the second: (1) *Deformities of Dr Samuel Johnson. Selected from his Works.* Edinburgh: Printed for the Author; and sold by W. Creech. And T. Longman, and J. Stockdale, London, 1782. — Second Edition. London: Printed for the Author; and sold by J. Stockdale; and W. Creech, Edinburgh, 1782. (2) *A Critical Review of the Works of Dr Samuel Johnson, Containing A Particular Vindication of Several Eminent Characters.* Edinburgh: Printed for J. Dickson, and W. Creech, 1783. — Second Edition. London. Printed for the Author, and sold by T. Cadell and J. Stockdale; at Edinburgh, by J. Dickson and W. Creech, 1783. — Another issue. London: Printed for R. Rusted, 1787.

(2) *Life of Johnson*, ed. G.B. Hill; rev., L.F. Powell (Oxford, 1934-1950), IV, 148.

information about its authorship has been brought to light. The evidence now available, when assembled, is highly convincing, perhaps conclusive, that James Thomson Callender is the chief instigator, if not the sole author, of these defamatory tracts.

For his intemperate views in *The Political Progress of Britain, or An Impartial Account of the Principal Abuses in the Government of this Country from the Revolution in 1688*, published in 1792, Callender was indicted for sedition in Edinburgh, whence he fled to America. Until 1796 he was a reporter of Congressional debates for the Philadelphia *Gazette*. With *The History of the United States for 1796; Including a Variety of Particulars Relative to the Federal Government Previous to that Period*,[3] 1797, he began to exercise his genius as a scandalmonger, which reached muck bottom in his attacks in the Richmond *Recorder* on Thomas Jefferson.

To establish that James Thomson Callender was the author of the *Deformities* and *A Critical Review* would illuminate his activities on both sides of the Atlantic. Students of Johnson have, as mentioned above, frequently noticed the ridicule in the *Deformities*, but they have seldom, if ever, detailed Callender's turbulent career in America. Similarly, students of American history have studied Callender's attacks on several early Americans, especially those on Thomas Jefferson; but they have been completely unaware, it seems, that the pamphleteer who wrote them may have begun his career by belittling Samuel Johnson.

The anonymous author of the *Deformities* reveals "the circumstances which gave it birth": William Shaw, author of *An Analysis of the Galic Language*, a "few months ago ... printed a pamphlet. He vilified decent characters. He denied the existence of Gaelic poetry, and his name was echoed in the newspaper as a miracle of candour." [4] Johnson was "the patron of this poor scribble." Therefore "the Doctor stands convicted of an *illiberal intention to deceive*." As punishment for this conviction the *Deformities* was prepared.

The *Deformities* has little, if any, plan, the author's strategy being to sting Johnson on every vulnerable spot. Johnson is guilty of "invidious and revengeful" remarks about Chesterfield; he fails to appreciate Gray — whose

---

(3) Note the similarity of this title with that of *The Political Progress*, its British counterpart.

(4) P. 61.

admiration for Macpherson "put him (to use his own words) *half mad*"; his remarks about many writers — Milton, Dryden, Arbuthnot, Swift, *et al.* — are prejudiced and contradictory, stupid even.

As *The Gentleman's Magazine* observed, the anonymous author, sensitive to criticism of Scotland, took violent exception to several of Johnson's comments in the recently published *Tour*. Also he is always on the defensive for Gaelic poetry — or the lack of it; Whitaker's attack, in his *History of Manchester*, on Johnson's neglect of his Gaelic sources is applauded; but Shaw's denial, in his *Analysis*, of the existence of Gaelic poetry is "without parallel ... in the annals of Grubean impudence."(5)

But the greater part of the sixty-two page pamphlet is directed at the *Dictionary*. It begins, for example, by pointing out that Johnson's admirers believe his *Dictionary* "to be the most capital monument of human genius. The studies of Archimedes and Newton are but a feather in the scale with this amazing work." But his "*malignity*," it continues, is so great as displayed in such definitions as those for "Excise, Gazeteer, and Pension" that "he would, in Queen Anne's reign, have had a fair chance of mounting the pillory." Interlarded throughout the sixty-three page diatribe are the *Dictionary*'s "wild blunders and risible absurdities" (as Johnson good humoredly labelled them); Definitions which are Latinized — "Window. 'An *aperture* in a building by which air and light are *intromitted.* ";(6) definitions which are empty — "Man. '1. Human being.   2. Not a woman.   3. Not a boy' ";(7) definitions which are circular — "fiddler. ... 'A musician, one that plays upon a fiddle' ";(8) definitions which are ribald — a list of seven naughty words, such as those unfound by the ladies to whom Johnson said, "What my dears! then you have been looking for them."(9) The definitions of terms in music, poetry, biology, anatomy expose Johnson's lack of learning. And the anonymous author concludes with the broad declaration that he "has attempted to illustrate" Johnson's "covetous and shameless prolixity — his corruption of our language — his very limited literature — his entire want of general

---

(5) LII (September 1782), 439.

(6) P. 25.

(7) P. 28.

(8) P. 29.

(9) [Henry Digby Beste], *Personal and Literary Memorials* (London 1829), p. 12.

learning — his antipathy to rival merit — his paralytick reasoning — his adherence to contradictions — his defiance of decency — his contempt for truth. . . . To collect every particle of *inanity* which may be found in our *patriot's* work is infinitely beyond the limits of a shilling pamphlet. We stop at the present, but the subject seems *inexhaustible*."[10]

Johnson, laughing off the *Deformities*, wrote Boswell on March 28, 1782, " 'The Beauties of Johnson' are said to have got money to the collector; if the 'Deformities' have the same success, I shall be still a more extensive benefactor. "[11] There is no record, it seems, of his opinion of *A Critical Review*. Even in the face of such reckless ridicule, Johnson was still content to leave his animadversions on Hanway's attack "the only instance," Boswell believed, "in the whole course of his life, when he condescended to oppose any thing that was written against him."[12]

A Critical Review, though ostensibly divided into ten sections, is as rambling as the *Deformities*. The anonymous author declares that he is "often at a loss which to admire most, the folly of" Johnson's "censures or the violence of his contradictions."[13] With this strategy declared, he goes through the *Rambler* and *Lives* and collects passages which he thinks he can make to seem foolish or contradictory — statements, among others, about Prior, Congreve, Swift, Gray, Pope, Milton, Thomson, Churchill, Chesterfield; he defends the "translator of Fingal," and heaps sarcasm on Johnson's "glorious affability, when in Scotland"; Section V deplores Johnson's "ridiculous censure of the fair sex"; Sections VIII and IX, in the self-same manner of the *Deformities*, ridicule the *Dictionary*. In the "Introduction" the author declares that, "from the wilderness of flowers that blossom" in the Doctor's "Immortal Dictionary," he plans "to gather a garland for his venerable brow."[13]

There can be little, if any, doubt that the *Deformities* and *A Critical Review* have a common origin. The paper, type, and make-up of the title-page indicate that they were issued from the same press. In the "Introduction" of *A Critical Review* the statement is made that "The author of the present

---

(10) Pp. 62-63.
(11) *Life of Johnson*, IV, 149.
(12) *Ibid.*, I, 314.
(13) P. 10.

trifle was last year induced to publish a few remarks on the writings of Dr Samuel Johnson. ... Like the former essay, these pages will endeavour to ascertain the genuine importance of Dr Johnson's literary character." In notes on pages 19, 37, 55, and 63 the *Deformities* is cited. Moreover the tell-tale word "deformities" appears in the text at least three times (pages 31, 43, and 50), the last time with a capital *D*. Is James Thomson Callender the author of the *Deformities* and *A Critical Review?* If he is, they light up the background of Callender's pamphleteering in America.

An attempt to identify the author of the *Deformities* was made by George Steevens when it appeared. In a letter to William Cole, 14 May 1782, he says that it was "written by a Club of Caledonian Wits."(14) *The Gentleman's Magazine* for September 1782, "reciting the circumstance" of the origin of the *Deformities*, contends that it is a revenge pamphlet inspired by *An Analysis of the Galic Language* by William Shaw ("Nadir" Shaw, in the *Deformities*), who "denied the existence of Gaelic poetry; and THEREFORE this Essayist, 'by fair and copious quotations from Dr. Johnson's ponderous performances, has attempted to illustrate' " his " 'prolixity,' " " 'corrupt language,' " " 'pedantry,' "(15) etc...

In February 1783, *The Monthly Review* briefly noted:

> This seems to be the production of some ingenious angry Scotchman, who has taken great pains to prove, what all the world knows, that there are many exceptionable passages in the writings of Dr. Johnson. There are, however, few spots in this literary luminary now pointed out that have not been discovered before. So that the present map must be considered rather as a monument to the delineator's malignity, than of his wit. — His *personalities* seem to indicate personal provocation; though perhaps it may well be all pure nationality. (16)

Though Boswell mentions the pamphlet and quotes a letter in which Johnson comments on it, neither he nor any of his editors before L.F. Powell try to identify the incensed author. In 1815 Robert Anderson said that

---

(14) Brit. Mus. Addit. MS. 6401, f. 175 *r*. Part of this letter is quoted by L.F. Powell in Boswell's *Life of Johnson*, IV, 499.

(15) LII, 439.

(16) LXVIII, 185.

the *Deformities* "is the production of Mr. Thomson Callender, nephew of the poet."[17]

When the *Deformities* was cataloged in the Bodleian in 1834,[18] it was attributed to John Callander of Craigforth. In *A Critical Review of the Works of Dr Samuel Johnson*, 1783, the statement is made that "Mr. Callander of Craigforth ... observes" that " 'Had the laborious Johnson been better acquainted with the oriental tongues, or had he understood the first rudiments of the northern languages from which the English and Scots derive their origin, his bulky volumes had not presented to us the melancholy truth, that unwearied industry, *devoid of settled principles*, avails only to add one error to another.' "[19] This blast, which is taken from the "Introduction" to Callander's *Two Ancient Scottish Poems, The Gaberlunzie Man and Christ's Kirk on the Green*, Edinburgh, 1782, may well have been the evidence that caused *A Critical Review* to be attributed to John Callander of Craigforth; then, because of the interconnections between it and the *Deformities* and because of their convincing similarity, the *Deformities* was also assigned to him. On the other hand, one might argue that the quoting from John Callander in *A Critical Review* should have been conclusive evidence for the Bodleian that he was not the author.

When the *Deformities* and *A Critical Review* were cataloged in the British Museum, in 1854 and 1862, they were likewise attributed to John Callander of Craigforth.[20] In 1915, Courtney and Smith seemed to doubt that John Callander wrote them; for, they noticed, "strangely enough no mention of them is made by Robert Chambers in his memoirs of Callander."[21] The *Catalogue of Printed Books in the Edinburgh University Library*, 1918,

---

(17) *Life of Samuel Johnson, LL.D. With Critical Observations on His Works* (Edinburgh, 1815, Third edition), p. 231. Of Callender's career in America, Anderson says only that "he was appointed reporter to Congress, and died a few years ago."

(18) There is no copy of *A Critical Review* in the Bodleian.

(19) P. 4.

(20) Most libraries, it seems, have followed the lead of the Bodleian in attributing the *Deformities* and (by comparison) *A Critical Review* to John Callander of Craigforth. In addition to the Bodleian and the British Museum, I have checked the New York Public, Pierpont Morgan, Yale, and University of Michigan libraries.

(21) William P. Courtney amd D. Nichol Smith, *A Bibliography of Samuel Johnson* (Oxford, 1915. Reissued with facsimiles, 1925), p. 136.

assigns *A Critical Review* to John Callander; it does not list the *Deformities*. Arthur G. Kennedy, in *A Bibliography of Writings on the English Language*, 1927, attributes the *Deformities* to John Callander; he lists the 1787 issue of *A Critical Review* as anonymous. In *A Dictionary of Anonymous and Pseudonymous English Literature*, 1926-1932, Halkett and Laing assign *A Critical Review* to John Callander on the authority of the British Museum; the *Deformities* also to John Callander on authority of a note by Chalmers in 1782.

No doubt, having followed the suspicion he expressed in 1915, and having ascertained the author, D. Nichol Smith, in the *CBEL Bibliography*, 1941, attributed both items to J.T. Callander, listing both editions of the *Deformities* in 1782 and both editions of *A Critical Review* in 1783. He does not mention the 1787 issue of *A Critical Review*. Finally L.F. Powell, *primus editorum*, in his revision of G.B. Hill's edition of Boswell's *Life* quoted from a letter by James Thomson Callender to John Stockdale, 4 October 1783, which says: "I will be greatly obliged to you, for delivering the remaining Copies of Deformities of Johnson to the bearer, and sending me his Receipt for them."[22] Dr. Powell thinks that this letter "shows" that Callender "was the author of the book."[23]

The information in this letter, Anderson's identification, a fairly plausible reason why the *Deformities* was so long attributed to John Callander, Steevens' suggestion of communal authorship, the similarity of the styles and contents of the two works, and the parallel circumstances of publication point to a reasonably safe conclusion that the *Deformities* and *A Critical Review* were written by a club of Caledonian wits, the chief spark of which was James Thomson Callender.

Recent studies of the history of the *Dictionary* have not added any information about the author of these satires. In "The Critical Reception of Johnson's *Dictionary* in the Latter Eighteenth Century,"[24] Gertrude Noyes, though she considers both publications, neither goes beyond the usual bibliographical sources nor speculates on the ability, background, or purpose of the author. In *Dr. Johnson's 'Dictionary,'* Sledd and Kolb, though

---

(22) Hyde Collection. See the *R.B. Adam Library*, III, 48.

(23) *Life*, IV, 499. Dr. Powell, like Robert Anderson, says that James Thomson Callender was a nephew of the poet Thomson, and gives the *DNB* as the source of his information. I cannot find the statement in the *DNB*.

(24) *Modern Philology*, LII (February 1955), 175-191.

they quote twice from the *Deformities,* say nothing about who wrote it, albeit their quotations would have been more pertinent had they established the reputation of the author.([25]) Without attempting to identify or characterize the author, W.K. Wimsatt, in his reply to Keast's review of his *Philosophic Words,* uses a passage of the *Deformities* to support his rebuttal. ([26])

Callender's pamphleteering in America, likewise, was extraordinarily vehement, even for a Scotch master of scurrility in the time of Peter Porcupine. A fugitive from Edinburgh, he arrived in Philadelphia in 1793. Jefferson, thinking Callender was a genius suffering persecution and, quite naturally, impressed with his *Political Progress of Britain,* contributed to his support. The life-and-death struggle between the Federalists and the Republicans was shaping up, and Callender soon joined the battle. Before it was over, the imbroglio had involved, or demanded the attention of, several of the most eminent men of the new republic — Washington, Adams, Monroe, Chase, Marshall, but most seriously Hamilton and Jefferson.

By 1797, Callender had secured information which enabled him to embarrass Hamilton. He published a letter by F.A. Muhlenberg, Speaker of the House, which declared that Jacob Clingman, a clerk employed by Muhlenberg, and one James Reynolds had "applied to me, for my aid and friendship, on behalf of himself and Reynolds" to secure a release

> from ... a charge ... for subornation or perjury, whereby they had obtained money from the treasury of the United States ... During the time this business was thus depending ... Clingman, *unasked,* frequently dropped hints to me, that Reynolds *had it in his power, very materially to injure the Secretary of the Treasury;* and that Reynolds knew several very improper transactions of his ... it was frequently added, that Reynolds said, *he had it in his power to hang the Secretary of the Treasury;* that he had frequently advanced money to him ... and other insinuations of an improper nature.([27])

---

(25) James H. Sledd and Gwin J. Kolb. *Dr. Johnson's 'Dictionary': Essays in the Biography of a Book.* Chicago: University of Chicago Press, 1955.

(26) *Philological Quarterly,* XXIX (April 1950), 88.

(27) *The History of the United States for 1796: Including a Variety of Particulars Relative to the Federal Government Previous to that Period* (Philadelphia, 1797), pp. 209-210. Quoted from Microcard Edition, ES 1427-1433.

Five years earlier, Muhlenberg, Senator Monroe, and Representative Abraham Venable had confronted Hamilton, then Secretary of the Treasury, with the rumor that he, involved with Reynolds, "was deeply concerned in speculation." Hamilton was able to convince them that he was a victim of blackmail of Reynolds' making. After Callender's exposé, however, Hamilton could not avoid a public explanation. His first plan was to ask his inquisitors to assert that they had seen the documents and that Callender was lying. Chiefly because of the reluctance of Monroe — no friend of Hamilton's — this plan to vindicate himself failed. In fact, Hamilton felt that Monroe was looking for further evidence with which to ruin him. There was talk of, and preliminary arrangements for, a duel. But Hamilton came to the conclusion that he would have to sacrifice his private reputation to clear his public actions. So he calmly wrote:

> The charge against me is a connection with one James Reynolds for purpose of improper pecuniary speculation. My real crime is an amorous connection with his wife for a considerable time, with his privity and connivance, if not originally brought on by a combination between the husband and wife with the design to extort money from me.[28]

Callender had scored his first great success as a scandalmonger.

His next targets were also Federalists. Under the secret patronage of Jefferson, Callender, in *The Prospect before Us*, 1800, assailed Adams and Washington. Among other charges, he declared that Adams is fomenting a war with France and "yoking us into an alliance with the British tyrant,"[29] wants to "curb the frontier population," and has heaped myriads of dollars upon William Smith ... a paper jobber who next to Hamilton himself is perhaps the most detested character on the continent." Also Adams is a "hoary headed incendiary," and, to cap his crime, a "professed aristocrat." Some charges in which Callender lashes through Adams to his predecessor, Washington, afford an example of his vituperation:

---

(28) David Loth, *Alexander Hamilton: Portrait of a Prodigy* (New York, [1939]), p. 249.

(29) "Trial of James Thomson Callender, for Sedition, on Tuesday the third of June, 1800." Richmond, (1804). Copy taken from the *Virginia Gazette*, July-August 1800. Quoted from Microcard Edition, ES 770-771.

The system of persecution has extended all over the continent, every person holding an office must either quit it, or think and vote exactly with Adams. ... Adams and Washington, have since been shaping these jobbers into Judges and Ambassadors. As their whole courage lies in want of shame, these poltroons, without risking a manly and intelligent defence of their own measures, raise an affected yelp against the corruption of the French directory; as if any corruption could be more venal, more notorious, more execrated, than their own. ...(30) Mr. Adams has only compleated the scene of ignominy, which Mr. Washington began. ... The last presidential felony will be buried by Congress in the same criminal silence as its predecessors.(31)

Callender ends his diatribe, "Take your choice then, between Adams, war and beggery and Jefferson, peace and competency."

Because of his remarks about Adams he was tried under the Sedition Law, fined $200, and sent to prison for nine months. While in prison he wrote two fiery pamphlets for which Jefferson advanced money under ambiguous terms.

Soon after Jefferson took office, Judge Samuel Chase, a staunch Federalist, was impeached for his bullying tactics, particularly in his conduct of Callender's trial. As a witness John Marshall, though another staunch Federalist, was forced to admit that Chase's rulings on at least four points of procedure in the trial were unheard of in legal procedure. Chase was not convicted, but his conduct led to a reform of the judicial system.

Jefferson pardoned Callender (and all others convicted under the unwise Sedition Law), and Callender's fine was remitted. But Callender was not satisfied; he wanted to be postmaster of Richmond. Jefferson refused to appoint him, in spite of the tone of blackmail which now pervaded his importunities. Soon he turned his political coat and was editing the most scurrilous anti-Jefferson paper in the country, to the infinite delight of the Federalists, who immediately circulated this erstwhile rag far and wide — even to the rarefied atmosphere of Beacon Hill.

---

(30) *Ibid.*, p. 11.

(31) *Ibid.*, p. 13.

Callender accused Jefferson of dishonesty and cowardice, but malice inspired his most injurious charges:

> It is well known that the man, *whom it delighted the people to honor*, keeps ... as his concubine, one of his own slaves. Her name is Sally. The name of her eldest son is Tom. His features are said to bear a striking resemblance to those of the president himself. ... By this wench Sally, our President has had several children. There is not an individual in the neighborhood of Charlottesville who does not believe the story; and not a few who *know it*. ... Behold the favorite ! the first born of republicanism ! the pinnacle of all that is good and great ! ... If the friends of Mr. Jefferson are convinced of *his* innocence, they will make an appeal. ... If they rest in silence, or if they content themselves with resting upon a *general denial,* they cannot hope for credit. The allegation is of a nature too *black* to be suffered to remain in suspense. We should be glad to hear of its refutation. We give it to the world under the firmest belief that such a refutation *never can be made.* The AFRICAN VENUS is said to officiate as housekeeper at Monticello. When Mr. Jefferson has read this article, he will find leisure to estimate how much has been lost or gained by so many unprovoked attacks upon J.T. Callender.[32]

Who had scored his most sensational hit as a scandalmonger.

Despite the fact that much of the *Recorder* is Billingsgate diatribe, such accusations left on Jefferson, as similar charges had left on Hamilton, a stain which can never be entirely effaced.

Callender's ignominious end came on July 17, 1803. *The Gentleman's Magazine* declared that he, "after experiencing many varieties of fortune as Iscariot Hackney ... drowned himself ... in James river"; [33] the coroner's jury, however, declared that his death was accidental, following intoxication.

These particulars of Callender's activities in America, removed from the *Deformities* and *A Critical Review* by two decades, provide an enlightening foreground to these early efforts of spleen.

---

(32) From the Richmond *Recorder*. As printed in the New York *Evening Post*, September 10, 1802. Quoted from *Jefferson Reader*, ed. Francis Coleman Rosenberger (New York, 1953), pp. 109-111.

(33) LXXIII (September 1803), 882.

Callender, it would seem, at least deserves a hearing. Did he possess extraordinary talents of a kind, as Jefferson on the basis of his *Political Progress of Britain* believed ? Or did most of his writings delineate rather his "malignity, than his wit" ? May one find in his turbulent career that he is consistently a champion of political justice ? Or was he "Iscariot Hackney" ? Is his criticism of Johnson, in part at least, valid ? Or is it "scurrilous and witless" ?[34] Those who answer these, and similar, questions will give added perspective to their accounts by connecting Callender's activities on both sides of the Atlantic — whether they are interpreting the charges against Jefferson in the Richmond *Recorder* or evaluating the *Deformities of Dr Samuel Johnson*.

FINDLAY COLLEGE,

OHIO.

---

(34) See L.F. Powell, Boswell's *Life of Johnson*, IV, 500.

JOYCE HEMLOW

Dr. Johnson and Fanny Burney— Some Additions To The Record

We shall go down hand in hand to posterity.

— SAMUEL JOHNSON TO FANNY BURNEY

Fanny Burney has sometimes been blamed for rot acceding to Boswell's request for information about Dr. Johnson.[1]

> "Yes, madam; you must give me some of your choice little notes of the Doctor's; we have seen him long enough upon stilts; I want to show him in a new light. Grave Sam, and great Sam, and solemn Sam, and learned Sam — all these he has appeared over and over. Now I want to entwine a wreath of the graces across his brow; I want to show him as gay Sam, agreeable Sam, pleasant Sam; so you must help me with some of his beautiful billets to yourself."[2]

In spite of her evasion of this request, Fanny Burney has nevertheless helped to build up the picture of "agreeable Sam " as everyone who has read her diaries or the extracts from them comprising the volume *Dr. Johnson & Fanny Burney*[3] will know. Many of the details, however, which would

---

(1) Charles Townsend Copeland, "Johnson and his Friendships," *Anniversary Papers* by Colleagues and Pupils of George Lyman Kittredge (Boston and London, 1913), p. 55–61.

(2) *Diary and Letters of Madame d'Arblay*, ed. Charlotte Barrett (4 vols., London, 1893), III, 299. This work will be referred to hereafter as *Diary*.

(3) Ed. Professor Chauncey Tinker. The full title is *Dr. Johnson & Fanny Burney. Being the Johnsonian Passages from the Works of Mme. d'Arblay* (New York, 1911).

have contributed to such a picture have been suppressed either by the aged
Madame d'Arblay herself or by the Victorian editors of the *Diary and Letters*.(4)
Much of the deleted materials is still extant in manuscript.*

In an age less squeamish than the mid-nineteenth century, readers may
perhaps agree with Fanny Burney and James Boswell that such anecdotes
will do the great Doctor no harm, tinged though they be, even in Fanny
Burney's writings, with the full-bloodedness of the eighteenth century. The
suppressed material includes accounts, more unguarded than those printed,
of dinner parties or evenings at St. Martin's Street or Streatham Park, and
additional testimony about the Doctor's "sportive humour," his "truly con-
vivial jocosity,"(5) the "gaiety of his ideas," and his laughter "so hearty,"
says Fanny Burney, as "to almost shake his seat as well as his sides." Besides
such lightsome matter the omitted passages include supplementary versions
of Dr. Johnson's famous quarrels and their unhappy effects, and there is,
finally, the attempt of the diarist to analyze her own feelings about the great
man she saw so constantly and at so close a range at Streatham.

Because of the "cruel infirmities" to which Dr. Johnson was subject,
as everybody knows, there is some difficulty about the "wreath of the graces"
which Boswell had in mind, at least such graces as arise from external
nature. As Mr. Blakeney observed, the doctor was "not much of a fine gentleman"; and Fanny Burney gleefully recorded the Irishman's alleviating
remarks: "not much of a fine gentleman, indeed, but a clever fellow — a
deal of knowledge — got a deuced good understanding !"(6) Fanny Burney's

---

* In the Henry W. and Albert A. Berg Collection of The New York
Public Library. I am grateful to the Library for permission to read the Burney
manuscripts, to collate the manuscripts of the diaries with the printed texts,
and to quote from such deletions from Fanny Burney's accounts of Dr. Johnson as hereafter appear.

(4) Madame d'Arblay's nieces, Charlotte Francis (Mrs. Barrett), to whom
the manuscripts were willed, and Fanny Phillips (Mrs. Raper), who sometimes acted as consultant to Charlotte. Madame d'Arblay herself worked on
the manuscripts for many years.

(5) *Diary*, I, 38–40; 56. Diary MS., p. 753. Cf. *Diary*, I, 136: "Dr. Johnson has more fun, and comical humour, and love of nonsense about him, than
almost anybody I ever saw ! I mean with those he likes; for otherwise he can
be as severe and as bitter as report relates him."

(6) *Diary*, I, 195.

description of Dr. Johnson and his visit to St. Martin's Street in 1777[7] is often quoted and her subsequent accounts are corroborative. "He has almost perpetual convulsive movements, either of his hands, lips, feet, or knees, and sometimes of all together,"[8] she observed, but — as she continued sympathetically —

> the sight of them can never excite ridicule, or, indeed, any other melancholy reflections upon the imperfections of Human Nature; for this, who is the acknowledged First Literary Man in this Kingdom, & who has the most extensive knowledge, the clearest understanding, & the greatest abilities of any Living Author, — has a Face the most ugly, a Person the most awkward, & manners the most singular, that ever were, or ever can be seen. But all that is unfortunate in his *exterior*, is so greatly compensated for in his *interior*, that I can only, like Desdemona to Othello, *"see his visage in his Mind."*[9]

She went on to tell about the originality and comprehensiveness of his language, the instruction and entertainment of his conversation, and the readiness of his wit. He has a "love of social converse that nobody, without Living under the same Roof with him would suspect."[10]

In the diaries of 1778-1783 we can still catch odds and ends of the conversation and echoes of the laughter at Streatham. The dinner parties there were brilliant. Fanny Burney delighted to tell how the wits "flashed away" with allusions and sarcasms gay, forcible, and spendid.[11] "O, Fanny, set this down as the happiest period of your life," advised Mr. Crisp. "Where will you find such another set ?"[12]

---

(7) *The Early Diary of Frances Burney, 1768-1778,* ed. Annie Raine Ellis (2 vols., London, 1913), II, 152-58. This work is hereafter cited as *Early Diary.*

(8) *Diary,* I, 22.

(9) Diary MS., p. 704.

(10) Diary MS., p. 728.

(11) *Diary,* I, 239, 258.

(12) *Diary,* I, 217.

In November of 1778 Streatham was the scene of a champagne party, which was to provoke the Victorian censors to more vigorous deletions than usual. "Monday was the day for our great party; and the doctor came home at Mrs. Thrale's request, to meet them," wrote Fanny in her diary, where she also scribbled annotations on the guest list:

> Mr. Cator, who was formerly a timber merchant, but having amassed a fortune of one million of pounds, he has left off business ...
>
> Mrs. Cator, his lady, a sort of Mrs. Nobody.
>
> Mr. Norman, another rich business leaver-off.
>
> Mrs. Norman, his lady; a pretty sort of woman, who was formerly a pupil of Dr. Hawkesworth ...
>
> Mr. George and Mr. Thomas Norman, her sons-in-law.
>
> Mr. Rice, of whom I know nothing but that he married into Mr. Thrale's family.
>
> Lady Ladd; ... own sister to Mr. Thrale. She is a tall and stout woman, has an air of mingled dignity and haughtiness, both of which wear off in conversation. She dresses very youthful and gaily, and attends to her person with no little complacency. She appears to me uncultivated in knowledge, though an adept in the manners of the world, and all that. She chooses to be much more lively than her brother; but liveliness sits as awkwardly upon her as her pink ribbons ...
>
> Miss Moss, a pretty girl, ... Mr. Rose Fuller, Mr. Embry, Mr. Seward, Dr. Johnson, the three Thrales, and myself close the party.[13]

The dinner, said Fanny, was a "sumptuous" affair of "three courses, and a most superb dessert."[13] The menu included venison and pineapples, though we learn this only indirectly through Fanny Burney's report of Rose Fuller's moralizing upon the consumption of luxuries at a time when *"poor old England* was in such danger."[14] The evening before, Mr. and Mrs. Thrale had taken Fanny Burney all round the paddock at Streatham and showed

---

(13) *Diary*, I, 85-89.

(14) Diary MS., p. 799-806.

her "their hot-houses, kitchen-gardens, &c. Their size and their contents are astonishing; but we have not once missed a pine-apple since I came, and therefore you may imagine their abundance; besides grapes, melons, peaches, nectarines, and ices."[13] Stretham hospitality had always been notable. No one except Mr. Blakeney had ever been known to find fault with it.

> "I am glad, Mr. Thrale," continued this hero, "you have got your fireplace altered. Why, ma'am, there used to be such a wind, there was no sitting here. Admirable dinners — excellent company — *très bon* fare — and, all the time, 'Signor Vento' coming down the chimney ! Do you remember, Miss Thrale, how, one day at dinner, you burst out a-laughing, because I said a *très bon* goose ?"[15]

After dinner Miss Moss played and sang, "to the great fatigue of Mrs. Thrale" and of Dr. Johnson, who refused to leave his wine for the "rapturous entertainment."[13] In the evening nearly everyone strolled upon the gravel walks before the windows and Fanny "was going to have joined some of them" when Dr. Johnson stopped her and asked how she did.

> "I was afraid, sir," cried I, "you did not intend to know me again, for you have not spoken to me before since your return from town."
>
> "My dear," cried he, taking both my hands, "I was not sure of you, I am so near-sighted, and I apprehended making some mistake."[13]

Then the great man drew her "very unexpectedly towards him" and kissed her. When the others went he drew a chair for her close to his own at the window, "and thus *tête-à-tête* we continued,"[13] writes the diarist, "almost all the evening" and "almost" (as the manuscript has it, though not the printed *Diary*) "almost in the Dark." "We have no candles at Streatham till we go into the Library,"[14] she explained. The doctor talked to her about his journey to the Hebrides and was good enough to wish that she had been along — "quite gravely, I assure you !"[13] adds Fanny for the benefit of the appreciative Susan, the sister to whom most of her early diaries were ad-

(15) *Diary*, I, 196.

dressed. This conception of Fanny in the Western Isles and Scottish Highlands must have amused them still more on the appearance of Rowlandson's
caricatures; for the Burney sense of the ridiculous did not spare even the
Burneys themselves. Dr. Johnson was indulgent to the young,[16] and his
kindness to unassuming youth is nowhere better illustrated than in his indulgence to Fanny Burney.[17] Perhaps in return she afforded him some
happiness in times like this when she listened with such gratified attention.

Presently they were disturbed. "By degrees, however, our party en-
creased: Mr. Embry ventured to approach us nearer, — & then Mr. Seward
came and flung himself upon the back of my sofa."[14] When all except the
house-guests had departed, Mrs. Thrale joined the group and "we had a
most nice general conversation"[14] until the candles were brought and everyone repaired to the Library. For some time Miss Burney had fancied "the
folks had all drunk too much champagne!" for Mr. Seward, who usually
was "as shy as any Girl can be," actually took "advantage of the Dark" to

---

(16) Thus on January 3, 1785, Fanny Burney wrote to Marianne Porte
(*Diary*, II, 2-3): "You can now only know him [Dr. Johnson] in his works;
and perhaps from his character of harshness and severity, you may think you
could there alone know him to advantage. But had you been presented to him,
you would not have found that the case. He was always indulgent to the young,
he never attacked the unassuming, nor meant to terrify the diffident."

I am indebted to Professor Raymond Klibansky of McGill University for
a reference which affords additional evidence of Dr. Johnson's kindness to the
young — namely, the opening sentences of a letter from Allan Ramsay to
Dr. William Hunter, Windmill Street, dated Bolt Court, June 1, 1778. The
letter is to be found in Dr. Hunter's *Letter Book*, in the possession of the Royal
College of Surgeons of England, London, by whose kind permission the following lines are quoted:

"Dr. Johnson with his usual humanity interests himself for a young artist
who lies ill of some distemper which requires the advice of a skillfull [sic] ana-
tomist, and has induced me to conspire with him in desiring that you would
be so good as to call upon the young man ..." (See also *Chamber's Journal*
[1906], p. 34, for a previous printing.)

(17) See Dr. Charles Burney's Memoranda — A Collection of miscellaneous holographs in the Berg Collection of the NYPL: "Dr. Johnson was more
indulgent and kind to her [Fanny] than to any female author after my acquaintance with him. Mrs. Lennox, Betty Carter, Mrs. Chapone, & Sally Fielding
... had enjoyed his favour. But he always said that no writer so young and
inexperienced had seen so deeply into character, or copied the manners of the
times with more accuracy."

detain her forcibly from joining the company.[14] Perhaps it was at this time and perhaps because of the champagne that Lady Ladd, who Mrs. Thrale thought would wear "Pink in her Coffin,"[14] had her historic fall. The conversation in the library was upon current politics and made, as Fanny thought, "but melancholy reporting."

Next morning the events of the preceding afternoon and evening were reviewed. "Dr. Johnson was quite in sportive humour," reported Fanny Burney, and "our breakfast was delightful." Mrs. Thrale informed the doctor that, like him, Lady Ladd had had the misfortune to fall down and hurt herself woefully.

> "How did that happen, madam?"
> "Why, sir, the heel of her shoe caught in something."
> "Heel?" replied he; "nay, then, if her ladyship, who walks six foot high" (N.B. this is a fact), "will wear a high heel, I think she almost deserves a fall."
> "Nay, sir, my heel was not so high!" cried Lady Ladd.
> "But, madam, why should you wear any? That for which there is no occasion, had always better be dispensed with ..."
> "However," continued he, "if my fall does confine me, I will make my confinement pleasant, for Miss Burney shall nurse me — positively!" (and he slapped his hand on the table), "and then, she shall sing to me, and soothe my cares."[13]

> She shall sing me a song,
> Of 2 Day's long,
> The Woodcock & the sparrow;
> Our little Dog has bit his Tail
> And he'll be Hang'd to-morrow.[14]

In the early days of their acquaintance Dr. Johnson had suggested that Fanny write a comedy, a farce called "Streatham," and Fanny had been delighted with his sense of the burlesque.[18] "How little did I expect at a distance, from this Lexiphanus, this great and dreaded Lord of English literature, a turn so comic and diverting for burlesque humour!"[19] The manuscript of the *Diary* for 1781 provides us with an example.[20] "While

(18) *Diary*, I, 56.
(19) Diary MS., p. 754.
(20) Diary MS., p. 1506-07.

we were thus alone one Evening we made an extempore Elegy, Dr. Johnson, Mrs. Thrale & myself *spouting* it out alternately, for Miss Thrale is no versifier, not even in this miserable way. The *occasion* was to *make fun* of an Elegy in a Trumpery Book we had just been reading, so I will try to recollect it. "(20)

I

Here's a Woman of the Town
Lies as Dead as any Nail!
She was once of high renown,—
And so here begins my Tale.

II

She was once a cherry plump
Red her cheek as Cath'rine Pear,
Toss'd her nose, & shook her Rump,
Till she made the neighbours stare.

III

There she soon became a Jilt,
Rambling often to & fro'
All her life was nought but guilt,
Till Purse & Carcase both were low.

IIII

But there came a country 'Squire
He was a seducing Pug!
Took her from her friends & sire,
To his own House her did Lug.

V

Black her eye with many a Blow
Hot her Breath with many a Dram
Now she lies exceeding low
And as quiet as a Lamb.

"So if any 3 people can do worse — let them!"

The doctor's presence was not always conducive to comfort and geniality, as certain people had learned to their embarrassment and woe. There was that evening at St. Martin's Street in 1778 when Dr. Johnson only awoke from profound reveries to reprove the haughty Fulke Greville and other gentlemen who, as Charlotte Burney said, "were so kind and considerate as to divert themselves by making a fire skreen to the whole room — Dr. Johnson, made them all *make off*, for when nobody would have imagined he had known the gentlemen were in the room, he said that 'if he was not *ashamed* he would keep the fire from the ladies too,' — this reproof (for a *reproof* it certainly was, altho' given in a very comical dry way) was productive of a scene as *good as a comedy*, for Mr. Suard tumbled on to the sopha directly, Mr. Thrale on to a chair, Mr. Davenant sneaked off the *premises* seemingly in as great a fright and as much confounded as if he had done any bad action, and Mr. Gruel [Greville], being left *solus* was obliged to stalk off in spight of his teeth [toothache], and it was pretty evidently against the grain."[21] Madame d'Arblay recalled how the lofty Greville shortly thereafter rang for his carriage, and no one at the party "ever asked, or wished for its repetition."[22]

Fanny Burney judged that dinner guests must have sometimes found Dr. Johnson "almost as amusing as a fit of the toothache !"[23] There was that dinner at Streatham when he "burst forth with a vehemence and bitterness almost incredible" — the occasion of "the grand Battle upon the Life of Lyttelton." Fanny Burney has left two accounts of this combat: one is printed in the *Diary and Letters* for the year 1781;[24] the other, a report of her conversation with Mr. George Cambridge at a blue party in 1783, is still in part buried among the "Confessions" of her attachment to that young clergyman — a somewhat tedious and painful record of the vicissitudes of eighteenth-century love.[25] She assured Mr. Cambridge that the quarrel was serious.

> "I never saw Dr. Johnson really in a passion but then: & dreadful, indeed, it was to see ! I wished myself away a thousand times. It was a frightful scene. *He* so red, poor Mr. Pepys so pale !"
>
> "But how did it begin ? What did he say ?"
>
> "O Dr. Johnson came to the point without much ceremony ! He called out aloud, before a large company, at dinner. What

(21) *Early Diary*, II, 286-87.

(22) *Memoirs of Doctor Burney* (3 vols., London, 1832), II, 101-14.

(23) *Diary*, I, 311.

(24) *Diary*, I. 354-58.

(25) Diary MS., p. 1843-47. Cf. *Diary* I, 547-51.

have you to say, sir, *to* me or *of* me ? Come forth, man !
I hear you object to my life of Lord Lyttelton. What are your
objections ? If you have anything to say, let's hear it. Come
forth, man, when I call you !"

"What a *call*, indeed ! — why then he fairly bullyed him into
a quarrel ?"

"Yes. And I was the more sorry, because Mr. Pepys had begged of *me*, before they met, not to let Lord Lyttelton be mentioned. Now I had no more power to prevent it than this
macaroon cake in my Hand."

"Certainly not. If you had made any such request to Dr. Johnson, he would have made you some odd speech, & then
gone on his way."

"Mrs. Thrale, perhaps, might have interfered; but a very pro-
voking accident happened to herself. She had called for a
Tumbler of water, & the Butler, by mistake, gave her a
Tumbler of champagne; but she drank it entirely off without
finding out what she was about. For she does every thing
with that sort of impetuosity, — but the moment she had
finished, she called out what is it you have given me ? —
& she grew so extremely frightened when she found it was
champagne, that she did nothing but terrify herself, &
swallow water, Glass after Glass, all Dinner Time. And that
occupied her so entirely, that she could attend to nothing at
all else. Otherwise *she* might perhaps have had power to call
them to order."[25]

Fanny was not so alarmed, however, as to miss the "one happy circumstance"
of the quarrel — namely, the presence of Mr. Cator.[24] This gentleman,
"who would by no means be prevented talking himself, either by reverence
for Dr. Johnson, or ignorance of the subject in question, ... gave his opinion,
quite uncalled, upon everything that was said by either party, and with an
importance and pomposity, yet with an emptiness and verbosity, that rendered the whole dispute, when in his hands, nothing more than ridiculous,
and compelled even the disputants themselves, all inflamed as they were,
to laugh." [24]

"As to this here question of Lord Lyttelton I can't speak to
it to the purpose, as I have not read his 'Life,' for I have only
read the 'Life of Pope;' I have got the books though, for
I sent for them last week, and they came to me on Wednesday,
and then I began them; but I have not yet read 'Lord Lyttel-

ton.' 'Pope' I have begun, and that is what I am now reading. But what I have to say about Lord Lyttelton is this here: Mr. Seward says that Lord Lyttelton's steward dunned Mr. Shenstone for his rent, by which I understand he was a tenant of Lord Lyttelton's. Well, if he was a tenant of Lord Lyttelton's, why should not he pay his rent ?''

"Who could contradict this ?" asks Fanny. And she goes on: "When dinner was quite over, and we left the men to their wine, we hoped they would finish the affair" but "when they were all summoned to tea, they entered still warm and violent." Mr. Cator had now begun to read the "Life of Lyttelton" that he might better understand the cause, "though not a creature," said Fanny, "cared if he had never heard of it."(24) Dr. Johnson still "harangued and attacked ... with a vehemence and continuity that quite concerned both Mrs. Thrale and myself, and that made Mr. Pepys, at last, resolutely silent, however called upon." "This now grew more unpleasant than ever," reported Miss Burney, "till Mr. Cator, having some time studied his book, exclaimed, —

> "What I am now going to say, as I have not yet read the 'Life of Lord Lyttelton' quite through, must be considered as being only said aside, because what I am going to say —"
> "I wish, sir," cried Mrs. Thrale, "it had been *all* said aside; here is too much about it, indeed, and I should be very glad to hear no more of it."
> This speech, which she made with great spirit and dignity, had an admirable effect. Everybody was silenced. Mr. Cator, thus interrupted in the midst of his proposition, looked quite amazed; Mr. Pepys was much gratified by the interference; and Dr. Johnson, after a pause, said, —
> "Well, madam, you *shall* hear no more of it; yet I will defend myself in every part and in every atom !"(24)

So ended the diary account of 1781; but additional comments are to be found in Miss Burney's conversation with Mr. Cambridge in 1783.

> "It was behaving ill to *Mrs. Thrale*, certainly, to quarrel in her house."
> "Yes, but he never repeated it; though he *wished* of all things to have gone through just such another scene with Mrs. Montagu, & to restrain was an act of heroic forbearance."

"Why I rather wonder he did not; for *she* was the Head of the
set of Lytteltonians."

"O, he knows that; he calls Mr. Pepys only her prime
Minister."(25)

Then Fanny told of the doctor's encounter with Mrs. Montagu, who "had
publicly declared — that she would never speak to him more !"

> She turned from him very stiffly, & with a most distant air,
> & without even courtesying to him ... However, he went
> up to her himself, *longing* to begin ! & very roughly said
> "Well, madam, what's become of your fine new House ? I
> hear no more of it ?"
> "But how did she bear this ?"
> "Why she was *obliged* to answer him; & she soon grew so
> frightened — as *every body* does, — that she was as civil as
> ever !"(25)

The "dear violent Doctor" was "very candid and generous in acknowledging"
that he had acted wrongly. He is "a superior Being in all great & essential
parts,"(26) wrote Fanny, and "too noble to adhere to wrong";(25) yet according to her letters to her father from Brighton in 1782,(27) she again found
cause to regret Dr. Johnson's belligerence and its effects:

> I am quite sorry to see how unmercifully he attacks & riots
> the people. He has raised such a general alarm, that he is
> now omitted in all cards of invitation sent to the rest of us.
> What pity that he will never curb himself ! nor restrain his
> tongue upon every occasion from such bitter or cruel speeches
> as eternally come from him ! ... Poor Mr. Pepys has been
> shook by him almost to Death: [In another letter of about
> the same time we read that "Mr. Pepys was so torn to pieces
> by him the other night, in a party at Home, that he suddenly
> seized his Hat, & abruptly walked out of the Room in the
> middle of the discourse."] & Mr. Coxe, a Brother of the
> Writer, had so rough a speech from him, the other Day, that
> he declares it has made him nervous ever since. Dr. Delap

(26) Diary MS., p. 3509.

(27) A. L. S. and A. L., dated Brighton, November 3 and 8, respectively,
1782, from Fanny Burney to her father Dr. Charles Burney. The Berg Collection of the NYPL.

confesses himself afraid of coming as usual to the House;
& Mr. Selwyn, having yesterday declined meeting him at
Mr. Hamilton's, ran away before his return Home, in the
utmost terror of being severely reprimanded for his refusal.[27]

"Dr. Johnson has his Health wonderfully well," reported Fanny to
Dr. Burney in November, 1782; yet he does not "spend his time very agreeably,"

> for he is dreaded too much to get any conversation, except by
> accident; & he has had no invitation since my arrival, but to
> one Dinner, at single speech Hamilton's. He has therefore
> passed most of his Evenings alone, & much to his dissatis-
> faction. He has, however, so miserably mauled the few who
> have ventured to encounter him, that there is little wonder
> they wave [*sic*] the ceremony of any meetings they can avoid.[27]

In 1783, as we learn from her conversation with Mr. George Cambridge,
Fanny thought Dr. Johnson "much softened."[25] "Why I am now," said he,
"come to that Time when I wish all bitterness & animosity to be at an
end."[25] He had been thinking just then of Mrs. Montagu.

> "I have never done her any serious harm, — nor would I; —
> though I *could* give her a *bite* ! — but she must provoke me
> first. In volatile talk, indeed, I may have spoken of her not
> much to her mind; for in the tumult of conversation, malice
> is apt to grow sprightly; & *there*, I hope, I am not yet dec-
> repid !"[25]

As James Fordyce informed the Deity in 1785:[28]

---

(28) "On the Death of Dr. Johnson," *Addresses to the Deity* (Boston, 1813),
p. 162-63. The first edition appeared in 1785, Dr. James Fordyce was the
author also of *Sermons to Young Women*, a popular courtesy book, which ran
to fourteen editions between 1766 and 1814. The pious and slightly lascivious
tone of the work soon made it the sport of satirists like Sheridan, who allowed
Lydia Languish to tear off its pages for curl papers; or like Jane Austen, who,
as every reader of *Pride and Prejudice* knows, gave it into the hands of the
sententious Mr. Collins to read to the yawning Lydia Bennet.

When trouble and anguish came upon thy aged servant [Dr. Johnson], when "his sleep went from him," when in solemn recollection he "communed with his own heart upon his bed," and examined himself in the view of his last and great account, he saw wherein he had offended. Then it was, that I heard him condemn, with holy self-abasement, the pride of understanding by which he had often trespassed against the laws of courteous demeanour, and forgotten the fallible condition of his nature.

At the close of 1784, those who were left of the Streatham group knew that Dr. Johnson was "going on to death very fast." "*Priez Dieu pour moi* !"[29] he had enjoined Fanny in November, 1783; and a year later on one of her visits to Bolt Court he had renewed the injunction, "Remember me in your prayers !"[29] "I longed to ask him so to remember *me* !"[29] she confided to Susan. Still later when he had sent a similar request through her father, she was moved to write: "I never felt so touched in my life, as at such a humility, from a man so good, so religious, so fitted to answer his accounts in another World !"[30] On December 7, the day when she had gone twice in vain to see him, she wrote thus to the Lockes of Norbury Park:

> My regard for him ... is sincere, respectful, & full of admiration; indeed I have always loved him as well as I could, & I ... *wish* I could love him more. Mr. Locke laughed when I said so, but I meant it in earnest; for when I think a character really estimable, I *want* to love it thoroughly. Will poor Dr. Johnson *see this* where he is going? No matter, for if he sees less than he expected, in finding how far, far more I love you, whom he will regard as a new acquaintance, he will see *more* than he expected in finding that, *with truth*, I loved him *at all*; for he perpetually told me, when we lived a good deal together, that I "cared not for him"; in which indeed he much wronged me, though I did not, because I *could* not, care for him as much as he desired; for, with all his partial kindness to *me*, his behaviour to others kept me in continual alarm.[31]

---

(29) *Memoirs of Doctor Burney*, II, 358-70; III, 1-171.

(30) Diary MS., p. 3609.

(31) A.L.S., dated December 7, 1784, from Fanny Burney to Mrs. William Locke. The Berg Collection of the NYPL. See Diary MS., p. 1933.

This attempt at self-analysis perhaps gives a less accurate indication of her feeling about the great man than the entry in her diary for December 20, 1784.

> Dec. 20th.— This day was the ever-honoured, ever-lamented Dr. Johnson committed to the earth. Oh, how sad a day to me ! My father attended, and so did Charles. I could not keep my eyes dry all day ! nor can I now in the recollecting it; but let me pass over what to mourn is now so vain.[32]

---

(32) *Diary,* I, 585.

J A M E S   H .   L E I C E S T E R

Johnson's Life of Shenstone:
Some Observations on the Sources

When Johnson wrote the *Lives of the Poets* he honoured his bargain with the booksellers by writing the lives and assessing the merits of a whole hierarchy of English poets ranging from the mediocre to the man of genius. Some aroused his admiration; others his aversion. Shenstone presented a subject for whom he had no marked predilection either as a poet or as a man. A Life in praise of Shenstone would have proved popular had he chosen to write it. Contemporary opinion was divided as to the virtues of Shenstone's sequestered retirement from the world, but as a poet he enjoyed a popularity approaching that of Gray;[1] as an exponent of the art of landscape gardening he was widely esteemed and his achievements at the Leasowes were justly acclaimed. But Johnson could not write with complete approbation of the man or his work. He judged Shenstone by his own scale of values and made his own robustly honest, if unsympathetic, assessment. If there was some common ground between poet and biographer, there were also fundamental differences of temperament and outlook. True to himself and life as he knew it, Johnson chose to write a Life of Shenstone which for the most part ran counter to the accepted views of his contemporaries. Faint praise, implied censure, direct reproof — such criticisms did not accord with the opinions of admirers and friends intent on honouring the memory of the man and advancing the reputation of the poet. Inevitably, Johnson's Life did not meet with universal approval and the work engendered controversy. Deferential murmurs and hostile criticisms were still reverberating long after Johnson had followed Shenstone to the grave.

As a biographer, Johnson had no first-hand knowledge of his subject. Both men had been at Pembroke College, Oxford, but Johnson left the uni-

---

(1) Marjorie Williams, *William Shenstone* (1935), p. 101.

veisity before Shenstone matriculated. Shenstone had a great admiration
for Johnson and his work, and expressed a keen desire to meet him which
was never fulfilled. Bishop Percy endeavoured to arrange an introduction
but did not succeed. Johnson thus afforded himself no occasion on which
to discover Shenstone's real abilities by his method of coming close to a man
in conversation. However, he had gleaned some information about the
poet from his conversations with contemporaries, doubtless discussed the
poems as they appeared, and exchanged anecdotes with acquaintances.
Boswell and others record such occasions. The poems themselves were in
part biographical but these did not present the factual details Johnson
required. He therefore looked around for biographical sources to supplement
his own limited knowledge. His "sources" may be listed as follows:

1. — Treadway Russell Nash, "Some particulars in the Life of William
   Shenstone," *The History and Antiquities of Worcestershire* (1781).

2. — Robert Dodsley, A biographical Preface and a description of the
   Leasowes, *The Works in Verse and Prose of William Shenstone*
   (1764).

3. — William Mason, *Memoirs of Gray's Life* (1775); for an extract
   from a letter concerning Shenstone.

4. — Johnson's memory — particularly for the anecdotal information.
A further source of biographical information which Johnson did not fully
exploit was

5. — Shenstone's Letters.

Having acquired sufficient data, Johnson used his material to present a Life
of Shenstone in accordance with his own assessment. He had formed his
opinion of Shenstone as a man and weighed his merits as a poet long before
he undertook to write the Life. Thus, when he turned to a biographical
source, he used the facts but not the opinions of other writers to illustrate
and support his own established and independent judgments.

Johnson's major biographical source, an account of Shenstone in
the *History of Worcestershire*, appeared fortuitously in the same year as the
Lives of the Poets. More than seven-tenths of Johnson's biographical material
derives from this account; indeed, the first nine paragraphs, with one small
exception, were taken entirely from it. The date of publication of this unlikely
source is of particular interest and raises some problems. Treadway Russell

Nash, D.D., first published his proposal for the *History and Antiquities of Worcestershire* in June, 1774, when he appealed for material likely to assist him in the compilation.[2] Subsequently the work was published in two volumes; the first appearing in 1781, and the second in 1782. It was the first volume which contained the Shenstone memoir.

Nash generally gave the source of his material and named the contributors, but for the account of Shenstone only a vague reference to the authorship was given: "For these particulars we are indebted to one or two of his intimate friends."[3] The dedication page bears the date 1 January 1781, and the work was published on 4th April, 1781.[4] In August of the same year it was reviewed in the *Gentleman's Magazine* which quoted from the work generally and made particular reference to Shenstone: "The account of Shenstone, under *Hales Owen*, is nearly the same with that given by Dr. Johnson, who was his fellow-collegian at Pembroke College, Oxford."[5] Johnson's Life of Shenstone in the final volume of the *Prefaces Biographical and Critical to the Works of the English Poets* had been reviewed three months earlier in the same magazine.[6] Quoting from *Prayers and Meditations*, Boswell recorded that

> IN 1781 Johnson at last completed his "Lives of the Poets," of which he gives this account: "Some time in March I finished the 'Lives of the Poets', which I wrote in my usual way, dilatorily and hastily, unwilling to work, and working with vigour and haste." [7]

(2) John Amphlett, *An Index to Dr. Nash's Collection for a History of Worcestershire* (1895), p.x.

(3) Treadway Russell Nash, "Some particulars in the Life of William Shenstone," *The History and Antiquities of Worcestershire* (1781), I, 528. Subsequent references to this edition appear in the text. The account of Shenstone has since been attributed to his friend and correspondent, John Scott Hylton. See F. and K.M. Somers, *Halas, Hales, Hales Owen* (Halesowen, Worcestershire: H. Parker, 1932), pp. 60f.

(4) The first "This day was published" notice appears in *The Morning Herald*.

(5) *Gentleman's Magazine*, LI, 374, Aug. 1781.

(6) Ibid., LI, June, 1781.

(7) *Boswell's Life of Johnson*, ed. G.B. Hill, revised and enlarged by L.F. Powell (Oxford, 1934-50), IV, 34.

Since the *History of Worcestershire* appeared on 4th April 1781, it would seem that Johnson's work preceded that of Nash. However, the evidence of a contemporary advertisement in *The Public Advertiser* for Tuesday, 15 May 1781, reveals that Johnson's work appeared six weeks after the publication of Nash. From this it follows that Johnson completed the Life of Shenstone after 4th April, and we must modify his own account that he finished the *Lives* some time in March. Alternatively, we must accept that he read the account of Shenstone prior to publication.

Rapid composition came naturally to Johnson. Writing in his "usual way with vigour and haste," and being pressed by his publishers, he would have welcomed a new book to supplement his limited material. The man who sat up all night and wrote forty-eight of the printed octavo pages of the Life of Savage at a sitting would have had no difficulty in despatching the Life of Shenstone during the few weeks following the publication of Nash's account so that it could be included in the tenth and final volume of the *Lives*.

On the day the *History of Worcestershire* was published, Henry Thrale died. This "very essential loss to Johnson" added to his duties,[8] but it did not prevent him from dining with Boswell at a club at the Queen's Arms, in St. Paul's Church-yard two days later. On the contrary, the loss of Henry Thrale led him to seek companionship. A letter to Mrs. Thrale, dated London 9 April 1781, provides a revealing glimpse of Johnson at this time: "Our sorrow has different effects; you are withdrawn into solitude, and I am driven into company."[9] Boswell records a succession of occasions on which he dined with Johnson in distinguished company during this period. About this time, we may imagine Johnson reading the Nash account of Shenstone in White's Fleet Street bookshop, or perhaps borrowing a copy from a friend, assimilating the details, and reproducing them again from his prodigious memory to supplement his own version. Boswell noted that "He had a peculiar facility in seizing at once what was valuable in any book, without submitting to the labour of perusing it from beginning to end."[10] Certainly, Johnson kept closely to the details supplied by Nash, including

---

(8) "he took upon him, with a very earnest concern, the office of one of his executors, the importance of which seemed greater than usual to him." Ibid., IV, 85.

(9) Johnson, *Letters*, ed. G.B. Hill (Oxford, 1892), No. 722.

(10) Boswell's *Life*, I, 71.

the erroneous ones. But his account was not a scrupulously accurate copy: the order of presentation was changed slightly, and there were minor discrepancies. His handling of the source indicates a familiarity with the text but not a precise transcription and suggests that he had not the book open before him as he wrote.

Johnson looked to publishers to send him copies of books, and if we accept that the account was seen before publication it is of interest to note that three of the London booksellers mentioned in the Advertisement for the *History of Worcestershire* were also numbered among the publishers of the *Lives of the Poets*. We must discount coincidence as an explanation of all the points of similarity between the two versions; nor is it likely that the "intimate friends" of Shenstone sought Johnson's assistance when preparing their account for Nash. In point of fact there is ample internal evidence to demonstrate that Johnson borrowed freely from Nash.

The Shenstone memoir in *The History of Worcestershire* is included in the chapter on Hales Owen headed by a geographical description:

> HALES-OWEN, formerly HALES, HALAS.
> This great parish, which is situated part in Shropshire, and part in Worcestershire, is bounded on the south by Clent and Frankley, on the north by Rowley, and West-Bromwich, on the east by Edgbaston, and Harborne, and on the west by Hagley, Pedmore, and Old Swinford; is no where contiguous to the county of Salop, but separated from it at least twelve miles. (I, 508).

Some twenty pages later follows the account of the poet together with an explanation for its inclusion:

> As we have given in this work an account of the parish of Hales-owen at large, although in strictness only part of it belongs to our subject; we doubt not but the reader will pardon the insertion of some particulars of the life of WILLIAM SHENSTONE esquire, the brightest ornament of this place, although he was born in that part of Hales-owen which lies within the county of Salop. Mr. Thomas Shenstone married Anne Penn ... By her he had two sons, WILLIAM our poet, and Joseph. William, the subject of this account, was born at the Leasowes on or about the 18th of November, 1714. (I, 528f.)

In using this information, Johnson omitted the laudatory epithet "the bright-est ornament" but accepted the topographical details. He reserved his critical judgments until later and at this stage showed more interest in the place than in the poet. Dodsley had also referred to the parish in his Description of the Leasowes: "THE Leasowes is situate in the parish of Hales-Owen, a small market town, in the county of Salop; but surrounded by other count-ies, and thirty miles from Shrewsbury, as it is near ten to the borders of Shropshire."[11] Johnson's account has points in common with both Nash and Dodsley, but he confused Dodsley's distance of Hales-Owen from the borders of Shropshire with that given from Shrewsbury — an error per-petuated by some later biographers who have used Johnson as a source. Johnson's version thus reads:

> WILLIAM SHENSTONE, the son of Thomas Shenstone and Anne Pen, was born in November, 1714, at the Leasowes in Hales-Owen, one of those insulated districts which, in the division of the kingdom, was appended, for some reason not now dis-coverable, to a distant county; and which, though surrounded by Warwickshire and Worcestershire, belongs to Shropshire, though perhaps thirty miles distant from any other part of it.[12]

It was Johnson's practice to discover, where possible, the place and full date of birth of the poets in the *Lives*. However, he omitted the inconclusive dating of the day. The parish register[13] would not have helped him here as it records only the baptismal date. Richard Graves later confirmed the birth-day as 18th November — the date now generally accepted by the authori-tative biographers. The place of birth is supported by Shenstone's own test-imony and we can now disregard the evidence of the Matriculation register which records that Shenstone was born in Wigstone Magna or Wigstone Parva, Leicestershire. It has since been proved that the official responsible for entering the names in the Matriculation register mixed the entries of two persons.[14]

---

(11) Shenstone, *Works*, II, 333.

(12) *Lives of the Poets*, ed. G.B. Hill (1905), III, 348. Subsequent re-ferences to the Life of Shenstone appear in the text.

(13) H. Sydney Grazebrook, *Extracts from the Parish Registers of Hales-owen, Co. Worcester.*

(14) See Myra M. Ward, "Shenstone's Birthplace," *MLN*, Nov. 1936, pp. 440f.

A dubious date given by Nash and copied by Johnson relates to the death of Shenstone's grandfather. The parish register records the burial on 11 August 1727. The two other dates given by Nash in the following passage accord with the parish records:

> His father had died in June 1724, and his grandfather in August 1726, before he was twelve years old, leaving him and his brother under their mother's care, who continued to superintend the farm till her death in 1732, a short time before he removed to Oxford. At her death, the guardianship of her two sons devolved on the rev. Mr. Tho. Dolman, rector of Brome, in this neighbourhood, but in the county of Stafford, who had married Mary Penn, their mother's sister; of whose paternal care, Mr. Shenstone often speaks with great respect. (I, 529).

Writing with vigour and haste, Johnson erred in stating that it was Shenstone's grandmother who managed the estate on the death of Thomas Shenstone. It was, as Nash records, Shenstone's mother who looked after her two children until her decease when the care of the estate devolved upon her brother-in-law. Johnson's version, which otherwise followed Nash closely, runs thus:

> When he was young (June 1724) he was deprived of his father, and soon after (August, 1726) of his grandfather, and was with his brother, who died afterwards unmarried, left to the care of his grandmother, who managed the estate.
>
> From school he was sent in 1732 to Pembroke-College in Oxford ...
>
> About the time when he went to Oxford, the death of his grandmother devolved his affairs to the care of the reverend Mr. Dolman of Brome in Staffordshire, whose attention he always mentioned with gratitude. (III, 349)

Johnson was indebted to Nash for the picturesque anecdote from Shenstone's childhood. The original version was as follows:

> From his earliest infancy he was remarkable for his great fondness for reading, so that when any of his family went to distant markets or fairs, he constantly importuned them to bring him presents of books; which, if they returned home later than his usual hour of going to rest, were always taken

up to bed to him; and sometimes when they had been forgotten, his mother had no other means to allure him to sleep, but by wrapping a piece of wood in paper like a book; which he would hug to his pillow, till the morning discovered the deception. (I, 529)

In using these details, Johnson added the cautionary "it is said that" to conclude the anecdote and improved the narrative by adopting a more logical order. In the Nash version it had preceded the account of Shenstone's early schooling; in Johnson's it followed this. His first dame, Sarah Lloyd,[15] is of particular interest since she inspired one of his most well known and best loved poems. Johnson himself rated it as the most pleasing of Shenstone's poems. Nash gave this account: "He received the first tincture of learning under a school-dame near the Leasowes, whose memory he afterwards immortalized in his poem of the School-Mistress, and whose name he has recorded in one of his letters." (I, 529) Johnson's paraphrase became:

> He learned to read of an old dame, whom his poem of *The School-mistress* has delivered to posterity; and soon received such delight from books that he was always calling for fresh entertainment, and expected that, when any of the family went to market, a new book should be brought him, which when it came was in fondness carried to bed and laid by him. It is said that when his request had been neglected, his mother wrapped up a piece of wood of the same form, and pacified him for the night. (III, 348)

He continued with details of Shenstone's schooling and, characteristically, named the schoolmaster:

> As he grew older he went for a while to the Grammar-school in Hales-Owen, and was placed afterwards with Mr. Crumpton, an eminent school-master at Solihul, where he distinguished himself by the quickness of his progress. (III, 348f.)

This, again, followed Nash closely:

> He for a short time attended the grammar school at Halesowen; whence he was removed to Solihull in Warwickshire,

---

(15) Sarah Lloyd is mentioned in a letter on the occasion of printing "The School-mistress": Shenstone, *Works*, III, 53.

under the care of the rev. Mr. Crumpton; who had the tuition
of many children, sons of the neighbouring nobility and gentry.
Here he made a quick progress in the Latin and Greek classics.
(1,529).

It is Johnson and not Nash who allowed Crumpton the title of "an
eminent schoolmaster." At this point we may ask what connotation the
adjective "eminent" implies. Was it inspired by Crumpton's teaching the
sons of the nobility and gentry, or is it an interpolation with some autobio-
graphical significance ? We can only speculate on the memories evoked by
the reference to Crumpton and Solihull. The story of Johnson's unsuccessful
application for the mastership of Shenstone's old school at Solihull, a few
weeks after his marriage, comes vividly alive in Greswold's letter to Wal-
mesley:

> all agree that he is an Excellent Scholar, and upon that account
> deserves much better than to be schoolmaster of Solihull. But
> then, he has the character of being a very haughty, illnatured
> Gent., & that he has such a way of distorting his Face (which
> though he can't help) the Gent. think it may affect some Young
> Ladds for these two reasons he is not approved on, the late
> Master, Mr. Crompton's huffing the Fœofees being still in
> their Memory.(16)

We may also speculate on the extent to which the morose pedagogue's
"huffing the Fœofees" determined the course of young Samuel Johnson's
career.

Continuing the story of Shenstone's education, Nash recorded that

> on the 24th of May, 1732, he was admitted a commoner of
> Pembroke College in Oxford. Of this college he continued a
> member near ten years [Mr. Shenstone finally left college,
> March 25, 1742 (Nash, footnote)], having at the end of the
> first four years put on a Civilian's gown, but with what design
> does not appear, for he never took any degree, and apparently
> never intended to follow any profession, as he had long before
> succeeded to his paternal estate ...

(16) Solihull, 30 August 1735;   Pembroke College MSS. quoted in
Appendix G, Boswell's *Life*, I, 531.

About the time that Mr. Shenstone was a member of Pembroke
College, that little seminary was distinguished for the great
number of men of genius and learning with which it abounded,
and who have since reflected such honour on this their original
place of education. With these Mr. Shenstone spent several
years in a most pleasing society, and contracted friendships
which only terminated with his life. (I, 529f.)

Johnson's version of this was a concise paraphrase:

From school he was sent in 1732 to Pembroke-College in
Oxford, a society which for half a century had been eminent
for English poetry and elegant literature. Here it appears that
he found delight and advantage; for he continued his name
in the book ten years, though he took no degree. After the
first four years he put on the Civilian's gown, but without
shewing any intention to engage in the profession. (III, 349)

Unlike Shenstone, Johnson does not appear to have contracted life-long
friendship with his contemporaries at Oxford. But he was peculiarly happy
in recalling how many of the sons of Pembroke were poets, and retained
to the last a love and regard for his College. Describing one of Johnson's
visits to Dr. Adams, in the June of the year following the publication of the
Lives of the Poets, Hannah More wrote:

You cannot imagine with what delight [Dr. Johnson] showed
me every part of his own college ... After dinner Johnson
begged to conduct me to see the college, he would let no one
show it me but himself, — "This was my room; this Shenstone's."
Then, after pointing out all the rooms of the poets who had
been of his college, "In short," said he, "we were a nest of
singing-birds."[17]

Some of Johnson's interpretations of the material taken from Nash
were called in question by contemporary critics. An example of this resulted
from Nash's account of Shenstone's early poetry:

While he was at college, he printed without his name, a small
volume of juvenile verses, with the following title: "Poems
upon various occasions, written for the entertainment of the
author, and printed for the amusement of a few friends prejudiced in his favour ... 1737." (I, 530).

---

(17) Hannah More, *Memoirs*, I, 261.

In his own account Johnson gave greater emphasis to the poetry than to his other studies: "At Oxford he employed himself upon English poetry; and in 1737 published a small *Miscellany*, without his name." (III, 349) Had he followed Nash more closely at this point and given the *Miscellany* its full title it would have been more evident to the reader that Shenstone's early verses were written for the diversion of his friends. The result was that Richard Graves later found it necessary to correct this and other false impressions and stressed that Shenstone "amused" himself with English poetry and "employed" himself in the study of mathematics, logic, natural and moral philosophy, and other sciences.(18)

Nash also gives a brief factual account of the years immediately following Shenstone's departure from Oxford:

> About the year 1739, he was much resident in London; and for some years following he divided his time between the metropolis, Bath, and Cheltenham, occasionally visiting the University. In the spring of the year 1740, he published his poem of "the Judgement of Hercules;" and in 1742, his "School-mistress;" both separately, in 8vo. (I, 530).

Johnson used this and added a detail of his own concerning the dedication to the first poem.(19) His more sophisticated account of this period, with perhaps a suggestion of aimlessness in his use of the verb "wandered", reads thus:

> He then for a time wandered about, to acquaint himself with life, and was sometimes at London, sometimes at Bath or any other place of publick resort; but he did not forget his poetry. He published in 1740 his *Judgement of Hercules*, addressed to Mr. Lyttelton, whose interest he supported with great warmth at an election: this was afterwards followed by *The School-mistress*. (III, 350).

In the next passage dealing with the death of Shenstone's uncle and the subsequent development of the Leasowes, Johnson's prejudice becomes evident. A comparison of the two passages shows his rather blunt statement

---

(18) *Recollection of Some Particulars in the Life of the late William Shenstone, Esq.* (London, 1788), p. 23.

(19) Shenstone refers to his support of George Lyttelton's candidature for the County of Worcestershire in 1740. Shenstone, *Works*, III, 26.

of the facts and, in the last line, a deflating comment nowhere paralleled in
the original.

Nash:

> In 1745 his uncle Dolman died, who had chiefly managed
> his estate; which had been occupied by Mr. John Shenstone
> of Perry Hill, in this parish, a distant relation, who, with his
> sons John and Thomas Shenstone, rented the farm as tenants.
> Mr. Shenstone began now to be more resident at the Leasowes,
> and at first boarded with his tenants; but not liking the rest-
> raint he was under, at length took the farm into his own hands;
> and soon began to display that genius and taste, which at
> length made the Leasowes to be so much admired and celeb-
> rated. (I, 530).

Johnson:

> Mr. Dolman, to whose care he was indebted for his ease and
> leisure, died in 1745, and the care of his own fortune now fell
> upon him. He tried to escape it a while, and lived at his house
> with his tenants, who were distantly related; but, finding that
> imperfect possession inconvenient, he took the whole estate
> into his own hands, more to the improvement of its beauty
> than the increase of its produce. (III, 350)

Continuing from the point where Shenstone assumed responsibility
for the management of the estate, Nash gave a highly commendatory description of the poet's achievements at the Leasowes; he extolled his skill and
praised his success as an innovator of landscape gardening:

> The manner of laying out ground in the natural style was
> quite in its infancy when Mr. Shenstone began his improve-
> ments, and excepting the walk through the High Wood (which
> was his earliest attempt) very little of what was executed at
> first now remains unaltered. By degrees he brought these de-
> lightful scenes to their present perfection; and long before he
> died, they had attracted the notice and procured him the
> friendship of persons the most distinguished for rank or genius.
> A description of the Leasowes, as left at his death in 1763,
> by Robert Dodsley, may be seen at the end of the 2nd volume
> of his Works. (I, 530)

None of this was used by Johnson. Acting on the hint in the final sentence,
he left the Nash narrative at this point and turned to the Dodsley descrip-

tion. This he used to advantage in his description of the gardener's art at the Leasowes. From the factual details of Dodsley's encomium, he produced a satirical version of his own suffused with Johnsonian prejudice. He returned to the Nash memoir a few paragraphs later and utilised details from the following extracts. The first provides an ingenuous description of Shenstone's disposition and circumstances which is not at all points reconcilable with that given by another of his "intimate friends", Richard Graves.

> As for Mr. Shenstone's moral character, it had all the virtues, and all the imperfections which attend a generous, easy, indolent disposition: with a strong glow of benevolence, and a readiness to serve his friends he had an equal disinclination to inspect and regulate his own affairs. This, with a total want of frugality, and the expence of keeping up the beauty of his extensive walks out of an income never more than 300*l*. per annum, occasioned often inconvenience extremely distressing to a man of fine sensibility; and sometimes ruffled a temper naturally mild and placid. (I,530)

The second dealt with Shenstone's financial circumstances immediately prior to his death:

> Having, as hath been before observed, impaired his fortune, not only by his taste for rural improvements, but by an unfortunate law-suit, in which he was involved with a near relation; he was upon the point of being made easy in his circumstances by a pension of 300*l*. per ann. which some powerful friends were procuring for him, when he was seized with a putrid fever, which put a period to his life at the Leasowes, about 5 o'clock on Friday morning the 11th of February, 1763. He was buried near his brother under a plain flat stone, inscribed with his name, on the south-side of Hales-owen churchyard. (I,531)

When Johnson drew upon this material he omitted the first part of the not entirely flattering moral character and made no mention of the law-suit. He expressed some doubt on the question of Shenstone's pension but used the occasion to pay him a generous tribute:

> He spent his estate in adorning it, and his death was probably hastened by his anxieties. He was a lamp that spent its oil in blazing. It is said that if he had lived a little longer he

would have been assisted by a pension: such bounty could not have been ever more properly bestowed; but that it was ever asked is not certain: it is too certain that it never was enjoyed.

He died at the Leasowes of a putrid fever about five on Friday morning, February 11, 1763, and was buried by the side of his brother in the church-yard of Hales-Owen. (III,352f.)

He had expressed a similar opinion concerning the pension some years earlier: "Poor Shenstone never tasted his pension. It is not very well proved that any pension was obtained for him. I am afraid that he died of misery."[20]

Two other small items from Nash were used by Johnson. The first concerned Shenstone's celibacy:

Mr. Shenstone was never married, but acknowledged it was his own fault, that he did not accept the hand of the lady whom he so tenderly loved, and whose charms he has so affectionately sung in his celebrated pastoral ballad, which is among the most admired of all his poems. (I,531)

Johnson accepted the biographical data but omitted the note of approbation concerning the poem. He reserved his judgment and regrets for the latter half of the Life in which he made his critical assessment of the poetry: "He was never married, though he might have obtained the lady, whoever she was to whom his *Pastoral Ballad* was addressed." (III, 353) The second item is contained in one of Nash's footnotes and concerned the origin of Elegy XXVI. This poem, known as "Elegy to Jessy", bears the superscription: "Describing the sorrow of an ingenuous mind, on the melancholy event of a licentious amour."

Among his Elegies is one on the unhappy fate of a young Lady, who is represented as having fallen a victim to the seduction of unlawful love; which some ignorant readers have imagined to be expressive of his own remorse for some such adventure in which he was himself concerned. It is but justice to his memory to declare, that this is entirely groundless; and that the subject of this Elegy is well known to his friends to have been suggested by the story of Miss Sally Godfrey in Richardson's Pamela. (I,531,n.f.)

[20] 19 Sept. 1774; Boswell's *Life*, V, 457.

Omitting the reference to the ignorant readers, Johnson included this vindication of Shenstone's moral character:

> His life was unstained by any crime; the *Elegy on Jessy*, which has been supposed to relate to an unfortunate and criminal amour of his own, was known by his friends to have been suggested by the story of Miss Godfrey in Richardson's *Pamela*. (III, 354)

Another significant omission on the part of Johnson relates to Dodsley. It concerned his precipitate publication of some of Shenstone's early works and criticised his edition of the posthumous works.

Nash:

> Yet many of the feebler performances, that clog his works and abate our reverence for his genius, are well known to his friends to have been dragged into notice contrary to his own intention or judgment, being either juvenile, or unfinished escapes, which he never would have suffered to be printed, had he lived to publish his works himself; as he often expressed great concern at the previous insertion of them in Dodsley's Miscellanies, to whom all his manuscripts had been sent, while he was disabled by a severe fit of illness from making a proper selection. Poor Shenstone wanted for his posthumous works such a friend and corrector as Parnell had in Pope. Yet, under all this disadvantage, he ever will deserve a place among our English classics. (I, 530).

This passage shows Dodsley in an unfavourable light and suggests that some bad feeling existed between poet and publisher. In a footnote, Nash referred his readers to what Shenstone had said on this subject in a letter to Graves, but did not quote from it. Had he done so, Shenstone's sentiments towards his editor would have been made plain. In the letter Shenstone confesses how mortified he had been by the first sight of Dodsley's *Miscellanies*, but continues: "To speak the truth, there are many things appear there very contrary to my intentions; but which I am more desirous may be attributed to the unseasonableness of my fever, than to my friend D[odsley]'s precipitation."[21] Dodsley had dealt kindly with Shenstone in the Preface to the Works; he was also Johnson's publisher and friend

---

(21) Letter to Graves, 30 May 1758; *Works*, III, 313.

Perhaps for these reasons, Johnson omitted the offending passage. Certainly, the Nash version tends to be misleading at this point, and Johnson had no wish to perpetuate error.

Almost all the material in Nash was utilised by Johnson, although he made no acknowledgement of his source. He employed paraphrase rather than transcription and made minor changes in accordance with the dictates of his own opinions and prejudices. Shenstone does not appear to the same advantage as he does in the original. Restraint, a change of emphasis but not conscious distortion, a significant omission, a nuance here and there, all contribute to impart a Johnsonian bias to the Nash version.

Johnson's second source, Robert Dodsley's biographical preface to the first collected edition of the works, appeared in the year following Shenstone's death. Dodsley's intent was to present the man to his readers in the most favourable light; in a manner befitting a friend in mourning. At the same time, in his capacity as publisher, his endeavour was to enhance the reputation of the poet and to popularise his works. This twofold motive for erecting a pious monument in a handsome edition of his works set a limitation on its merits as a factual biographical source. Johnson used the Preface with reservation: he knew the particular difficulties and temptations of the contemporary biographer as well as the advantages. Dodsley's account contained some information also to be found in Nash, as well as additional details. Johnson made little attempt to collate the two. Thus in using Nash exclusively for the opening paragraphs he omitted some interesting and not insignificant details from Dodsley. An observation on Shenstone's disposition was used, and on this occasion Johnson acknowledged his source: "He is represented by his friend Dodsley as a man of great tenderness and generosity, kind to all that were within his influence, but, if once offended, not easily appeased." (III,353) Dodsley also considers Shenstone's lack of economy and provides a brief picture of his personal appearance. On these topics Johnson made his most extensive use of the Preface. Dodsley recorded that

> He was no œconomist; the generosity of his temper prevented him from paying a proper regard to the use of money; he exceeded therefore the bounds of his paternal fortune, which before he died was considerably encumbered. But when one recollects the perfect paradise he had raised around him, the hospitality with which he lived, his great indulgence to his servants, his charities to the indigent, and all done with

an estate not more than three hundred pounds a year, one should rather be led to wonder that he left any thing behind him, than to blame his want of œconomy.[22]

Johnson paraphrased part of this but made no comparable attempt to mitigate the faults by remarking on Shenstone's generosity and achievements. He represents him as being "inattentive to œconomy, and careless of his expences". (III,353)

Johnson had lived with poverty and always exhibited a sympathetic understanding of the poor; his charity was devoid of sentiment. He judged by his own standards, and had no cause to feel humbled at Shenstone's benevolence to those within his circle. Shenstone collected sham ruins and the statues of men in his garden: Johnson the ruins of real men and women within and about his household.

From his personal knowledge of Shenstone, Dodsley gave an authoritative account of his appearance and mode of dress:

> His person, as to height, was above the middle stature, but largely and rather inelegantly formed: his face seemed plain till you conversed with him, and then it grew very pleasing. In his dress he was negligent, even to a fault; though when young, at the university, he was accounted a BEAU. He wore his own hair, which was quite grey very early, in a particular manner; not from any affectation of singularity, but from a maxim he had laid down that, without too slavish a regard to fashion, every one should dress in a manner most suitable to his own person and figure. In short, his faults were only little blemishes, thrown in by nature, as it were on purpose to prevent him from rising too much above that level of imperfection allotted to humanity.[23]

Here, again, Johnson had some things in common with his subject. He, too, was clumsy in form, negligent of his clothes and, as a young man, had worn his own hair at a time when the practice excited ridicule.[24] In his maxim concerning dress, Shenstone had distinguished between the fashions of a younger man and those of an older man: "A MAN's dress in the former

---

(22) pp. iii f.
(23) pp. iv f.
(24) See Boswell's *Life*, I, 94.

part of life should rather tend to set off his Person, than to express riches, rank or dignity: In the latter, the reverse."[25] Dodsley's rather sweeping reference to this principle does not bring out the distinction. Johnson's acceptance of this version without comment suggests that he did not turn to *Men and Manners* to verify Dodsley's assertion. He omitted the intimate little description of the poet's face and the reference to the beau. If Dodsley's description is not over-flattering, he nevertheless makes a gracious attempt to remove any suggestion of incivility towards his friend. Johnson was not moved either to excuse the blemishes or to speculate on nature. In less deferential language he accepted Shenstone for what he was:

> in his person larger than the middle size, with something clumsy in his form; very negligent of his cloaths, and remarkable for wearing his grey hair in a particular manner, for he held that the fashion was no rule of dress, and that every man was to suit his appearance to his natural form. (III,353f.)

On the subject of Shenstone and marriage, Dodsley is more informative than Johnson and Nash. Dodsley adds speculation to the known fact:

> It was perhaps from some considerations on the narrowness of his fortune, that he forbore to marry; for he was no enemy to wedlock, had a high opinion of many among the fair sex, was fond of their society, and no stranger to the tenderest impressions. One, which he received in his youth, was with difficulty surmounted. The lady was the subject of that sweet pastoral, in four parts, which has been so universally admired; and which, one would have thought, must have subdued the loftiest heart, and softened the most obdurate.[26]

Johnson found no place for such speculation in his own account. He himself had found the narrowness of his fortune no insurmountable obstacle to marriage with one financially his superior. Indeed, marriage brought some alleviation to his circumstances. Johnson's version reads: "He was never married, though he might have obtained the lady, whoever she was, to whom his *Pastoral Ballad* was addressed." (III, 353)

---

(25) Shenstone, *Works*, II, 164.

(26) p. iv.

Dodsley's Preface comprises a biographical sketch followed by a brief appraisal of Shenstone's works. Whilst Johnson made direct use of this biographical material, he chose to make his own independent evaluation of the works. Nevertheless, some of these critical observations were made in contradistinction to Dodsley, as if to correct or modify the judgments popularised in the collected edition. Writing in a eulogistic vein and glossing over Shenstone's faults, Dodsley was out to prove his poet great; or at least that he had the qualities, if not the determination, to achieve greatness:

> His character as a writer will be distinguished by simplicity with elegance, and genius with correctness. He had a sublimity equal to the highest attempts; yet from the indolence of his temper, he chose rather to amuse himself in culling flowers at the foot of the mount, than to take the trouble of climbing the more arduous steps of PARNASSUS.[27]

Johnson assented to Shenstone's claim to simplicity, but reduced "elegance" to easiness. He doubted whether Shenstone could ever have reached Parnassus, even if his temperament had been less indolent. Johnson knew the enemy Indolence himself and chose to fight against it. He judged by achievement rather than aspiration, and was thus more forthright in enumerating Shenstone's defects than Dodsley had been:

> The general recommendation of Shenstone is easiness and simplicity; his general defect is want of comprehension and variety. Had his mind been better stored with knowledge, whether he could have been great I know not; he could certainly have been agreeable. (III,359)

On a previous occasion he had assessed the poet in more picturesque language:

> To some lady who was praising Shenstone's poems very much, and who had an Italian greyhound lying by the fire Johnson said, "Shenstone holds amongst poets the same rank your dog holds amongst dogs; he had not the sagacity of the hound, the docility of the spaniel, nor the courage of the bull-dog, yet he is still a pretty fellow".[28]

---

(27) p.v.

(28) *Johnsonian Miscellanies*, ed. G.B. Hill (Oxford, 1897), II, 5.

Dodsley's manifest approval of Shenstone's retirement from the world
is evident throughout his Preface. During the last years of Shenstone's life,
he paid an annual visit to the Leasowes. He thought highly of his friend's
achievements as a landscape gardener, and paid a further tribute to his memory by adding "A Description of the Leasowes" to the second volume of
the *Works*. In this enthusiastic and imaginative account, Dodsley conducts
his reader round the estate, displaying to advantage every detail of the place,
re-creating every aspect as Shenstone himself intended it to be seen. Johnson
made some use of this attempt to perpetuate the beauties of the Leasowes
— but not altogether to Shenstone's advantage. In his Description Dodsley
enthused over the visual beauty of the Leasowes; one magnificent scene he
described as follows:

> if a boon companion could enlarge his idea of a punchbowl,
> ornamented within with all the romantic scenery the Chinese
> ever yet devised, it would, perhaps, afford him the highest
> idea he could possibly conceive of earthly happiness.(29)

Johnson's idea of earthly happiness embraced humanity. While there were
beggars on the streets of London and indigent families in the villages, he
would have found greater admiration for Shenstone had he contrived with
nature to harvest the fecundity of the soil. There is thus a note of censure
in Johnson's remark that Shenstone managed his estate "more to the
improvement of its beauty than the increase of its produce." (III,350) His
observations on these improvements cast doubt on their true merit. Without enthusing over the achievements, he allowed some praise and then only
with reservations. As part of a life's work the Leasowes did not weigh heavily
in Johnson's scales of absolute values. Furthermore, it was achieved, so he
thought, at a price beyond the poet's means. The details summarised in
Johnson's account are all to be found in the "Description". At one point
on the "tour" Dodsley conjectures the purpose of Shenstone's benches:

> I must observe once for all, that a number of these extempore
> benches (two stumps with a transverse board) seem chiefly
> intended as hints to spectators, lest in passing cursorily thro'
> the farm they might suffer any of that immense variety the
> place furnishes, to escape their notice.(30)

(29) Shenstone, *Works*, II, 360.
(30) Ibid., II, 337.

At other points he describes such details as: "a pleasing serpentine walk", "a long winding vale, with the most graceful confusion", "a new theatre of wild shaggy precipices", "a mound that pounds up the water", and "a small babbling rill ... forming little peninsulars, rolling over pebbles ... falling down small cascades, all under cover, and taught to murmur very agreeably". He enthuses over each spectacle and vista:

> one of the most beautiful cascades imaginable is seen by way of incident, through a kind of vista, or glade, falling down a precipice over-arched with trees, and strikes us with surprize. It is impossible to express the pleasure which one feels on this occasion, for though surprize alone is not excellence, it may serve to quicken the effect of what is beautiful. I believe none ever beheld the grove, without a thorough sense of satisfaction; and were one to chuse any one particular spot of this perfectly Arcadian farm, it should, perhaps, be this.(31)

On a rainy day in mid-September, some seven years before he wrote the Life, Johnson visited the Leasowes with the Thrales as they were returning from their journey into North Wales. His brief record of the occasion contrasts with Dodsley's lavish description and suggests reluctance rather than rapture at the prospect of viewing the cascades: "It was rain, yet we visited all the waterfalls. There are, in one place, fourteen falls in a short line."(32) Dodsley had been enraptured by the "striking cascades": characteristically, Johnson was content to count them.

This was by no means his first visit to a cascade on the Welsh tour. After recording the dimensions of the "very noble ruin" of Ruthin Castle, he wrote: "We then went to see a cascade. I trudged unwillingly, and was not sorry to find it dry."(33) The memory of the Leasowes had now long since faded. However, the author of *Rasselas*, with Dodsley's description before him, would find no difficulty in recreating the scene with verisimilitude. Johnson's objective and concentrated details comprise the essence of Dodsley's description bereft of his rapturous admiration and unqualified praise. Any doubts as to the achievement of the Leasowes were all Johnson's own:

---

(31) Ibid., II, 365.

(32) "A Journey into North Wales, in The Year 1774," Boswell's *Life*, V, 457.

(33) Ibid., V, 442.

Now was excited his delight in rural pleasures, and his ambition of rural elegance; he began from this time to point his prospects, to diversify his surface, to entangle his walks, and to wind his waters, which he did with such judgement and such fancy as made his little domain the envy of the great and the admiration of the skilful: a place to be visited by travellers, and copied by designers. Whether to plant a walk in undulating curves, and to place a bench at every turn where there is an object to catch the view; to make water run where it will be heard, and to stagnate where it will be seen; to leave intervals where the eye will be pleased, and to thicken the plantation where there is something to be hidden, demands any great powers of mind, I will not enquire: perhaps a sullen and surly speculator may think such performances rather the sport than the business of human reason. But it must be at least confessed that to embellish the form of nature is an innocent amusement, and some praise must be allowed by the most supercilious observer to him who does best what such multitudes are contending to do well. (III, 350f.)

Dodsley included with the "Description" some commendatory verses in praise of the Leasowes. These verses by Shenstone's friends contain many allusions to fairies and nymphs, groves, birdsong, and the bleat of the lambkins. Fairies are also referred to in some lines inscribed on a tablet at Shenstone's root-house. The opening and closing lines were as follows:

Here in cool grot, and mossy cell,
We rural fays and faeries dwell ...

But harm betide the wayward swain,
Who dares our hallow'd haunts profane !

Dodsley quoted the inscription and added the following observation: "THESE sentiments correspond as well as possible with the ideas we form of the abode of fairies; and appearing deep in this romantic vally, serve to keep alive such enthusiastic images while this sort of scene continues."(34) Such power of fancy over reason was too much for Johnson. To him fairies were a legacy from a barbarous state and had no place in a rational age. He did not quote the verses, but used the fairies and the lambkins to introduce a jarring note of realism into his narrative. Shenstone was not always free of creditors, although Graves later dismissed as a "groundless surmise"

---

(34) Shenstone, *Works*, II, 336.

the allegation that duns haunted the Leasowes.([35]) Johnson, however, play-fully introduced the story, and the fairies, at this point:"In time his expences brought clamours about him, that overpowered the lamb's bleat and the linnet's song; and his groves were haunted by beings very different from fauns and fairies." (III, 352)

Johnson enjoyed such anecdotes and used them to enliven his biogra-phical writings; but his use of a biographical detail was determined by the prerequisites of relevance and significance. How much of the essential Shen-stone does Johnson communicate to the readers through the use of anecdotal material ? First there is the story from infancy, taken from Nash, to which I have already referred. Some of his contemporaries took this as an "idle jest",([36]) but it is not without its significance. Books, poetry, literature, were an essential part of Shenstone's life. Here, the child was father of the man, and books remained a life-long love. The second anecdote concerns the relationship between Shenstone and his neighbour, Lord Lyttelton of Hagley. It does credit neither to Shenstone nor to Lyttelton. Johnson's story of the supposed rivalry between the two was later called in question and aroused controversy. Since the "sources" provide no justification for assuming that any serious rivalry existed, Johnson's interpolation is of particular interest. He bore no malice to Shenstone and had no personal motive for making the "little fellow" appear ridiculous. It is to be noted, however, that the contro-versial passage begins and ends with observations not on Shenstone but on life. Writing in the full wisdom of his years, Johnson was more concerned with the underlying truths of human nature and its frailties as illustrated in the anecdote than in the petty rivalry itself. Having defined the praise due to Shenstone, Johnson continued:

> but, like all other modes of felicity, it was not enjoyed with-out its abatements. Lyttelton was his neighbour and his rival, whose empire, spacious and opulent, looked with disdain on the *petty State* that *appeared behind it*. For a while the inhabi-tants of Hagley affected to tell their acquaintance of the little fellow that was trying to make himself admired; but when by degrees the Leasowes forced themselves into notice, they took care to defeat the curiosity which they could not suppress,

---

(35) *Recollection*, pp. 72f.

(36) Robert Potter, *The Art of Criticism; as exemplified in Dr. Johnson's Lives of the Most Eminent English Poets* (London, 1789), p. 172.

by conducting their visitants perversely to the inconvenient
points of view, and introducing them at the wrong end of a
walk to detect a deception; injuries of which Shenstone
would heavily complain. Where there is emulation there
will be vanity, and where there is vanity there will be folly.
(III, 351f.)

No one challenged the general truth expressed in the concluding sentence,
but his critics seized upon the particular incident. The third "anecdote" is
again significant. Johnson used it to support and illustrate his contention that
"The Pleasure of Shenstone was all in his eye", and continued, "he valued
what he valued merely for its looks; nothing raised his indignation more
than to ask if there were any fishes in his water." (III, 352) Again, this is
not just an idle jest. It represents the gulf between writer and subject instanc-
ed above. The divergence of opinion as to the relative importance of beauty
and utility was manifest in the controversies of the century: the problem is
unresolved today. Johnson demanded a more fruitful yield from the bounties of nature than an aesthetic experience. In this respect he represented the
rationalists. Mrs. Piozzi recorded that

> Johnson used to laugh at Shenstone for not caring whether
> there was anything good to eat in the streams he was so fond
> of, "as if (says he) one could fill one's belly with hearing soft
> murmurs or looking at rough cascades."(37)

There were fish, however, in his streams, as one uninvited visitor of the
Johnsonian school discovered. Shenstone's first impulse on this occasion was
to deliver the poacher over to Justice. On learning of his wretched circumstances, however, he reflected otherwise:

> I make a material Distinction between a *Robber* and a *Pilferer*;
> nor can I assign the former Appellation to a poor Wretch,
> who, in his Hunger, has taken two or three *Fishes*, or as many
> *Loaves* ... Then again, the Wife and five Children ! — The
> poor Fellow subsists, chief Part of the Year, only by carrying
> News-Papers round the Country. Had He been shut up, what
> was to have supported the ragged Family meanwhile ? I am
> beside inclined to think, that half a Crown, and a little whole-

---

(37) Mrs. Piozzi, *Anecdotes of the Late Samuel Johnson, LL.D.*, in *Johnsonian Miscellanies*, I, 323.

some Admonition, that is, if he be not a practised and stubborn Offender, might go as far towards amending his Morals, as an Acquaintance with the Inside of a Prison, and the Conversation of such Associates as he might find there.[38]

Johnson and Shenstone may have been on opposite sides in the controversy of Reason, but a concern for humanity was common to them both.

The penultimate anecdote concerns Shenstone's house and adds point to the concluding story of the duns who haunted the groves. It is illustrative of Johnson's conception of a man who put luxury before necessity, ornament before utility, who mistook the shadow for the substance:

> His house was mean, and he did not improve it; his care was of his grounds. When he came home from his walks he might find his floors flooded by a shower through the broken roof; but could spare no money for its reparation. (III, 352)

Again the anecdote started controversy. Graves questioned the validity of Johnson's "intelligence" on the point. He denied that the house was, in fact, mean or neglected.[39] Percy, writing from first-hand knowledge, supported this:

> Johnson had committed great mistakes with respect to Shenstone ... He grossly misrepresented both his circumstances and his house, which was small but elegant, and displayed a great deal of taste in the alteration and accommodation of the appartments, &c.[40]

Since Johnson used anecdotes more to the disadvantage than to the advantage of Shenstone, it is not surprising that they were read with mixed pleasure by his critics. Some aroused a lively, controversial interest; others proved highly contentious; the least innocuous raised protests in some quarters. But to Johnson, a story revealed a man, and a man illumined life. It was life that concerned Johnson in old age more than the chronicling of half a hundred poets.

---

(38) *The Letters of William Shenstone*; Arranged and Edited with Introduction, Notes and Index, by Marjorie Williams (Oxford, 1939), pp. 605f.

(39) *Recollection*, pp. 71f.

(40) John Nichols, *Illustrations of the Literary History of the Eighteenth Century* (1848), VII, 151.

When Johnson wrote the Life of Shenstone there were already in existence two published collections of the poet's letters and a volume of Lady
Luxborough's letters to Shenstone.[41] These valuable sources of biographical information were not exploited by Johnson. Dodsley was aware of the
value of Shenstone's letters as "an authentic history of his mind", and he
published his own edition of them five years after the two earlier volumes
of the *Works*. In addition to their biographical importance, he fully appre-
ciated their literary merit and was confident that they would provide an agreeable entertainment for his readers. In the Preface to the Letters he was at
pains to justify their publication and quoted Shenstone's own sentiments,
expressed in a letter to Graves, in support of his claims:

> I confess to you that I am considerably mortified by
> Mr. W[histler]'s conduct in regard to those Letters (meaning
> his own letters to that gentleman's brother); and, rather than
> they should have been so unnecessarily destroyed, would
> have given more money than it is allowable for me to men-
> tion with decency. I look upon my Letters as some of my
> *chef-d'œuvres*; and could I be supposed to have the smallest
> pretensions to propriety of style or sentiment, I should imagine
> it must appear principally in my Letters to his brother, and
> one or two more friends. I consider them as the records of a
> friendship that will be always dear to me, and as the history
> cf my mind for these twenty years past.[42]

Johnson had discussed this same topic with Boswell, whilst on the tour to
the Hebrides. He agreed that it was wrong of the brother of one of his cor-
respondents to burn his letters, and added "Shenstone was a man whose correspondence was an honour."[43] It is all the more remarkable, therefore,
that Johnson ignored the letters. Had he read them sympathetically, he would
have met Shenstone on more intimate terms and learned more of the man

---

(41) "Letters to particular Friends, from the Year 1739-1763," *The Works
in Verse and Prose of William Shenstone*, ed. J. Dodsley (1769), Vol. III.
*Select Letters between the late Duchess of Somerset, Lady Luxborough, Miss
Dolman, Mr. Whistler, Mr. R. Dodsley, William Shenstone, Esq. and others*, ed.
Thomas Hull, 2 vols. (1778).
Lady Luxborough, *Letters written by the late Right Honourable Lady
Luxborough to William Shenstone, Esq.* (1775).

(42) Shenstone, *Works*, III, p. vii.

(43) Boswell's *Life*, V, 268.

pictured within. Had this closer acquaintance been allowed to modify the preconceived image, he would have been spared much of the adverse criticism which followed. Johnson knew the value of letters to the biographer, but he was also aware of the pitfalls. For him, truth and sincerity were fundamental to the practice of biography. Letters were, therefore, not to be taken unreservedly as a reliable reflection of the writer's character; they were to be used with caution. In the Life of Pope he was not convinced that "the true characters of men may be found in their letters, and that he who writes to a friend lays his heart open before him."[44] Boswell had no such misgivings when he turned to Johnson's letters to provide a "view of his mind", in the Life. Here, he was extending the possibilities of Mason's biographical method in *Memoirs of Gray's Life* (1775), and was at a loss to conceive why Johnson had depreciated this work so unreasonably.

Johnson's reference to Shenstone's letters comes at the conclusion of the biographical portion of the Life; they are not included in his assessment of the works. Furthermore, he avoided direct comment and allowed Gray to pass judgment and characterize the writer. When we remember Johnson's own sentiments towards Gray, we may detect a touch of irony in his choice of such an unsympathetic assessment:

> What Gray thought of his character, from the perusal of his *Letters*, was this: "I have read too an octavo volume of Shenstone's *Letters*. Poor man ! he was always wishing for money, for fame, and other distinctions; and his whole philosophy consisted in living against his will in retirement, and in a place which his taste had adorned; but which he only enjoyed when people of note came to see and commend it. His correspondence is about nothing else but this place and his own writings, with two or three neighbouring clergymen, who wrote verses too". (III, 354)

Had Johnson perused the Letters himself and found the character revealed therein at variance with that discovered by Gray, he would have said so. As it was, he quoted him without comment. From this we may assume either that he was not conversant with the Letters, or that he maintained a silence of assent. His critics did not remain silent; both Gray and Johnson were challenged on their disparaging interpretation. Alluding to the strictures in the

---

(44) *Lives*, III, 206.

Life of Gray, Robert Potter considered Johnson's use of the quotation doubly
unjust: "he introduces Gray with his knotted club to knock down the gentle
Shenstone, to be himself knocked down at last by our blind Polypheme in
the wantonness of his might."[45]

To the modern reader, Shenstone's letters can give delight as a charming revelation of the interests, way of life, changing temperament and passing
moods of an eighteenth century man of taste. He had no Boswell to record
his conversations, but his letters do something of this for him. They also
serve as a commentary on and a corrective to those passages in Johnson where
he followed his established practice of departing from the source in order to
generalise and expound his own opinions. The Letters are particularly
illuminating when read in conjunction with his evaluation of Shenstone's
achievements in the realm of landscape gardening. In an age when landscape art was becoming increasingly popular, Shenstone had secured an en-
viable reputation as a successful exponent. Johnson's reflections angered his
contemporaries. His general opinions were questioned and his particular references to Shenstone were challenged. Johnson maintained that "The pleasure
of Shenstone was all in his eye; he valued what he valued merely for its looks."
(III, 352) The letters suggest that Shenstone's aesthetic meant something
more than "appeal to the eye;" it had also to satisfy his sense of fitness and
his intellectual integrity. Just as the appeal to the ear of an old ballad was
not sufficient, in his opinion, to merit inclusion in Percy's collection if it
proved to be spurious, so he would not allow inferior design to masquerade
as art, however attractive it might appear to the eye of the philistine.

Johnson also represents Shenstone as having little care for the economy
of his estate, and maintained that in neglecting his house at the expense of
his grounds "He spent his estate in adorning it, and his death was probably
hastened by his anxieties. He was a lamp that spent its oil in blazing." (III,352)
If he spent his oil in blazing he at least took pains to trim the wick. His letters
do not suggest that he was habitually careless or unmindful of his economy.
Sometimes he found his financial restrictions oppressive and he suffered under
his burden; on other occasions he could smile at himself as an impecunious
aesthete. He does not appear over-indulgent in the use of his limited income;
he over-spent at times, but was a slave neither to economy nor to prodi-
gality:

---

(45) *Art of Criticism*, p. 172.

> You [Jago] cannot think how much you gratified my vanity when you were here, by saying, that if this place were yours, you thought you should be less able to keep within the bounds of *œconomy* than myself. — God knows, it is pain and grief to me to observe her rules at *all*; and *rigidly* I never can. — How is it possible to possess improveable scenes, and not wish to improve them ? and how is it possible, with œconomy, to be at the expence of improving them upon my fortune ? To be continually in fear of excess in perfecting every trifling design, how irksome ! to be restrained from attempting *any*, how vexatious ! Œconomy, that invidious old matron ! on occasion of every frivolous expence, makes such a hellish squalling, that the murmur of a cascade is utterly lost to me.[46]

Sometimes the old matron was too much with him. Nevertheless, he did not allow himself to be impressed merely by the cost of landscape gardening as practised on the grand scale by his richer neighbours. He smiled at his own modest outlay in comparison with that of his "rivals" at Hagley. His letters to Lady Luxborough and other friends contain much helpful technical advice founded on the dual principles of economy and artistic expediency:

> *Balls* will suit the Simplicity of your Dorick Buildings better than *Urns*, and will come five times Cheaper.[47]
>
> I am a degree more frugal than you; for I only use quicklime, and either blue or yellow sand to take away the objection which I have to whited walls.[48]

Yet the success of his estate was in no way proportional to his limited expenditure; the imposing list of visitors testifies to the high esteem he enjoyed as an exponent of his art.

The last of Johnson's own general comments is of particular interest since he stated it twice. It appears first in the biographical section: "His mind was not very comprehensive, nor his curiosity active; he had no value for those parts of knowledge which he had not himself cultivated." (III, 354) And again, in the critical section, as a final summing up of his poetry:

---

(46) Shenstone, *Works*, III, 120.

(47) *Letters*, ed. M. Williams, p. 227.

(48) Shenstone, *Works*, III, 214.

> The general recommendation of Shenstone is easiness and simplicity; his general defect is want of comprehension and variety. Had his mind been better stored with knowledge, whether he could have been great I know not; he could certainly have been agreeable. (III, 359)

Shenstone would have concurred, at least in part, with this; but he did not always under-estimate his own abilities. His reputation rested upon his gardening and his poetry, and he wished the honours to be divided equally between the two. For this reason he criticised a proposed inscription, composed by his friend Richard Graves, because it placed more emphasis on his skill in gardening than on his accomplishment in poetry. Nevertheless, the tenor of his existence was one of rustic retirement and cultured leisure. He lived out his days among the commonplaces of the country scene far from "the full tide of human existence at Charing Cross".[49] When not absorbed by his own estate he would be writing to friends advising them on theirs; giving sound practical advice on painting and decorating, or the making of quills sealing wax and papier mâché, and attending generally to the business of friendship and correspondence. Locally he interested himself in the affairs of the parish, the new turn-pike road from Hagley to Birmingham, or the provision of a new set of bells for the church.

But there was more to Shenstone than perhaps Johnson realised. The letters, for all the daily round and common task of the sequestered life, contain a wider comprehension and variety than he allowed. By ordinary standards, Shenstone's knowledge and interests were neither completely parochial nor unimportant. His correspondence with Percy and the detailed advice and assistance he gave towards the compilation of the *Reliques*, the critical comments scattered through his letters, and his own achievements as a writer,

---

(49) "JOHNSON. 'Why, Sir, Fleet-street has a very animated appearance; but I think the full tide of human existence is at Charing-cross.' " Boswell's *Life*, II,337.

Cf. "Our conversation turned upon living in the country, which Johnson, whose melancholy mind required the dissipation of quick successive variety, had habituated himself to consider as a kind of mental imprisonment. 'Yet, Sir [said Boswell], there are many people who are content to live in the country.' JOHNSON. 'Sir, it is in the intellectual world as in the physical world; we are told by natural philosophers that a body is at rest in the place fit for it; they who are content to live in the country, are *fit* for the country.' " Ibid., IV, 338.

reveal a comprehension and curiosity more extensive than Johnson would allow. It is only when Shenstone is measured against Johnson himself that his limitations become more apparent, and we see how few were the points at which he touched life.

Three other aspects of Shenstone's life, not developed by Johnson, are manifest in his Letters: his love of visitors, his dependence upon friends, and his indolence. The social pleasures that his gardens brought him began to mean as much to Shenstone as the pleasures of the eye. He made no attempt to conceal his delight at the popularity of the Leasowes, which to him was proportionate to the numbers, and rank, of his visitors. In 1749 he wrote to his friend Jago: "It is now Sunday evening, and I have been exhibiting myself in my walks to no less than a hundred and fifty people, and that with no less state and vanity than a Turk in his seraglio."[50] Quantity was not enough; he wished for quality too. He lists the names of the wealthy and the famous as so many butterflies caught in the net of his garden. The sound of titles and the glitter of nobility were sufficient reward for his labours and brought satisfaction and purpose to his existence. His success continued with the years. But visitors were a transient delight, and even they could not minister to his deeper needs. Imposing as the roll of visitors might be, it was but a luxury. For Shenstone, the necessity of life was friendship. This he had in common with Johnson: both depended upon friends and companions. Visitors flattered his vanity, but friends sustained his existence. At times the temporary absence of the coaches and coronets could leave him dispirited; at others their presence could leave him unmoved. But the irrecoverable loss of a friend or beloved relative struck at his very heartstrings and left him bewildered. The finality of death shook his existence and drove him to pour out his soul in letters. Such a time was one of spiritual introspection and self-evaluation. Again, there is a comparison with Johnson himself; but whereas he lived under the awful fear of death and final judgment, Shenstone derived some comfort from the erection of a memorial urn and enjoyed a pleasing melancholy in sepulchral contemplation.

For the most part, Shenstone was content to lead a quiet, sequestered life, regulated by the seasons and enlivened by his diversions, with no great desire to seek ambition or find adventure beyond the confines of the Leasowes. His letters and his friends justified his existence to himself. But his

---

(50) Shenstone, *Works*, III, 183.

life was made up of things as well as people. Indolence, ill-health, melancholy, were combatted to some extent by material possessions. He could lose himself in his collection of coins or curios without being entirely dominated by them, and was able to rationalise and justify this use of his time. From his trifles he derived a therapeutic value after his hypochondriacal illness. His letters are full of the trivialities of a rustic life, and innocent, inexpensive amusements. Trifles meant a great deal to him and became part of his philosophy of life:

> Mean time, do not despise others that can find any needful amusement in what, I think, Bunyan, very aptly called *Vanity Fair*. I have been at it many times this season, and have bought many kinds of merchandize there. It is a part of philosophy, to adapt one's passions to one's way of life; and the solitary, unsocial sphere in which I move makes me think it happy that I can retain a relish for such trifles as I can draw into it.[51]

If he could not defeat Indolence he was content to make a truce with it. At times he considered his poems as part of the inebriation of trifles. Sometimes indolence kept him from them: sometimes he turned to poetry to keep off indolence.

Here there is a gulf between subject and biographer. Shenstone made some endeavour to contain indolence, and his writings were a palliative or an escape. Johnson knew indolence and fought against it. Ever conscious of the task unfinished and the work yet to be done, he did not turn to his writings for relief from boredom. Nor could he look upon time as a void to be filled, but rather as an allotted span for the filling of which he would be called to account. For Shenstone the passing mood determined the effort: Johnson insisted that a man might write at any time "if he will set himself *doggedly* to it."[52] Johnson, too, could enjoy trifles in his own way and on his own terms; but he refused to deceive himself by specious rationalisation into accepting time mis-spent or the avoidance of a task. His religious contemplations before any new literary venture or serious study contrast markedly with Shenstone's attitude:

> Grant, O Lord, that I may not lavish away the life which Thou hast given me on useless trifles, nor waste it in vain searches after things which Thou hast hidden from me.

(51) Ibid., III, 198.
(52) Boswell's *Life*, V, 40.

Enable me, by Thy Holy Spirit, so to shun sloth and negligence, that every day may discharge part of the task which Thou hast allotted me.[53]

Shenstone could reconcile his indolence and his trifles with the purpose of his existence, and could come to terms with his inactivity:

You speak of my dwelling in the Castle of Indolence, and I verily believe I *do*. There is something like enchantment in my present inactivity; for, without any kind of lett or impediment to the correction of my trifles that I see, I am in no wise able to make the least advances. I think within myself I could proceed if you were here; and yet I have reason to believe, if you *were* here, we should only ramble round the groves, and chat away the time; and perhaps *that*, upon the *whole*, is of full as much importance.[54]

No one loved good talk with friends more than Johnson, but he would not willingly chat away the time. He found no enchantment in Indolence but an enemy on the Devil's side against whom he had to wrestle.

Shenstone's retirement from the buffets of the world to the tranquillity of the Leasowes was viewed variously by his contemporaries. Some identified him with the character of Graves' Columella,[55] a recluse dedicated to poetry and romance. To these he appeared an admirable example of the simple life; to others he symbolised the anti-social escapist. Certainly Shenstone had no delusions as to his own way of life, and the hum-drum was not obscured by romance. In a happy conversational mood he once wrote to Jago and described the "notable incidents" in his life as amounting to "about as much as the tinsel of your little boy's hobby horse." In the same letter he gave his friend a recipe for happiness. Anticipating Voltaire by some twelve years,[56] he would have him cultivate his garden:

I find no small delight in rearing all sorts of poultry; geese, turkeys, pullets, ducks, &c... one may easily habituate one's self to cheap amusements; that is, *rural* ones (for all town amusements are horridly expensive); — I would have you

---

(53) "Before any New Study;" Nov. 1752. *Prayers and Meditations*.

(54) Shenstone, *Works*, III, 170f.

(55) See R. Graves, *Columella; or, the Distressed Anchoret* (1779).

(56) *Candide*, published 1759.

cultivate your garden; plant flowers, have a bird or two in the hall (they will at *least* amuse your children); write now and then a song; buy now and then a book; write now and then a letter.[57]

As such, this is a faithful picture of his life at the time. It has all the charm of a pastoral ballad; but to Johnson it was just as far removed from real life as he knew it. The Leasowes to him was not the best of all possible worlds. He observed laconically: "He spent his estate in adorning it, and his death was probably hastened by his anxieties." (III, 352) The romantic idyll was shattered. However charming and worthwhile the quiet retirement from the world might appear to his contemporaries, Johnson could not accept it as a complete justification of time and talent. His comment on the "Elegies" could apply equally well as an epitome of rustic retirement: "The peace of solitude, the innocence of inactivity, and the unenvied security of an humble station can fill but a few pages." (III, 355) To Johnson all this was insufficient to fill a human life. For him, at least, it represented a false view. Solitude drove him into company; inactivity tortured his soul; poverty was a bitter memory. In consequence he found more to pity than to praise in Shenstone. He had shown that escape from the Happy Valley to the world beyond did not of itself lead to true happiness.[58] Conversely, he had no wish to deceive his readers into false hopes of happiness through retirement from the world to the groves and gardens of the Leasowes.

---

(57) Shenstone, *Works*, III, 159f.

(58) *Rasselas* published 1759.

JOHN HARDY

Two Notes on Johnson:

(1) A Suggested Approach to the Criticism
(2) Locke as a Possible Source of *Metaphysical.*

(1) A Suggested Approach to the Criticism

Since commitment to judgment is fundamental to Johnson's criticism, a satisfactory account of his critical practice can only be offered from a knowledge of why particular judgments themselves are made. That these judgments are *individual* judgments could be demonstrated by comparing Johnson with other critics identifiable with the neo-classical critical tradition. But histories of literature and of criticism do not often exhibit any appreciable perception of Johnson's individual or distinctive qualities as a critic; nor is this deficiency always remedied by more specialized commentaries on the criticism.

One tradition of commentary, which descends most obviously from Macaulay,[1] has tended to conceal the individuality under a picture of eccentricity. Its evidence for a myopic and "prejudiced" critic has been inferred from its interpretation of Boswell's *Life of Johnson,* to which it has seemed to regard the *Lives of the Poets* as at best supplementary. An example of this tradition is to be found in Professor C.B. Tinker's two essays on Johnson in *Essays in Retrospect*; their ultimate emphasis is indicated by "Johnson's bulky and impressive figure."[2] Professor Tinker has, of course, made an individual contribution to this tradition; his sympathy and deeper understanding have resulted in its refinement. But while he seems to realize that the man is significantly present in the criticism ("there are frequently at work

---

(1) Compare Bertrand H. Bronson's "The Double Tradition of Dr. Johnson," *JELH* XVIII (1951), pp. 92-3.

(2) Yale, 1948, p. 34; though only the first essay ("Johnson as Monarch," pp. 23-33) is concerned with the criticism.

in his mind great fundamental convictions which are at the very heart and
center of the man")(3), his formulation of this fact reverts to Macaulayan
patterns (though, of course, his appraisal differs from Macaulay's); it does
not sufficiently dissociate the Johnson of the criticism from what has been
described as "a character out of a great book":(4)

> Johnson's criticism is not a *system* ... Though we still read
> the *Lives of the Poets*, we do not do so to find out what to
> think about Milton and Pope, but rather to enjoy the humor
> and the humors, the audacities and the prejudices of a man
> of genius, who even in his aberrations is always amusing and
> always stimulating.(5)

In "The Theoretical Foundations of Johnson's Criticism" Professor
W.R. Keast has challenged Professor Tinker's description of Johnson as a
critic having "tastes" but no "system."(6) He argues that Johnson had "a
coherent view of literature and a coherent body of assumptions concerning
both its practice and its evaluation," and it is "on the basis of these assumptions concerning the nature of literature and the task of criticism" that Johnson is seen to develop "the scheme of analysis which underlies his discussions
of technical problems, works and genres, and individual authors."(7) This
reaction proves compensatory by serving to discourage any "psychological"
interpretations that appear irresponsible. The essay also demonstrates the
originality of Johnson's "conception of literature"(8) when compared with
that of his predecessors. This originality is shown to consist in his treatment
of literature as "a mode of activity" of a therefore "peculiarly tentative and
experimental character,"(9) and in the related insistence on the importance
of the reader as "antecedent to art, in the sense that the properties involved

---

(3) *ibid.* p. 28.

(4) By James L. Clifford in *Johnsonian Studies* (Minneapolis, 1951): "The
Victorians were generally content to take Johnson as a character out of a great
book" (p. 2).

(5) *loc. cit.*

(6) *Critics and Criticism*, ed. R.S. Crane (Chicago, 1952), p. 389.

(7) *ibid.* pp. 391, 399.

(8) *ibid.* p. 397.

(9) *ibid.* pp. 397, 404.

in [Johnson's] definition of the proper reader are derived from an examination of human nature and not from an examination of literature." (**10**) But
in pursuing his discussion in terms of "the four elements in the literary process — author, work, nature, and audience,"(**11**) Professor Keast introduces
a methodization which must leave somewhat inadequately considered the
most important factor in any final description of the criticism, namely, the
individual reader or critic himself. This can be best illustrated from his explanation of Johnson's objection to religion as a subject for poetry:

> Religion and mythology are both poor subjects for poetry;
> they differ, of course, in many respects, but the reason for
> their inadequacy is the same — neither is "level with common
> life," neither offers anything on which the imagination can
> rest while the mind compares the life represented with the life
> it knows.(12)

Johnson's "aesthetic" reason for disallowing Sacred Poetry corresponded
to part of Rymer's objection to the subject of Cowley's *Davideis*(13) and may
be summarized as follows: since Sacred Story was not a part of Nature, it
was not a proper object of poetic imitation. But Johnson's total objection to
Sacred Poetry was far more complex than this. The above quotation, however, by not conveying the measure of this complexity, virtually fails to
suggest grounds for distinguishing between the objections of Rymer and
Johnson. It does not attempt to explain Johnson's "submissive reverence, and
an imagination over-awed and controlled."(14) Such an expunging of Johnson's personal response and individuality as a reader must inevitably denature
the criticism.

Unlike Dryden, Johnson could not but have found the symposiac method uncongenial. His insistence on the validity of the reader's response
not only detected the arbitrariness of certain "rules", but represented a cri-

---

(10) *ibid.* p. 403.

(11) *ibid.* p. 399.

(12) *ibid.* pp. 401-2.

(13) See *Critical Essays of the Seventeenth Century*, ed. J.E. Spingarn,
II, 171, where Rymer's Preface to Rapin (1674) is reprinted.

(14) *Life of Cowley*, par. 147. (*Lives of the Poets*, ed. G.B. Hill, I, 49.)

tical criterion according to which the externality of independent lines of argument became in practice impossible. What Johnson's criticism is continually revealing to us is the judicial response of Johnson as reader (and this yet remains to be more relevantly and fully described). Although such responses exist at numerous levels, Johnson always argues (or has argued) out each matter with *himself*. The personally realized quality of his dialectic both inspires the confidence with which he can pronounce judgment and immediately differentiates him from other critics within seemingly the same critical tradition.

(2) Locke as a Possible Source of
Johnson's *Metaphysical*

Johnson's use of the term *metaphysical* to describe the poets of the school of Donne has caused a good deal of puzzlement. G.B. Hill's commentary is confusing rather than illuminating: after citing several *loci* containing irrelevant associations, he ambiguously glosses *metaphysical* as *"unnatural, unreal, fantastic."*[1]

A recent note does nothing to dispel the confusion: John Crossett suggests that Johnson was using the term as an equivalent of the Longinian *para physin* ("contrary to nature, exceeding nature") by a substitution for the uncoined "paraphysical" — "too inkhorn even for him, as it is for us today" (*Boston University Studies in English*, 1960, p. 123). It would, however, have been particularly uncharacteristic of Johnson to have used a word with a vague or imprecise meaning, and he might therefore be expected to have avoided such a shift. Mr. Crossett tries to make the substitution more probable by suggesting that Johnson might have felt compelled to find an equivalent term which was precedented in English:

> The word "metaphysical" appeared in his dictionary where he quotes Shakespeare and gives as the secondary definition "supernatural" or "preternatural." The word as traced by the *OED* has, as far back as Marlowe, a history of meaning that which "is above or goes beyond the laws of nature." Dryden also seems to have used the term in this sense in his famous passage on Donne: "He affects the metaphysics, not only in his satires, but in his amorous verses, *where nature only should reign.*[2]

---

(1) *Lives of the Poets*, ed. G.B. Hill, I, 67-8. (The quotation from Leslie Stephen's account in the *Dict. Nat. Biog.* contains the most relevant part of Hill's Appendix.)

(2) p. 123.

This method of argument obliterates the distinction between what deviates from nature in the sense expressed in the *Life of Cowley* (par.101) and what is "belonging to an operation or agency which is more than physical or natural; supernatural", which is the remainder of the *OED* definition under which the examples from Marlowe and Shakespeare are comprised. It must be pointed out that Johnson's secondary definition is not merely "supernatural or preternatural" but "in *Shakespeare* it means supernatural or preternatural," and the single example from Shakespeare is quoted ("the golden round,/Which fate and metaphysical aid doth seem/To have thee crown'd withal"). Dryden's use of the term cannot then be similarly glossed.

Dryden's use of the term (1693) is commonly accepted as Johnson's original. Dryden is comparing Dorset with Donne:

> You equal Donne in the variety, multiplicity, and choice of thoughts; you excel him in the manner and the words. I read you both with the same admiration, but not with the same delight. He affects the metaphysics, not only in his satires, but in his amorous verses, where nature only should reign; and perplexes the minds of the fair sex with nice speculations of philosophy, when he should engage their hearts, and entertain them with the softnesses of love. In this (if I may be pardoned for so bold a truth) Mr. Cowley has copied him to a fault; so great a one, in my opinion, that it throws his *Mistress* infinitely below his Pindarics and his latter compositions, which are undoubtedly the best of his poems, and the most correct.[3]

To Donne Johnson, unlike Dryden, would not have attributed "choice of thoughts" (which in the Augustan age, particularly after Locke's differentiation of *wit* and *judgment* in 1690, would have suggested *judgment*), or have agreed that the "thoughts" of metaphysical and non-metaphysical poets were able to be equated: it was "the cast of his sentiments" (par. 62)[4] which differentiated Donne even from Ben Jonson (and the *Dictionary* defined "sentiment" as "thought; notion; opinion"). Nevertheless certain points made by Dryden recur in Johnson: Donne could be read with "admiration" but not with "delight"; Cowley copied him in his "amorous verses" where especially

---

(3) *Essays of John Dryden,* ed. W.P. Ker (Oxford, 1900), II, 19.

(4) All paragraph references are to the *Life of Cowley* in G.B. Hill's edition of the *Lives of the Poets.*

"nature only should reign" (and it is from such verses that Johnson predominantly quotes).

Arthur H. Nethercot's research into the use of the term before Johnson is generally informative:

> The use of the term "metaphysical" in connection with certain poets or with certain types and styles of poetry was far from uncommon in the seventeenth and eighteenth centuries, and ... there were various sources from which Johnson might have got the suggestion for his phrase, altho[ugh] probably the responsibility was mainly Dryden's.

> The earliest writer known to have used the term with a poetical application was the Italian poet Testi (1593-1646), who, with Marino especially in mind, defended his preference of classical to Italian models thus:

> *poichè lasciando quei concetti metaphysici ed ideali di cui sono piene le poesie italiane, mi sono provato di spiegare cose più domestiche.*([5])

Two instances of the use of the term in English with reference to Italian poetry are here recorded. (1) Chesterfield wrote to his son as follows:

> The *Pastor Fido* of Guarini is so celebrated, that you should read it; but in reading it, you will judge of the great propriety of the characters. A parcel of shepherds and shepherdesses, with the *true pastoral simplicity*, talk metaphysics, epigrams, *concetti*, and quibbles, by the hour, to each other (8 February O.S. 1750).

(2) Joseph Warton's *Essay on the Writings and Genius of Pope* (1756, and reviewed by Johnson) referred to Petrarch as follows:

> There appears to be little valuable ... except the purity of his diction. His sentiments even of love, are metaphysical and farfetched (p. 66).

While assenting to the general conclusion of this research, and allowing the similarity between Italian and English *metaphysical* poetry (Johnson himself

---

(5) *Modern Language Notes*, XXXVII (1922), pp. 12-13. I am indebted to this research for its reference to George Campbell's *Philosophy of Rhetoric*, from which I later quote.

believing that "this kind of writing" was "borrowed from Marino and his
followers," par. 62). one can at least argue that, even if Testi had made *metaphysical* fashionable as a literary term, it would not seem to have desig-
nated, at least in Englishmen's minds, a particular school of poets within
Italian literature. The measure of deliberateness with which Johnson introduces the term suggests that he was conscious both of some innovation and,
at the same time, of a more specifically acknowledged background of association from which the term could inherit a descriptive and critical currency.
Such a background could have been supplied for Johnson (and for Dryden)
by Locke.([6])

That "the authors of this race ... drew their conceits from recesses of
learning not much frequented by common readers of poetry" (par. 65) expresses a *prima facie* disapproval in a critical *corpus* which insists on both the
importance of the common reader and the "universal language" of poetry.([7])
A derogatory application of *metaphysical* to poets "singular in their thoughts"
(par. 54) might have been suggested to Johnson by Locke's vilification of the
learning and logic of pre-empiricist philosophy. In his chapter "Of the Abuse
of Words" Locke discusses *"wilful* faults" in the use of language.([8]) His first
example concerns words which do not stand for any "clear and distinct
ideas":

> Their authors or promoters, either affecting something sin-
> gular, and out of the way of common apprehensions, or to sup-
> port some strange opinions, or cover some weakness of their
> hypothesis, seldom fail to coin new words, and such as, when
> they come to be examined, may justly be called *insignificant*
> [i.e. meaningless] *terms*;

and Locke regards "the Schoolmen and Metaphysicians" as "the great mint-
masters of this kind of terms." Later in the same chapter Locke writes:

---

(6) Johnson makes several complimentary references to Locke: for example,
the *Idler* Nos. 24, 66 (where the philosophy of Locke is opposed to that of "the
ancient metaphysicians"). in *John Locke and English Literature of the Eighteenth
Century* (New Haven, 1936), Kenneth MacLean shows a probable influence of
Locke on Dryden by comparing Dryden's pre- and post-1690 conceptions of
wit (p. 64).

(7) See, for example, the *Life of Dryden*, par. 255, and the *Life of Gray*,
par. 51.

(8) *An Essay Concerning Human Understanding*, III, x.

> Another abuse of language is an *affected obscurity* ... The
> Peripatetick philosophy has been most eminent in this way ...
> This is unavoidably to be so, where men's parts and learning
> are estimated by their skill in disputing.... This, though a
> very useless skill, and that which I think the direct opposite
> to the ways of knowledge, hath yet passed hitherto under the
> laudable and esteemed names of *subtlety* and *acuteness*. (9)

The *Life of Cowley* contains some verbal parallels: for example, "singular,
strange, subtlety, acuteness" — though "acuteness" gains a different valua-
tion from Johnson. More convincing is the care with which Johnson seems to
have chosen his first examples of *metaphysical* poetry. Johnson's method is
to follow his reasoned critical statement with illustrative quotations, and
those which illustrate the introduction of the term seem reminiscent of the
logic and learning of the philosophical tradition denigrated by Locke. The
first is from Cowley's "The Tree of Knowledge":

> The sacred tree midst the fair orchard grew ...
> That right Porphyrian tree which did true logick shew (par. 65).

Porphyry's Introduction to the *Categories* became a medieval compendium
of Aristotelian logic. The second is from Cowley's "Elegy upon Anacreon":

> Love was with thy life entwin'd ...
> Th' antiperistasis of age
> More enflam'd thy amorous rage (par. 66).

Johnson's *Dictionary* refers to "antiperistasis" (under which this example from
Cowley is quoted) as "an exploded principle in the Peripatetick philosophy."
In the critical commentary connecting his first half-dozen quotations, Johnson reinforces the point of such examples by the phrases "too scholastick" and
"more abstruse and profound" (pars. 69, 70)(10)

---

(9) *ibid.* III, x, 6,7,8.

(10) Johnson's third example contains "an allusion to a Rabbinical opinion
concerning Manna" (par. 67). Locke's attribution of "an *affected obscurity*"
was made more fully as follows: "Though the Peripatetick philosophy has been
most eminent in this way, yet other sects have not been wholly clear of it"
(III, x, 6). For Johnson's attitude towards "the subtilties of the schools" and
"the chimeras of metaphysicians" compare also his *Life of Boerhaave*, par. 22
(*Works*, 1825, vi, 273-4).

Perhaps the most interesting association of *metaphysics* with Cowley', poetry before Johnson occurs in George Campbell's *Philosophy of Rhetorics* published in London in 1776. In discussing "The unintelligible   From want of meaning" under the subheading "The learned", Campbell writes:

> I know not a more fruitful source [of learned nonsense] thay-scholastical theology: . . . of the same kind of school-metaphy-sics are these lines of Cowley:
> Nothing is there to *come*, and nothing *past*,
> But an eternal *now* does always last.
> What an insatiable appetite has this bastard-philosophy for absurdity and contradiction !([11])

Campbell was principal of Marischal College, and Johnson met him when he visited Aberdeen. I know of no certain evidence that Johnson read Camp-bell's book before writing the *Life of Cowley*, but there is some internal evidence which suggests that he might have seen it.([12]) Campbell himself had read Locke, concurring with his opinion of "the scholastic art of syllo-gizing":

> It is long since I was first convinced, by what Mr. Locke hath said on the subject, that the syllogistic art . . . serves more to display the ingenuity of the inventor . . . than to assist the diligent inquirer in his researches after truth . . . In a word, the whole bears the manifest indications of an artificial and ostentatious parade of learning, calculated for giving the ap-pearance of great profundity, to what in fact is very shallow.([13])

It might therefore be suggested, particularly in view of Mr. Crossett's explanation of the term, that although *metaphysical* "modes of writing" (par. 64) came to be criticized in relation to established Aristotelian and Longinian criteria, the term itself would not have been understood by the contemporary reader as derived from such criteria. Nature was the Augustan touchstone for testing the quality of poetry, and it was Johnson's central charge against the

---

(11) II, 79-82.

(12) Johnson's definition of metaphysical *wit* (par. 56) seems to be a com-posite of Campbell's discussion of *wit* (I,45), and his own discussion of Browne's style in his earlier *Life of Browne* (*Works*, 1825, VI, 500).

(13) I, 163-4.

"metaphysical poets" that they were not poets of Nature. But their "unnaturalness" is originally the result of their being *metaphysical* (in the sense of "school-metaphysics"). When they were then judged according to established critical criteria, they proved to be unrepresentative, and consequently unaffecting:

> Of thoughts so far-fetched as to be not only unexpected but unnatural, all their books are full ... The difficulties which have been raised about identity in philosophy are by Cowley with still more perplexity applied to Love (pars. 71, 72).

This coupling of the representative and the affecting is common in Johnson, and explains his attempt in the *Life of Cowley* to dissociate versified *wit* from poetry.(14)

---

(14) Just as the procedure of "the Schoolmen and Metaphysicians" was unacceptable to the empirical search for truth, so "the modes of writing" of the metaphysical poets appeared unpoetic to Johnson's eyes. That he used *metaphysical* with "school-metaphysics" in mind can also be inferred from the one passage in the *Life of Cowley* where he wrote specifically "metaphysical poetry" (par. 112). In his poems "*for* and *against* Reason" the poet had undertaken to argue *ingeniously* on opposite sides of the same topic as though acting the parts of both opponent and respondent in a scholastic disputation. And it was in a similar pair of poems (Cowley's "Against Hope" and "For Hope") that Johnson thought "scholastick speculation can be properly admitted" (par. 99). We have accepted Johnson's term, but not as a term of reproach. Perhaps this is why it has seemed difficult to ascertain Johnson's meaning.

WARREN FLEISCHAUER

Johnson, *Lycidas,* and
The Norms of Criticism

In 1944 Joseph Wood Krutch assured us that "to most people, even to most of those not especially qualified to judge either Milton or poetry, the lines [of *Lycidas*] themselves confute the arguments against them and prove Johnson wrong, even though they may not make it clear how one who seems so sensible can be."[1] Since Krutch's popular biography, nothing, at least to my knowledge, has appeared to reverse the judgments implicit in his remark that *Lycidas* is a great poem, Johnson a great critic, and that the great critic's condemnation of the great poem is to be attributed to some inexplicable perversity. So Jean H. Hagstrum (1952) described Johnson's critique of *Lycidas* as "usually regarded as his greatest critical faux pas,"[2] and elsewhere accounted for Johnson's blundering by his not having liberated himself fully from the neoclassical dogma "that the familiar lay in the idea or the sentiment, which should express the common sense of mankind and thus could not be expected to be original, and that the unfamiliar lay in linguistic decoration of one kind or another, in agreeable turns of phrase, in illustration, in metaphor and simile, in versification." Therefore, concluded Mr. Hagstrum, Johnson found *Lycidas* "deficient because 'there is no nature, for there is no truth; there is no art, for there is nothing new.' "[3] Less recondite but equally erroneous is Walter Jackson Bate's observation that "Johnson's response to Lycidas is merely one of his quaint misfires; the poem struck his stock antipathy to anything that savored of the pastoral tradition, and his remarks were foolishly haggled over during the nineteenth

---

(1) Joseph Wood Krutch, *Samuel Johnson* (New York, 1944), p. 486.

(2) Jean H. Hagstrum, *Samuel Johnson's Literary Criticism* (Minneapolis, 1952), p. 45.

(3) *Ibid.*, p. 161.

century."(4) To professional Milton scholars, such as Professors James Holly Hanford(5) and Merritt Y. Hughes,(6) Johnson's critique of *Lycidas* is not merely "quaint," but a demonstration of lamentable prejudice; and yet one is perhaps most dismayed to find a critic describing Johnson's strictures on *Lycidas*, as did Sir Leslie Stephen,(7) as perfectly "true" and perfectly "outrageous." Jesting Pilate could not have been more cavalier.

A generation this side of Sir Leslie, we have Paul Elmer More referring airily to Johnson's "well known deficiency of ... imagination," and compounding that trite and false charge with another, intended perhaps to exculpate Johnson, but only libelling him:

> To Dr. Johnson all this masquerade of sheep and shepherds is "easy, vulgar, and therefore disgusting," a cheap device cf images without passion and without art. Johnson had good reason to be suspicious of a genre that has invited so many weak poets to indulge in flim-flam. But he should not have forgotten how all through the Old Testament, from the call that came to Amos, "who was among the herdsmen of Tekoa," and all through the New Testament, from the angelic vision that broke upon the shepherds who were "abiding in the field" about Bethlehem, to the parable that Jesus spake to his disciples, "I am the good shepherd and know my sheep," — how all through the Bible this pastoral allegory of the Church runs like the very music of religion.(8)

More's indictment of Johnson's collapse of memory so stupendous that it would remove the critic from the Judaeo-Christian tradition is eloquent, but not convincing. Dr. Johnson knew the Scriptures at least as well as did Dr. More, and he knew, far better than Milton, the differences and similarities between a crozier and a sheephook.

---

(4) Walter Jackson Bate, *The Achievement of Samuel Johnson* (New York, 1955), p. 219.

(5) James Holly Hanford (ed.), *The Poems of John Milton*, 2nd ed. (New York, 1953), p. 22.

(6) Merritt Y. Hughes (ed.), *Paradise Regained, The Minor Poems, and Samson Agonistes* (New York, 1937), pp. xlviii-xlix.

(7) Leslie Stephen, *Samuel Johnson*, English-Men-of-Letters Series (New York, n.d.), p. 189.

(8) Paul Elmer More, *On Being Human* (Princeton, 1936), p. 198.

Yet if Johnson is damned as a critic with a memory senile, on the one hand, on the other he is chided for not having an attitude toward poetic diction sufficiently infantile. Robert Bridges once suggested that, if Johnson had "become again as a little child, he might have liked *Lycidas* very well."(9) With all the deference that we can muster for the laureated dead, we can scarcely bring ourselves to conceive of Samuel Johnson piping down neo-Blakean valleys wild the namby-pamby pleasures of *Lycidas*, and Bridges' fatuous remark should be rejected by professional Miltonians with as much indignation as it was renounced by one professional Johnsonian, the late R.W. Chapman, who, in his Presidential Address to the Johnson Society of Lichfield (1928), scornfully remarked the outrageousness of Bridges'(10) suggestion, then called attention to the critic who, familiar to every Johnsonian sealed of the tribe, alone had the courage even to raise the question as to whether Johnson was, then, utterly wrong about *Lycidas*.

In the 1907 Leslie Stephen Lecture at Cambridge University, Sir Walter Alexander Raleigh demanded:

> And yet when the noise of the shouting shall have died away, it may be questioned whether most of the points attacked by Johnson would ever be chosen by admirers of *Lycidas* for special commendation. Is there nothing artificial and far-fetched about the satyrs and the fauns with cloven heel ? Is the ceremonial procession of Triton, Camus, and St. Peter an example of Milton's imagination at its best ? In short, do the beauty and wonder ... derive from the allegorical scheme ... ? But I am almost frightened at my own temerity, and must be content to leave the question unanswered.(11)

However, the question haunted Raleigh. He returned to it in a later essay on *The Lives of the Poets:*

> Why should a poet pretend to be a shepherd, and translate real passion into the jargon of a rustic trade ? The famous

---

(9) Robert Bridges, "Poetic Diction in English" in *English Critical Essays, XXth Century,* ed. by Phyllis M. Jones, Oxford World Classics (London, 1935), p. 10.

(10) R.W. Chapman, *Johnsonian and Other Essays and Reviews* (Oxford, 1953), pp. 50-51.

(11) Walter Raleigh, *Six Essays on Johnson* (Oxford, 1910), pp. 28-29.

criticism on *Lycidas* was not primarily dictated by personal or
political hostility to Milton; the substance of it is repeated in
many passages of the Lives ... Where Johnson repeats a thought
many times, it is always worthwhile to pause, and look for
his meaning. He found *Lycidas* lacking in that deep personal
meaning ... which to him was the soul of an elegy ... [And
here Raleigh quoted, as had Johnson before him, the lines
from *Lycidas* about the "uncouth swain's" having driven
with Lycidas oft a-field]. The hot partisans of Milton have
not yet answered Johnson's criticism. Is the grey fly a real
grey fly ? If it is, what is it doing among the allegorical flocks ?
If not, what does it mean ?([12])

Raleigh quoted Johnson's simple verse tribute to Dr. Robert Levett, "a poor
thing, perhaps," he conceded, "to set beside the splendours of *Lycidas*; yet
it has in it all that Johnson looked for, half puzzled, in that greater elegy,
and looked for in vain. It tells us more of Levett than of Johnson; in *Lycidas*,
we are told more of Milton than of Edward King."([13])

By Raleigh's remarking Milton's preoccupation with Milton rather than
with Edward King, he points forward to that solution, widely accepted in
our time, that *Lycidas* is a great poem because Milton did not mean it.([14])
But Raleigh's anticipation of E.M.W. Tillyard is merely accidental, and
the essential value of his criticism is its suggestion that we examine Johnson's strictures on *Lycidas* not against the backdrop of nineteenth-century
criticism, but as part and pith of the *Lives* as these were written by Johnson
and read by his contemporaries.

We may start with James Boswell, who, if he is not highly to be esteemed
as a critic of Johnson's works, can yet be trusted as a journalist to record
the fact that his contemporaries would have clamored against what our own
contemporaries regard as the critic's "greatest critical *faux pas*" or a "quaint
misfire." Boswell records nothing of the sort. He notes that "against the
Life of Milton, the hounds of Whiggism have opened in full cry."([15]) But
Boswell makes no particular mention of *Lycidas*, though he can demand,
"Of Milton's great excellence as a poet, where shall we find such a blazon

(12) *Ibid.*, pp. 151-152.
(13) *Ibid.*, p. 153.
(14) E.M.W. Tillyard, *Milton* (London, 1930), pp. 76-85.
(15) James Boswell, *Life of Johnson* (Oxford, 1934), IV, p. 40.

as by the hand of Johnson ?"[16] Still he says nothing of any contemporary protest against Johnson's strictures on *Lycidas*, and his silence must be valued as golden.

Like Boswell, Hawkins is quick to record the protest of readers of the *Lives* against Johnson's judgment of Prior's "Henry and Emma," of the poetry of Lyttleton and Gray. Indeed, Hawkins observes that the entire University of Cambridge was in arms over Johnson's *Life of Gray*. But Sir John mentions nothing of Cantabrigian wrath or even perturbation over Johnson's strictures on *Lycidas*, even among the "hounds of Whiggism."[17]

Let us track the hounds to their kennel, *The Monthly Review* for August, 1779. There the Whig reviewer notes, with great understatement, that "Milton's character is drawn in no amiable colours,"[18] and he attempts, heroically, to erase the streaks of the tiger wherever Johnson has numbered them. But on Johnson on *Lycidas* this hound of Whiggism comes easily to heel. He is brief: "... Dr. Johnson's censures are severe, and *well enforced* [italicizing mine]; he is of opinion no man could have fancied ... he read *Lycidas* with pleasure, had he not known its author."[19] Nowhere is vindicated more fully Raleigh's later observation that Johnson's "criticism on *Lycidas* was *not* [italics mine] primarily dictated by personal or political hostility to Milton" than it is in these fawnings of an indisputable hound of Whiggism, such as, probably, the Rev. Robert Potter was not. If Potter had been a hound of Whiggism, he would certainly have snarled at Johnson's *Life of Milton* for its biographical detail. But Potter's several pamphlets on the *Lives* assail Johnson not for that monarchical biographer's limning Milton as a "surly republican," but for his treatment of the poetry of Shenstone, Collins, and Gray. Though Potter quotes from *Lycidas* to justify Gray's "big language," as he calls it, he is strangely silent on Johnson's strictures on Milton's poem.[20]

---

(16) *Ibid.*

(17) Sir John Hawkins, *The Life of Samuel Johnson, LL.D.* (Dublin, 1787), pp. 472-475.

(18) John Ker Spittal (ed.), *Contemporary Criticisms of Dr. Samuel Johnson* (London, 1923), p. 226.

(19) *Ibid.*

(20) Robert Potter, *An Inquiry into Some Passages in Dr. Johnson's Lives of the Poets; Particularly His Observations on Lyric Poetry, and the Odes of Gray* (London, 1783), pp. 1-31, *passim*, esp. p. 27; also *The Art of Criticism; As Exemplified in Dr. Johnson's Lives of the Most Eminent English Poets* (London, 1789), pp. 1-250, *passim*.

Or let us turn to the "Preface" by Thomas Warton to his 1790 edition of Milton's *Minor Poems*. A sound scholar, Warton makes no mention of Johnson's strictures, of which he must certainly have been aware; but, more importantly, Warton's exhaustive tabulation of the manner in which the period, 1637-1790, had ignored Milton's minor poems, *Lycidas* included, would indicate that better than a century and a half of major English criticism should be consigned to that infancy which Bridges believed prerequisite for the appreciation of *Lycidas*.[21] To Warton's chronicle of neglect, I can add comments only from two early *Lives* of Milton. Edward Phillips remarked of *Lycidas*, "that most excellent Monody," that "Never was the loss of Friend so Elegantly lamented,"[22] and while that judgment is directly opposed to Johnson's, it does indicate that Milton's nephew, no more than Johnson, had not acquired the Tillyardean art of psychoanalytically looking "behind the poem." Jonathan Richardson the Elder, in the "Life of the Author" prefixed to the work (1734) co-authored by him and his son, cites Sir Henry Wotton's praise of *Comus*, in a letter from Wotton to Milton, then adds: "As great an Encomium have I heard of *Lycidas* as a Pastoral, and that when *Theocritus* was not forgot; *Theocritus*, of whom *Virgil* was but an Imitator in his Pastorals, as he was of *Homer* in his *Aeneis*."[23] What was the encomium of *Lycidas* heard by Richardson the Elder, he fails to mention, but in the eighteenth-century pre-Johnsonian biographical notices of Milton, the rest is silence. In the Miltonic biographies of John Aubrey, John Phillips, Anthony à Wood, and John Toland, there is no mention of the poem, whose annals, like those of poverty, are brief. The infamous passage from Johnson's *Milton* on *Lycidas* is the first critique of that poem by a major English literary critic, and the evidence points toward the fact that the critique satisfied the moiety of the readers of the *Lives*. Recalling that Johnson had remarked in the "Preface" to *Shakespeare* that Shakespeare "has long outlived his century, the term commonly fixed as the test of literary merit,"[24] one concludes

---

(21) Thomas Warton, "Preface to Milton's *Minor Poems*" in *English Critical Essays, XVIth-XVIIIth Centuries*, Oxford World Classics (London, 1940), pp. 451-60.

(22) Edward Phillips, "The Life of Mr. John Milton" (1694) in *The Early Lives of Milton*, ed. by Helen Darbishire (London, 1932), p. 54.

(23) Jonathan Richardson the Elder, "The Life of Milton, and a Discourse on *Paradise Lost*" in Darbishire (ed.), *op. cit.*, p. 212.

(24) Samuel Johnson, *The Works of Samuel Johnson, LL.D.* (Oxford, 1825), V, p. 105.

that *Lycidas*, far from its having outlived a century, had endured, by 1779, a century and a half of neglect in the *consensus gentium*.

However, there are indications that poetic taste, even as Johnson was writing his *Lives*, was becoming receptive to *Lycidas*. Johnson himself tells us that "one of the poems on which much praise has been lavished is *Lycidas*."(25) Further, Mrs. Thrale warned Johnson in a letter dated August 20, 1780, that "the admirers of *Lycidas* will be angry no doubt."(26) Of these admirers, we hear something in a conversation, preserved, between Johnson and Anna Seward, whom the critic once told that he would hang a dog that read *Lycidas* twice. When she demanded what would become of her who could say it by heart, Johnson exploded: "Die in a surfeit of bad taste !"(27) Finally, William Cowper in a letter, dated October 31, 1779, to the Rev. William Unwin, had anticipated Mrs. Thrale's warning by remarking that Johnson had "passed sentence of condemnation of *Lycidas*, and ... taken occasion, from that charming[!] poem to expose to ridicule (what is indeed ridiculous enough) the childish prattlement of pastoral compositions, as if *Lycidas* was [*sic*] the prototype and pattern of them all."(28) With the Cowpers and the Sewards, we feel the oncoming wave of the future. But to understand Johnson's "greatest critical *faux pas*" or "quaint misfire," we need only to abandon Raleigh's "temerity" and to follow his suggestion: "Where Johnson repeats a thought many times, it is always worthwhile to pause, and look for his meaning."(29) If we examine, once again, what Johnson did say about *Lycidas*, we shall find that his strictures on that poem are based on norms to which he appeals, time and again, throughout his criticism.

Imprimis, Johnson declared that *Lycidas* was a poem "of which the diction is harsh, the rhymes uncertain, and the numbers unpleasing."(30) Johnson's remark about the uncertainty of the rhyme is the most easily justifiable of his strictures. With the greatest theorists and practitioners of

---

(25) *Ibid.*, VII, p. 119.

(26) Hesther Lynch Thrale, *The Letters of Mrs. Thrale*, ed. by R. Brimley Johnson (New York, 1926), p. 60.

(27) Hugh Kingsmill, *Samuel Johnson* (New York, 1934), p. 209.

(28) William Cowper, *Complete Works*, ed. by T.S. Grimshawe (London, 1876), p. 40.

(29) Raleigh, *Six Essays*, p. 151.

(30) *Works*, VII, p 119.

Augustan literature, Johnson regarded rhyme as a self-imposed obstacle for
the poet to overcome, intended not only to ornament lines, but to act as a
constraint upon the poet, preventing much automatic writing and, at the same
time, giving that assurance of form which every reader had a right to expect.
In criticism, these arguments are at least as old as Dryden, and by Johnson's
day they had been confirmed by better than a century of prescriptive practice,
of which Johnson's views are only the abstraction. Even so, they are scarcely
hide-bound. Johnson thought the sonnet form ill adapted to the English
language, which, lacking the inherent facility of the Italian for rhyme, forced
sound to tyrannize over sense, as it did in the Spenserian stanza. Yet as an
Aristotelian who consistently assailed the "Pindarick folly" of the Augustan
age, and, although he accepted blank verse in tragedy, Milton's epics, and
Thomson's *Seasons*, he censured Dryden's first *Cecilia* ode for its rhymes being
"too remote from one another" to fulfill their function.[31] For the same reason
and consistent to his norm, Johnson censured the rhymes of *Lycidas* as "uncertain." In *Lycidas* Johnson found the irregularity of the rhymes particularly
reprehensible because of Milton's simultaneous abandonment of conventional meter. Like Wordsworth a generation later, Johnson could not assent
to the poet's setting the reader adrift in limbo; somehow the reader had to
be given the assurance of form, of which, however, rhyme was only one of
several means.

As in rhyme, so in meter, Johnson, who once defined poetry simply as
"metrical composition," inevitably found *Lycidas* deficient. True, as a critic,
Johnson not only condoned, but required a variation of meter to relieve the
ear. However, such a variation presumed a pattern the like of which one will
look for vainly in *Lycidas*. Johnson, who also reprehended Dryden's *Threnodia Augustalis* for the "irregularity of its meter,"[32] might well be expected
to condemn *Lycidas*, a poem far more licentious in this respect and according
to the Johnsonian norms, than Dryden's. Though Mr. Hagstrum assures
us that Johnson's metrical system "was essentially that of Edward Bysshe,"[33]
Johnson is in fact both more tolerant and flexible in his criticism than was
Bysshe, and he made his concession historically to seventeenth-century
metrical laxity elsewhere than in his critique of *Lycidas*, when he censured

---

(31) *Ibid.*, p. 325.

(32) *Ibid.*, p. 324.

(33) Hagstrum, *op. cit.*, p. 194.

Dryden's *Threnodia* for metrical irregularity with the extenuation that it was something "to which the ears of that age ... were accustomed."[34] And that Johnson, in his strictures on the rhymes and numbers of *Lycidas* was speaking for *his* age, rather than for Milton's or the pre-Romantic day a-dawning, is confirmed for us by the comment, thirty years before the publication of the *Lives,* in a 1748 letter from William Shenstone to Richard Jago: "The censure you have passed upon Milton's *Lycidas,* so far as it regards the metre which he has chosen, is unexceptionably just; and one would imagine, if that argument concerning the distance of the rhymes were pressed home in a public essay, it should be sufficient to extirpate that kind of verse forever,"[35]

Now rhyme in these latter days delights us not, nor meter either, but modern critics have found Johnson's censure of *Lycidas* for "diction harsh" simply incomprehensible, partly because the poem has been extolled for what Belloc calls "that verse the clarions of which ring out unchanged in fresh glory after three hundred years,"[36] but mainly because modern critics have not bothered to discover what Johnson meant by "harsh" and by "diction." Yet thirty years ago Joseph Epes Brown noted that Johnson's use of the word "harsh" had caused more trouble than anything else in the whole canon of Johnsonian criticism. Brown made clear that Johnson most often used "harsh" to indicate not merely what is offensive to the ear, but what is grating to the whole aesthetic sense,[37] a usage found everywhere in Johnson's criticism, confined not only to lines of verse lacking "music", but extended to figures of speech, tangled syntax, words in unusual signification, even to Warburtonian emendations and explications of Shakespearean text, to anything unduly labored or strained, either stylistically or intellectually. That Johnson so used "harsh" to describe the "diction" of *Lycidas* is certain because his meaning of "diction" is broader than, though inclusive of, our more constricted modern meaning, which our abridged dictionaries list merely as "choice of words". Now Johnson's *Dictionary* interchangeably defines the word "diction" as "style," and the word "style" as "diction." Further, Johnson critically employs the words "diction" and "style" interchangeably.

---

(34) *Works,* VII, p. 324.

(35) William Shenstone, *The Letters of William Shenstone,* ed. by Marjorie Williams (Oxford, 1939), p. 133.

(36) Hilaire Belloc, *Milton* (Philadelphia, 1935), p. 120.

(37) Joseph Epes Brown (ed.), *The Critical Opinions of Samuel Johnson* (Princeton, 1926), p. 125.

If we thus adjust ourselves to Johnson's critical vocabulary, we should have
no difficulty in our seeing why he found the "diction harsh," if, at the same
time, we can determine the Johnsonian norm for poetic diction.

The best statement anywhere of Johnson's norm for poetic diction is
in *The Idler*, No. 77, where Johnson outlines his beau ideal of "easy poetry,"
precisely the opposite of "harsh poetry." "Easy poetry," he tells us, harkens
back to Horace, and is "such as 'every reader hopes to equal, but after long
labour finds unattainable.'" Johnson readily acknowledges that "[t]his is
a very loose description, in which only the effect is noted," and he adds that
"the qualities which produce this effect remain to be investigated."[38] Pro-
ceeding to investigate the cause of the effect, he describes "easy poetry" as

> that in which natural thoughts are expressed without violence
> to the language. The discriminating character of ease appears
> principally in the diction; for all true poetry suffers by harsh
> or daring figures, by transposition, by unusual acceptations
> of words, and by any license which would be avoided by a
> writer of prose. Where any artifice appears in the construc-
> tion of the verse, that verse is no longer easy.[39]

The norm thus set forth by Johnson in *The Idler*, No. 77, made inevitable
his stricture of *Lycidas* for "diction harsh," and indeed of the general Miltonic style, of which he asserts elsewhere in his Life of *Milton* that

> throughout all Milton's works there prevails an uniform pe-
> culiarity of *diction* [italicizing mine], a mode and cast of ex-
> pression which bears little resemblance to that of any former
> writer.... This novelty has been ... imputed to his laborious
> endeavours after words suitable to the grandeur of his ideas.
> Our language, says Addison, sunk under him. But the truth
> is, he had formed his style by a perverse and pedantic prin-
> ciple.[40]

"Perverse" and "pedantic" are but synonyms for the Johnsonian "harsh."
Yet Johnson describes the poet as "master of his language in its full extent;
and [as having] selected the melodious words with such diligence that from

---

(38) *Works*, IV, p. 376.
(39) *Ibid.*
(40) *Ibid.*, VII, p. 140.

his book alone the Art of English Poetry might be learned."[41] No, it was not the music of *Lycidas* to which Johnson was deaf. He heard it well enough. It was rather that, for Johnson, there was more to style, to "diction," than mere music. Of our twentieth-century selves it is true, as T.S. Eliot observes, that "we forgive much to sound" where Johnson "forgave much to sense."[42] But we may have been so charmed by mermaids' singing that we forget what song they sang.

Not so Johnson. He was closer by far in his critique on *Lycidas* to Milton than are modern critics, for he knew that, not only in the Johnsonian but also in the Miltonic sense, the style of *Lycidas* was "harsh," and was "perversely" and "pedantically" intended to be "harsh" by the poet. Milton himself calls attention to those poetical "berries *harsh* [italicizing mine] and crude," plucked by the "uncouth swain," and later referred to as (1.189) "his Dorick lay." In fact, a deliberate harshness of style was one of the conventions of the pastoral, as a genre of poetry, as Johnson himself had explained in *The Rambler*, No. 37, when he observed that poets

> having the mean and despicable condition of a shepherd always before them, conceive it necessary to degrade the language of pastoral by obsolete terms and rustic words which they very learnedly call *Dorick* [italicizing mine] without reflecting that they thus become authors of a mangled dialect, which no human being ever could have spoken ...[43]

Examples of Dorick style abound in English poetry, most conspicuously in Edmund Spenser's *The Shepheardes Calendar*, "Aegloga Nona," which Johnson quotes:

> Diggon Davie, I bidde her god day:
> Or Diggon her is, or I missaye.
> Her was her while it was daye light,
> But now her is a most wretched wight.
> For day, that was, is wightly past,
> And now at earst the dirke night doth hast.

(41) *Ibid.*, pp. 140-141.
(42) T.S. Eliot, *On Poetry and Poets* (New York, 1957), p. 193.
(43) *Works*, II, pp. 182-183.

And Milton, Johnson knew and we are confidently told, stood in direct line
of descent from Spenser. Of course, in *The Rambler*, No. 37, with massive
common sense, Johnson bludgeoned this silly neoclassical rationalization,[44]
which Pope had abandoned in his pastorals and which Gay had burlesqued
in his, as effectively as he elsewhere pulverized the silly neoclassical dramatic
unities. Mr. Hagstrum to the contrary, Johnson liberated himself sufficiently
from neoclassical dogma to write sound criticism that went to the heart of
the matter, not merely to the mere *pericardium* of *Lycidas*, and that evaluated
its style for what Milton himself had called it — "harsh."

Writing with the masculine grandeur of generality, Johnson might have
specified many ways in which *Lycidas* could be justly arraigned for "diction
harsh." First, the inversion of word order, which Johnson elsewhere censured
in his general remarks on the Miltonic style as "the disposition of the words,"
is obviously "harsh," in the Johnsonian sense of "transposition." Secondly,
the celebrated figure of "blind mouths," however luscious to modern metaphysical or surrealistic taste, could have been only "harsh or daring" to Johnson. Thirdly, the syntax is violent, *i.e.*, "harsh," as in such lines as Walter
Alexander Raleigh singled out in *Lycidas* as characteristic of its style:

> But now my oat proceeds,
> And listens to the Herald of the Sea.[45]

These are the specific items which, for Johnson, made the "diction harsh,"
but we may add to them.

Let us turn to the restricted signification of "diction" as the "unusual
acceptations of words." In the instance of Johnson, we deal with a critic who
had compiled a monumental *Dictionary* and who, therefore, is qualified
uniquely among critics to determine such "acceptation." The celebrated
"grey-fly" of *Lycidas*, 1. 28, is literally not in Johnson's lexicon, though
the word "scrannel" (1. 124) is, but he confessed, citing its use only in
Lycidas, "Of this word I know not the etymology, nor any other example,"
and hazarded a definition as "vile; worthless. Perhaps grating to the sound."
Of the Miltonic word "use," 1. 137, Johnson correctly gave the definition,
for which *Lycidas* is the only citation, as "to frequent," then correctly labled

---

(44) *Ibid.*, p. 183.
(45) Walter Raleigh, *Milton* (New York, 1900), p. 223.

it "obsolete" in this particular signification. To Johnson, the word "swart," l. 138, had a special signification of "unusual acceptation": "In Milton *swart* seems to signify black; gloomy; malignant." The word *beaked* (1.94) is cited only from *Lycidas*, another unusual acceptation. But of this verbal criticism there could be no end. Johnson knew whereof he wrote when he described *Lycidas* as having a "diction harsh."

Even so, we are not done, for Milton's diction in *Lycidas* contained other elements repulsive to Johnson's norms for poetic style. These elements are accurately described by Hagstrum's *Samuel Johnson's Literary Criticism*, and may here be briefly listed: (1) participal epithets (e.g., "the mellowing year," l. 5, and "honour'd flood," 1.85); (2) expletives (e.g., "doth," 1.16, and "did,". l. 60); (3) stock adjectives ending in -*y* (e.g., "watry," l. 12, and "watry" again, l. 167); and (4) harsh elisions (e.g., "th'abhorred shears," l. 75).[46] Now these are not items noted in modern criticism, but they were prescriptively censured in Augustan criticism and consciously avoided by better poets in their verse. Taken singly, none of them would have been sufficient cause for Johnson's strictures on the *Lycidean* diction; but, lumped in the aggregate and considered with other elements more obviously "harsh" in the Miltonic style, they made the poem seem to him, with his disciplined taste and sensitivity to style, an absolute abomination.

These "berries harsh and crude" can be justified on the basis that *Lycidas* is a poem neoclassically falling into the genre of the pastoral, but the explanation, traceable back at least as far as Raleigh, that Johnson disliked *Lycidas* because it was a pastoral, is not acceptable.[47] Johnson said that the "form" of *Lycidas* is "that of a pastoral, easy, vulgar, and therefore disgusting,"[48] but he did not say that *Lycidas* was a pastoral. This distinction, which Johnson made, is of the first importance. To Samuel Johnson, *Lycidas* was an elegy in the pastoral vein, though nothing could be easier than to multiply Raleigh's three citations of Johnson's negative reaction to the pastorals of Hammond, Shenstone, and Lyttleton, into many more such instances, to demonstrate, even more emphatically than did Raleigh, that Johnson's *Lives* (except in the one instance of Pope's pastorals) invariably condemned the pastoral recipe. Johnson tolerated Pope's pastorals alone, because he re-

---

(46) Hagstrum, *op. cit.*, p. 102 f.

(47) James Holly Hanford, *A Milton Handbook*, 4th ed. (New York, 1946), p. 168, is right when he uses the word "pastoralism."

(48) *Works*, VII, p. 120.

garded these, as did Pope himself, and as they were, as the juvenalia of a prodigy, tolerable as the first public flight of a fledgling poet into versification. But the case was altered with Milton, who, as Johnson knew, had written *Lycidas* after he had already distinguished himself with *L'Allegro* and *Il Penseroso*. Nor would Johnson have praised *Lycidas*, as it has been praised, as the culmination of the Renaissance tradition of pastoral poetry. No one insisted more often than did Johnson that no poet ever became great by imitation alone, and he knew well enough the entire pastoral tradition, sacred and semi-sacred, pagan and demi-pagan, from Theocritus, through Spencer and Milton, to Shenstone and Lyttleton, *ad nauseam,* in all its hyper-mellowed decadence.

But Johnson did not reject all poems because they were pastorals, though it is still widely assumed in some of the highest Johnsonian scholarly circles that Johnson could abide no pastorals whatsoever. For example, the editors of the first volume of the new Yale edition of Johnson's *Works* perpetuate this vulgar error in the commentary to Johnson's desultory journal for the year 1734, where Johnson notes his reading of *"Theocrati Idyllium."* The scholiast blunders: "And remembering [Johnson's] later antipathy to pastorals, particularly of the eighteenth-century sort, one wonders what his reaction was to one of the Greek fathers of the pastoral, in one of his most typical idylls, 'Thyrsis.' "[49] Fortunately, one need not wonder long, if he discovers that, long before Johnson wrote the *Lives,* he had written *Rambler,* No. 36, devoted to the reason as to why true pastorals please.

True pastorals please because, Johnson knew, as do we all know, that every man needs, at times, an Arcadia:

> The images of true pastoral have always the power of exciting delight; because the works of nature, from which they are drawn, have always the same order and beauty, and continue to force themselves upon our thoughts, being at once obvious to the most careless regard, and more than adequate to the strongest reason, and severest contemplation. Our inclination to stillness and tranquillity is seldom much lessened by long knowledge of the busy and tumultuary part of the world. In childhood we turn our thoughts to the country, as to the region of pleasure; we recur to it in old age as a port of rest,

---

(49) E.L. McAdam, Jr., with Donald and Mary Hyde, eds., *Diaries, Prayers, and Annals,* The Yale Edition of *The Works of Samuel Johnson* (New Haven, 1958), I, p. 35, n.

and perhaps with that secondary and adventitious gladness, which every man feels on reviewing those places, or recollecting those occurrences, that contribute to his youthful enjoyments, and bring him back to the prime of life, when the world was gay with the bloom of novelty, when mirth wantoned at his side, and hope sparkled before him.[50]

In a humane way, Johnson sympathetically anticipated Bridges' adjuration to become again as a little child to read true pastoral, such as Theocritus, if not *Lycidas*. And the distinction is very important, because *Lycidas* was, for Johnson, not "true pastoral;" it was, and is, neo-pastoral.

To Johnson "true pastoral" was exemplified by Theocritus, and by Theocritus alone, and Johnson's definition of pastoral, in its true sense, derived from Virgil, is identical in *The Rambler*, No. 37, and the *Dictionary*. Pastoral is, wrote Johnson, "a poem in which any action or passion is represented by its effects upon a country life."[51] Later, in *The Adventurer*, No. 92, Johnson manifested, once again, his sincere admiration for Theocritus, who alone did write "true pastoral" in this sense, which Wordsworth was to attempt to return to in "Michael," but in which Theocritus united "elegance and simplicity," and, in thus doing, succeeded so well that "his countrymen, despairing to excel, forebore to imitate him." Not mentioning Moschus and Bion, Johnson submits Virgil's pastorals to critical examen, and, true to his norm that no poet was ever great by imitation alone, declares that Virgil in his ten pastorals could advance "very little claim to the praise of an inventor." Still, Johnson accepts Horace's verdict on Virgil as a pastoral poet, "that the rural muses have appropriated to him their elegance and sweetness," in short, not their "simplicity" or naturalness. With Virgil, Johnson ends the pastoral tradition of antiquity, "the earlier ages", though he makes passing exception of one Calphurnius, a truly "obscure author of the lower ages."[52]

A quarter of a century after *The Adventurer*, No. 92, Johnson continued and concluded his history of the pastoral, coupling with the name of the renowned Calphurnius that of the equally famous Nemesian, then proceeded to trace the Renaissance tradition through Petrarch, Mantuan, Sannazarro's

---

(50) *Works*, II, p. 177.
(51) *Ibid.*, p. 181.
(52) *Ibid.*, IV, pp. 73-74.

Arcadia, Tasso's and Guarini's "Sylvan Dramas," to Spenser and the time
when Johnson, and he alone, had earned the right to observe yawningly that
"all nations of Europe filled volumes with Thyrsis and Damon, and Thesyl-
lis and Phyllis."[53] Indeed, he knew that the longer the pastoral tradition
in poetry had endured, the more artificial it had become. With each stage
of its transmission, it was a further step from Theocritan reality; and imitation, begot incestuously upon imitation, had only raised pastoral decadence
to a higher power. The momentum thus gained had made pastoral the more
effete, sterile, merely "literary," and the more unnatural, corrupt, and hence,
to Johnson, the less venerable, in the tradition which he knew so well.

Therefore, he speaks with magisterial authority when he mentions Virgil's
famous fifth pastoral, which, Johnson declared, "thousands have laboured to
imitate," whose images are thus "easily invented," and in which, in both the
original and the imitations thereof, "there are few sentiments of rational
praise or natural lamentation." What Johnson had earlier said of Virgil, he
later said, in other words, of *Lycidas,* and it was the entire Renaissance tradi-
dition, of which *Lycidas* is indeed the culmination in English literature,
which Johnson had in mind when, in *The Rambler,* No. 37, he averred that

> It is ... improper to give the title of pastoral to verses in
> which the speakers, after a slight mention of their flocks, fall
> to complaints of errours in the church, and corruptions in
> the government, or to lamentations of the death of some illus-
> trious person, whom, when once the poet has called a shep-
> herd, he has no longer any labour upon his hands, but can
> make the clouds weep, and lillies wither, and the sheep hang
> their heads, without art or learning, genius or study.[54]

Here, as elsewhere, Johnson's contempt for the purely formular in literature
is withering, vast, and consistent. In *The Rambler,* No. 4, Johnson recalls
"a remark made by Scaliger upon Pontanus, that all his writings are filled
with the same images; and that if you take from him his lillies and his roses,
his satyrs and his dryads, he will have nothing left that can be called poetry.
In like manner, almost all the fictions of the last age will vanish, if you deprive them of a hermit and a wood, a battle and a shipwreck."[55] Further,

---

(53) *Ibid.,* VIII, pp. 390-391.
(54) *Ibid.,* II, p. 184.
(55) *Ibid.,* p. 15.

Johnson based his praise of Shakespeare, in great part, on that poet's avoidance of the mere literary recipe: "Upon every other stage, the universal agent is love.... To bring a lover, a lady and a rival into the fable; to entangle them in contradictory obligations, perplex them with oppositions of interest, and harrass them with violence of desires inconsistent with each other; to make them meet in rapture and part in agony; to fill their mouths with hyperbolical joy and outrageous sorrow; to distress them as nothing human ever was distressed; to deliver them as nothing human ever was delivered, is the business of a modern dramatist." But Shakespeare, added Johnson, "caught his ideas from the living world, and exhibited what he saw before him,"[56] whereas he thought that Milton, particularly in *Lycidas*, "saw nature, as Dryden expresses it, 'through the spectacles of books.' "[57] In all his critical writings, Johnson adheres, as did Newman after him, to the Aristotelian principle that literature imitates nature, not other literature nor super-nature. For Johnson, this principle was a norm of criticism.

But what is not a Johnsonian norm is that urged upon tender minds not qualified, in Mr. Krutch's phrase, "to judge either Milton or poetry," by Cleanth Brooks and Robert Penn Warren in their *Understanding Poetry*. Johnson, Messrs. Brooks and Warren assert,

> attacked *Lycidas*, because the pastoral imagery, having no basis in biographical fact [we are back to that pestiferous grey-fly again], indicates insincerity on the part of the poet. For instance, does a poet in writing a poem ever try to make the reader have an experience identical with that caused by a bereavement ?[58]

The answer to the question of Milton's sincerity in *Lycidas*, which Johnson raises and which Professor Tillyard attempts to answer, is *not* to be made the basis for that other question which Messrs. Brooks and Warren directly raise. For, though Johnson had written of *Lycidas* that "where there is leisure for fiction, there is little grief,"[59] he had also written, not inconsistently, in

---

(56) *Ibid.*, V, p. 107.

(57) *Ibid.*, VII, p. 131.

(58) Cleanth Brooks and Robert Penn Warren, *Understanding Poetry* (New York, 1939), pp. 611-612.

(59) *Works*, VII, p. 119.

his *Life of Waller*, that "Poets, indeed, profess fiction; but the legitimate end of fiction is the conveyance of truth."[60]

In every respect, Johnson was too sound an Aristotelian to accept art on any other grounds than that it is representational in the Aristotelian sense only of "imitative," imitative of nature. Of even the mimetic art, Johnson derived his view from this Aristotelian canon, when he emphatically censured Garrick's anticipation of Stanislavsky with the remark that, if Garrick actually believed he were Shakespeare's Richard III every time he performed the role of that monster on the stage, then he deserved to be hanged "every time he performed it."[61] "It is false," Johnson asserted, "that any representation is mistaken for reality,"[62] and he later observed of the metaphysical school of Donne and Cowley that, "if the father of criticism has rightly denominated poetry ... an imitative art, these writers will, without great wrong, lose their right to the name of poets, for they cannot be said to have imitated anything; they neither copied nature nor life, neither painted the forms of matter, nor represented the operations of the intellect."[63] Indeed, Johnson's adherence to the fundamental critical concept of Aristotelian imitation is so demonstrably consistent that no one should presume that he would accept the merely neoclassical imitation evident to him in *Lycidas*. When Johnson deprecates "imitation" in *Rasselas* ("I soon found, that no man was ever great by imitation"), [64] he had in mind the *Lycidean* or neoclassical kind of "imitation," which his *Dictionary* had defined as a "kind of middle translation." Yet Johnson's own position is made clear by his observation, in his *Life of Dryden*, that "plain prosaic meaning" is not necessary for delight in poetry[65].

However, Johnson's toleration of the absence of "plain prosaic meaning" in a poem means not his bland acceptance of utter opacity, as is indicated by his remark, in the biographical part of his *Life of Milton* that *Lycidas* revealed the poet's "malignity to the Church by some lines which are interpreted as threatening its extinction."[66] Though Johnson's chief concern is Milton's

---

(60) *Ibid.*, p. 196.
(61) Boswell, *op. cit.*, IV, p. 244.
(62) *Works*, V, p. 120.
(63) *Ibid.*, VII, p. 15.
(64) *Ibid.*, I, p. 221.
(65) *Ibid.*, VII, p. 315.
(66) *Ibid.*, p. 72.

anti-episcopacy, the phrase "are interpreted" is characteristic of a critic who wrote the English language with Grecian precision, who himself forebore interpreting the vague, and who knew, as well as anyone earlier, then, or since, the conventional nature of the famous digression. With the reticence of the phrase "are interpreted," characteristic of a writer to whom a prudent caution was habitual, Johnson paused later to puzzle over the allegory. What is that "grim wolf with privy paw ?" Is it, as Professor Hanford believes, a probable reference to Rome, or, as he alternately suggests, a possible allusion to the Devil ?[67] Or, we ourselves may as plausibly ask, to Sin or to the Society of Jesus ? And what of that ominously poised weapon, the "two-handed engine ?" Is it the Biblical sword of God's vengeance, as Hanford believes,[68] or is it as Professor Merritt Y. Hughes suggests, the two houses of Parliament ?[69] But let us turn from scholarly speculation and rise to criticism with other questions: Were scholarly cruxes ever the essence of poetry ? Are we, as readers of poetry, to share the professional Milton scholars' delight in these cruxes ? Are we to accept Professor Hanford's romantic aesthetic judgment, which his scholarly proclivities to their best to defeat, that "the menacing vagueness of the figure adds to its effectiveness ?"[70] Or are we to say simply with Johnson "that the representation may be allegorical, but the true meaning is so uncertain and remote that it is never sought because it cannot be known when it is found,"[71] if, of course, it could be found ?

The confusion of Johnson's critics becomes absolute when they attempt to account for the final paragraph of his strictures on *Lycidas*:

> The poem has yet a grosser fault. With these trifling fictions are mingled the most awful and sacred truths, such as ought never to be polluted with such irreverend combinations. The shepherd likewise is now a feeder of sheep, and afterwards an ecclesiastical pastor, a superintendent of a Christian flock. Such equivocations are always unskillful; but here they are indecent, and at least approach to impiety, of which, however, I believe the writer not to have been conscious.[72]

---

(67) Hanford (ed.), *op. cit.*, p. 148, n. to l. 128.

(68) *Ibid.*

(69) Hughes (ed.), *op. cit.*, p. 292, n. to ll. 128-131.

(70) Hanford (ed.). *op. cit.*, p. 148, n. to l. 130.

(71) *Works*, VII, p. 120.

(72) *Ibid.*

Noted above is Paul Elmer More's deploring Johnson's forgetfulness "how all through the Bible this pastoral allegory of the Church runs like the very music of religion," but the plain fact is that Johnson did not forget. He only did not confound the Scriptural tradition with the pagan, and ever consciously distinguished between the two traditions. In *The Adventurer*, No. 92, though only incidentally, of pastoral in its wider sense, Johnson had remarked "that it has long subsisted in the east, the *Sacred Writings* sufficiently inform us."[73]

But the co-editors of a recent edition of Milton's *Minor Poems*, perhaps taking their cue from More, solemnly aver that "by Dr. Johnson's time, the two meanings of *Pastor* had, for a serious mind, become so far divorced that Johnson must have thought Milton was taking advantage of a connotation as frivolous as that which joins the discrepant meanings in a pun."[74] In this instance, one need not consult historical suppositions; he need consult only Johnson's *Dictionary*, where "pastor" is defined, in its first signification, as "1. A shepherd," with two citations from Dryden; and "2. A clergyman who has care of a flock; one who has souls to feed with doctrine." Alas, in the groves of our Academe, if not on the hillocks of our Arcadia, those hungry sheep are still looking up, unfed.

However, Messrs. Brooks and Hardy may inadvertently have suggested what is basic to Johnson's ultimate rejection of *Lycidas*. The synthesis of Christian and pagan imagery may indeed jell for an avowed agnostic like Sir Leslie Stephen or Joseph Wood Krutch, who would regard St. Peter as fabulous as Apollo. That synthesis may have coalesced into habitual thought even for a theist come late to the Anglican fold, like Paul Elmer More. The synthesis may be made, unconsciously, even as Johnson suggests, by one who, like Milton, can be accurately described by T.S. Eliot as "a Christadelphian, and perhaps not a very orthodox Christadelphian at that,"[75] rather than as a Christian. To New Critics, such as Messrs. Brooks, Warren, and Hardy, who find the essence of poetry in the *discordia concors* of baroque poetry, the synthesis is too easily accomplished. To all such persons as these, Johnson's rejection of *Lycidas* for its intermingling of Christian and pagan elements would naturally appear bigoted.

---

(73) *Ibid.*, IV, p. 73.

(74) Cleanth Brooks and John Edward Hardy (eds.), *Poems of Mr. John Milton* (New York, 1951), p. 180.

(75) Eliot, *op. cit.*, p. 168.

But to Johnson, who was loyal to his norms, his judgment of *Lycidas*, in this his climactic stricture against its "grosser fault," could not have been otherwise. Ever and everywhere, Johnson inveighed against mythology when it was employed, not merely frivolously in poetry, but when it was conjoined with those "most awful and sacred truths." For example, he reproved Dryden, who "sometimes connects religion and fable too closely without distinction."(76) He was quick to chide Pope, whose wishing of "peace" to the "shade" of Nicholas Rowe, in an epitaph, was for Johnson "too mythological to be admitted into a Christian temple ... Let fiction at least cease with life," admonished Johnson, "and let us be serious over the grave."(77) Johnson would have agreed with Eliot, who admits "that I have never felt happy in the spectacle of Fr. Camus and St. Peter marching in the same procession, like a couple of professors down King's Parade on their way to hear the university sermon."(78) Eliot, perhaps, belongs to the Church ironic, but Johnson was of the Church militant. For him that baroque synthesis of Christian and pagan in *Lycidas* never crystallized, as it did for many critics, such as More or Bridges, whose easy lapse into Scriptural language in their reproof of Johnson indicates that they regarded *Lycidas* as a fifth Gospel, its perusal as the equivalent of attending divine services. "Become again as a little child," in Bridges' phrase, they find that *Lycidas*, in More's phrase, belongs to a tradition "from the call that came to Amos ... to the parable that Jesus spake to his disciples," and that it is "like the very music of religion," so much like it, in fact, that they forget, as Johnson did not, the "like" of the simile. To such critics *Lycidas* is "the very music of religion."

It was not so to Johnson. Too stern a Churchman to confound a seventeenth-century Independent with an Old Testament prophet or with the Second Person of the Trinity, he was also too orthodox a Christian to look upon *Lycidas* as an extension of the Gospel. He would not rob Peter to pay Apollo. He did not, would not, could not confuse the poetical experience with the religious. Here Johnson's critical norm is most emphatic because, not only is it the corollary of the principle that art is, in the Aristotelian sense, imitative of nature, not of the supernatural, but it is at one with his religious dogma. So, in a footnote to Shakespeare's *Merry Wives of Windsor*,

---

(76) *Works*, VII, p. 343.

(77) *Ibid.*, VIII, pp. 353-354.

(78) Eliot, *op. cit.*, p. 190.

Johnson ejaculates: "There are laws of higher authority than those of criticism."([79]) So he wrote, in his *Life of Waller*, that "contemplative piety, or the intercourse between God and the human soul, cannot be poetical," that "[m]an, admitted to implore the mercy of his Creator and plead the merits of his Redeemer, is already in a higher state than poetry can confer;"([80]) and so, ultimately, he found the devotional poetry of Watts, "like that of others, unsatisfactory."([81])

Therefore, the question as to whether Johnson was right in his critique of *Lycidas* may, after a thorough examination of the evidence, be answered affirmatively. It is not, certainly, that Johnson did not understand *Lycidas*; it is rather that modern critics have not understood Johnson's critique of *Lycidas* as an integral part and pith of his *Lives of the English Poets*, at one with his norms of criticism. It fulfills his own definition of "real criticism" as given extemporaneously to Boswell, October 16, 1769, as "the beauty of thought, formed on the workings of the human heart."([82]) Johnson was true to his norms, and therefore not false to *Lycidas*.

---

(79) Samuel Johnson (ed.), *The Plays of William Shakespeare*, 2nd ed. (London, 1768), II, p. 541, n. 4.

(80) *Works*, VII, p. 213.

(81) *Ibid.*, VIII, p. 386.

(82) Boswell, *op. cit.*, II, p. 88.

GWIN J. KOLB

Textual Cruxes in *Rasselas*

Recent interpretations of three passages in *Rasselas* highlight both the puzzling character of the passages and the need for a closer study of them.(1) In support of his conclusion(1) that the prince's party returns, at the end of the tale, only to Abyssinia and not to the Happy Valley, Professor George Sherburn cites the italicized portion of the following sentence in chapter I: "Such was the appearance of security and delight which this retirement [the Happy Valley] afforded, that they to whom it was new always desired that it might be perpetual; and *as those, on whom the iron gate had once closed, were never suffered to return*, the effect of longer experience could not be known."(2) Although not made explicit, Professor Sherburn's reading may be paraphrased as follows: once any person, and especially a permanent resident, had left the Valley ("those, on whom the iron gate had once closed"), he was "never suffered to return" to the Valley.

(2) In his essay on "The Importance of Imlac,"(3) Professor Agostino Lombardo, arguing the "extreme" "ironic" treatment of the poet, refers to what he takes to be a marked disparity between two of Imlac's remarks in chapter XII: after first stressing the futility of Rasselas's scheme to "make deliberately my *choice of life*" and thus to achieve happiness, the poet concludes by telling the prince: "... yet, if your determination is fixed, I do not counsel you to despair. Few things are impossible to diligence and skill."

---

(1) "Rasselas Returns — to What ?" *PQ*, XXXVIII (1959), 383-84.

(2) All quotations from *Rasselas* are drawn from R.W. Chapman's edition (Oxford, 1927) of the tale.

(3) *Bicentenary Essays on "Rasselas,"* ed. Magdi Wahba (Cairo, 1959), pp. 31-49, esp. pp. 48-49.

(3) Mr. Mahmoud Manzalaoui, discussing "*Rasselas* and Some Mediaeval Ancillaries,"(4) asserts that at the end of the book Imlac "is even more
undecided than the prince. Even his vague contentment 'to be driven along
the stream of life,' is, we are told, a wish that he knew could not be
obtained" (the actual passage in chapter XLVIII reads: "Of these wishes
that they had formed they well knew that none could be obtained").

By examining the context of each passage, we may be able to test the
validity of these three interpretations.

(1) The first six paragraphs of *Rasselas* consist of a brief exhortation to
the reader followed by information about the prince, the practice of confin-
ing the "sons and daughters of Abissinian royalty," and the Happy Valley
itself, described as a place in which "all the diversities of the world were
brought together, the blessings of nature were collected, and its evils extracted
and excluded." The seventh paragraph, containing the passage under discussion, reads thus:

> The valley, wide and fruitful, supplied its inhabitants with
> the necessaries of life, and all delights and superfluities were
> added at the annual visit which the emperour paid his children,
> when the iron gate was opened to the sound of musick; and
> during eight days every one that resided in the valley was
> required to propose whatever might contribute to make se-
> clusion pleasant, to fill up the vacancies of attention, and les-
> sen the tediousness of time. Every desire was immediately
> granted. All the artificers of pleasure were called to gladden
> the festivity; the musicians exerted the power of harmony,
> and the dancers shewed their activity before the princes, in
> hope that they should pass their lives in this blissful captivity,
> to which these only were admitted whose performance was
> thought able to add novelty to luxury. Such was the appearance
> of security and delight which this retirement afforded, that
> they to whom it was new always desired that it might be per-
> petual; and *as those, on whom the iron gate had once closed,
> were never suffered to return, the effect of longer experience could
> not be known.* Thus every year produced new schemes of de-
> light, and new competitors for imprisonment [my italics].

In order to determine the meaning of the italicized passage, we must
look carefully at the preceding remarks in the paragraph. Once a year, we

---

(4) *Ibid.*, pp. 59-73, esp. p. 69.

are told, the "iron gate" to the Happy Valley "was opened to the sound of musick," and the emperor (accompanied by his train, presumably) entered for a visit with "his children." Among other functions, the visit provided the means of increasing both the ostensible pleasures of the royal prisoners and the number of people in the Valley. For a period of eight days, every person who lived "in the valley was required" to suggest ways of brightening the possible dullness of confinement. Entertainers (whose ranks included a poet[5] at least once) added their talents to the "festivity." Specifically, Johnson says, "musicians" and "dancers" — necessarily members of the emperor's party — displayed their skills "in hope" of spending "their lives in this blissful captivity, to which" only those entertainers "were admitted whose performance" added "novelty" to "luxury." So delightful were appearances in the Valley Johnson continues, that "they to whom" the experience "was new" (i.e., the contestants, since the royal children automatically became permanent inmates until "the order of succession" elevated one or more of them "to the throne" [p. 8]) "always desired that" their residence "might be perpetual."

Next follows the passage which Professor Sherburn offers as proof that Rasselas and his party could not return, at the end of the book, to the Happy Valley. Viewed in its context, however, the passage seems susceptible of two different interpretations, neither of which really supports Professor Sherburn's conclusion. Only one appears altogether consistent with what is said in the succeeding sentence, but the other receives irresistible support from a passage in chapter V of the tale. The first reading may be paraphrased as follows: since the unsuccessful entertainers ("those, on whom the iron gate had once closed") "were never" permitted to compete a second time in the Valley ("were never suffered to return"), the effect on happiness of a "longer experience" than eight days "could not be known" to anyone outside the Valley (excluding, supposedly, the emperor's train). "Thus," we are told, "every year produced *new* schemes of delight, and *new* competitors for imprisonment" (my italics). According to this interpretation, therefore, the crucial passage cannot apply to the prince's party at the end of the book, since no member of it — neither Rasselas, Nekayah, Pekuah, Imlac, nor the astronomer — has ever been an unsuccessful contestant.

---

(5) In chapter XII, Imlac tells Rasselas that he "waited for the time when the gate of the *happy valley* should open," that his "performance" as poet "was distinguished with favour," and that he "resigned" himself "with joy to perpetual confinement."

The second reading, suggested to me by Mr. Donald Eddy, provides an alternative explanation for the attitude toward permanent residence ("desired that it might be perpetual") held by temporary dwellers ("they to whom it was new") in the Valley: since those persons once admitted as permanent residents to the Valley ("those, on whom the iron gate had once closed") "were never suffered to return" to the outside world, any difference between temporary and lasting residence ("the effect of longer experience") "could not be known" to anyone outside the Valley. That this is the intended sense of the passage seems clear from a remark at the beginning of chapter V: looking for a means of escape from the Valley, Rasselas "saw himself confined ... by the gate, through which none that once had passed it were ever able to return." If, however, "those, on whom the iron gate had once closed" are identified as permanent dwellers *in* the Valley rather than unsuccessful contestants *outside*, the meaning of the next sentence becomes rather cloudy. Why, then, one may ask, the emphasis on "new schemes" and "new competitors" "every year?" In reply, Johnson, had Boswell actually put the question to him, might have growled: Sir, gates shut people *out* as well as *in*. And though such an answer may not remove all ambiguity from the sentence referred to, the essential point, for the immediate purpose of this discussion, appears indisputable: the probable meaning of the key passage cited by Professor Sherburn enables us to draw no conclusion about the re-admittance to the Valley of permanent residents who had earlier escaped from confinement.

(2) In chapter XII Imlac concludes the story of his life, and Rasselas asks the poet "to teach [him] the way to break [his] prison." Imlac replies:

> 'Sir ... your escape will be difficult, and, perhaps, you may soon repent your curiosity. The world, which you figure to yourself smooth and quiet as the lake in the valley, you will find a sea foaming with tempests, and boiling with whirlpools: you will be sometimes overwhelmed by the waves of violence, and sometimes dashed against the rocks of treachery. Amidst wrongs and frauds, competitions and anxieties, you will wish a thousand times for these seats of quiet, and willingly quit hope to be free from fear.'
>
> 'Do not seek to deter me from my purpose, said the prince: I am impatient to see what thou hast seen; and, since thou art thyself weary of the valley, it is evident, that thy former state was better than this. Whatever be the consequence of

my experiment, I am resolved to judge with my own eyes of the various conditions of men, and then to make deliberately my *choice of life.*'

'I am afraid, said Imlac, you are hindered by stronger restraints than my persuasions; yet, if your determination is fixed, I do not counsel you to despair. Few things are impossible to diligence and skill.'

Do Imlac's remarks in the first and third paragraphs justify Professor Lombardo's comment that the poet, after "showing [Rasselas] at once how the world really is," reveals himself to be the victim "of a hope which remains alive in the teeth of all evidence ?"(6) For the answer to this question, we must examine closely the exchange between Imlac and Rasselas. Imlac begins by noting' the difficulty of escape from the Valley and by stressing the disillusionment of Rasselas, if free, with the outside world. The prince responds by asking Imlac not to dissuade him from his plan and by rejecting the poet's description of life beyond the Valley. Imlac's reply in paragraph three is clearly directed, or so it seems to me, to Rasselas's initial remark ("Do not seek to deter me from my purpose"). Specifically, the poet reminds the prince that an iron gate and towering peaks ("stronger restraints"), not "my persuasions," prevent him from launching his investigations into the "various conditions of men." Despite these formidable obstacles, however, Imlac continues, Rasselas, if his "determination is fixed," should not "despair" of escaping from the Valley — for, the poet generalizes, "few things are impossible to diligence and skill."

The answer to the question posed above should now be obvious. Imlac's second set of remarks do not contradict his earlier set, although at a hasty glance they may appear to do so. In the first paragraph, he tells Rasselas the truth about the world outside the Happy Valley; in the third, he exhorts Rasselas not to give up hope of escaping from the Valley. Professor Lombardo's comment, we must therefore conclude, rests on a misreading of the text.

(3) The famous last chapter of *Rasselas* contains descriptions, it will be recalled, of the "various schemes of happiness which" the prince and his party "had formed" during their survey of "the various conditions" of life. Pekuah, the maid of honor, longed for retirement as "prioress" in the "convent of St. Anthony"; Nekayah, the princess, "desired first to learn all sciences,

---

(6) *Bicentenary Essays*, p. 48.

and then purposed to found a college of learned ladies, in which she would preside"; Rasselas himself "desired a little kingdom, in which he might administer justice in his own person, and see all the parts of government with his own eyes." "Imlac and the astronomer," unlike the other members of the group, "were contented to be driven along the stream of life without directing their course to any particular port." Then Johnson begins the final paragraph of the tale with this statement: "Of these wishes that they had formed they well knew that none could be obtained."

On the basis of this sequence of passages, Mr. Manzalaoui has inferred that Imlac's "vague contentment 'to be driven along the stream of life' is ... a wish that he knew could not be obtained."(7) Now admittedly the content and location of the statement beginning "Of these wishes" suggest its applicability to all instances which it covers. Admittedly, also, the statement refers to the specific wishes of Pekuah, Nekayah, and Rasselas. With respect to the comment about Imlac and the astronomer, however, the relationship is much less certain. For, though the proximity of the comment and the generalization might seem to imply antecedents of the latter in the former, the plain fact remains that Imlac and the astronomer have expressed desires for nothing at all ("were contented to be driven along the stream of life") and that therefore *these wishes*" "*they* had formed" (my italics) cannot refer to longings of the senior members of Rasselas's party. Mr. Manzalaoui's inference was prompted, one may guess, by the relative, rather confusing positions of the two sentences.

UNIVERSITY OF CHICAGO

---

(7) *Ibid.*, p. 69.

JAMES L. CLIFFORD AND DONALD J. GREENE

A BIBLIOGRAPHY OF JOHNSONIAN STUDIES 1950-1960

With Additions and Corrections

1887 - 1950

A Supplement to

JOHNSONIAN STUDIES

1887 - 1950

CONTENTS

PREFATORY NOTE

In Section A of this supplement we have provided additions and corrections to the 1887-1950 list (including notices of new editions and reissues appearing between 1950 and 1960 of works included in that list); and in Section B we have added a bibliography of Johnsonian studies first published in the decade of the 1950's. The general principles of compilation are those stated in the "Prefatory Note" to *Johnsonian Studies, 1887-1950* (University of Minnesota Press, 1951), to which the reader is referred. As before, some selectivity has been exercised in the choice of items. In Section B, items have been arranged under the same subject classifications (twenty-four sections in all) as in the earlier list. A similar system of numbering of items has been followed, except that numbers in Section B have the letter "S" prefixed to them. In other words, a number *without* "S" before it *always* refers to an item in the 1887-1950 list; a number *with* "S" *always* to an item in the 1950-1960 supplement. There is one slight variation in procedure from the earlier work. When a book has been published in more than one country, by different publishers, an attempt has been made to supply the names of both where it seemed that doing so might be of use to students.

It may be well to repeat what was said by your senior editor in the earlier Preface about the significance of the asterisk placed before some items. In order to help readers to select the more important scholarly references recourse has been made to a dangerous device — that of giving a special mark to items which may have particular utility, either historically or critically. At the risk of appearing arbitrary or prejudiced, we have felt that the value of some selectivity for many who may casually consult the list far outweighs any possible criticism of individual choices. The basis of selection has always been usefulness, stress being laid on (1) new discoveries, (2) new critical approaches, whether they appear completely convincing or not, (3) sound historical summations or literary evaluations.

The lack of a complete subject index for the earlier list has disturbed some users. Certainly such a tool could be very valuable. But to compile one that would be genuinely comprehensive — and only if it were genuinely comprehensive would it be thoroughly dependable — would be a most time-consuming and arduous task. Perhaps if, at some future time, a revised edition of the complete list is undertaken, it may be possible to attempt such an index. Meanwhile, it is our hope that the 1950-1960 supplement is not so large that the classified table of contents cannot serve users of it fairly well for the same purpose; and we have tried to make the index of names (of authors, editors, and reviewers) more useful by adding a word or two indicating the subject of many of the entries.

We are happy to be able to express gratitude to many scholars in various parts of the world for their assistance in making this supplement as detailed and accurate as it is. Not everyone can be mentioned, but our warm thanks go in particular to Allen T. Hazen, Donald and Mary Hyde, Lawrence C. McHenry, Jr., Robert B. Orlovich, L.F. Powell, and Arthur Sherbo, who have given generously of their time and energy to improving it, and to Magdi Wahba, through whose generous support it has been published. Finally, for the omissions and careless errors, which any list of such size and diversity must inevitably have, we ask your forbearance.

J.L.C and D.J.G.

A Survey of

JOHNSONIAN STUDIES, 1950-1960

Ten years ago, when assessing the reputation of Samuel Johnson from his own day to the mid-twentieth century, one could point to certain obvious changes. From being cherished as an eccentric but lovable companion, from being dismissed as a wrongheaded and prejudiced bigot, he had become once more a respected thinker and man of letters. Indeed, it was possible to say that the wheel of critical appreciation had made a full turn.

As the following list abundantly proves, the decade of the 1950's brought no retreat from the new concern with Johnson the creative writer and critic. A quick glance at certain sections of the bibliography affords striking evidence. In Section VI ("Clubs and Associations"), VII ("Homes and Places"), and VIII ("Pictures, Relics, etc."), the earlier list for the years 1887 to 1950 included a total of 146 entries. The same sections in the 1950-60 bibliography provide the meager sum of 22. By way of contrast, in Section XVII, the number of critical works on *Rasselas* listed between 1887 and 1950 was 36; between 1950 and 1960 there are 42 — six *more* during the last ten years than in all the previous sixty-three. Of course, conclusions from these figures might be pressed too far: it could be argued that the law of diminishing returns in the search for Johnsonian "association items" set in long ago, and it is true that the bicentenary, in 1959, of the publication of *Rasselas* probably inspired the writing of a number of pieces that might not otherwise have been written. Still, after making all possible allowances of this kind, such figures do show that students of today are more interested in Johnson "the great highbrow" than in Johnson "the Great Clubman," to use F.R. Leavis's incisive epithets (see item 1133). Not that the clubbable side has been completely forgotten. New "Johnson Societies" have come into existence during the last decade, and there are rumors that others are projected. But the "Transactions" of the young Johnson Society of the Great Lakes Region (S 651) disclose little interest in trying to reproduce the conviviality of the Cheshire Cheese. Pleasant as the punchbowls and churchwarden pipes of older celebrations were, and still are, much more important to our post-war sensibility are Johnson's wisdom and his deep understanding of human motives. He has become an inspiration and a comfort, as well as a witty and amusing companion.

The amount of scholarly activity during the 1950's is astonishing. Although the following list, like its predecessor, is somewhat selective, it nevertheless does include well over 500 separate items, considerably more than a quarter of the total number listed for the sixty-three years covered by the earlier volume (¹). In no earlier decade have so many written so much about so many aspects of Johnson — a state of affairs which must be encouraging to anyone who believes, as presumably any user of this compilation does, that the great moralist has something of major import to say to the twentieth century.

To be sure, a review of the work of the 1950's brings the impression that to some extent, at least, it has been a transitional era. Despite the decisive change in Johnson's general reputation, one has to admit the editing of Johnson's writings has nevertheless fallen far behind the rise in critical estimation. In 1950 it was possible to say that "it would be difficult to find another major author of the past who stands so desperately in need of a thorough modern re-editing." The situation has not materially changed. Although in the latter half of the decade of the 1950's, there came the announcement of the new Yale Edition of the Works of Samuel Johnson (S 100), with Herman W. Liebert as Chairman of the Editorial Committee and Allen T. Hazen as General Editor, so far only one volume has appeared (S 1925), and that had been started long before the edition was planned. The bicentenaries of the *Dictionary*, *Rasselas*, the *Rambler* and the *Idler* came and went, bringing no adequate scholarly texts. It appears inevitable that great group projects move slowly. Thus it remains for the next supplement to record the gradual appearance of properly annotated editions of the periodical essays, of *Rasselas*, of the political writings, the Shakespearian criticism, and the *Lives of the Poets*. How happy we shall all be to watch this great edition slowly come alive!

In another way, too, the past decade has seemed like an interlude. Some of the giants of the last generation of Johnson scholars — Aleyn Lyell Reade,

_____

(1) Even when the 70 or so "new" items of our addenda to the 1887-1950 list are included, the total comes to well under 2,000. For the great majority of the entries in Section A below, we are indebted to the vigilance of the users of the 1887-1950 list; we hope the users of the present one will be equally thoughtful in sending in notices of errors and important omissions.

R.W. Chapman — are gone, the completion of the *magnum opus* of each (249, S 1850) almost coinciding with the date at which the present list opens; though others, like L..F. Powell, are happily still with us, working away with accustomed skill and enthusiasm. Yet the publication in 1950 of the final volumes of Powell's revision of the Boswell-Hill *Life* (314) seemed to mark the culmination of a great era of Johnsonian scholarship. Any decade that follows the completion of three such monumental works as Reade's *Gleanings*, Chapman's *Letters*, and Powell's *Life* is bound to give a feeling of anticlimax. Who among the next generation of Johnson scholars are going to take the places of these men ?

Such complaints are not intended to minimize the important contributions of the decade of the 1950's. Seven volumes of the Yale–McGraw-Hill edition of the Boswell Papers have now appeared (S 303–S 309), and the project is approaching the period of the "great conversations" of the late 1770's, when it will perhaps be of most interest and use to Johnsonians. We do now have the first real edition of Johnson's private papers — journals, prayers, religious self-examinations, medical diaries (S 1925). One of the most important aspects of all this work has been the number of seemingly small but very significant items of Johnsoniana that have been recovered, frequently from the efforts of early editors to suppress them. Painstaking and ingenious methods of infra-red ray photography have enabled scholars to decipher passages erased because they conflicted with the "image" of Johnson it was wished to create — the image which to a large extent *was* created and which prevailed in the nineteenth century. It now appears, so the edtiors of Johnson's diaries write (S 1939), that Strahan, their first editor, was "interested in creating and preserving a conventional pattern of Johnson's religion and marriage." In "instances where Johnson is talking about his relations with Tetty or about his religious doubts and scruples, Strahan, with an eye to posterity, has crosshatched Johnson's words so thoroughly that they cannot be read by ordinary means." And it appears that Boswell, to some degree, seconded Strahan's efforts, for a somewhat unexpected light is cast on Johnson's marital life by the recovery of evidence, suppressed by Boswell, of Johnson's determination to marry again after Tetty's death (S 206), and of Johnson's "innocent" dalliance with Mrs. Desmoulins on (though not in) his bed, with Tetty asleep in the next room (S 203, Chap. XVII, from the Boswell Papers at Yale). Another exciting discovery is the text of Johnson's earliest known English poem (see S 203, Chap. IV). It is difficult not to speculate what Wordsworth, not to mention later romantic critics, would have said had he known its title —"To a Daffodil." Trivial as such discoveries may appear at first glance, they should at least serve as a warning against attempting over-subtle interpretations of Johnson on the basis of incomplete or censored earlier accounts of his life and work.

Except for such minor finds, there have been no extensive additions to our biographical knowledge of Johnson during the last decade. There were no spectacular discoveries of Boswell papers. Nor were there any exciting sales of Johnsoniana, though the great Hyde Collection continues to grow in size and usefulness under the skilled hands of its owners (S 9, S 10, S 11). The holdings of an earlier collector, Chauncey B. Tinker, have been described for students in a sumptuous catalogue, prepared by Robert Metzdorf (S 14). And a number of catalogues of Johnsonian exhibitions contain important information (S 7, S 18, etc.).

For the most part, however, the period was one of consolidation and use of earlier discoveries. Your senior editor's *Young Sam* (or *Young Samuel*) *Johnson* (S 203) attempted to make available in a continuous narrative the findings of a host of earlier scholars and antiquarians. As its dedication made clear, this biography owed its very existence to the devoted labors of such men as Aleyn Lyell Reade and Percy Laithwaite. Through their efforts, and from the Boswellian discoveries of the 1940's, it was at last possible to fashion a portrait of Johnson as a young man. One might add that the future happy hunting ground for biographers must be Johnson's middle years — the 1750's and 1760's — the time of his greatest literary productivity. What, for example, was Johnson doing day by day in 1760 and 1761, one of the most obscure periods, for which Boswell can offer only scattered guesses ? Where are the new Reades and Laithwaites, willing to devote long years to the patient uncovering of minutiae connected with Johnson's friends and colleagues during this dark period ? In 1950 we expressed a hope that they would soon make their appearance. We are still waiting. Is it too much to hope that the bibliography of the 1960's will be able to record a wealth of new evidence ? Or will the same sad complaint be repeated ?

We should, of course, be ungrateful did we not show proper regard for the appearance in the past decade of a number of important critical and full-scale biographical studies of close associates of Johnson at various periods in his life. Of these the most distinguished is Joyce Hemlow's biography of Fanny Burney (S 425), which can assuredly be called "definitive." Miss Hemlow was fortunate in being able to track down a wealth of exciting new evidence (now in the British Museum, the Berg Collection of the New York Public Library, and the private library of J.M. Osborn), which illumines the whole amazing Burney family. If Clarence Tracy had been able to uncover similar caches of material about the enigmatic Richard Savage (S 1404), we should know a great deal more about the obscure years of Johnson's early life. Unfortunately, although Tracy has examined all existing evidence, time has more effectively obscured the solution to the problem of Savage's paternity than it did the scandals of the Burney tribe, despite all Fanny's efforts at suppression. Ralph Wardle's study of Goldsmith (S 458) will be useful for factual details, but critically it leaves much to be desired. Percy Scholes' biography of Sir John Hawkins (S 453) is another disappointment, for it is consistently marred by an irrational animus against its subject. Happily Sir John's reputation as a biographer has been convincingly defended in an admirable study by Bertram H. Davis (S 409). Davis is also preparing a modern abridged edition of Hawkins' *Life of Johnson*. Among other important works we should mention the printing by F.W. Hilles of recently discovered manuscripts by Sir Joshua Reynold (S 448); the valuable gleanings by Edward Ruhe from the collections of Thomas Birch (S 449, S 450); and various essays included in the anniversary volume collected by Hilles, entitled *New Light on Dr. Johnson* (S 957).

Although there have been thorough studies of some other close friends of Johnson (notably of Hawkesworth [S 416] and Baretti [S 435, S 457]), there are still more who would repay serious examination. One need mention only a few — the elusive William Guthrie, who clearly must have been an important influence on Johnson in the early years of his connection with the *Gentleman's Magazine*; Dr. Richard Bathurst, for whom Johnson had such affection; Thomas Birch, Topham Beauclerk, William Strahan. Any Johnsonian can think of others. If some of them seem too minor to deserve a whole book to themselves, a volume containing shorter biographical studies of several such figures would be welcome.

Perhaps the statement in the earlier "Survey" which was most dubious was that on page 7: "Thanks to Boswell and Mrs. Thrale, we know fairly conclusively what Johnson wrote. And thanks to the work of W.P. Courtney [and other scholars] we have identified most of it." The discovery of hitherto unidentified small Johnsonian pieces, or at least the attribution of such pieces to Johnson, has proceeded merrily apace during the 1950's. These have been mostly, though by no means always, pieces of unsigned journalism in the *Gentleman's* and *Literary Magazines* and other periodicals to which Johnson has long been known to have contributed (e.g., S 1387, S 2003–S 2008, S 2010–S 2015, S 2017, S 2022, S 2023). It may be pointed out that E.A. Bloom's survey of Johnson's work as a journalist (S 2001) had been in substance completed before much of this work appeared. Perhaps the most forceful argument that has been advanced in justification of this kind of activity is that in some of the early and middle years when Johnson had nothing to live on but what his pen could provide, the amount of writing hitherto ascribed to him by the traditional canon is so scanty that it is hard to see how he could have survived. Possibly a meticulous biographer, working with the minutiae of Johnson's economic life, together with a historian of journalism, who could provide concrete information about rates of payment and details of the way in which periodicals of the time were conducted, could shed useful light on this problem. Many of the new attributions labor under the disadvantage that almost the only evidence for them is "internal," and certainly one would feel happier about them if more corroborative "external" evidence were forthcoming — just as one would welcome more evidence about similar older ascriptions, made by Boswell and others, which have long formed part of the traditional canon of Johnson's works.

The new preoccupation with matters of canon has stimulated interest in the analysis of Johnsonian prose style (e.g., S 15, S 1386a, S 1387). One scholar, S. Krishnamurti, has had the enterprise to subject some pieces whose ascription to Johnson has not been entirely certain to a mathematical test, devised by the eminent statistician G. Udny Yule, of the frequency of occurrence of the same nouns (S 1382–S 1385). The results in all cases are consistent with an attribution to Johnson. Perhaps future advances in methods for the analysis of style by statistical mathematicians working with the formidable aid of electronic computers and the like may in time enable some of these questions of the Johnson canon to be satisfactorily cleared up. But this moves us into an area full of complex problems. The same kind of minute and exact analysis is necessary when a satisfactory text has to be established from variant or dubious readings found in manuscripts and early printed editions of Johnson's writings; and William B. Todd has recently shown how modern techniques of textual criticism may usefully be applied to Johnson's works (S 1705, S 1723; see also S 1700).

With the new emphasis on Johnson the creative writer, there has come a wealth of stimulating criticism of his major poems. The relationship of *London* and *The Vanity of Human Wishes* to the satires of Juvenal has been expertly analyzed by John Butt, Henry Gifford, and Mary Lascelles (S 1432, S 1437, S 1442); and there have been discerning general discussions by T.S. Eliot, Ian Jack, Susie I. Tucker, and Henry Gifford (S 920, S 1440, S 1454). Particular notice should be taken of a number of valuable studies, by such scholars as Bertrand H. Bronson, Macdonald Emslie, and Chester Chapin, of Johnson's use of personification and his mastery of other metaphoric effects (S 1431, S 1433, S 1435). No longer can there be any doubt that Johnson is firmly entrenched as one of the major poets of the Augustan Age in England.

During the past decade two of Johnson's greatest works, the *Dictionary of the English Language* and *Rasselas*, celebrated their bicentennials, and the occasions were marked by an amount of ceremonial recognition that must have satisfied even the most ardent Johnsonians. They were further marked, of course, by the publication of numerous studies dealing with these works: indeed, some forty critical studies of each are noted in Sections XVI and XVII below. Pride of place must go to James Sledd and Gwin Kolb's careful and judicious assessment of the *Dictionary* (S 1573). Together with an important article by the same authors (S 1561), it places Johnson where he belongs, in the main stream of "lexicographical tradition," and proves conclusively that more profitable results will be obtained from examining, not the supposed idiosyncrasies and deviations of Johnson's thought, but rather the traditions in which it lies.

If from a scholarly perspective *Rasselas* did not fare quite so well in its bicentenary decade, no doubt the reason is simply that it presents a more difficult problem. One cannot easily examine the context of philosophical and theological thought in which it was written with quite the same thoroughness with which Sledd and Kolb have examined the context of historical lexicography in which the *Dictionary* was compiled. A multitude of pleasant and useful shorter pieces, however, appeared in 1959, which testify to the continued vitality of Johnson's moral tale in our century. And through the enthusiasm of Magdi Wahba an anniversary volume was published, fittingly enough, in Cairo (S 1627). One recent doctoral dissertation should be especially mentioned (S 1650), for it apparently settles the vexed question of Johnson's sources for the setting of *Rasselas*.

If we lightly pass over the bicentenary of Johnson's meeting with Boswell, in May, 1963, the next important anniversary to be celebrated will be that of Johnson's *Shakespeare*, in 1965. A lively and no doubt salutary controversy was stirred up by the publication in 1956 of Arthur Sherbo's book on Johnson as editor of Shakespeare (S 1687). The *casus belli* was Sherbo's thesis that the content of the famous Preface and of some of Johnson's notes was not so original as had been formerly assumed, a thesis which some other students felt to be expressed in a way that made it almost tantamount to a charge of plagiarism and caused them to retort, with some heat, "in defence of Johnson." If, as we have suggested in the paragraphs above, there is a healthful tendency in Johnson studies generally to see Johnson "in the tradition" rather than as idiosyncratic, it is possible that more such controversies will develop in the future, the dividing line between immoral "plagiarism" and laudable "traditionalism" being often not easy to determine. (A similar controversy once raged over Johnson's great musical contemporaries, Bach and Handel, some nineteenth-century musicologists assiduously calling attention to the unscrupulous way in which they stole tunes without acknowledgement from their predecessors and their contemporaries, and even from themselves. Nowadays the matter seems to worry scarcely anyone.) Moreover, Sherbo is to be thanked for making easily available the full text of Johnson's annotations to Shakespeare (S 1670).

Ten years ago it was possible to point with pride to the rediscovery in our century of the positive merits of Johnson's literary criticism. To back up the claim there was an impressive list of celebrated authorities. One more might have been added, for it is now nearly twenty years since Yvor Winters proclaimed that a great critic is the rarest of all literary geniuses, and added that "perhaps the only critic in English who deserves that epithet is Samuel Johnson."[1] Happily, in recent years there has been even greater emphasis on investigating Johnson's techniques and on explaining the reasons for his greatness. In the forefront have been Jean Hagstrum (S 928); W.R. Keast (S 937); W.K. Wimsatt, Jr. (S 981); and Walter Jackson Bate (S 906). And there have been scores of shorter special studies which ought also to be recommended (notably S 919, S 920, S 1790, S 1795). Bate's *The Achievement of Samuel Johnson*, indeed, attempts to explain not only Johnson the critic, but also Johnson the moralist, and Johnson the compelling personality. All these studies are impressive pieces of work, and illumine aspects of a great

---

(1) *The Anatomy of Nonsense* (1943) p. 240.

man's mind which needed analysis. Yet a perusal of the more thoughtful reviews of these books must lead to the conclusion that in spite of all that has been done, much of Johnson's mind has yet to be travelled over — a prospect that will not be too disheartening to any genuine Johnsonian.

Bate makes one claim which may startle some casual readers. In discussing Johnson's interest in human frustration and the devious effects of blocked wills, Bate insists that the *Rambler* and other serious writings of Johnson provide "the closest anticipation of Freud to be found in psychology or moral writing before the twentieth century." Yet so far there have been no major objections to, or even detailed discussions of, this broad assertion. Perhaps in the future more work should be done on the exact nature of Johnson's analysis of character and his understanding of unconscious motives.

A considerable section of the earlier "Survey" was devoted to expounding a possible approach to the question of Johnson's political and social thinking less fatuous than the nineteenth century's dismissal of him as a bigoted and rather stupid "Tory." "He was in no sense a statesman," Macaulay wrote. "He never willingly read or thought or talked about affairs of state." Three books published during the last decade call attention to the fact that he at least *wrote* a very great deal about them. *Dr. Johnson and the English Law* by E.L. McAdam, Jr. (S 945) records some of the results of his brilliant discovery of Johnson's collaboration with Sir Robert Chambers in the long series of lectures (1,200 pages in manuscript) that Chambers delivered to the law students of Oxford University as successor to Blackstone as Vinerian Professor. Johnson's ideas about the legal foundations of "affairs of state," transmitted through Chambers' students, must have had a considerable influence on the general climate of legal and political opinion in England in the latter part of the eighteenth century. The excerpts McAdam prints cortain some of Johnson's most powerful writing and thinking, and the lectures form a document at least as profoundly revealing of the bases of Johnson's ideas about the problems of the human situation as do *Rasselas* and the *Rambler*. Any modern student who ignores them when trying to frame general conclusions about Johnson's "controlling ideas" does so at his own peril.

The longest continuous single work that Johnson ever wrote is the series of Parliamentary "debates" printed for a number of years in the early 1740's in the *Gentleman's Magazine*, a document of at least half a million words in length, a most formidable repository of political and moral wisdom, both theoretical and practical, which has hitherto hardly been studied seriously.

Benjamin Hoover has supplied a useful introduction to such study (S 1702), in which he demonstrates the untenability of many of the things that used to be said about the *Debates*. Although in many details and in actual wording they come from Johnson's own imagination, they do rest on a solid foundation of fact about what went on in the two Houses. Moreover, they are not grossly prejudiced and partisan. Instead of presenting a collection of faceless individuals delivering colorless truisms, they are full of lively characterization and incisive thinking and expression.

Finally, your junior editor's *The Politics of Samuel Johnson* (S 1701) attempts to survey all of the political parts of Johnson's known writings (and there turn out to be a very large number of them, in almost every part of his adult life). More important, perhaps, the author has studied the drastically revised picture of the political structure of eighteenth-century Britain which in the last thirty years has replaced the simple old Whig-versus-Tory myth in responsible modern historiography. His conclusion reinforces what was suggested in the earlier "Survey": Johnson's political conservatism was of the kind that follows naturally from a rigorously skeptical and empiricist turn of mind; it is so far from being bigoted and fearful that it can even accommodate itself, on occasion, to revolutionary ideas — as, for instance, the idea of a rebellion by the Negro slaves in the West Indies. That such forceful claims should arouse active opposition in those who cling to the traditional interpretations is obvious, and there will no doubt be many replies. For which let us rejoice. Honest controversy is the lifeblood of serious scholarship.

In the years ahead, then, let us go on arguing about what Johnson wrote, and said, and exactly what he meant, for popular half-truths continue to be uttered, and he is still often praised for the wrong reasons. Let us use him constantly for what is always so necessary — to clear our minds of cant. Let us use him, as we should all great writers of the past: as a friend, as a goad, and for intellectual and moral inspiration. And may the next decade of Johnsonian studies be as pleasant to record as this one has been.

Section A

Additions and Corrections

to

JOHNSONIAN STUDIES, 1887-1950

❦

Section B

A Bibliography of

JOHNSONIAN STUDIES, 1950-1960

ABBREVIATIONS

ELH	*ELH, a Journal of English Literary History*
JEGP	*Journal of English and Germanic Philology*
JHI	*Journal of the History of Ideas*
JNL	*Johnsonian News Letter*
MLN	*Modern Language Notes*
MLQ	*Modern Language Quarterly*
MLR	*Modern Language Review*
MP	*Modern Philology*
N & Q	*Notes and Queries*
PBSA	*Papers of the Bibliographical Society of America*
PMLA	*Publications of the Modern Language Association of America*
PQ	*Philological Quarterly*
RES	*Review of English Studies*
SP	*Studies in Philology*
SR	*Saturday Review* [New York]; formerly *Saturday Review of Literature*
TLS	*Times Literary Supplement* [London]

A) Additions and Corrections

to

JOHNSONIAN STUDIES, 1887-1950

Unless other directions are given,

"3a[new]" means that the entry is to be inserted, as an additional item in the list, immediately after existing item 3;

"10" or "10a" (without "[new]") means that the indicated change or addition is to be made to existing item 10 or 10a.

Item No.

3a[new] . BIRD, LOIS MAY MARIE. "American Criticism of Samuel Johnson, LL.D., 1807-1938: A Contribution to Bibliography" (typewritten) Madison, Wisconsin: University of Wisconsin Library School, 1938

10 . *Add:* Compiled by A. W. Evans.

14a[new] . CHAPMAN, R. W. "The Numbering of Editions in the Eighteenth Century" [deals with the *Rambler, Idler, Adventurer,* and *Lives of the Poets*], *RES,* III (January 1927), 77–79.

21 . *Add:* 2nd ed., 1950.

23a[new] . FIELDS, ANNIE (MRS. JAMES T.). "A Third Shelf of Old Books," *Scribner's,* XVI (September 1894), 343–52. (A description of her and her husband's collection, containing Johnson material. With facsimile of letter to James Compton [Chapman No. 811.1].)

26 . After *"Era"* add "[a descriptive pamphlet]".

28 . After *"Era"* add "[a descriptive pamphlet]".

39 . *Add:* By R. W. Chapman.

42 . *Add:* See also [Iowa State University] *Doctoral Dissertations: Abstracts and References,* VI (1953), 428–29.

51a[new]. POTTLE, FREDERICK A. "Printer's Copy in the Eighteenth Century" [problems of Johnson and Boswell bibliography], *PBSA*, XXVII (1933), Part 2, 65–73.

112a. *Add:* Reviewed by Gwin J. Kolb, *MP*, XLIX (August 1951), 70–72.

114. *Add:* Replaced by item S 111.

116a. *Add:* See item S 110.

121. To the footnote following this item (bottom of p. 22), add "Unfortunately it is not the best text."

143. *Add:* 2nd ed., 1956.

200. *Add:* See also pp. 296, 337, 375.

211a[new]. "Early Life of Johnson" ["review" of Boswell's *Letters to Temple*; *Boswelliana* (1856); Croker's ed. of Boswell's *Life* (1847)], *Quarterly Review*, CIII (April 1858), 279–328.

219. *Add:* Reviewed by Edmur d Wilson, *The New Yorker*, November 18, 1944, pp. 84–90 [see item S 980].

233a [new]. MAZZINGHI, T.J. "Dr. Johnson's Early Life" [letter about Whitby tutoring], *N&Q*, November 29, 1884, pp. 421–22.

249. *Add:* (Part XI: *Consolidated Index of Persons, Parts I to X*, 1952.)

258. *For* 1897 *read* 1847.

263a[new]. TALBOT, WILLIAM. "Birmingham's First Bookseller" [Michael Johnsor], *Publisher's Circular and Bookseller's Record*, CXXXVII (December 17, 1932), 719.

269. To following entry ("*See also*"), add "408a, 1059a."

280a[new]. "The Case of Samuel Johnson," *Canadian Journal of Medicine and Surgery*, LXII (September 1927), 57–61.

281a[new]. DUMONT, Dr. [of Monteux]. "Sur l'état pathologique de Samuel Johnson," *L'Union Médicale* (Paris), XI (June 18, July 2, 1857), 297–98, 321–23.

281b[new]. EAST, TERENCE. "Dr. Samuel Johnson: His Medical History as Recorded by James Boswell," *British Heart Journal*, IV (1942), 43–48.

284. *Add:* Reprinted in *Great Men: Psychoanalytic Studies*, pp. 175–85. New York: International Universities Press, 1956.

285. *For* HUCHISON *read* HUTCHISON.

296a[new]. TREVES, SIR FREDERICK. "Samuel Johnson," *Cassell's Magazine of Fiction*, February 1924, pp. 38–44.

303 . *Add:* Reprinted (full text, but with less annotation) as *Boswell's Column.* London: William Kimber, 1951.

305 . **Add:** Second corrected edition of Hill-Powell, in progress.

318a[new]. ————— . With an introduction by Herbert Askwith. Text of "Malone's sixth edition." 1 vol. New York: Random House (Modern Library "Giant") [1931 and frequently reissued].

319 . *Add:* Reissued, with a new index, 1953; with further corrections, 1957; and paperbound, 1960.

319a . *Add:* (For later editions of this, and subsequent volumes of the Boswell Papers, see items S 303 to S 309.)

338a[new]. GORDON, GEORGE. "Boswell's Life of Johnson," *More Companionable Books,* pp. 31-36. London: Chatto and Windus, 1947.

351a[new]. LIEBERT, HERMAN W. "The Boswell Papers" [their acquisition by Yale], *Yale Alumni Magazine,* XIII (October 1949), 14-16.

355 . *Add to main entry:* [by R.W. Chapman; a review of item 373, Vols. I-VI].

380₂[new]. SAINTSBURY, GEORGE. "Some Great Biographies," in *Collected Essays and Papers,* I, 409–33. London: J.M. Dent, 1923. (Earlier appeared in *Macmillan's Magazine,* June, 1892.)

392a[new]. WILSON, F. P. "Table Talk" [Boswell's reports of Johnson's conversation considered as in the "ana" genre], *Huntington Library Quarterly,* IV (October 1940), 27–46.

394 . To the following entry ("*See also*"), add "51a, 211a, 281b, 699, 819, 852a, 1116a, 1730a, 1746a."

401a[new]. ADDLESHAW, S. "The Swan of Lichfield: Anna Seward and Her Circle," *Church Quarterly Review,* CXXIV (April–June 1937), 1-34.

*408a[new]. "The Autobiography of Sylvanus Urban" [Johnson's early association with the *Gentleman's Magazine*], *Gentleman's Magazine,* CCI (July to December 1856), 1-9, 131-40, 267-77, 531-41, 667-77; CCII (January to April 1857), 3-10, 149-57, 282-90, 379-87.

415a[new]. BAVERSTOCK, J.H. *Treatises on Brewing* [contains letters of Henry Thrale], pp. xvii-xviii. London: G. and W.B. Whittaker, 1824.

417a[new]. BELL, WALTER GEORGE. "Dr. Johnson's Womankind," in *More About Unknown London,* pp. 174-88. London: John Lane, 1921.

444. Add: Reprinted in *Studies in the Literature of the Augustan Age: Essays Collected in Honor of Arthur Ellicott Case*, ed. R.C. Boys, pp. 50-60. Ann Arbor, Michigan: George Wahr Publishing Co., 1952.

446. (a) *Add:* 2nd ed., 1953.
   (b) After notice of review by Virginia Woolf, add "[reprinted in item 613a]."

451. *Add:* Reviewed by Virginia Woolf, *TLS*, July 29, 1909 [reprinted in item S 461].

469a[new]. DONNELLY, LUCY M. "The Celebrated Mrs. Macaulay," *William and Mary Quarterly*, VI (April 1949), 173-207.

470a[new]. EMDEN, CECIL S. "Oriel Friends of Dr. Johnson" [William Seward and Sir Richard Musgrave], *Oriel Papers*, pp. 133-46. Oxford: Clarendon Press, 1948. See also item S 413.

483. *Add:* See also item S 403.

511a[new]. KRISHNAMURTI, S. "Sir Robert Chambers: A Johnsonian in India," *Journal of the University of Bombay*, XVIII (September 1949), 1-5.

542a[new]. PEPYS, W.W. *A Later Pepys. The Correspondence of Sir William Weller Pepys, Bart., Master in Chancery*, 1758-1825, ed. Alice C.C. Gaussen. 2 vols. London: J. Lane, 1904.

574a[new]. SADLER, ERNEST A. "The Mansion, Ashbourne", *Journal of the Derbyshire Archaeological and Natural History Society*, LIII for 1932 (1933), 39-50.

600. *Add:* 2nd ed., 1951.

613a[new]. WOOLF, VIRGINIA, "Mrs. Thrale" [review of item 446], in *The Moment and Other Essays*, pp. 45-49. London: Hogarth Press, 1947; New York: Harcourt, Brace, 1948.

656a [new]. ESCOTT, T. H. S. *Club Makers and Club Members*, pp. 37-38, 136-39, etc. London: T. Fisher Unwin, 1914.

660a[new]. "The Johnson Club" [stems from item 661], *Unwin's Chap Book*, 1899-1900, pp. 14-16. London: T. Fisher Unwin, 1900.

699[new]. *Insert in Section VII before Item* 700:
   ADCOCK, A. ST. J. "Homes and Haunts of Johnson and Boswell," in *Famous Houses and Literary Shrines of London*, pp. 68-88. London: J.M. Dent, 1912.

703. *Add*: Reprinted in *Provincial Letters and Other Papers*, pp. 17–36. London: Smith, Elder and Co., 1906.

707a[new]. CHANCELLOR, E. BERESFORD. "The Age of Johnson," in *Literary Ghosts of London*, pp. 202–28. London: Richards, 1933.

711b[new]. *Insert after item* 711a:
DENT, ROBERT K. and HILL, JOSEPH. "Samuel Johnson and His Home," in *Historic Staffordshire*, pp. 294-303. Birmingham: Midland Educational Co., 1896.

722a[new]. FREEMAN, H.B. "Dr. Johnson and Lichfield," *Evening Standard* (London), October 7, 1904.

724a[new]. GRANT, ARTHUR. "The Ladies of the Vale" [spires of Lichfield cathedral], in *In the Old Paths*, pp. 159-72. London: Constable, 1913.

732aa[new]. *Insert before item* 732a:
KIRKE, HENRY. "Dr. Johnson in Derbyshire," *Journal of the Derbyshire Archaeological and Natural History Society*, XXXII (1910), 113-22.

737a[new]. MORTIMER, JOHN. "Ashbourne and Dr. Johnson," *Manchester Quarterly*, XXIII (1904), 54-61.

757a[new]. TIMMINS, SAMUEL. "Dr. Johnson in Birmingham," *Transactions of the Archaeological Section of the Birmingham and Midland Institute* (1876), 1-8.

803. *Add*: See also item S 785.

819[new]. *Insert in Section IX before item* 820:
B., A. "Mrs. Emmet. What Boswell Missed," *The Times* (London), March 20, 1923.

823. *Add*: See also *Radio Times* (London), May 16, 1952, pp. 6, 18.

826a[new]. GEORGE, DANIEL. "The Lost Diary of Dr. Johnson," *The Saturday Book*, VI (1946), 260-63.

838a[new]. LINKLATER, ERIC. *The Raft and Socrates Asks Why: Two Conversations* [Johnson a character in the latter], pp. 54-121.   London: Macmillan, 1942.

852a[new]. ROSE, KENNETH. "Portrait the Second: Boswell Meets Johnson," in *Georgiana: Seven Portraits*, pp. 10-15. London: Frederick Muller, 1947.

908a[new]. ALLODOLI, ETTORE. "Poliziano e Johnson" [and Johnson on some other Renaissance figures], *La Rinascita* (Florence), V (September 1942), 459-71.

910a. *Add:* (November 25, 1950), 516–19; (December 9), 541–44; (December 23), 561-63. (Chiefly a list of scientists quoted in the *Dictionary.*)

929a[new]. BENSON, ARTHUR C. "Dr. Johnson," in *Where No Fear Was,* pp. 106–18. London: Smith, Elder, 1914.

942. *Add:* Also *Unwin's Chap Book,* 1899-1900, pp. 17–19.

950. *Add:* 2nd ed., 1953.

967a[new]. BULLARD, SIR READER WILLIAM. *Samuel Johnson: A Public Lecture* (with Persian translation by L. Suratgar) [lecture given at the University of Teheran, November 2, 1943, by the British Ambassador]. Teheran: British Council, [1943].

986a[new]. CHESTERTON, G. K., "The Real Dr. Johnson," in *The Common Man,* pp. 118–21. London: Sheed and Ward, 1950. Earlier appeared in the *Daily Graphic* (London), 1909 (see John Sullivan, *G.K. Chesterton: A Bibliography,* 1958, p. 124).

1009a[new]. DAWSON, GEORGE. "Dr. Samuel Johnson," in *Biographical Lectures* pp. 159–71. London: Kegan Paul, Trench, 1887.

1028a[new]. DOYLE, A. CONAN. Chapter III [a general appreciation of Johnson] in *Through the Magic Door,* pp. 51–68. New York: McClure, 1908 and later reissues. Originally serialized in *Cassell's Magazine,* 1906.

1059a[new]. GRAY, W. FORBES. "The Douglas Cause: An Unpublished Correspondence" [Andrew Stuart's, concerning his *Letters to Lord Mansfield,* 1773; see *Life,* April 27, 1773], *Quarterly Review,* CCLXXVI (January 1941), 69-80.

1071a. *Add:* Reprinted in volume in honor of Arthur E. Case (cf. *ante,* item 444), pp. 88–103.

1095a[new]. HOLDSWORTH, SIR WILLIAM S. "Johnson's England," *Law Quarterly Review,* L, 99 (July 1934), 337-53. Review article based on item 1115.

1115. *Add:* See also item 1095a.

1116a[new]. JOWETT, BENJAMIN. "Addresses on ... Boswell and Johnson, and Johnson's own writings and character," in *Essays on Men and Manners,* ed. P. Lyttelton Gell. London: John Murray, 1895. (Apparently never published. "It seems to exist only in a proof-state. Balliol has a number of paper-bound, crown 8vo, imperfect copies." Not seen; information from Sir Geoffrey Faber, *Jowett,* 1957, p. 432.)

1124a[new] . KNOX, RONALD A ."Dr. Johnson," in *English Wits*, ed. Leonard Russell, pp. 29-46. London: Hutchinson, 1940. Reprinted in Ronald A. Knox, *Literary Distractions*, pp. 83-96. London: Sheed and Ward, 1958.

1133 . *Add:* Reprinted as "Johnson and Augustanism," in *The Common Pursuit*, pp. 97-115. London: Chatto and Windus; New York: George W. Stewart, 1952.

1137a[new] . LEYBURN, ELLEN D. "Bishop Berkeley: Metaphysician as Moralist" [considers Johnson in relation to Berkeley], in item 903, pp. 319-28.

1141 . *Add:* Reprinted (as separate essays) in *Essays on Life and Literature* pp. 57-146. London: J.M. Dent; New York: E.P. Dutton, 1951 (Everyman's Library).

1148 . *Add:* See item S 945.

1158 . *Add:* Reviewed by Donald F. Hyde, *PQ*, XXIX (July 1950), 282–83; E.L. McAdam, Jr., *MLN*, LXVI (January 1951), 64–66.

1160a[new] . MAIS, S.P.B. "Dr. Samuel Johnson, 1709-84," in *The Best of Their Kind*, pp. 163-78. London: Richards, 1949.

1178a . *Add:* See item S 955.

1180 . *Add:* Reprinted in *Essays Light and Serious*, ed. W.G. Langford, pp. 34–35. Toronto: Longmans (Canada), 1954.

1184a[new] . NAPIER, S. ELLIOTT. "Doctor Johnson: A Literary Anomaly," *Australian National Review*, December 1, 1937, pp. 40-43.

1230a . *Add:* Reprinted (with additions) 1954 (item S 960).

1314a[new] . SWAINE, D.J. "Samuel Johnson's Interest in Scientific Affairs," *Journal of Chemical Education*, XXIV (August 1948), 458-59.

1340 . *Add:* See also (March 2, 1901), 176; (March 23), 237; (April 13), 295-96.

1346 . *Add:* Reprinted (paperbound), Cambridge, Mass.: Walker-De Berry, 1960.

1381 . *Add:* Discussed by W.K. Wimsatt, Jr., *JNL*, IX, 3 (June 1949), 10–12.

1411 . *Add:* See item S 1404.

1435 . *Add:* Reprinted as "Poetry in the Eighteenth Century," in *The Pelican Guide to English Literature*, Vol. IV, pp. 271-77. Penguin Books, 1957.

1450a[new]. NEILSON, GEORGE. "Johnson, Burton, and Juvenal" [Burton and Sir Edward Coke quote *Res angusta domi* — source of "Slow rises worth" in *London*], *N&Q*, December 9, 1893, p. 465.

1482b[new]. *Insert after item* 1482a:

ÖFTERING, MICHAEL. "Die Geschichte der Schönen Irene in der französischen und deutschen Literatur," *Zeitschrift für vergleichenden Literaturgeschichte*, (neue Folge) XIII (1899), 27–45, 146–65. See also his Munich dissertation, *Die Geschichte der "Schönen Irene" in den modernen Literaturen*, Würzburg, 1897.

1506a[new]. Facsimiles of *Ramblers* 5 and 60 in Augustan Reprint Society Publication No. 22 (1950), ed. B.H. Bronson (see item 1425).

1514a[new]. DAVIDSON, FRANK. "Hawthorne's Use of a Pattern from the *Rambler*," *MLN*, LXIII (December 1948), 545–48.

1540. *Add:* Continued 338-41, 516-19, 541-46, 561-63.

1551. *Add:* See also items S 1568 and S 1571.

*1555a[new]. FLASDIECK, HERMANN M. Chapter IV, "Das Zeitalter Johnsons," in *Der Gedanke einer englischen Sprachakademie in Vergangenheit und Gegenwart*, pp. 101–43. Jena: Verlag der Frommanschen Buchhandlung, 1928.

1557a[new]. GORDON, J.W. "The English Dictionary," *Quarterly Review*, CCXL (July 1923), 164-82.

1576. *Add:* See also C.A. Ward, in *N&Q*, May 24, 1890, p. 406.

1591a[new]. SKEAT, W.W. "'Kidnapper'" [identifies Addison quotation in *Dictionary* entry for this word — *Spectator* No. 311], *N&Q*, May 4, 1907, pp. 345-46.

1592a[new]. STARK, EULA GENEVIEVE, "Samuel Johnson's Reading for the *Dictionary*" (master's thesis, University of Chicago, 1928).

1604. *Add:* Reviewed by Anna Granville Hatcher, *MLN*, LXVII (February 1952), 125–29. See also Donald Davie, "Berkeley and 'Philosophic Words,'" *Studies* (Dublin), XLIV (Autumn 1955), 319–24.

1607. To following entry ("*See also*") add "910a".

1620. In line 11, for "Home Memorial Press" read "Howe Memorial Press."

1623. *Add:* Tr. into French by J. Staquet. Brussels: Éditions La Boétie, 1946.

1629. *Add:* Reprinted in *Hilaire Belloc: An Anthology of His Prose and Verse*, ed. W.N. Roughead, pp. 266 — 72. Philadelphia: J.B. Lippincott, 1951.

1655. For "item 633" read "item 663."

1664[new]. *Insert in Section XVIII before item* 1665:
BRONSON, BERTRAND H. *Joseph Ritson: Scholar-at-Arms*, II, 429–54, etc. [discussion of Johnson's Shakespeare]. Berkeley: University of California Press, 1938.

1668a. *Add:* See item S 1678.

1676a[new]. LOVETT, DAVID. "Shakespeare as a Poet of Realism in the Eighteenth Century," *ELH*, II (November 1935), 267–89.

1694a[new]. WILSON, J. DOVER. "Introduction: Back to Johnson," in *The Fortunes of Falstaff*, pp. 1–14. Cambridge: Cambridge University Press, 1944.

*1699[new]. *Insert in Section XIX before item* 1700:
EVANS, MEDFORD. "Johnson's Debates in Parliament" (unpublished dissertation, Yale University, 1933).

1717a[new]. BRACEY, ROBERT. "To Paris with Dr. Johnson," *Blackfriars*, XIV (April 1933), 281–88. Review article based on item 1760.

1730a[new]. GATENBY, E. V. "Johnson and Boswell in Scotland," *Studies in English Literature* (Tokyo), IX (1929), 341–54.

1746a[new]. MACLEAN, CATHERINE M. "Dr. Johnson in the Highlands," *English Review*, XXXIX (November 1924), 686–90.

1801a. *Add:* See item S 1787.

1805. *Add:* Reprinted in *The Importance of Scrutiny*, ed. Eric Bentley, pp. 55–75. New York: Grove Press, 1948.

1823. *Add:* Reprinted in *Literary Essays*, pp. 94–99. London: Chatto and Windus, 1948; New York: Harcourt, Brace, 1949. (First printed in *Independent Review*, X, July 1906, as a review of item 1770 [ed. G.B. Hill, 1905]).

1824. *Add:* Reprinted in *The Forlorn Demon*, pp. 112–30. Chicago: Henry Regnery, 1953.

1850. After "nearing completion" add "[published 1952 — see item S 1850]."

1915. To the following entry ("*See also*"), add "23a."

1934a[new] . BROWN, STUART GERRY. "Dr. Johnson and the Christian Tradition" (dissertation, Princeton University, 1937). Ann Arbor, Michigan: University Microfilms [1952].

1960 . *For* PILLIANS *read* PILLANS.

2027a[new] . HENNIG, JOHN. "Young Johnson and the Jesuits" [Father Lobo], *The Month,* CLXXXII (November-December 1946), 440–49.

2030a . *Add:* See item S 1936.

2063a[new] .*Proposals for Printing* ... *Bibliotheca Harleiana* [1742]. Facsimile (introductory note by R.W. Chapman). Oxford: Clarendon Press, 1926.

2077 . For *"Bath and Wilts Chronicle and Herald,* December 21, 1937, p. 6" read *"Bath Chronicle and Herald,* December 23, 1937, p. 13."

2078 . To the following entry (*"See also"*), add "908a."

Additions and Corrections
to Index of Names,
JOHNSONIAN STUDIES, 1887-1950

1. References to be added to names already included in the index:

BELL, WALTER G., 417a

BRACEY, ROBERT, 1717a

BRONSON, BERTRAND H., 1506a, 1664

BROWN, STUART G., 1934a

CHAPMAN, ROBERT W., 14a, 39, 355, 2063a

CHESTERTON, GILBERT K., 986a

DENT, ROBERT K., 711b

EMDEN, CECIL S., 470a

ESCOTT, THOMAS H.S., 656a

GAUSSEN, ALICE C.C., 542a

GRAY, W. FORBES, 1059a

HILL, JOSEPH, 711b

KNOX, MGR. RONALD A., 1124a

KOLB, GWIN J., 112a

KRISHNAMURTI, S., 511a

LEYBURN, ELLEN D., 1137a

LIEBERT, HERMAN W., 351a

MCADAM, E. L., JR., 1158

POTTLE, FREDERICK A., 51a

SADLER, ERNEST A., 574a

SAINTSBURY, GEORGE, 380a

WARD, C.A., 1576

WIMSATT, WILLIAM K., JR., 1381.

WOOLF, VIRGINIA, 451, 613a

2. Changes to be made in existing entries:

After "Couper, W.J.," change "1772" to read "1722."

For "Huchison, Robert, 285," read "Hutchison, Sir Robert, 285," and insert in correct alphabetical place.

For "Pillians, T.D.," read "Pillans, T.D."

3. New entries, to be inserted in correct alphabetical place:

ADCOCK, A. ST. J., 699

ADDLESHAW, S., 401a

ALLODOLI, ETTORE, 908a

ASKWITH, HERBERT, 318a

B., A., 819

BAVERSTOCK, JAMES H., 415a

BENSON, ARTHUR C., 929a

BENTLEY, ERIC, 1805

BIRD, LOIS M.M., 3a

BULLARD, SIR READER W., 967a

CHANCELLOR, E. BERESFORD, 707a

DAVIDSON, FRANK, 1514a

DAVIE, DONALD, 1604

DAWSON, GEORGE, 1009a

B) A Bibliography

of

JOHNSONIAN STUDIES, 1950-1960

GENERAL

I. — BIBLIOGRAPHY

(Includes exhibition and sale catalogues, and general descriptive bibliography. Descriptive bibliography of individual works is listed in the sections dealing with those works.)

S1. *Abstracts of English Studies.* Monthly. Champaign, Illinois: National Council of Teachers of English. Vol. I, 1958–. Annual indexes list incidental references to Johnson in (selected) studies of other literary figures and topics.

S2. CHAPMAN, R.W. "The Congreve Manuscripts" [six early MSS of Johnson], *Bodleian Library Record*, V (1955), 118.

S3. ————. "Manuscript Hunting in Two Continents" [with facsimile of restoration of letter "edited" by Mrs. Piozzi], *New Colophon*, II, part 8 (1950), 370-78.

S4. CLIFFORD, JAMES L. "The Eighteenth Century," in *Contemporary Literary Scholarship: A Critical Review*, ed. Lewis Leary, pp. 97-99 [Johnson]. New York: Appleton-Century-Crofts, 1958.

★S5. ————. *Johnsonian Studies*, 1887-1950: *A Survey and Bibliography*. Minneapolis: University of Minnesota Press, 1951. Reviewed by Mary C. Hyde, *PBSA*, XLV (4th quarter, 1951), 365–67; H.W. Liebert, *PQ*, XXXI (July 1952), 277–78; R.W. Chapman, *RES*, n.s. III (July 1952), 299–300; E.L. McAdam, Jr., *MLN*, LXVII (November 1952), 498; Gwin J. Kolb, *MP*, L (February 1953), 215-16.

S6. DAVIS, HERBERT. "Recent Studies of Swift and Johnson," in *Sprache und Literatur Englands und Amerikas. Band III: Die wissenschaftliche Erschliessung der Prosa*, ed. Gerhard Müller-Schwefe, with Hermann Metzger, pp. 11-25 [contains in Johnsonian portion some factual inaccuracies]. Tübingen: Niemeyer, 1959.

*S7. *Dr. Samuel Johnson* ... [catalogue of] *An Exhibition of Books, Manuscripts, Views and Portraits arranged jointly by the Reference Library and the Museum and Art Gallery 14th September to 4th October 1959*. Birmingham: City of Birmingham Public Libraries, 1959.

*S8. FABIAN, BERNHARD. "Samuel Johnson: Ein Forschungsbericht," *Die Neueren Sprachen*, 1959, No. 9 (September), 393-407; No. 10 (October), 441-54.

S9. HYDE, DONALD and MARY. "The Hyde Collection," *The Book Collector*, IV (Autumn, 1955), 208-16.

*S10. HYDE, MARY C. "The History of the Johnson Papers," *PBSA*, XLV (2nd quarter, 1951), 103-16.

S11. ———. "A Library of Dr. Samuel Johnson" [description of the Hyde collection], *Vassar Alumnae Magazine*, XLV (May 1960), 2-6.

S12. *Johnson's Books: Catalogue of an Exhibition of Books in the Birmingham Library* [commemoration of 250th anniversary of Johnson's birth]. Birmingham: Birmingham Library, 1959.

S13. MAHONEY, JOHN L. "Dr. Johnson at Work: Observations on a Columbia Rare Book" [*Poems of Collins*, 1771, with Hammond's *Elegies*, marked by Johnson], *Columbia Library Columns*, X (November 1960), 20-23. See item 27.

*S14. METZDORF, ROBERT F. *The Tinker Library: A Bibliographical Catalogue of the Books and Manuscripts Collected by Chauncey Brewster Tinker*. New Haven: Yale University Library, 1959.

S15. MOSER, EDWIN. "A Critical Examination of the Canon of the Prose Writings of Samuel Johnson" (dissertation, New York University, 1959). Abstract in *Dissertation Abstracts*, XX (1960), 3283-84.

S16. [POWELL, L.F.] "Samuel Johnson," in *Cambridge Bibliography of English Literature*, Vol. V (Supplement), ed. George Watson, pp. 462-68. Cambridge: Cambridge University Press, 1957.

*S17. "Samuel Johnson" (annual entries, 1925–1949), in *English Literature, 1660–1800: A Bibliography of Modern Studies Compiled for Philological Quarterly*, ed. R.S. Crane *et al.* 2 vols. Princeton: Princeton University Press, 1950–52. Continued annually in the July number of *Philological Quarterly*. Further cumulative printings are expected.

*S18. *Samuel Johnson, LL.D. (1709-1784). An Exhibition of First Editions, Manuscripts, Letters, and Portraits to Commemorate the 250th Anniversary of his Birth, and the 200th Anniversary of the Publication of his Rasselas. September 22 — November 28, 1959.* New York: The Pierpont Morgan Library, 1959. Foreword by Herbert Cahoon.

S19. SHERBO, ARTHUR. "The Cancels in Dr. Johnson's *Works* (Oxford, 1825)," *PBSA*, XLVII (4th quarter, 1953), 376–78.

S20. ———. "Johnson and J. Roberts, Publisher" [published three books by Johnson, not one, as Boswell says], *JNL*, XV, 4 (December 1955), 12.

*S21. TAYLOR, FRANK. "Johnsoniana from the Bagshawe Muniments in the John Rylands Library: Sir James Caldwell, Dr. Hawkesworth, Dr. Johnson, and Boswell's Use of the 'Caldwell Minute,'" *Bulletin of the John Rylands Library*, XXXV (September 1952), 211–47. See also XXXIV (March 1952), 249–50.

See also item S1549.

II. — EDITIONS

WORKS

*S100. *The Yale Edition of the Works of Samuel Johnson*, general editor, Allen T. Hazen. New Haven: Yale University Press, 1958 —. (For Vol. I, all so far published, see item S1925).

SELECTIONS

S110. *Selected Prose and Poetry*, ed. with introduction and notes by Bertrand H. Bronson. New York: Rinehart and Co. (Rinehart Editions), 1952. [Previously listed as item 116a.] Enlarged edition, *Rasselas, Poems, and Selected Prose*, 1958.

S111. *Selections from Samuel Johnson, 1709-1784*, ed. R.W. Chapman. London: Oxford University Press, 1955.

ANTHOLOGIES

(SPECIFICALLY LIMITED TO ANTHOLOGIES OF 18TH-CENTURY WORKS)

S140. *The Pelican Book of English Prose. Vol. III: Eighteenth-Century Prose, 1700-1780*, ed. D.W. Jefferson [numerous short excerpts]. Harmondsworth, Middlesex: Penguin Books, 1956.

III. — BIOGRAPHY

(SEPARATE BIOGRAPHIES AND MISCELLANEOUS BIOGRAPHICAL INFORMATION)

S200. ATKINSON, A.D. "A Johnson Conversation" [identification of an undated remark in Cooke's *Life* with conversation of April 9, 1778, in Boswell], *N&Q*, February 17, 1951, p. 79.

S201. [BEARD, G.W.] "Some Johnsonian Addenda" [entries in Johnson's diaries omitted by Boswell; letters from Sir William Boothby to Michael Johnson], *The Times* (London), December 14, 1953, p. 10.

S202. CLIFFORD, JAMES L. "The Complex Art of Biography, or All the Dr. Johnsons," *Columbia University Forum*, I (Spring, 1958), 32–37. Revised and reprinted as "A Biographer Looks at Dr. Johnson", in item S957, pp. 121–31.

★S203. ———. *Young Sam Johnson*. New York: McGraw-Hill, 1955. *Young Samuel Johnson* [contains small variations from American edition]. London: Heinemann, 1955. Reviewed by Carlos Baker, *New York Times Book Review*, April 17, 1955, pp. 1, 22; John Raymond, *New Statesman and Nation*, December 24, 1955, pp. 860–61; Arthur Sherbo, *JEGP*, LV (January 1956), 162–64; J.H. Hagstrum, *MLN*, LXXI (February 1956), 131–33; John Beer, *Cambridge Review* LXXVII (April 21, 1956), 497–99; R.P. McCutcheon, *MP*, LIII (May 1956), 282–84; W.R. Keast, *MLQ*, XVIII (December 1957), 342–44.

S204. DAVIS, BERTRAM H. "Another Johnsonian Anecdote" [about a toast to Miss Williams; from *Liber Facetiarium*, 1811], *JNL*, XV, 4 (December 1955), 12.

S205. HILLES, FREDERICK W. *Dr. Johnson Rebuked: A Hitherto Unrecorded Incident in His Life as Revealed in a Letter from Dr. Samuel Glasse.* New Haven: privately printed for The Johnsonians [Yale University Press], 1952. [With facsimile of letter.]

*S206. HYDE, DONALD and MARY. *Dr. Johnson's Second Wife.* Somerville, New Jersey: privately printed [Princeton University Press], 1953. [With facsimile of four pages of Boswell's transcript of Johnson's diary.] Reprinted in *Manuscripts*, VI (Spring, 1954), 144-54. Revised and reprinted in item S957 [with facsimile of one page of Boswell's transcript], pp. 133-51.

S207. "A Johnson Anecdote" [in *The Weekly Entertainer*, 1786], *JNL*, XII, 1 (February 1952), 11.

S208. "Johnson and Stourbridge," *JNL*, XII, 3 (September 1952), 1-2.

S209. JOYCE, MICHAEL. *Samuel Johnson.* London: Longmans, Green, 1955.

S210. NORMAN, CHARLES. *Mr. Oddity: Samuel Johnson, LL.D.* Drexel Hill, Pennsylvania: Bell Publishing Co., 1951; London: John Murray, 1952.

S211. ———. *The Pundit and the Player: Dr. Johnson and Mr. Garrick: A Biography for Young People*, illustrated by Bruno Frost. New York: David McKay Co., 1951.

S212. PEARSON, HESKETH. *Johnson and Boswell: The Story of Their Lives.* London: Heinemann; New York: Harper and Brothers, 1958.

S213. POTTLE, FREDERICK A. "The Dark Hints of Sir John Hawkins and Boswell" [revision of item 238], reprinted in item S957, pp. 153-62.

S214. QUAINTANCE, RICHARD E., JR. "A Johnson Anecdote" [comment on Henry Mackenzie], *JNL*, XVIII, 4 (December 1958), 9-10.

S215. ROBERTS, S.C. *Samuel Johnson.* London: Longmans, Green, for the British Council and the National Book League, 1954 (*Writers and Their Work*).

S216. SCARLETT, E.P. "The Historic Shudder" [reprints an anecdote of Johnson from the *Monthly Magazine*, February 1798], *The New Trail* (University of Alberta Alumni Association), IX (Spring 1951), 29-30.

S217. "Some Little Known Remarks of Johnson" [from Henry Francis Cary's *Lives of English Poets*, 1846], *JNL*, XIII, 3 (September 1953), 11-12.

S218. "Some New Anecdotes of Johnson" [from Bodleian MS Eng. Misc. e 8, formerly MS collection of Philip Bliss], *JNL*, XIII, 4 (December 1953), 11. See also Bertram H. Davis, in *JNL*, XIV, 1 (March 1954), 11-12.

S219. TODD, WILLIAM B. "A Johnsonian Anecdote" [version in *London Evening Post*, 1773, of a quip to Robertson about the "kirk"], *JNL*, XV, 3 (September 1955), 12.

*S220. TYERS, THOMAS. *A Biographical Sketch of Dr. Samuel Johnson* [reprint of revised version issued as a separate pamphlet in 1785, with marginal additions by Tyers], introduction by Gerald D. Meyer. Los Angeles: Augustan Reprint Society, 1952 (Publication No. 34).

S221. WILLS, GEOFFREY. "Ceramic Causerie: Dr. Samuel Johnson and Chelsea" [rebuts a story in Thomas Faulkner's *History of Chelsea*, 1829 (I, 273), that Johnson experimented in manufacturing china and "afterwards gave a dissertation on this very subject in his works"], *Apollo*, LXI (January 1955), 14. See item 211.

S222. WIMSATT, WILLIAM K., JR. "A Philadelphian Meets Johnson" [John Ewing], *TLS*, January 1, 1960, p. 7.

See also items S2, S12, S21, and Sections IV to VIII below.

MEDICAL AND PSYCHOLOGICAL WORKS

*S275. BEATTIE, P.H. "The Ocular Troubles of Dr. Johnson and Mr. Pepys," *Proceedings of the Royal Society of Medicine*, XLVI (August 1953), 591–96.

S276. BENTON, ARTHUR L. and ROBERT J. JOYNT. "Early Descriptions of Aphasia" [deals with Johnson's aphasia], *American Medical Association Archives of Neurology*, III (August 1960), 119-20.

S277. BISHOP, P. JAMES. "Samuel Johnson's Lung" [an illustration of it found in Matthew Baillie, *A Series of Engravings ... to Illustrate ... Morbid Anatomy*, 1803], *Tubercle*, XL (December 1959), 478-81.

S278. CHASE, PETER PINEO. "The Ailments and Physicians of Dr. Johnson," *Yale Journal of Biology and Medicine*, XXIII (April 1951), 370-79.

*S279. CRITCHLEY, MACDONALD. "The Study of Language-Disorder: Past, Present, and Future" [Johnson's aphasia in 1783], in *The Centennial Lectures, Commemorating the One Hundredth Anniversary of E.R. Squibb and Sons*. New York: G.P. Putnam's Sons, 1959.

S280. "Dr. Johnson s Doctors," *New England Journal of Medicine,* CCLXI (September 17, 1959), 618.

S281. KENNEY, WILLIAM. "Dr. Johnson and the Psychiatrists" [a review of psychiatric studies of Johnson], *American Imago,* XVII (Spring 1960, 75–82.

S282. MACKEITH, RONALD. "Samuel Johnson, My Patient, " *The New Rambler,* June 1958, pp. 13–28. Reprinted in *Oxford Medical School Gazette,* XI (March 23, 1959), 4–12.

See also items S404, S405, S411, S907a.

IV. — BOSWELL

(WORKS AND EVENTS CONNECTED WITH JOHNSON)

EDITIONS

S300. *The Life of Samuel Johnson, LL.D.*
Abridged, with an introduction, by Bergen Evans [text follows that of item 314]. New York: Random House, 1952 (Modern Library).
Tr. into German (abridged and with an introduction) by Fritz Güttinger (with *The Journal of a Tour to the Hebrides*) [*Dr. Samuel Johnson: Leben und Meinungen; mit dem Tagebuch einer Reise nach den Hebriden*]. Zürich: Manesse-Verlag, 1951 (Manesse Bibliothek der Weltliteratur).
Tr. into Norwegian (abridged) by Solveig Tunold. Oslo: H. Aschehoug and Co., 1951.
Tr. into French by J.P. Le Hoc [*La Vie de Samuel Johnson*]. Paris: Gallimard, 1954 (Les Classiques Anglais).
Tr. into Serbo-Croat (abridged and with an introduction) by Stjepan Kresić. Zagreb: Kultura Publishing Co., 1958.

S301. *The Journal of a Tour to the Hebrides with Samuel Johnson, LL. D.*
Ed. with introduction and notes by Jack Werner, with 20 illustrations by Rowlandson. London: MacDonald and Co.; New York: Coward-McCann, 1956.
Ed. with introduction by L.F. Powell. London: J.M. Dent; New York: E.P. Dutton, 1958 (Everyman's Library).
With introduction by T.C. Livingstone. London: Collins, 1958 (New Collins Classics).
Tr. into German (abridged) by Fritz Güttinger, 1951. See item S300.

S302. *The Journal of a Tour to Corsica; and Memoirs of Pascal Paoli.* Ed. Morchard Bishop. London: Williams and Norgate, 1951.

The Yale Edition of the Private Papers of James Boswell

*S303. Vol. 1. *Boswell's London Journal, 1762–1763,* ed. Frederick A. Pottle with preface by Christopher Morley. New York: McGraw-Hill; London: Heinemann, 1950.

Limited edition. London: Heinemann, 1951. Includes an essay by F.A. Pottle, "The History of the Boswell Papers," pp. xi-xlii.

Reprinted (paperbound). New York: New American Library, 1956 (Signet Books).

Tr. into French by Mme. [Émile-Robert] Blanchet, with preface by André Maurois [*Les Papiers de Boswell: Amours à Londres, 1762–1763*]. Paris: Hachette, 1952.

Tr. into German by Fritz Güttinger (*Boswells Londoner Tagebuch*]. Zürich: Diana Verlag, 1953.

S304. Vol. 2. *Boswell in Holland, 1763–1764,* ed. F.A. Pottle. New York: McGraw-Hill; London: Heinemann, 1952.

S305. Vol. 3. See item S448 (Sir Joshua Reynolds, *Portraits*).

S306. Vol. 4. *Boswell on the Grand Tour: Germany and Switzerland, 1764,* ed. F.A. Pottle. New York: McGraw-Hill; London: Heinemann, 1953.

Tr. into German by Fritz Güttinger [*Boswells Grosse Reise: Deutschland und die Schweiz, 1764*]. Zürich: Diana Verlag, 1955.

Tr. into French by Celia Bertin, with preface by André Maurois [*Les Papiers de Boswell (2): Boswell Chez les Princes: Les cours allemandes, Voltaire, J.J. Rousseau, 1764*]. Paris: Hachette, 1955.

S307. Vol. 5. *Boswell on the Grand Tour: Italy, Corsica, and France, 1765-1766,* ed. Frank Brady and F.A. Pottle. New York: McGraw-Hill; London: Heinemann, 1955.

S308. Vol. 6. *Boswell in Search of a Wife, 1766–1769,* ed. Frank Brady and F.A. Pottle. New York: McGraw-Hill, 1956; London: Heinemann, 1957.

S309. Vol. 7. *Boswell for the Defence, 1769-1774,* ed. W.K. Wimsatt, Jr., and F.A. Pottle. New York: McGraw-Hill, 1959; London: Heinemann, 1960.

CRITICISM

S325. ADAMS, SARAH F. "Boswell's *Life of Samuel Johnson*" [cancels in copy of 1st edition], *Yale Library Gazette*, XXIX (July 1954), 35-36.

S326. ALTICK, RICHARD D. "The Secret of the Ebony Cabinet" [history of the Boswell papers], in *The Scholar Adventurers*, pp. 16-36. New York: Macmillan, 1950. Reissued in Macmillan Paperbacks, 1960.

S327. AUDIAT, PIERRE. "Héros Inattendus" [includes discussion cf *London Journal*], *Revue de Paris*, Année 59 (September 1952), 163-66.

S328. BALDWIN, LOUIS. "The Conversation in Boswell's *Life of Johnson*," *JEGP*, LI (October 1952), 492-506.

S329. BROOKS, ALFRED RUSSELL. "The Literary and Intellectual Foundations of James Boswell" (dissertation, University of Wisconsin, 1959). Abstract in *Dissertation Abstracts*, XIX (1959), 1752-53.

S330. BUTT, JOHN. "Boswell, Johnson, and Garrick" [earlier publication of an anecdote recorded in the *Life*], *JNL*, X, 4 (August 1950), 12.

S331. ———. *James Boswell* [inaugural lecture as Professor of Rhetoric and English Literature, December, 1959]. Edinburgh: University of Edinburgh, 1960.

S332. COLLINS, P.A.W. "Boswell's Contact with Johnson" [the two were in each other's company on a total of about 425 days], *N&Q*, April, 1956, pp. 163-66.

S333. ———. *James Boswell*. London: Longmans, Green, for the British Council and the National Book League, 1956 (*Writers and Their Work*).

S334. GÜTTINGER, FRITZ. "Boswell und Dr. Samuel Johnson" [part of introduction and samples of a German translation from the *Life*— see item S300], *Neue Schweizer Rundschau* (Zürich), XIX (May 1951), 29-38.

★S335. HART, EDWARD. "The Contributions of John Nichols to Boswell's *Life of Johnson*," *PMLA*, LXVII (June 1952), 391-410. See also Arthur Sherbo, *PQ*, XXXII (July 1953), 260-61.

S335a. HART, FRANCIS R. "Boswell and the Romantics: a Chapter in the History of Biographical Theory," *ELH*, XXVII (March 1960), 44-65.

S336. HORNE, COLIN J. "Boswell, Burke, and the *Life of Johnson*" [sale comparable to that of Burke's *Reflections on the French Revolution*], *N&Q*, November 11, 1950, pp. 498-99.

S337. [LIEBERT, HERMAN W.] *To Honor the Two Hundred and Seventeenth Anniversary of the Departure of Samuel Johnson and David Garrick to Try Their Fortunes in the Great Metropolis, 2 March 1737* [with facsimile of page of MS of the *Life*]. New Haven: privately printed for Halsted B. Vander Poel [Yale University Press], 1954. For similar title [1955] see item S1852.

S338. LONSDALE, ROGER. "Dr. Burney and the Integrity of Boswell's Quotations," *PBSA*, LII (4th quarter, 1959), 327–31.

S339. MARTIN, SAMUEL. *An Epistle in Verse Occasioned by the Death of James Boswell, Esquire, of Auchinleck* [1795], introduction by Robert Metzdorf. Hamden, Connecticut: Shoe String Press, 1952.

S340. McKILLOP, ALAN D. "Johnson and Ogilvie" [Ogilvie challenged Boswell's account of the conversation of July 6, 1763], *JNL*, XV, 4 (December 1955), 3–4.

S341. MONK SAMUEL H. "Samuel Johnson Quotes Addison" [an unrecognized quotation in the *Life*], *N&Q*, April 1957, p. 154.

S342. REID, B.L. "Johnson's Life of Boswell," *Kenyon Review*, XVIII (Autumn 1956), 546–75.

S343. ROBERTS, S.C. "More Boswell Letters," *TLS*, January 1, 1954, p. 16.

S344. SHELDON, ESTHER K. "Boswell's English in the *London Journal*," *PMLA*, LXII (December 1956), 1067–93.

S345. SHERBO, ARTHUR. "Gleanings from Boswell's *Notebook*," *N&Q*, March 1956, pp. 108–112.

S346. STEWART, MARY MARGARET. "The Search for Felicity: A Study of the Religious Thought of James Boswell in the Light of the Religious Developments of Eighteenth Century England and Scotland" [mentions influence of Johnson] (dissertation, Indiana University, 1959). Abstract in *Dissertation Abstracts*, XX (1960), 4392.

*S347. WAINGROW, MARSHALL. "Five Correspondences of James Boswell Relating to the Composition of the Life of Johnson" (unpublished dissertation, Yale University, 1951). A much enlarged edition, entitled "The Correspondence and Other Papers of James Boswell Relating to the *Life of Johnson*," is to be published shortly by Heinemann in London.

*S348. WIMSATT, WILLIAM K., JR. "James Boswell: The Man and the Journal," *Yale Review*, XLIX (Autumn 1959), 80–92.

See also items S20, S21, S200, S201, S206, S212, S409, S908, S917, S925, S960, S1380, S1449, S1713, S1719, S1722.

V. — JOHNSON'S PERSONAL RELATIONSHIPS

S400. ALLISON, JAMES. "Mrs. Thrale's Marginalia in Joseph Warton's *Essay*," *Huntington Library Quarterly*, XIX (February 1956), 155–64.

S401. BLOOM, EDWARD A. "Dr. Johnson's Landlord" [Richard Russell-Bolt Court, 1765–76], *N&Q*, August 1954, pp. 350–51.

S402. ———. "The Paradox of Samuel Boyse," *N&Q*, April 1954, pp. 163–65.

S403. BOYCE, BENJAMIN. "Johnson and Chesterfield Once More" [comment on item 483], *PQ*, XXXII (January 1953), 93–96.

S404. BRAIN, SIR RUSSELL. "Thomas Lawrence, M.D., P.R.C.P. (1711-83)" [relationship with Johnson], *Medical History*, I (October 1957), 293–306.

S405. CARTER, H.S. "Samuel Johnson and Some Eighteenth-Century Doctors," *Glasgow Medical Journal*, XXXII (July 1951), 218–27.

S406. CLIFFORD, JAMES L. "The Mystery of Dr. Johnson's Brother," *The Listener*, November 22, 1951, pp. 869–70.

S407. COCHRANE, PETER. "Tetty's Tombstone," *Manchester Guardian*, January 5, 1953, p. 3.

S408. COOKE, ARTHUR. "Anecdotes of Johnson and Garrick" [by Sir Richard Kaye], *JNL*, XIII, 3 (September 1953), 10.

*S409. DAVIS, BERTRAM HYLTON. *Johnson Before Boswell: A Study of Sir John Hawkins' Life of Samuel Johnson*. New Haven: Yale University Press, 1960. (A revision of "Sir John Hawkins' *Life of Johnson*: A Reappraisal" [dissertation, Columbia University, 1956]. Ann Arbor, Michigan: University Microfilms, 1956.) Reviewed in *The Times* (London), July 28, 1960, p. 13; *The Economist*, September 24, 1960, pp. 1190, 1195. An edition by Davis of Hawkins' *Life*, abridged, is to appear in 1961.

S410. DERRICK, MICHAEL. "Dr. Johnson's Monastic Cell Where He Thought of Ending His Days" [see item S443], *The Tablet*, CCV (March 19, 1955), 274.

S411. DOUBLEDAY, F.N. "Some Medical Associations of Samuel Johnson," *Guy's Hospital Reports*, CI, 1 (1952), 45-51.

S412. DUGGAN, G.C. "Boulter's Monument: A Poem" [Samuel Madden], *Dublin Magazine*, XXIX (October-December 1953), 20-27.

S413. E[MDEN], C[ECIL] S. "More Oriel Friends of Dr. Johnson" [John Myddelton and Thomas Apperley; see item 470a], *The Oriel Record* (Oxford), 1954, pp. 12-16.

S414. FIFER, C.N. "Dr. Johnson and Bennet Langton," *JEGP*, LIV (October 1955), 504-06. Reprinted in *Studies by Members of the English Department, University of Illinois, in Memory of John Jay Parry*, pp. 44-46. Urbana, Illinois: University of Illinois Press, 1957.

S415. FOSTER, W.E. "Samuel Johnson and the Dodd Affair," in item 663 (1951-52), pp. 36-49.

S416. GALLAGHER, ROBERT E. "John Hawkesworth: A Study toward a Literary Biography" (dissertation, Northwestern University, 1957). Abstract in *Dissertation Abstracts*, XVII (1957), 3002.

S417. GILLIS, WILLIAM. "Johnson and Macpherson" [letter from Sir William Forbes on the Johnson-Macpherson controversy], *JNL*, XV, 1 (March 1955), 7-8.

S418. GRAY, JAMES. "Beattie and the Johnson Circle," *Queen's Quarterly*, LVIII (Winter 1951-52), 519-32.

S419. ———. "Dr. Johnson and the King of Ashbourne" [John Taylor], *University of Toronto Quarterly*, XXIII (April 1954), 242-52.

S420. GREENE, DONALD J. "Johnson, Jenkinson, and the Peace of Paris," *JNL*, XI, 4 (September 1951), 8-11.

S421. HADEN, D.J. "Dr. Johnson's Headmaster at Stourbridge" [John Wentworth], *Birmingham Post*, September 16, 1952.

S422. [HANSON, L.F.] "Johnson, Percy, and Sir William Chambers" [annotation by Percy on Johnson's connection with Chambers' writings on China], *Bodleian Library Record*, IV (December 1953), 291-92.

*S423. HEMLOW, JOYCE. "Dr. Johnson and Fanny Burney – Some Additions to the Record" [passages cut out of the diary], *Bulletin of the New York Public Library*, LV (February 1951), 55-65.

*S424. ———. "Dr. Johnson and the Young Burneys," in item S 957, pp. 319-39.

*S425. ———. *The History of Fanny Burney*. Oxford: Clarendon Press, 1958. Reviewed in *TLS*, March 21, 1958, p. 152; by V.S. Pritchett, *New Statesman and Nation*, March 22, 1958, pp. 380–81; A.D. McKillop, *MLR*, LIV (January 1959), 98-99; J.L. Clifford, *MLN*, LXXIV (November 1959), 644-46.

S426. HILLES, FREDERICK W. "David Garrick and Sir Joshua" [based on item S448], *SR*, October 11, 1952, pp. 20-21, 30.

S427. HYDE, MRS. DONALD F. [MARY C.] "Tetty and Johnson," in item 663 (December 1957), pp. 34-46.

S428. [ISHAM, RALPH] "Dr. Johnson's Barber" [identified as "Mr. Collett"], *JNL*, XIII, 3 (September 1953), 1-2, 9.

*S429. JONES, W. POWELL. "Johnson and Gray, a Study in Literary Antagonism," *MP*, LVI (May 1959), 243–53.

S430. KETTON–CREMER, R.W. "Johnson's Last Gifts to Windham," *The Book Collector*, V (Winter 1956), 354–56.

S431. LEICESTER, J.H. "Dr. Johnson and William Shenstone," *The New Rambler*, June 1960, pp. 29-42.

S432. LEWIS, WILMARTH S. "The Young Waterman," in item S957, pp. 1-7. Earlier appeared in *Virginia Quarterly Review*, XXV (January 1949), 66–73.

*S433. [LIEBERT, HERMAN W.] *A Constellation of Genius* [account of Baretti's trial for murder and Johnson's evidence, with facsimiles of original documents]. New Haven: privately printed for The Johnsonians [Yale University Press], 1958.

S434. Low, D.M. "Edward Gibbon and the Johnsonian Circle," *The New Rambler*, June 1960, pp. 2–14.

S435. LUBBERS-VAN DER BRUGGE, CATHARINA J.M. *Johnson and Baretti: Some Aspects of Eighteenth-Century Literary Life in England and Italy*. Groningen: J.B. Wolters, 1951. Reviewed by E.A. Bloom, *JEGP*, LI (July 1952), 450-52; G.A. Bonnard, *English Studies*, XXXIII (October 1952), 224-26.

S436. ———. "A Lost Pamphlet of Giuseppe Baretti" [*The Voice of Discord*, and Johnson's help], *English Miscellany* (Rome), X (1959), 157- 88.

S437. LUCAS, F.L. "Johnson's *Bête Grise*" [Thomas Gray], *The New Rambler*, June 1960, pp. 15-28.

S438. McHenry, Lawrence C., Jr. "Doctors Afield: Robert Anderson, M.D., and His Life of Samuel Johnson," *New England Journal of Medicine*, CCLXI (September 17, 1959), 605-07.

S439. Mathias, Peter. "Henry Thrale and John Perkins," *The Brewing Industry in England*, 1700–1830, pp. 265-76, etc. Cambridge: Cambridge University Press, 1959.

S440. Metzdorf, Robert F. "Isaac Reed and the Unfortunate Dr. Dodd," *Harvard Library Bulletin*, VI (Autumn 1952), 393-96.

*S441. Mild, Warren. "Johnson and Lauder: A Re-examination," *MLQ*, XIV (June 1953), 149–53.

S442. Miller, Clarence A. *Sir John Hawkins: Dr. Johnson's Friend-Attorney-Executor-Biographer: A Reorientation of The Knight, The Lady, and Boswell.* Washington, D.C.: privately printed for the author, 1951.

*S443. Osborn, James M. *Dr. Johnson and the Contrary Converts* [James Compton and John Walker]. New Haven: privately printed for The Johnsonians [Yale University Press], 1954. Revised and reprinted in item S957, pp. 297–317.

*S444. ———. "Dr. Johnson's Intimate Friend" [Stephen Barrett], *TLS*, October 9, 1953, p. 652.

S445. Powell, L.F. "Edmund Southwell, His Sisters, and Dr. Johnson," *TLS*, December 30, 1960, p. 845.

*S446. Quinlan, Maurice J. "Dr. Franklin Meets Dr. Johnson" [item 550], reprinted in item S957, pp. 107–20.

S447. Reynolds, Frances. *An Enquiry Concerning the Principles of Taste* [materially helped by Johnson], introduction by James L. Clifford. Los Angeles: Augustan Reprint Society, 1951 (Publication No. 27).

S447a. ———. "Some Unpublished Recollections of Dr. Johnson" ["copied by her niece, Theophila Gwatkin, in whose family they have been preserved" — contains variants of the version published in item 505], *The Tablet*, CXCVIII (December 22, 1951), 464–66; (December 29, 1951), 484–85.

*S448. Reynolds, Sir Joshua. *Portraits by Sir Joshua Reynolds*, ed. with introduction and notes by Frederick W. Hilles. New York: McGraw-Hill; London: Heinemann, 1952. [Vol. 3 of *The Yale Edition of the Private Papers of James Boswell* — see items S303–S309].

*S449 . RUHE, EDWARD. "Birch, Johnson, and Elizabeth Carter: An Episode of 1738–1739," *PMLA*, LXXIII (December 1958), 491–500.

S450 . ———. "Hume and Johnson" [dinner guests together in 1763], *N&Q*, November 1954, pp. 477–78.

S451 . SARASON, BERTRAM D. "George Croft and Dr. Johnson," *N&Q*, March 1953, pp. 106–07.

S452 . SCHOLES, PERCY A. "Johnson's Two Musical Friends — Burney and Hawkins," *Canadian Music Journal*, I (Autumn 1956), 7–19.

S453 . ———. *The Life and Activities of Sir John Hawkins*. London: Oxford University Press, 1953. Reviewed by B.H. Bronson, *MLN*, LXIX (November 1954), 521–24.

S454 . SHERWIN, OSCAR. "A Man with a Tail — Lord Monboddo," *Journal of the History of Medicine and Allied Sciences*, XIII (October 1958), 435–65.

S455 . TAYLOR, E.G.R. "A Reward for the Longitude" [work of Zachariah Williams], *Mariner's Mirror*, XLV (February 1959), 59–66, (November), 339–41.

S456 . *Three Centuries* [history of the Barclay-Perkins brewery]. London: Barclay, Perkins Co., 1951.

S457 . TUCCI, GERALD ALFRED. "Baretti and the Shakespearean Influence in Italy: A Study in Eighteenth Century Polemics in Italy" (dissertation, New York University, 1960) [discusses influence of Johnson]. Abstract in *Dissertation Abstracts*, XX (1960), 4664.

S458 . WARDLE, RALPH M. *Oliver Goldsmith*. Lawrence, Kansas: University of Kansas Press, 1957. Reviewed by Morris Golden, *MLN*, LXXIII (June 1958), 442–44; K.C. Balderston, *PQ*, XXXVIII (July 1959), 327–28.

S459 . WEDGWOOD, SIR JOHN. "Wedgwood and Johnson" [the first Josiah Wedgwood], in item 663, December 1959, pp. 51–54.

S460 . WILLOUGHBY, EDWIN E. "The Unfortunate Dr. Dodd: The Tragedy of an Incurable Optimist," in *Essays by Divers Hands* (Royal Society of Literature), XXIX (1958), 124–43.

S461 . WOOLF, VIRGINIA. "A Friend of Johnson" [Baretti], in *Granite and Rainbow*, pp. 187–91. London: Hogarth Press; New York: Harcourt, Brace, 1958. Reprint of a review of item 451 (1909).

See also item S280.

VI. — CLUBS AND ASSOCIATIONS

S650 . FIFER, C.N. "The Founding of Dr. Johnson's Literary Club," *N&Q*, July 1956, pp. 302-03.

S651 . THE JOHNSON SOCIETY of the Great Lakes Region. Corresponding Secretary, Warren L. Fleischauer, John Carroll University, Cleveland, Ohio. Organized in 1959 [see *JNL*, June 1959, p. 3; December 1959, pp. 3-4, etc.]. Issues "Transactions" of the annual meetings.

S652 . THE JOHNSONIANS (New York City). At annual dinner in September issues privately-printed pamphlets — see items 435, 515, 2038, S205, S206, S433, S443, S707, S783, S1789, S1868, S1939. See also S957. A list of members was printed in 1951.

The following periodicals, listed in Section VI of *Johnsonian Studies, 1887-1950*, continued to be published 1950-60:
  Item 663 (*Transactions* of The Johnson Society [Lichfield]; annually). W. Richards, Hon. General Secretary.
  Item 668 (*Johnsonian News Letter*; four times a year). John H. Middendorf now co-editor.
  Item 672 (*The New Rambler*; irregularly — about twice a year). Rev. F.N. Doubleday now editor (address: Hartland, Moores Rd., Dorking, Surrey).

VII. — HOMES AND PLACES

S700 . BARTEL, ROLAND, ed. *Johnson's London: Selected Source Materials for Freshman Research Papers*. New York: D.C. Heath and Co., 1956.

S701 . BEVAN, BRYAN. "Dr. Johnson's Year," *Coming Events in Britain* (British Travel Association), July 1959, pp. 12-15.

S702 . CHRISTIAN, ROY. "Johnson's Lichfield," *Coming Events in Britain* (British Travel Association), September 1952, p. 25.

S702a . *Dr. Johnson and Birmingham: an Account of the Birmingham Celebrations of the 250th Anniversary of the Birth of Dr. Samuel Johnson*, ed. Eric Knight. Birmingham: Birmingham and Midland Institute, 1960.

S703 . HOPEWELL, S. "Johnson and His Times," in *The Book of Bosworth School*. Leicester: W. Thornley and Son, 1950. [Many errors; does not use Reade.]

S704 . HOPKINS, MARY ALDEN. *Dr. Johnson's Lichfield.* New York: Hastings House, 1952; London: Peter Owen, 1956.

★S705 . LAITHWAITE, PERCY. *Dr. Samuel Johnson and His Birthplace* [revised edition]. Lichfield: Johnson Birthplace Committee, 1955.

S706 . ———. "The Beginnings of Lichfield," in item 663, 1950.

S707 . [LIEBERT, HERMAN W.] *Dr. Johnson and Oxford.* [in honor of R.W. Chapman]. Privately printed for The Johnsonians, 1950.

S708 . LOCKSPEISER, SIR BEN. "City of Philosophers" [Lichfield], in item 663, December 1953, pp. 18–30.

S709 . MEYNELL, ROSEMARY, "Johnsonian Mysteries in Derbyshire," *Derbyshire Countryside,* July-September 1952, pp. 64–65.

S710 . OGDEN, C.R.B. "Dr. Johnson in Bedfordshire," *Bedfordshire Magazine,* V (Winter 1955–56), 93–97.

See also items S208, S221.

VIII. — PICTURES, RELICS, ETC.

S779 . BROWN, T.J. "English Literary Autographs: VI. Samuel Johnson," *The Book Collector,* II (Summer 1953), 143.

S780 . "Dr. Johnson: An Imaginary Portrait" ["The Infant Johnson" by Reynolds, now in the Hyde collection], *The Book Collector,* I (Summer 1952), 94–95. See comment by E. Rosenbaum, *TLS,* July 11, 1952, p. 453, and C. Roy Huddleston, *Book Collector,* I (Autumn 1952), 192.

S781 . *Garrick, Johnson, and the Lichfield Circle: An Exhibition of Paintings* [Lichfield Coronation Festival]. Lichfield, 1953. Introduction by K.J. Garlick.

S782 . LETTS, MALCOLM. "Dr. Johnson's Cat," *TLS,* November 7, 1952, p. 732.

S783 . L[IEBERT], H[ERMAN] W. *Johnson's Head: The Story of the Bust of Dr. Samuel Johnson Taken from the Life by Joseph Nollekens, R.A., in 1777.* With plates. New Haven: privately printed for the Johnsonians [Yale University Press], 1960.

S784 . NUTTALL, GEOFFREY F. "Johnson's Fighting Septuagint" [with which he knocked down Osborne; it still survives], *TLS,* March 27, 1959, p. 177.

S785. [WAINGROW, MARSHALL]. "Johnson's Degree Diplomas" [Boswell received them from Hawkins, not from Frank Barber; see item 803], *Bodleian Library Record*, III (December 1951), 238–39.

See also items S1796, S1939 (portrait of Tetty).

IX. — FICTION

(JOHNSON IN FICTION AND DRAMA)

S820. BLUNDEN, EDMUND. "Lives of the Poets: If Dr. Johnson Had Lived Rather Longer" [imaginary lives of Coleridge and Wordsworth], *TLS*, May 20, 27, 1955, pp. 276, 292.

S821. HART, CHARLES R. *Samuel Johnson: A Portrait* [a play in 11 scenes]. Eton, Windsor: Shakespeare Head Press, 1959.

S822. KRUTCH, JOSEPH WOOD. "The Last Boswell Paper," *SR*, July 21, 1951, pp. 13–15. Reprinted New York: P. and F. Duschnes, 1951.

S823. WATT, T.S. "A Pension for Johnson," *Punch*, June 17, 1953, pp. 712–14.

See also item S909.

X. — GENERAL STUDIES OF JOHNSON

(STUDIES OF PARTICULAR WORKS AND PARTICULAR ASPECTS OF HIS THOUGHT ARE LISTED IN LATER SECTIONS)

*S900. ABRAMS, MEYER H. "Dr. Johnson's Spectacles" [revision of item 900], reprinted in S957, pp. 177–87.

S901. ATKINS, J.W.H. "The Great Cham of Literature: Johnson," in *English Literary Criticism: 17th and 18th Centuries*, pp. 268–313. London: Methuen and Co., 1951.

S902. ATKINSON, A.D. "Dr. Johnson's English Prose Reading," *N&Q*, February 1953, pp. 60–63; March, 107–10; May, 206–10; July, 288–93; August, 344–46.

S903. ———. "Dr. Johnson and the Royal Society," *Notes and Records of the Royal Society of London*, X (April 1953), 131–38.

S904. ———. "Dr. Johnson and Sweden," *English*, VIII (Spring 1951), 184–88.

S905. BALDESHWILER, SISTER JOSELYN. "Johnson's Doctrine of Figurative Language" (dissertation, Fordham University, 1954).

★S906. BATE, WALTER JACKSON. *The Achievement of Samuel Johnson*. New York: Oxford University Press, 1955. Reviewed by E.R. Marks, *Kenyon Review*, XVIII (Spring 1956), 311–18; Arthur Sherbo, *JEGP*, LV (April 1956), 326–28; Gwin J. Kolb, *PQ*, XXXV (July 1956), 302–04; J.H. Hagstrum, *MP*, LIV (August 1956), 66–69; in *TLS*, March 16, 1957, p. 162; by Ian Watt, *MLN*, LXXII (November 1957), 546–49; J.C. Bryce, *RES*, n.s. IX (May 1958), 217–19.

★S907. BLOOM, EDWARD A. "The Allegorical Principle" [Johnson's ideas of allegory], *ELH*, XVIII (September 1951), 163–90.

S907a. BRAIN, SIR RUSSELL. *Some Reflections on Genius and Other Essays*, with drawings by Norman Smith. London: Pitman Medical Publishing Co., 1960. Reprints items 279, 954, and S1710 and adds two other essays on Johnson.

★S908. BRONSON, BERTRAND H. "The Double Tradition of Dr. Johnson," *ELH*, XVIII (June 1951), 90–106. Reprinted in *Eighteenth-Century English Literature: Modern Essays in Criticism*, ed. J.L. Clifford, pp. 285–99. New York: Oxford University Press, 1959 (Galaxy Books).

S909. CARR, H. WILDON. "Berkeley and Dr. Johnson: An Imaginary Dialogue" [on Johnson's "refutation" of Berkeley], *The Personalist*, XLI (Winter 1960), 13–14.

S910. CHAMBERLIN, WILLIAM HENRY. "Immortal Sam," *National Review* (New York), December 5, 1959, pp. 528–30.

S911. CHAPIN, CHESTER F. "Dr. Johnson's Approval of a Passage in Rousseau," *N&Q* November 1959, pp. 413–14.

S912. ———. "Johnson, Rousseau, and Religion," *Texas Studies in Literature and Language*, II (Spring 1960), 95–102.

S913. CHAPMAN, R.W. *Johnsonian and Other Essays and Reviews*. Oxford: Clarendon Press, 1953. Reprints items 978, 983, 1432, reviews of items 217, 218, 303, 306, 373, 1855.

S914. CLIFFORD, JAMES L. "Johnson and the Americans", *The New Rambler*, January 1959, pp. 13–18.

S915 . ————. "Johnson's Works in Our Day," in item 663, December 1958, pp. 37–49.

S916 . DAICHES, DAVID. *Critical Approaches to Literature* [in particular, pp. 241-60, "Possibilities and Limitations of a Method"]. New York: Prentice-Hall, 1956.

S917 . DE BEER, E.S. "Macaulay on Croker, Boswell, and Johnson," *The New Rambler*, July 1952, p. 5.

S918 . DE SELINCOURT, AUBREY. "Dr. Johnson," in *Six Great Englishmen*, pp. 43-72. London: Hamish Hamilton, 1953.

★S919 . DONNER, H.W. "Dr. Johnson as a Literary Critic" [inaugural lecture as Professor of English Language and Literature in the University of Uppsala], *Edda* (Oslo), LIV (1954), 325-37.

S919a EARISMAN, DELBERT L. "Samuel Johnson's Satire" (unpublished dissertation, Indiana University, 1960). Abstract in *Dissertation Abstracts*, XXI, 620.

★S920 . ELIOT, T.S. "Johnson as Critic and Poet," in *On Poetry and Poets*, pp. 162-92. London: Faber and Faber; New York: Harcourt, Brace, 1957.

S921 . EMLEY, EDWARD. "Dr. Johnson and Modern Criticism," *Philological Papers: University of West Virginia*, Series 52, No. 4-1 (October 1951), 66-82.

S922 . ————. "Dr. Johnson and the Writers of Tudor England" (dissertation, New York University, 1958).

S923 . FINNERTY, SISTER M. JEAN CLARE. "Johnson the Moralist: Friend and Critic of the Clergy and Hierarchy" (dissertation, Fordham University, 1959).

S924 . FUSSELL, PAUL, JR. *Theory of Prosody in Eighteenth-Century England*, pp. 24-26, 41-44, and passim. New London, Connecticut: Connecticut College, 1954.

S925 . GILLIS, WILLIAM. "Johnson, Boswell, and Fergusson" [poems on Johnson and Boswell attributed to the Scottish poet], *JNL*, XIV, 2 (June 1954), 6-7.

S926 . GRAHAM, W.H. "Dr. Johnson and Royalty," *Contemporary Review*, No. 1081 (January 1956), 36-38.

S926a . GRAY, JAMES. "Dr. Johnson and the 'Intellectual Gladiators' " [on Restoration comedy], *Dalhousie Review*, XL (Autumn 1960), 350-59.

S927. GREENE, DONALD J. " 'No Warbler He' – a Contemporary Tribute to Johnson" [*The Authors*, by Daniel Hayes, 1766], *N&Q*, June 1953, pp. 243-44. See also Walter Armytage, *N&Q*, September 1953,p. 506.

*S928. HAGSTRUM, JEAN H. *Samuel Johnson's Literary Criticism*. Minneapolis: University of Minnesota Press, 1952. Reviewed by Ian Jack, *PQ*, XXXII (July 1953), 274–76; W.K. Wimsatt, Jr., *MLN*, LXIX (February 1954), 128–30; D. J. Greene, *RES*, n.s. V (April 1954), 200–03; M.H. Abrams, *Kenyon Review*, XVI (Spring 1954), 307–13.

S929. HALEY, SIR WILLIAM. "The 250th Anniversary of the Birth of Dr. Johnson," in item 663, December 1959, pp. 54–61.

S930. ———. "Dr. Samuel Johnson: Journalist," in item 663, December, 1960, pp. 29–39.

S931. HAVENS, RAYMOND D. "Solitude and the Neoclassicists," *ELH*, XXI (December 1954), 251–73.

S932. HUBBLE, DOUGLAS V. "Samuel Johnson in Friendship," in item 663, December 1956, pp. 21–31.

S933. HUMPHREYS, A.R. "Johnson," in *The Pelican Guide to English Literature*, ed. Boris Ford, Vol. IV, pp. 399–419. Penguin Books, 1957.

*S934. JONES, MARJORIE. "Housman and Johnson: Some Similarities," in item 663, December 1959, pp. 12–36.

S935. KALLICH, MARTIN. "The Association of Ideas in Samuel Johnson's Criticism," *MLN*, LXIX (March 1954), 170–76.

S936. KEAST, W.R. "Johnson and Intellectual History," in item S957, pp. 247-56.

*S937. ———. "The Theoretical Foundations of Johnson's Criticism," in *Critics and Criticism, Ancient and Modern*, ed. R.S. Crane, pp. 389-407. Chicago: University of Chicago Press, 1952. See also Jean H. Hagstrum, *PQ*, XXXII (July 1953), 276–78.

S938. KENNEY, WILLIAM. "The Modern Reputation of Samuel Johnson" (dissertation, Boston University, 1956). Abstract (separate pamphlet), Boston: Boston University Graduate School, 1956.

S938a. KIRK, RUSSELL. "Samuel Johnson the Statist" [largely an attack on S1701], *Kenyon Review*, XXII (Autumn 1960), 679–86.

S939. KRONENBERGER, LOUIS. "Johnson and Boswell", *The Republic of Letters*, pp. 89–123. New York: Knopf, 1955. See item 116.

S940 . KRUTCH, JOSEPH WOOD . "The Great Talker," *New York Times Magazine*, September 12, 1959.

S941 . LASCELLES, MARY. "Johnson's Last Allusion to Mary, Queen of Scots" [in *Letters* No. 972; other references by Johnson to Mary], *RES*, n.s. VIII (February 1957), 32–37.

S942 . ———. "A Physician in a Great City" [Johnson], in item 663 (1951–52), pp. 25–35.

S943 . LUCAS, F.L. *The Search for Good Sense*, pp. 27–128. London: Cassell; New York: Macmillan, 1958. Reviewed by Paul Fussell, Jr., *PQ*, XXXVIII (July 1959), 292.

S944 . McADAM, E.L., JR. "Dr. Johnson as Bibliographer and Book Collector," in item S957, pp. 163–75.

*S945 . ———. *Dr. Johnson and the English Law* [item 1148]. Syracuse, New York: Syracuse University Press, 1951. Reviewed by Lester E. Denonn, *American Bar Association Journal*, XXXVIII (April 1952), 305; Gwin J. Kolb, *PQ*, XXXI (July 1952), 279–80; George D. Hornstein, *Columbia Law Review*, LIII (January 1953), 136–38.

S946 . ———. "Johnson, Percy, and Warton" [relation between Johnson's work with Percy on *Reliques* and his edition of Shakespeare], *PMLA*, LXX (December 1955), 1203–04.

S946a . McGUFFIE, HELEN LOUISE, "Samuel Johnson and the Hostile Press" [contemporary attacks], (unpublished dissertation, Columbia University, 1961).

S947 . MANCHESTER, WILLIAM. "H. L. Mencken at Seventy-Five: America's Sam Johnson," *SR*, September 10, 1955, pp. 11–13, 64–65. See also D.J. Greene, *JNL*, XVIII, 2 (June 1958), 5–6.

S948 . MATTHEWS, ROGER G. "Homage to Samuel Johnson," *The Rising Generation* (Tokyo), CV, 10 (October 1, 1959), 530-34.

S949 . METZDORF, ROBERT F. "Thackeray and Johnson," *The New Rambler*, July 1952, pp. 6-8.

S949a . MEYNELL, LAURENCE. [Johnson and "true civility"] in item 663, December 1954, pp. 15–23.

S950 . MICHOT, PAULETTE. "Doctor Johnson on Copyright," *Revue des langues vivantes* (Brussels), XXIII (1957), 137–47.

*S951 . MIDDENDORF, JOHN H. "Dr. Johnson and Mercantilism," *JHI*, XXI (January-March 1960), 66–83.

★S952. MINER, EARL R. "Dr. Johnson, Mandeville, and 'Publick Benefits',"
Huntington Library Quarterly, XXI (February 1958), 159–66.

S953. MOLIN, SVEN E. "Criticism in Vacuo" [an attack on item S978],
University of Kansas City Review, XXIV (December 1957), 156-60.
Reply by Wellek, and comment by Molin, XXIV (June 1958), 283-86.

S954. MOORE, J.R. "An Early Allusion to Samuel Johnson ?" [as "the pretty
ingenious gentleman at St. John's Gate" in *A Dialogue in the Shades*,
1745], *JNL*, XVII, 2 (July 1957), 8–9.

S955. MOORE, ROBERT E. "Dr. Johnson on Fielding and Richardson "[item
1178a], *PMLA*, LXVI (March 1951), 162-81.

S956. MORGAN, IRA L. "Contemporary Criticism of the Works of Samuel
Johnson" (dissertation, University of Florida). Abstract in *Dissertation
Abstracts*, XIV (1954), 2071.

★S957. *New Light on Dr. Johnson: Essays on the Occasion of His 250th Birth-
day*, ed. Frederick W. Hilles. New Haven: Yale University Press, 1959.
(Essays included have been separately listed.) Reviewed by Sir Harold
Nicolson, *Observer*, March 6, 1960; in *TLS*, May 20, 1960, p. 324;
by Ian Jack, *PQ*, XXXIX (July 1960), 333-35; Jacques Chauvin,
Études Anglaises, XIII (July-September 1960), 379–80.

S958. PETTIT, HENRY. "Dr. Johnson and the Cheerful Robots" [attitude
toward science], *Western Humanities Review*, XIV (Autumn 1960),
381–88.

S959. POWELL, L.F. "A Friend of Johnson: Dr. Birkbeck Hill," *The New
Rambler*, January 1960, pp. 4-10.

★S960. RADBRUCH, GUSTAV. "Dr. Johnson und sein Biograph" [expansion of
item 1230a], in *Gestalten und Gedanken: Zehn Studien*, pp. 49–69, 211-12.
Stuttgart: K.F. Koehler, 1954.

S961. ROBERTS, S.C. *Dr. Johnson and Others*. Cambridge: Cambridge
University Press, 1958. Reprints items 1244, 1248, S1942.

S962. ———. "Johnson in Parody," in item S957, pp. 285—96.

S963. SAVAGE, OLIVER D. "Johnson and Dickens: A Comparison," *The
Dickensian*, LXVIII (December 1951), 42–44.

S964. SHERBO, ARTHUR. "George III, Franklin, and Dr. Johnson" [quota-
tions from Shakespeare used by the King to characterize Franklin and
Johnson], *N&Q*, January 19, 1952, pp. 37-38.

S965. ———."Tribute to Johnson" [in essay "On Gratitude" in *The Student* — perhaps by Christopher Smart], *JNL*, XIX, 2 (June 1959), 11.

S966. S[IEBURG], F[RIEDRICH]. "Der Dr. Johnson" [partly a notice of item S300, ed. Güttinger], *Die Gegenwart* (Frankfurt a/M), VII, 12 (1952), 373–74.

S967. "Un Siècle avant Solférino" [Johnson's ideas adumbrate those of Henri Dunant, inspirer of the Geneva Convention and the Red Cross], *Revue Internationale de la Croix Rouge* (Geneva), XXXIII (December 1951), 969–71. Contains a French translation, by J.C. de Watteville, of Johnson's Introduction to *Proceedings of the Committee . . . for Cloathing French Prisoners of War.*

S968. SOUTH, HELEN P. "Dr. Johnson and the Quakers," *Bulletin of Friends Historical Association*, XLIV (Spring 1955), 19–42.

S969. SPECTOR, ROBERT D. "Dr. Johnson's Swallows" [who hibernate under water; contemporary theories about them], *N&Q*, December 22, 1951, pp. 564–65.

S970. SUTHERLAND, JAMES R. *The English Critic* [inaugural lecture as Lord Northcliffe Professor of Modern English Literature, University College, London], pp. 9–12 and passim. London: University College [H. and K. Lewis Co.], 1952. See also *TLS*, December 12, 1952, p. 819.

S971. THOMAS, ALAN G. "Dr. Johnson and the Book Trade," *Books and the Man* (Antiquarian Booksellers Association annual), 1953, pp. 31–37.

S972. TODD, WILLIAM B. "Cowper's Commentary on the *Life of Johnson*," *TLS*, March 15, 1957, p. 168.

S973. TUCKER, SUSIE I. "Dr. Johnson, Mediaevalist," *N&Q*, January 1958, pp. 20–24.

S974. VAN LIERE, EDWARD J. "Doctor Johnson and the Weather," *Philological Papers: University of West Virginia*, Series 52, No. 4–1 (October 1951), 40–48.

S975. DE VEDIA Y MITRE, MARIANO. "El Doctor Johnson y la Obsesion de la Muerte," *La Nacion* (Buenos Aires), January 21, 1951, 2nd section, p. 1.

S976. VOITLE, ROBERT B., JR. *Samuel Johnson the Moralist.* Cambridge, Mass.: Harvard University Press (expected early in 1961).

S977. WATT, IAN. "Dr. Samuel Johnson after 250 Years," *The Listener*, September 24, 1955, pp. 476–79.

S978. WELLEK, RENÉ. "Dr. Johnson," in *A History of Modern Criticism*, I, 79-104. New Haven: Yale University Press, 1955. See item S953.

S979. WHITE, ERIC. "Dr. Johnson and Opera," *TLS*, March 28, 1958, p. 169.

S980. WILSON, EDMUND. "Reexamining Dr. Johnson" [review of item 219], reprinted in *Classics and Commercials*, pp. 244-49. New York: Farrar, Straus, and Cudahy, 1950; London: Allen, 1951. Reprinted in *A Literary Chronicle*, 1920-1950, pp. 328-30. New York: Doubleday, 1956 (Anchor Books).

S981. WIMSATT, WILLIAM K., JR. "The Neo-Classic Universal: Samuel Johnson," Chapter 15 in W.K. Wimsatt, Jr., and Cleanth Brooks, *Literary Criticism: A Short History*. New York: Alfred A. Knopf; London: Routledge, 1957.

XI. — JOHNSON'S PROSE STYLE

S1380. BERNARD, F.V. "Two Errors in Boswell's *Life of Johnson*" [that Johnson disapproved of parentheses and "the former and the latter"], *N&Q*, July-August 1959, pp. 280-81.

S1381. BUTT, JOHN. "Blair on Johnson" [criticism of Johnson's style in students' notes of Blair's lectures], *JNL*, XX, 1 (March 1960), 9-10.

S1382. KRISHNAMURTI, S. "Dr. Johnson's Use of Monosyllabic Words," *Journal of the University of Bombay*, XIX (September 1950), 1-12.

S1383. ———. "Frequency-Distribution of Nouns in Dr. Johnson's Prose Works" [application to Johnson of techniques described in G. Udny Yule, *The Statistical Study of Literary Vocabulary*], *Journal of the University of Bombay*, XX (September 1951), 1-16.

S1384. ———. "Vocabulary Tests: Applied to the Authorship of the 'New Essays' Attributed to Dr. Johnson" [Yule's "characteristic" test seems to confirm Johnson's authorship of the "Weekly Correspondent" essays (see item 2054)], *Journal of the University of Bombay*, XXII (September 1953), 1-5.

S1385. ———. "Vocabulary Tests Applied to (Dr. Johnson's) Authorship of the 'Misargyrus' Papers in *The Adventurer*" [seems to be confirmed by use of Yule's "characteristic,"] *Journal of the University of Bombay*, XXI (September 1952), 47-62.

S1386. MORGAN, EDWIN. " 'Strong Lines' and Strong Minds: Reflections on the Prose of Browne and Johnson," *Cambridge Journal*, IV (May 1951), 481–91.

S1386a. ROCKAS, LEO. "The Description of Style: Dr. Johnson and His Critics" (unpublished dissertation, University of Michigan, 1960). Abstract in *Dissertation Abstracts*, XXI, 338–39.

S1387. SHERBO, ARTHUR. "The Case for Internal Evidence (5): The Uses and Abuses of Internal Evidence" [attributes to Johnson "An Essay on Elegies" in the *Universal Museum*, 1767], *Bulletin of the New York Public Library*, LXIII (January 1959), 5-22. Attacked by Ephim G. Fogel, *ibid*. (May, June, 1959), 223–36, 292–308. Reply by Sherbo, *ibid*. (July 1959), 367–71.

S1388. WATT, IAN. "The Ironic Tradition in Augustan Prose from Swift to Johnson," *Restoration and Augustan Prose*, pp. 19–46. Los Angeles: W.A. Clark Memorial Library, 1957.

INDIVIDUAL WORKS

XII. — LIFE OF SAVAGE

S1400. *The Life of Richard Savage*
Ed. Cyril Connolly, in *Great English Short Novels*, pp. 9-85. New York: Dial Press, 1953.
Ed. Richard Evan Lyon (dissertation, University of Chicago). Chicago: University of Chicago, Department of Photoduplication (microfilm), 1958.

*S1401. BOYCE, BENJAMIN. "Johnson's *Life of Savage* and Its Literary Background," *SP*, LIII (October 1956), 576-98.

S1402. MORGAN, H.A. "Johnson's Life of Savage," *Contemporary Review*, CXCV (January 1959), 38-41.

S1403. SHERBO, ARTHUR. "Johnsoniana: An Obituary Notice and an 'Abstract' from the Life of Savage," *N&Q*, February 2, 1952, pp. 51–54.

*S1404. Tracy, Clarence R. *The Artificial Bastard: A Biography of Richard Savage* [item 1411]. Toronto: University of Toronto Press; Cambridge, Mass.: Harvard University Press, 1953. Reviewed by Benjamin Boyce, *PQ*, XXXIII (July 1954), 294–95; J.L. Clifford, *MLN*, LXX (May 1955), 373-74; M.J.C. Hodgart, *RES*, n.s. VI (July 1955), 323–24. See also S1430.

XIII. — NONDRAMATIC POEMS

EDITIONS

S1420. *The Vanity of Human Wishes*, in *The Late Augustans: Longer Poems of the Later Eighteenth Century*, ed. Donald Davie, pp. xxii-xxiii, 14-24. London: Heinemann, 1958.

CRITICISM

S1430. Bernard, F.V. "The Dreaded Spy of London" [an allusion to Savage in *London*], *N&Q*, September 1958, pp. 398–99.

*S1431. Bronson, Bertrand H. "Personification Reconsidered" [revision of item 1430 and review of item S1433 in *MLN*], in item S957, pp. 189–231.

*S1432. Butt, John. "Pope and Johnson in Their Handling of the Imitation," *The New Rambler*, June 1959, pp. 3–14. Reprinted in item S957, pp. 19-34, as "Johnson's Practice in the Poetical Imitation."

*S1433. Chapin, Chester F. *Personification in Eighteenth-Century English Poetry*, pp. 98–115. New York: Columbia University Press, 1955. Reviewed by A.D. McKillop, *PQ*, XXXV (July 1956), 254-55; E.R. Wasserman, *JEGP*, LV (October 1956), 651–54; B.H. Bronson, *MLN*, LXXI (November 1956), 533–41.

S1433a. Coffey, Warren J. "The Poetry of Samuel Johnson" (unpublished dissertation, University of Wisconsin, 1960). Abstract in *Dissertation Abstracts*, XXI, 615.

S1434. Davie, Donald. *Purity of Diction in English Verse*, pp. 45–47, 82–90 and elsewhere. London: Chatto and Windus, 1952.

*S1435. EMSLIE, MACDONALD. "Johnson's Satires and 'The Proper Wit of Poetry'," *Cambridge Journal,* VII (March 1954), 347–60.

S1436. ———. "Johnson's *The Vanity of Human Wishes*" [lines 23–26, 99–102, 137–40], *The Explicator,* XII (November 1953), 1–2.

S1437. GIFFORD, HENRY. "*The Vanity of Human Wishes,*" *RES,* n.s. VI (April 1955), 157-65. See also Christopher Ricks, *RES,* n.s. XI (November 1960), 412-13.

S1438. GREENE, DONALD J. "Johnson on Garrick ?" [veiled slurs on Garrick in *London* ?], *JNL,* XIV, 3 (September 1954), 10–12. See also Mary Lascelles, *JNL,* XV, 1 (March 1955), 11–12.

S1439. JACK, IAN. "The 'Choice of Life': Johnson and Matthew Prior" [influence of *Solomon* on *Vanity of Human Wishes* and *Rasselas*], *JEGP,* XLIX (October 1950), 523-30.

*S1440. ———. " 'Tragical Satire': *The Vanity of Human Wishes,*" in *Augustan Satire,* pp. 135–45. Oxford: Clarendon Press, 1952.

S1441. KOLB, GWIN J. "Johnson Echoes Dryden" [*The State of Innocence*], *MLN,* LXXIV (March 1959), 212–13.

*S1442. LASCELLES, MARY. "Johnson and Juvenal," in item S957, pp. 35–55.

S1443. LEAVIS, F.R. "Johnson as Poet" [reprint of review in *Scrutiny* of item 1423], in *The Common Pursuit,* pp. 116-20. London: Chatto and Windus; New York: George W. Stewart, 1952.

S1444. LIEBERT, HERMAN W. " 'We Fell upon *Sir Eldred*' " [Johnson as reviser of Hannah More's verses], in item S957, pp. 233–45.

S1445. MOHR, EUGENE V. "Dr. Johnson's Latin Poems: A Translation and Commentary" (Master's thesis, Columbia University, 1952).

S1446. RICKS, C.B. "Wolsey in *The Vanity of Human Wishes,*" *MLN,* LXXIII (December 1958), 563–68.

S1447. SCHOFF, FRANCIS G. "Johnson on Juvenal" [*Vanity of Human Wishes*], *N&Q,* July 1953, pp. 293-96.

S1448. SHERBO, ARTHUR. "The Text of *The Vanity of Human Wishes,*" *N&Q,* May 10, 1952, pp. 205–06.

S1449. SMITH, D. NICHOL. "A Boswell Fragment" [recovery of note recording emendation to *Vanity of Human Wishes*; see *Life,* III, 358, n.1], *Meanjin,* XI (Spring 1952), 292-93.

*S1450. ———. "Johnson's Poems" [item 1461], reprinted in item S957, pp. 9–17.

S1451. SPRINGER-MILLER, FRED. "Johnson and Boileau" [use of Boileau's *First Satire* — reference to George II in *London*], *N&Q*, November 10, 1951, p. 497.

S1452. TUCKER, SUSIE I. and HENRY GIFFORD. "Johnson's Latin Poetry," *Neophilologus*, XLI (July 1957), 215–21.

S1453. TUCKER, SUSIE I. and HENRY GIFFORD. "Johnson's *On the Death of Dr. Robert Levet*," *The Explicator*, XV (April 1957), 9.

*S1454. TUCKER, SUSIE I. and HENRY GIFFORD. "Johnson's Poetic Imagination," *RES*, n.s. VIII (August 1957), 241–48.

S1455. TUCKER, SUSIE I. "The Steeps of Fate" [line 125 of *Vanity of Human Wishes*], *N&Q*, August 1957, p. 354.

S1456. "*The Vanity of Human Wishes*" [lines 15–20], *N&Q*, August 1957, pp. 353–54.

S1457. WILLIAMS, HAROLD. "China to Peru," *N&Q*, October 27, 1951, p. 479.

See also items S412, S1525.

XIV. — DRAMATIC WORKS

S1475. MAXWELL, J.C. "*Othello* and Johnson's *Irene*," *N&Q*, April 1957, p. 148.

S1476. METZDORF, ROBERT F. "Johnson at Drury Lane" [revision of item 1482a], reprinted in S957, pp. 57–64.

S1477. MORAN, BERNA. "The Irene Story and Dr. Johnson's Sources" [fails to use item 1476], *MLN*, LXXI (February 1956), 87–91.

XV. — RAMBLER, ADVENTURER, IDLER

EDITIONS

S1500. *The Rambler* [selections], with introduction by S.C. Roberts. London: J.M. Dent; New York: E.P. Dutton, 1953 (Everyman's Library).

CRITICISM

S1510. BLOOM, EDWARD A. "Symbolic Names in Johnson's Periodical Essays," *MLQ*, XIII (December 1952), 333–52.

S1511. COHEN, B. BERNARD. "Hawthorne's 'Mrs. Bullfrog' and *The Rambler*," *PQ*, XXXII (October 1953), 382–87.

S1512. ELDER, A.T. "Irony and Humour in the *Rambler*," *University of Toronto Quarterly*, XXX (October 1960), 57–71.

S1513. FOX, ROBERT C. "Dr. Johnson, Bishop Wilkins, and the Submarine ' [*Rambler* 105], *N&Q*, August 1958, pp. 364, 368.

S1514. GRAHAM, W.H. "Dr. Johnson's *The Rambler*," *Contemporary Review*, CLXXXIV (July 1953), 50–53.

S1515. GREANY, HELEN T. "Johnson and the Institutes" [Quintilian's], *N&Q*, October 1958, p. 445.

S1516. GRIFFITH, PHILIP M. "A Study of the *Adventurer* (1752-1754)" (dissertation, University of North Carolina, to be completed 1961).

S1517. HEINLE, EDWIN C. "The Eighteenth Century Allegorical Essay" (dissertation, Columbia University, 1957). Abstract in *Dissertation Abstracts*, XVII (1957), 1763.

S1518. ROBERTS, S.C. "The Author of the *Rambler*," *The New Rambler*, January 1959, pp. 2–12.

S1519. SHERBO, ARTHUR. "Translation of the Mottoes and Quotations in *The Adventurer*," in item S1687, pp. 145–74.

S1520. ———. "Father Lobo's *Voyage to Abyssinia* and *Ramblers* 204 and 205," *N&Q*, September 1, 1951, p. 388.

S1521. ———. "The Making of *Ramblers* 186 and 187" [borrowings from Hans Egede, *A Description of Greenland*, 1745], *PMLA*, LXVII (June 1952), 575–80.

S1522. ———. "The Mottoes to *Idlers* 88 and 101," *JNL*, XIII, 4 (December 1953), 10–11.

S1523. ———. "The Translation of the Motto for *The Adventurer* No. 126," *N&Q*, November 10, 1951, 497–98.

S1524. ———. "The Translations of Mottoes and Quotations in Johnson's *Rambler*," *N&Q*, June 21, 1952, pp. 278–79. See also W.H.J., *N&Q*, July 19, 1952, p. 328.

S1525. ————. "Two Notes on Johnson's Revisions" [*Adventurer* and Mary Masters' poems], *MLR*, L (July 1955), 311–15.

S1526. WATSON, MELVIN R. *Magazine Serials and the Essay Tradition, 1746–1820* [contains discussion of Johnson's periodical essays]. Baton Rouge: Louisiana State University Press, 1956 (L.S.U. Studies, Humanities Series No. 6).

See also item S1385.

XVI. — THE *DICTIONARY*

S1540. ARRIETA, RAFAEL ALBERTO. "El Diccionario del Altillo," *La Prensa* (Buenos Aires), August 7, 1960.

S1541. ATKINSON, A.D. "Dr. Johnson and Newton's *Opticks*," *RES*, n.s. II (July 1951), 226–37.

S1542. ————. "Dr. Johnson and Some Physico-Theological Themes" [use of Burnet's *Sacred Theory of the Earth*], *N&Q*, January 5, 1952, pp. 16–18; April 12, pp. 162–65; June 7, pp. 249–53.

S1543. ————. "Donne Quotations in Johnson's Dictionary," *N&Q*, September 1, 1951, pp. 387–88.

S1544. ————. "A Prospect of Words," *N&Q*, October 11, 1952, pp. 452–54; October 25, pp. 475–77.

*S1545. BALDERSTON, KATHARINE C. "Dr. Johnson's Use of William Law in the Dictionary," *PQ*, XXXIX (July 1960), 379–88.

S1546. BOYCE, BENJAMIN and DOROTHY G. "Dr. Johnson's Definitions of 'Tory' and 'Whig'," *N&Q*, April 1953, pp. 161–62.

S1547. CLIFFORD, JAMES L. "Dr. Johnson's Dictionary: A Memorable Achievement of the Mind," *New York Times Book Review*, April 10, 1955, p. 7. Reprinted in item S1549, pp. 3-6.

S1548. CONGLETON, J.E. "Johnson's Dictionary, 1755–1955," *South Atlantic Bulletin* (South Atlantic Modern Language Association), XX (March 1955), 1–4.

S1549. *An Exhibition in Honor of the 200th Anniversary of the Publication of Johnson's Dictionary, 15 April 1755*, with introduction by John R. Turner Ettlinger. New York: Columbia University Libraries, 1955.

S1550. FLEMING, LINDSAY. "Dr. Johnson's Use of Authorities in Compiling His Dictionary of the English Language," *N&Q*, June 1954, pp. 254–57; July, pp. 294–97; August, pp. 343–47.

S1551. ———. "Johnson, Burton, and Hale" [copies of Burton and Hale used by Johnson located], *N&Q*, April 1957, p. 154.

S1552. FUSSELL, PAUL, JR. "A Note on Samuel Johnson and the Rise of Accentual Prosodic Theory" [revised definition of "versification" in *Dictionary*, 1773], *PQ*, XXXIII (October 1954), 431–33.

S1553. GILBERT, VEDDER M. "Altercations of Thomas Edwards with Samuel Johnson" [over the *Dictionary*], *JEGP*, LI (July 1952), 326–35.

S1554. GREENE, DONALD J. " 'Sooth' in Keats, Milton, Shakespeare, and Dr. Johnson" [crux in *Eve of St. Agnes* explained by definition in *Dictionary*], *MLN*, LXV (December 1950), 514–17. See also C.A. Luttrell, *N&Q*, September 15, 1951, pp. 405-07, and reply by Greene, *N&Q*, May 10, 1952, pp. 204-05.

S1555. HUDSON, WILSON M. "Whitaker's Attack on Johnson's Etymologies" [in his *History of Manchester*, 1775], *Huntington Library Quarterly*, XIV (May 1951), 285–97.

S1556. KEAST, W.R. "Johnson's *Plan of a Dictionary*: A Textual Crux" [three paragraphs intended deleted], *PQ*, XXXIII (July 1954), 341–47.

*S1557. ———. "The Preface to *A Dictionary of the English Language*: Johnson's Revision and the Establishment of the Text,' *Studies in Bibliography* (University of Virginia), V (1952–53), 129-46.

S1558. ———. "Self-quotation in Johnson's Dictionary," *N&Q*, September 1955, pp. 392–93. See also June 1956, p. 262.

S1559. ———. "Some Emendations in Johnson's Preface to the *Dictionary*," *RES*, n.s. IV (January 1953), 52–57.

*S1560. ———. "The Two *Clarissas* in Johnson's *Dictionary*" [quotations are from *A Collection . . . . of Moral and Instructive Sentiments*, appended to Vol. VIII, 1751], *SP*, LIV (July 1957), 429–39.

S1560a. KOLB, GWIN J. and JAMES H. SLEDD. "The History of the Sneyd-Gimbel and Pigott-British Museum Copies of Dr. Johnson's *Dictionary*," *PBSA*, LIV (4th Quarter 1960), 286–89.

*S1561. KOLB, GWIN J. and JAMES H. SLEDD. "Johnson's *Dictionary* and Lexicographical Tradition," *MP*, L (February 1953), 171-94.

*S1562. KOLB, GWIN J. and JAMES H. SLEDD. "The Reynolds Copy of Johnson's *Dictionary*," *Bulletin of the John Rylands Library*, XXXVII (March 1955), 446-75.

S1563. LEHNERT, MARTIN. "Das englische Wörterbuch in Vergangenheit und Gegenwart," *Zeitschrift für Anglistik und Amerikanistik* (Berlin), IV (June 1956), 265-323.

S1564. LIEBERT, HERMAN W. "Johnson's *Dictionary*, 1755-1955," *Yale Library Gazette*, XXX (1955), 27-28.

S1565. MICHELL, H. "Arrack" [in *Dictionary* and *Rambler* 16], *N&Q*, May 26, 1951, p. 237. See also A.D. Atkinson, July 7, p. 306, and T.O. Mabbott, July 21, p. 328.

*S1566. NOYES GERTRUDE E. "The Critical Reception of Johnson's *Dictionary* in the Latter Eighteenth Century," *MP*, LII (February 1955), 175-91.

*S1567. ORSZÁGH, LASZLO. "Johnson Lexikográfiai Modszere" [commemorates 200th anniversary of the *Dictionary*], *Filológiai Közlöny* (Magyar Tudományos Akadémia, Budapest), II (1956), 251-65. Summaries in Russian and English, p. 339.

S1568. SHERBO, ARTHUR. "Dr. Johnson Marks a Book List" [appended to Vol. VIII of Warburton's *Shakespeare* — see item 1551], *N&Q*, November 22, 1952, p. 519.

S1569. ———. "Dr. Johnson Quotes One of His Amanuenses," *N&Q*, June 21, 1952, p. 276.

S1570. ———. "Dr. Johnson's *Dictionary*: A Preliminary Puff" [by "W.S." (William Strahan ?) in *Gentleman's Magazine*, 1749], *PQ*, XXXI (January 1952), 91-93.

S1571. ———. "Dr. Johnson's *Dictionary* and Warburton's *Shakespeare*" [further description of copy mentioned in item 1551], *PQ*, XXXIII (January 1954), 94-96.

*S1572. ———. "Dr. Johnson's Revision of His *Dictionary*" [more than 700 changes noted in words under "M" between 1755 and 1773 editions], *PQ*, XXXI (October 1952), 372-82.

*S1573. Sledd, James H. and Gwin J. Kolb. *Dr. Johnson's Dictionary: Essays in the Biography of a Book.* Chicago: University of Chicago Press, 1955. Reviewed by D.T. Starnes, *MLN*, LXXI (April 1956), 309–11; D.J. Greene, *JEGP*, LV (April 1956), 331–34; W.K. Wimsatt, Jr., *PQ*, XXXV (July 1956), 308-10; J.C. Bryce, *RES*, n.s. IX (May 1958), 219–20.

S1574. Sledd, James H. and Gwin J. Kolb. "Johnson's Definitions of *Whig* and *Tory*," *PMLA*, LXVII (September 1952), 882-85.

S1575. Tillotson, Geoffrey. "Johnson's Dictionary," *Spectator*, April 29, 1955, pp. 527–28.

S1576. Tucker, Susie I. "Dr. Watts Looks at the Language" [indebtedness to Watts in *Dictionary*], *N&Q*, July-August 1959, pp. 274–79.

*S1577. Wimsatt, William K., Jr. "Johnson's Dictionary: April 15, 1955," in item S957, pp. 65–90 (with facsimile of a page of Bacon's *Essays* marked by Johnson).

S1578. ———. "Samuel Johnson and Dryden's *Du Fresnoy*" [use of translation of *The Art of Painting* in *Dictionary*], *SP*, XLVIII (January 1951), 26–39.

See also item S1677.

XVII. — RASSELAS

EDITIONS

S1620. *Rasselas*

Reprinted (in full) in item S110 and item 143 (1956).

S1623. *Rasselas* (translations).

Tr. into Spanish, with an introduction, by Mariano de Vedia y Mitre [*La Historia de Raselas, Principe de Abisinia*]. Buenos Aires: Guillermo Kraft [1951].

Tr. into Arabic by Kamel el Mohandes and Magdi Wahba, with fifty illustrations by S. Diamantis [four reproduced in item S1627]. Cairo: Anglo-Egyptian Bookshop, 1959. The illustrations by Diamantis have been separately reprinted.

CRITICISM

S1625. BARNETT, GEORGE L. "*Rasselas* and *De Senectute*," *N&Q*, November 1956, pp. 485–86.

S1626. ————. "*Rasselas* and *The Vicar of Wakefield*," *N&Q*, July 1957, pp. 303-05.

S1627. *Bicentenary Essays on Rasselas*, ed. Magdi Wahba. Supplement to *Cairo Studies in English*, 1959. Individual essays are listed separately in this section. Reviewed by Gwin J. Kolb, *PQ*, XXXIX (July 1960), 336-39.

S1628. BREDVOLD, LOUIS I. "*Rasselas* and the *Miscellanies* of John Norris," *JNL*, XVI, 1 (March 1956) 3-4.

S1629. CLIFFORD, JAMES L. "Candide and Rasselas," *New York Times Book Review*, April 19, 1959, pp. 4, 14.

S1630. ————. "Some Remarks on *Candide* and *Rasselas*," in item S1627, pp. 7-14.

S1631. DINA ABDUL-HAMID AL AOUN. "Some Remarks on a Second Reading of *Rasselas*" [emphasizes its place in the tradition of tracts on a princely education], in item S1627, pp. 15-20.

S1632. DUNCAN-JONES, E.E. "Marvell, Johnson, and the First Sunset" [*Rasselas*, Chap. 35, and *The First Anniversary of the Government Under Oliver Cromwell*, lines 337–40], *TLS*, April 3, 1959, p. 193.

S1633. FISHER, MARVIN. "The Pattern of Conservatism in Johnson's *Rasselas* and Hawthorne's *Tales*," *JHI*, XIX (April 1958), 173-96.

S1634. GOODYEAR, LOUIS E. "*Rasselas*' Journey from Amhara to Cairo Viewed from Arabia," in item S1627, pp. 21-29.

S1635. GUZZO, ORLANDO. *Il "Candide" Inglese: "Ras Selas" di Samuele Johnson*. Torino [Turin]: Edizioni di "Filosofia," 1951 (La Filosofia nella Letteratura, No. 3).

S1636. HONIG, EDWIN. "Crusoe, Rasselas, and the Suit of Clothes," *University of Kansas City Review*, XVIII (Winter 1951), 136–42.

S1637. HOVEY, RICHARD B. "Dr. Samuel Johnson, Psychiatrist," *MLQ*, XV (December 1954), 321–35.

S1638. JOHNSON, J.W. "Rasselas and His Ancestors," *N&Q*, May 1959, pp. 185–88.

S1639. JOOST, NICHOLAS. "Whispers of Fancy; or, the Meaning of *Rasselas*," *Modern Age*, I (Fall 1957), 166–73.

S1640. KENNEY, WILLIAM. "Johnson's *Rasselas* after Two Centuries," *Boston University Studies in English*, III (Summer 1957), 88–96.

S1641. ————. "*Rasselas* and the Theme of Diversification," *PQ*, XXXVIII (January 1959), 84-89.

S1642. KOLB, GWIN J. "Johnson's 'Dissertation on Flying' " [revision of item 1641], reprinted in item S957, pp. 91–106.

S1643. ————. "The 'Paradise' in Abyssinia and the 'Happy Valley' in *Rasselas*," *MP*, LVI (August 1958), 10–16.

★S1644. ————. "The Structure of *Rasselas*," *PMLA*, LXVI (September 1951), 698–717.

S1645. ————. "The Use of Stoical Doctrines in *Rasselas*, Chapter XVIII," *MLN*, LXVIII (November 1953), 439–47.

★S1646. LASCELLES, MARY. "*Rasselas* Reconsidered," in *Essays and Studies by Members of the English Association*, n.s. IV (1951), 37–52.

S1647. LAWRENCE, R.G. "Dr. Johnson and the Art of Flying," *N&Q*, August 1957, pp. 348-51.

S1648. LEYBURN, ELLEN D. " 'No Romantick Absurdities or Incredible Fictions' : The Relation of Johnson's *Rasselas* to Lobo's *Voyage to Abyssinia*," *PMLA*, LXX (December 1955), 1059-67.

S1649. LINK, FREDERICK M. "*Rasselas* and the Quest for Happiness," *Boston University Studies in English*, III (Summer 1957), 121-23.

★S1650. LOCKHART, DONALD MERRITT. "Father Jeronymo Lobo's Writings Concerning Ethiopia, Including Hitherto Unpublished Manuscripts in the Palmella Library" (unpublished dissertation, Harvard University [Department of Romance Languages], 1958). Discusses, pp. 70–79, Johnson's translation of Lobo-Legrand and, pp. 86–141, the sources of *Rasselas*.

★S1651. LOMBARDO, AGOSTINO. "The Importance of Imlac," in item S1627, pp. 31–49. Translated by Barbara Arnett Melchiori.

S1652. MAHMOUD, FATMA MOUSSA. "*Rasselas* and *Vathek*," in item S1627, pp. 51–57.

S1653. MANZALAOUI, MAHMOUD. "*Rasselas* and Some Mediaeval Ancillaries," in item S1627, pp. 59–73.

★S1654. Metzdorf, Robert F. "The First American 'Rasselas' and Its Imprint," *PBSA*, XLVII (4th quarter, 1953), 374–76.

S1655. ———. "Grand Cairo and Philadelphia: The Frontispiece to the 1768 Edition of Johnson's *Rasselas*," in item S1627, pp. 75–80.

S1656. Moore, John Robert. "Conan Doyle, Tennyson, and *Rasselas*," *Nineteenth Century Fiction*, VII (December 1952), 221–23.

S1657. ———. "*Rasselas* and the Early Travelers to Abyssinia," *MLQ*, XV (March 1954), 36–41.

S1658. ———. "*Rasselas* in Retrospect," in item S1627, pp. 81-84.

S1659. Osgood, C.G. "Johnson and Macrobius" [Chap. VIII of *Rasselas*], *MLN*, LXIX (April 1954), 246.

S1660. Pakenham, Thomas. "Gondar and the Mountain" [where Abyssinian princes were imprisoned], *History Today*, VII (March 1957), 172–81. See also his *The Mountains of Rasselas* [an account of the author's travels in Ethiopia]. London: Weidenfeld and Nicolson; New York: Reynal and Co., 1959.

S1661. Rawson, C.J. "The Continuation of *Rasselas*" [Cornelia Knight's *Dinarbas*], in item S1627, pp. 85–95.

S1662. Sherburn, George. "Rasselas Returns—To What ?", *PQ*, XXXVIII (July 1959), 383–84.

S1663. Tillotson, Geoffrey. "Time in *Rasselas*," in item S1627, pp. 97-103.

S1664. Wahba, Magdi. "A Note on the Manner of Concluding in *Rasselas*," in item S1627, pp. 105–110.

S1665. Whitley, Alvin. "The Comedy of *Rasselas*," *ELH*, XXIII (March 1956), 48–70.

S1666. Willard, Nedd. "*Zadig* and *Rasselas* Considered," in item S1627, pp. 111–123.

See also item S1439.

XVIII. — SHAKESPEARE

EDITIONS

★S1670. *Johnson's Notes to Shakespeare*, ed., with an introduction to each volume, by Arthur Sherbo. Los Angeles: Augustan Reprint Society. Vol. I, Comedies (Publication No. 59-60), 1956. Vol. II, Histories (Publ. No. 65-66) 1957. Vol. III, Tragedies (Publ. No. 71-73), 1958

S1671. *Preface to Shakespeare, with Proposals for Printing the Dramatic Works of William Shakespeare* (1756) [text "reprinted from *Johnson on Shakespeare*" — item 1683]. London: Oxford University Press, 1957.

S1672. *Samuel Johnson: Preface to Shakespeare e Altri Scritti Shakespeariani,* ed. with introduction and notes by Agostino Lombardo [contains *Miscellaneous Observations on Macbeth*, Drury Lane Prologue, *Rambler* 168, Proposals (1756), Preface, and selected notes]. Bari: Adriatica Editrice, 1960 (Biblioteca Italiana di Testi Inglesi, Vol. IV).

S1673. *Samuel Johnson on Shakespeare,* ed. with introduction by W.K. Wimsatt, Jr. New York: Hill and Wang, 1960 [Dramabook].

CRITICISM

S1675. ADLER, JACOB H. "Johnson's 'He That Imagines This' " [in Preface to Shakespeare], *Shakespeare Quarterly*, XI (Spring 1960), 225-28.

S1676. BADAWI, M.M. "The Study of Shakespearian Criticism," *Cairo Studies in English* (1959), pp. 98–117.

S1677. BERNARD F.V. "Johnson and *Lear*" [quoted copiously in *Dictionary* despite Johnson's disclaimer of having re-read it], *JNL*, XVII, 1 (March 1957), 7-8.

S1678. EASTMAN, ARTHUR M. "Johnson's Shakespeare and the Laity: A Textual Study" [see item 1668a], *PMLA*, LXV (December 1950), 1112-21.

S1679. FLEISCHAUER, WARREN L. "Dr. Johnson's Editing and Criticism of Shakespeare's Lancastrian Cycle" (unpublished dissertation, Western Reserve University, 1951).

S1680. "Johnson's Shakespeare Folios" [letter of George Steevens, wanting to get rid of leaves in his First Folio "scribbled on" by Johnson], *JNL*, XIII, 4 (December 1953), 10.

S1681. LIEBERT, HERMAN W. "Proposals for Shakespeare, 1756," *TLS*, May 6, 1955, p. 237.

S1682. MONAGHAN, T.J. "Johnson's Additions to His *Shakespeare* for the Edition of 1773," *RES*, n.s. IV (July 1953), 234–48. See also Arthur Sherbo, *PQ*, XXXIII (July 1954), 283-84.

*S1683. SCHOLES, R.E. "Dr. Johnson and the Bibliographical Criticism of Shakespeare," *Shakespeare Quarterly* XI (Spring 1960), 163-71.

S1684. SHERBO, ARTHUR. "Dr. Johnson on *Macbeth*: 1745 and 1765," *RES*, n.s. II (January 1951), 40–47.

S1685. ———. "Johnson and a Note by Warburton" [on *King Lear*, reprinted as Johnson's by Raleigh and others], *JNL*, XVI, 1 (March 1956), 11–12.

*S1686. ———. "The Proof-Sheets of Dr. Johnson's Preface to Shakespeare," *Bulletin of the John Rylands Library*, XXXV (September 1952), 206–10.

*S1687. ———. *Samuel Johnson, Editor of Shakespeare, with an Essay on The Adventurer*. Urbana, Illinois: University of Illinois Press, 1956 (Illinois Studies in Language and Literature, Vol. 42). Reviewed by H.K. Miller, *PQ*, XXXVI (July 1957), 378–79; Arthur M. Eastman, *Shakespeare Quarterly*, VIII (Autumn 1957), 548–49; G.A. Bonnard, *Erasmus*, XI (January 1958), 43–45; M.R. Ridley, *RES*, n.s. IX (February 1958), 91–93; W.K. Wimsatt, Jr., *MLN*, LXXIII (March 1958), 214–17. See also Arthur M. Eastman, "In Defense of Dr. Johnson," *Shakespeare Quarterly*, VIII (Autumn 1957), 493–500, and reply by Sherbo, IX (Summer 1958), 433.

S1688. ———. "Sanguine Expectations: Dr. Johnson's *Shakespeare*," *Shakespeare Quarterly*, IX (Summer 1958), 426–28.

S1689. TUCKER, SUSIE I. "Johnson and Lady Macbeth" [connotations of "blanket," "dun," "knife," etc.], *N&Q*, May 1956, pp. 210–11.

See also item S457.

XIX. — POLITICAL WRITINGS

(INCLUDES DISCUSSIONS OF JOHNSON'S POLITICAL VIEWS)

*S1700. GREENE, DONALD J. "*The False Alarm* and *Taxation No Tyranny*: Some Further Observations" [variant issues; see item S1705], *Studies in Bibliography* (University of Virginia), XIII (1960), 223-31.

*S1701. ——. *The Politics of Samuel Johnson.* New Haven: Yale University Press, 1960. (A revision of "The Politics of Samuel Johnson" [dissertation, Columbia University]. Ann Arbor, Michigan: University Microfilms, 1954.) Reviewed by Medford Evans, *National Review* (New York), May 7, 1960, pp. 306-07; H.W. Liebert, *New York Herald Tribune Book Review*, May 29, 1960, p. 6; Milton Hindus, *The New Leader*, August 29, 1960, pp. 26–27; in *The Economist*, September 24, 1960, pp. 1190, 1195; by John A. Rycenga in *Modern Age*, V (Winter 1960-61), 95-98; by W.R. Ward in *Parliamentary Affairs*, *XIV* (Winter 1960-61) 125-26.

*S1702. HOOVER, BENJAMIN B. *Samuel Johnson's Parliamentary Reporting.* Berkeley and Los Angeles: University of California Press, 1953 (University of California Publications, English Studies, No. 7). Reviewed by Arthur Sherbo, *JEGP*, LIII (October 1954), 640–41; Benjamin Boyce, *MLQ*, XVII (March 1956), 75–76; John Butt, *RES*, n.s. VII (October 1956), 433-35.

S1702a LYLES, ALBERT M. "The Hostile Reactions to the American Views of Johnson and Wesley," *Journal of the Rutgers University Library*, XXIV (1960), 1–13.

S1703. METZDORF, ROBERT F. "Samuel Johnson in Brunswick" [early German translation of *Taxation No Tyranny*], *MLN*, LXVIII (June 1953), 397-400.

S1704. SIDNEY, JOSEPH. "The Political Thought of Samuel Johnson" (dissertation, University of Chicago). Chicago: University of Chicago Department of Photoduplication [microfilm], 1957.

*S1705. TODD, WILLIAM B. "Concealed Editions of Samuel Johnson" [*The False Alarm* and *Taxation No Tyranny*], *The Book Collector*, II (Spring 1953), 59-65.

See also items S945, S951.

XX. — *A JOURNEY TO THE WESTERN ISLANDS OF SCOTLAND*
AND OTHER TRAVEL JOURNALS

S1710. BRAIN, W. RUSSELL. "Dr. Johnson and the Kangaroo" [he imitated one in an inn at Inverness], *Essays and Studies by Members of the English Association*, n.s. IV (1951), 112–17. Reprinted in item S907a, pp. 48-54.

S1711. CORNU, DONALD. "The Historical Authenticity of Dr. Johnson's 'Speaking Cat'" [incident mentioned in *Life*, III, 246], *RES*, n.s. II (October 1951), 358–70.

S1712. CURWEN, H. DARCY. "In Search of Johnson" [account of his trip to the Hebrides], *Harvard Alumni Bulletin*, LXIII (November 5, 1960), 146, 148.

S1713. FLETCHER, EDWARD G. "Mrs. Piozzi on Boswell and Johnson's Tour" [annotations on copy at Harvard], *Texas Studies in English*, XXXII (1953), 45–58.

S1714. GRAHAM, W.H. "Dr. Johnson in Scotland," *Contemporary Review*, CXCIII (February 1958), 78–82.

S1715. GREENE, DONALD J. "Yeats's Byzantium and Johnson's Lichfield" [echo in Yeats of Johnson's "monuments of sacred magnificence" ?], *PQ*, XXXIII (October 1954), 433–35.

S1716. ——–. "Johnsonian Critics," *Essays in Criticism*, X (October 1960), 476–80 (largely an attack on item S1717).

S1717. HART, JEFFREY. "Johnson's *A Journey to the Western Islands*: History as Art," *Essays in Criticism*, X (January 1960), 44–59. See item S1716.

S1718. LINDSAY, LILIAN. "Dr. Johnson and Scotland," *The New Rambler*, July 1951, pp. 5–8.

S1719. McLAREN, MORAY. *The Highland Jaunt*. London: Jarrolds, 1954; New York: William Sloane, 1955. See also his "Dr. Johnson's Island" [Coll], *New Statesman and Nation*, January 24, 1953, pp. 88–89.

S1720. OSBALDESTON-MITFORD, MRS. "Skye as Johnson Saw It," *The New Rambler*, January 1952, pp. 5–8.

S1721. SHERBO, ARTHUR. "The Text of Johnson's *Journey to the Western Islands of Scotland*: 'Bayle' or 'Boyle' ?", *N&Q*, April 26, 1952, pp. 182–84.

S1722. STUCLEY, ELIZABETH. *A Hebridean Journey with Johnson and Boswell*. London: Christopher Johnson, 1956.

*S1723. TODD, WILLIAM B. "The Printing of Johnson's *Journey* (1775)," *Studies in Bibliography* (University of Virginia), VI (1953–54), 247–54.

XXI. — THE LIVES OF THE POETS

EDITIONS

S1770. *Selections from the Lives of the Poets*, ed. Warren L. Fleischauer [lives of Savage, Pope, Collins, Gray; excerpts from Cowley, Milton, Dryden, Addison]. Chicago: Henry Regnery Co., 1955.

CRITICISM

S1780. ALLISON JAMES. "Joseph Warton's Reply to Dr. Johnson's *Lives*" [Warton's *Essay on Pope*, Vol. II, 1782], *JEGP*, LI (April 1952), 186–91.

*S1781. BOYCE, BENJAMIN. "Samuel Johnson's Criticism of Pope in the *Life of Pope*," *RES*, n.s. V (January 1954), 37–46. See also item S1790.

S1782. CARNIE, R.H. "Lord Hailes's Notes on Johnson's *Lives of the Poets*," *N&Q*, February to November, 1956, pp. 73–75, 106–08, 174–76, 343–46, 486–89.

S1783. CARROLL, RICHARD A. "Johnson's *Lives of the Poets* and Currents of English Criticism, 1750–1779" (dissertation, University of Michigan). Ann Arbor, Michigan: University Microfilms, 1950. Abstract in *Microfilm Abstracts*, X, 4 (1950), 208–09.

S1784. CROSSETT, JOHN. "Did Dr. Johnson Mean 'Paraphysical' ?", *Boston University Studies in English*, IV (Summer 1960), 121–24.

S1785. DARBISHIRE, HELEN. *Milton's Paradise Lost*, p. 7 ff. [concerned with Johnson's criticism of Milton]. London: Oxford University Press 1951.

S1786. GRENANDER, M.E. "*Samson's* Middle: Aristotle and Dr. Johnson." [Johnson's critique of Milton's *Samson Agonistes*], *University of Toronto Quarterly*, XXXIV (1955), 377–89.

*S1787. HART, EDWARD. "Some New Sources of Johnson's *Lives*" [item 1801a], *PMLA*, LXV (December 1950), 1088–1111.

S1788. HILL, D.M. "Johnson as Moderator" [in *Life of Milton*], *N&Q*, December 1956, pp. 517–22.

S1789. HILLES, FREDERICK W. *Johnson on Dr. Arbuthnot* [alterations in the *Life of Pope*]. New Haven: privately printed for The Johnsonians [George Grady Press], 1957. Facsimiles of a page from Johnson's MS and two pages of his proof sheets.

*S1790. ———. "The Making of *The Life of Pope*," in item S957, pp. 257–84. Facsimile of a page from Johnson's MS—a different page from that in item S1789.

S1791. HORSMAN, E.A. "Dryden's French Borrowings" [Johnson's charge in his *Life of Dryden* is correct], *RES*, n.s. I (October 1950), 346–51.

*S1792. JOHNSON, MAURICE. "A Literary Chestnut: Dryden's 'Cousin Swift'" [discusses Johnson's part in the legend], *PMLA*, LXVII (December 1952), 1024–34. Discussion, with J.R. Moore, *PMLA*, LXVIII (December 1953), 1232–39.

S1793. KEAST, W.R. "Editing Johnson's *Lives*," *The New Rambler*, June 1959, pp. 15–29.

S1794. LIEBERT HERMAN W. "Johnson's Revisions" [in the "character" of Collins, 1763, for the *Life of Collins*], *JNL*, XI, 2 (April 1951), 7–8.

*S1795. PERKINS, DAVID. "Johnson on Wit and Metaphysical Poetry," *ELH*, XX (September 1953), 200–17.

S1796. ROWAN, D.F. "Johnson's *Lives*: An Unrecorded Variant and a New Portrait," *The Book Collector*, I (Autumn 1952), 174.

XXII. — LETTERS

EDITIONS

*S1850. *The Letters of Samuel Johnson, with Mrs. Thrale's Genuine Letters to Him*, ed. R.W. Chapman [item 1850]. 3 vols. Oxford: Clarendon Press, 1952. Reviewed by Sir Harold Williams, *MLR*, XLVIII (July 1953), 339–41; in *TLS*, September 18, 1953, pp. 589–91; by Mary Lascelles, *RES*, n.s. V (January 1954), 88–93; E.L. McAdam, Jr., *PQ*, XXXV (July 1956), 304–06; Robert Wieder, *Études Anglaises*, IX (October-December 1956), 350–52.

S1851. *Selected Letters of Samuel Johnson*, ed. R.W. Chapman. London: Oxford University Press, 1951 (World's Classics). A revision of item 1858.

S1852. [LIEBERT, HERMAN W.] *To Honor the Two Hundred and Eighteenth Anniversary of the Departure of Samuel Johnson and David Garrick to Try Their Fortunes in the Great Metropolis, 2 March 1737* [with facsimile of letter to George Huddesford, February 26, 1755 (Chapman No. 63)]. New Haven: privately printed for Dorothy and Halsted Vander Poel [Yale University Press], 1955.

CRITICISM

S1860. CLIFFORD, JAMES L. "A New Johnson Correspondent" [Mrs. Way of Denham Place], *TLS*, May 30, 1952, p. 368.

S1861. COMYN, J.R.G. "Two Letters of Dr. Johnson" [to Dr. Burney], *TLS*, August 26, 1960, p. 545.

S1862. EAVES, T.C. DUNCAN. "Dr. Johnson's Letters to Richardson," *PMLA*, LXXV (September 1960), 377–81.

S1863. GRAHAM, W.H. "Dr. Johnson's Letters," *Contemporary Review*, CLXXXV (January 1954), 26–28.

S1864. "The Indulgence of Children" [Johnson's letters to Queeney Thrale], *TLS*, November 19, 1954, pp. i-ii of Children's Book Supplement.

S1865. IRVING, WILLIAM H. "Johnson and the Johnsonian Tinge," in *The Providence of Wit in the English Letter Writers*, pp. 286–306. Durham, North Carolina: Duke University Press, 1955.

S1866. KOLB, GWIN J. "The Address of Dr. Johnson's Last Letter to William Windham," *N&Q*, May 1957, p. 213.

S1867. —— –. "Notes on Four Letters by Dr. Johnson: Addenda to Chapman's Edition," *PQ*, XXXVIII (July 1959), 379–83.

S1868. McADAM, E.L., JR. *Dr. Johnson and the King's Library* [Johnson's letter to F.A. Barnard, May 28, 1768 (Chapman No. 26); facsimile]. New York: Privately printed for The Johnsonians [Harvard University Printing Office], 1955.

S1869. SHERBO, ARTHUR. "'Impransus'" [Chapman No. 10], *JNL*, XIII, 2 (May 1953), 12.

S1870. ———. "Dr. Johnson and 'Topsel on Animals': A Conjecture" [Chapman No. 11; 'Topsel' used for *Marmor Norfolciense* ?], *N&Q*, March 15, 1952, pp. 123–24.

S1871. ———. "Dr. Johnson's Letters" [additional notes to item S1850], *JNL*, XX, 3 (September 1960), 10–11.

S1872. VIETS, HENRY R. "Johnson and Cheyne" [identification of quotations in Chapman Nos. 338, 426, 493], *TLS*, February 5, 1954, p. 89.

See also items S420, S941, S1938.

XXIII. — DIARIES, PRAYERS, SERMONS

(INCLUDES DISCUSSIONS OF JOHNSON'S RELIGIOUS BELIEFS)

EDITIONS

*S1925. *Diaries, Prayers, and Annals*, ed. E.L. McAdam, Jr., with Donald and Mary Hyde. New Haven: Yale University Press, 1958 (Vol. I of *The Yale Edition of the Works of Samuel Johnson* [item S100]). Reviewed by Fredson Bowers, *JEGP*, LVIII (January 1959), 132–37; in *TLS*, March 6, 1959, pp. 121–22; by Margery Bailey, *PQ*, XXXVIII (July 1959), 331–333; by Maurice J. Quinlan, *MLQ*, XX (September 1959), 287–88.

*S1926. ASTON, HENRY HERVEY (actually Samuel Johnson), *A Sermon Preached at the Cathedral Church of Saint Paul, Before the Sons of the Clergy* [1745], ed. with an introduction by James L. Clifford. Los Angeles: Augustan Reprint Society, 1955 (Publication No. 50). See item 2061.

CRITICISM

S1930. BALDERSTON, KATHARINE C. "Doctor Johnson and William Law," *PMLA*, LXXV (September 1960), 382–94.

S1931. BENNETT, HIRAM R. "Samuel Johnson, Churchman," *Anglican Theological Review*, XL (October 1958), 301–09.

S1932. BRODERICK, JAMES H. "Dr. Johnson's Impossible Doubts," *South Atlantic Quarterly*, LVI (April 1957), 217–23.

S1933. DE BEER, E.S. "Johnson's θ φ" [in *Prayers and Meditations*], *N&Q*, December 1955, pp. 537–38.

S1934. GRAHAM, W.H. "Dr. Johnson and Law's *Serious Call*," *Contemporary Review*, CXCI (February 1957), 104–06.

S1935. GREENE, DONALD J. "Johnson and Newman" [parallels between a Latin verse prayer of Johnson and "Lead, Kindly Light"], *JNL*, XVIII, 3 (October 1958), 4–6. See also Sister M. Jean Clare, *JNL*, XX, 1 (March 1960), 12.

*S1936. HYDE, DONALD and MARY. "Johnson and Journals," *New Colophon*, III (1950), 165–97 [item 2030a]. See also E.L. McAdam, Jr., *PQ*, XXX (July 1951), 275–76.

S1937. JOOST, NICHOLAS. "Poetry and Belief: Fideism from Dryden to Eliot," *Dublin Review*, No. 455 (1st Quarter, 1952), 35–53.

S1938. MAY, GEORGE LACEY. "Religious Letters of Dr. Johnson," *Church Quarterly Review*, CLIV (April-June 1953), 168–75.

*S1939. [McADAM, E.L., JR., MARY C. and DONALD F. HYDE, GEORGE MILNE], *The Johnsons Photographed* [restoration of passages in Johnson's diaries erased by George Strahan; facsimiles]. New York: privately printed for The Johnsonians, 1956.

S1940. NORTH, RICHARD. "The Religion of Dr. Johnson," *Hibbert Journal*, LVI (October 1957), 42–46.

*S1941. QUINLAN, MAURICE J. "The Reaction to Dr. Johnson's *Prayers and Meditations*," *JEGP*, LII (April 1953), 125–39.

S1942. ROBERTS, S.C. "Dr. Johnson as a Churchman," *Church Quarterly Review*, CLVI (October-December 1955), 372–80. Reprinted in item S961.

S1943. STAMM, ISRAEL S. "Some Aspects of the Religious Problem in Haller" [contrasts the religious thought of Albrecht von Haller, 1708-77, with that of his contemporary, Johnson], *Germanic Review*, XXV (February 1950), 5–12.

*S1944. SUTHERLAND, RAYMOND C. "Dr. Johnson and the Collect," *MLQ*, XVII (June 1956), 111–17.

S1945. SWANSEA AND BRECON, EDWARD WILLIAMSON, BISHOP OF. "Dr. Johnson and the Prayer Book," *Theology*, LIII (October 1950), 363–72.

*S1946. WILLIAMS, PHILIP. "Samuel Johnson's Central Tension: Faith and the Fear of Death," *Tōhoku Gàkuin Daigaku Ronshu* [Journal of Literary Studies, North Japan College, Sendai], Nos. 33-34 September 1958, pp. 1–35.

See also items S201, S206, S346, S410.

XXIV. — MISCELLANEOUS WORKS

S2000. BLACK, D.A.K. "Johnson on Boerhaave," *Medical History*, III (October 1959), 325–29.

S2001. BLOOM, EDWARD A. *Samuel Johnson in Grub Street* [as journalist]. Providence, Rhode Island: Brown University Press, 1957 (Brown University Studies, No. XXI). Reviewed by C.R. Tracy, *PQ*, XXXVII (July 1958), 337–38; S.C. Roberts, *MLR*, LIII (October 1958), 567–68; D.J. Greene, *MLN*, LXXIV (February 1959), 169–72; Henry Gifford, *RES*, n.s. X (May 1959), 201–02.

S2002. BRAHAM, LIONEL. "Johnson's Edition of Roger Ascham," *N&Q*, August 1956, 346–47.

S2002a. GIBBS, F.W. "Dr. Johnson's First Published Work ?" [attribution of a translation of Boerhaave's *Elementa Chemiae* (1732)], *Ambix*, VIII (February 1960), 24–34.

S2003. GREENE, DONALD J. "Dr. Johnson and 'An Authentic Account of the Present State of Lisbon' " [not Johnson's], *N&Q*, August 1957, p. 351.

*S2004. ———. "Johnson's Contributions to the *Literary Magazine*," *RES*, n.s. VII (October 1956), 367–92.

*S2005. ———. "Johnson and the *Harleian Miscellany*" [attributes ten short prefaces signed "J"], *N&Q*, July 1958, pp. 304–06.

*S2006. ———. "Some Notes on Johnson and the *Gentleman's Magazine*," *PMLA*, LXXIX (March 1959), 75–84.

S2007. ———. "Was Johnson Theatrical Critic of the *Gentleman's Magazine* ?", *RES*, n.s. III (April 1952), 158–61.

S2008. KOLB, GWIN J. "Dr. Johnson and the *Public Ledger*: A Small Addition to the Canon," *Studies in Bibliography* (University of Virginia), XI (1958), 252–55.

S2009. ———. "A Note on the Publication of Johnson's 'Proposals for Printing the *Harleian Miscellany*'," *PBSA*, XLVIII (2nd quarter, 1954), 196–98.

S2010. LEED, JACOB. "Samuel Johnson and the *Gentleman's Magazine*, an Adjustment of the Canon" [*Account of the Conduct of the Duchess of Marlborough*, 1742], *N&Q*, May 1957, pp. 210–13.

⋆S2011. ———. "Samuel Johnson and the *Gentleman's Magazine:* Studies
in the Canon of His Miscellaneous Prose Writings, 1738–1744" (dissertation, University of Chicago). Chicago: University of Chicago
Department of Photoduplication [microfilm], 1958.

⋆S2012. ———. "Two New Pieces by Johnson in the *Gentleman's Magazine* ?"
[letters by Pamphilus, 1738], *MP*, LIV (May 1957), 221–29. See items
S2014, S2018.

S2013. ———. "Two Notes on Johnson and *The Gentleman's Magazine*"
[attributes "Foreign Books," 1741–43, and "The Art of Deciphering,"
1742], *PBSA*, LIV (2nd quarter, 1960), 101–110.

S2014. LIEBERT, HERMAN W. "Johnson and Gay" ["Pamphilus" letter,
October 1738], *N&Q*, May 12, 1951, p. 216. See items S2006, S2012,
S2018.

⋆S2015. McADAM, E.L., JR. "Dr. Johnson and Saunders Welch's *Proposals,*"
RES, n.s. IV (October 1953), 337–45.

S2016. McCUTCHEON, ROGER P. "Johnson and Dodsley's *Preceptor,* 1748,"
Tulane Studies in English, III (1952), 125–32.

⋆S2017. McHENRY, LAWRENCE C., JR. "Dr. Samuel Johnson's Medical
Biographies" [in James's *Medicinal Dictionary* (see items 2024, 2025);
also attributes life of Oribasius], *Journal of the History of Medicine and
Allied Sciences*, XIV (1959), 298–310.

S2018. McLEOD, A.L. "Notes on John Gay" [letter by Pamphilus, *Gentleman's Magazine,* October 1738], *N&Q*, January 20, 1951, p. 32. See
items S2006, S2012, S2014.

⋆S2019. RUHE, EDWARD. "The Two Samuel Johnsons" [translations of
Sarpi's *History of the Council of Trent*], *N&Q*, October 1954,
pp. 432-35.

S2020. SCHNECK, JEROME. "Hermann Boerhaave and Samuel Johnson,"
Journal of the American Medical Association, CLXI, 14 (August 4, 1956),
1414-15.

S2021. SHERBO, ARTHUR. "Dr. Johnson and Joseph Warton's Virgil" [various
critical remarks extracted from Johnson's works and inserted in Warton's
notes; also discusses Johnson's part in Fawkes' *Theocritus*], *JNL*, XVIII,
4 (December 1958), 12; XIX, 1 (March 1959), 10.

S2022. ———. "A Possible Addition to the Johnson Canon" [review of Keysler's *Travels* in *Literary Magazine*, 1756], *RES*, n.s. VI (January 1955), 70–71. See item S2004.

S2023. ———. "Two Additions to the Johnson Canon" [letter to *Daily Advertiser*, April 1739, and "Foreign History," *Gentleman's Magazine*, November 1747], *JEGP*, LII (October 1953), 543–48.

S2024. WAGLEY, MARY F. and PHILIP F. "Comments on Samuel Johnson's Biography of Sir Thomas Browne," *Bulletin of the History of Medicine*, XXXI (July-August 1957), 318–26.

See also items S2, S15, S422, S436, S440, S441, S455, S945, S967, S1384, S1387, S1520, S1650, S1870.

INDEX OF NAMES

SECTION B

References are to item numbers, not pages. An attempt has been made to indicate the subject matter of most entries, except for very general discussions.

CONTRIBUTORS

CHESTER F. CHAPIN : Assistant Professor of English at the University of Michigan.

JAMES L. CLIFFORD : Professor of English at Columbia University. Author of *Hesther Lynch Piozzi* and *Young Sam Johnson*. Co-editor of the *Johnsonian News Letter*.

JAMES E. CONGLETON : Chairman of the Department of English at Findlay College, Findlay, Ohio. Author of *Theories of Pastoral Poetry in England, 1684–1798*.

The Rev. F.N. DOUBLEDAY, M.R.C.S.: Editor of *The New Rambler*, Journal of the Johnson Society of London.

J.D. FLEEMAN : Working at Oxford on a study of the texts of the Collected Works of Samuel Johnson, from 1787 to 1825.

WARREN FLEISCHAUER : Professor of English at John Carroll University, Cleveland, Ohio. Corresponding Secretary of the Johnson Society of the Great Lakes Region.

DONALD J. GREENE : Associate Professor of English at the University of New Mexico, Albuquerque. Author of *The Politics of Samuel Johnson*.

JOHN P. HARDY : Former Queensland Rhodes Scholar. Senior Demy of Magdalen College, Oxford.

JEFFREY HART : Assistant Professor of English at Columbia University.

JOYCE HEMLOW: Professor of English at McGill University. Author of *The History of Fanny Burney*.

A.J. HUMPHREYS : Professor of English at the University of Leicester. Author of *The Augustan World*.

R.K. KAUL : Lecturer in English, Punjab University, Chandrigarh, India.

GWIN J. KOLB : Associate Professor of English at the University of Chicago. Co-author of *Dr. Johnson's Dictionary*.

J.H. LEICESTER : Post-graduate research scholar at Birkbeck College in the University of London.

L.F. POWELL : Editor of Boswell's *Life of Johnson*; magister egregius.

ARTHUR SHERBO : Associate Professor of English at Michigan State University. Author of *Samuel Johnson, Editor of Shakespeare, with an Essay on the Adventurer*.

A.J. TILLINGHAST : Post-graduate research scholar at the University of Nottingham.

IAN WATT : Associate Professor of English at the University of California. Author of *The Rise of the Novel*.

S.O.P.-PRESS
(Société Orientale de Publicité)
Cairo